Praise for *An Introduction to Masculinities*

"This is the book that I've been waiting for someone to write! Kahn integrates theory and research from the social sciences into a coherent account of the diverse meanings of 'masculinities'. Most books on men's studies are either highly focused on a particular analytic framework, or provide broad surveys with little theoretical depth. Kahn identifies the major paradigms through which masculinities can be conceptualized. As a result, readers will gain a 'meta' awareness of how men's lives are being constructed and analyzed, both by professionals and lay people in everyday life. This book is truly an accomplishment."

Michael Addis, Clark University

"*An Introduction to Masculinities* is a comprehensive overview of a wide range of perspectives on masculinities. It provides students with an excellent road map to guide them through important theories and issues in a complex field."

Dr. Harry Brod, Professor of Philosophy and Humanities,
Department of Philosophy and World Religions, University of Northern Iowa

"I have just finished reading Dr. Kahn's new book *An Introduction to Masculinities* and am extremely impressed by the quality of the work. A high quality introductory text on masculinity is much needed and long overdue. This is the book we have been waiting for.

As one of the founders of the field of feminist psychology, I am pleased to see Kahn's deep understanding of the approach and the use of its constructivist perspectives and tools to bring an understanding to current ideas about masculinities.

The writing is accessible, lively and consistently interesting. The author speaks directly to the student in a way that is pertinent and involving. The content is made understandable without sacrificing either depth or complexity. The many important concepts to which the student is introduced are clearly explained in a writing style that is both engaging and personal. All texts should be this clear and this interesting."

Ellyn Kaschak, Professor of Psychology, Author of Engendered
Lives *and Editor,* Journal of Women and Therapy

"Dr. Kahn has written a clear, wide-ranging and thoughtful introduction to contemporary issues and research about masculinities. Students and teachers will find this a valuable guide to complex and important problems."

Raewyn Connell, University of Sydney, Author of Masculinities

"I am grateful to Jack Kahn for this careful, compendious, well-researched yet reader-friendly book. As a teacher, Kahn is skilled at explaining complex gender ideas and connecting them with our daily experiences and feelings. All students will find a lot to interest them here. I appreciate Kahn's historical accuracy and integrity in showing how feminist thinking led to the development of thinking about masculinities. His book will especially help readers to recognize the gender constructs that have been in us and around us while we were pressured to believe that gender patterns are innate."

Peggy McIntosh, Ph.D., Associate Director, Wellesley Centers for Women, Wellesley College

"Kahn makes a unique and valuable contribution to the fields of masculinities and gender studies. Speaking to students with a masterful blend of personal and academic writing, he makes the social and psychological complexities of these issues accessible in an introductory text."

Dr. Steven Botkin, Executive Director,

An Introduction to Masculinities

Jack S. Kahn

Curry College

A John Wiley & Sons, Ltd., Publication

This edition first published 2009
© 2009 Jack S. Kahn

Blackwell Publishing was acquired by John Wiley & Sons in February 2007.
Blackwell's publishing program has been merged with Wiley's global Scientific,
Technical, and Medical business to form Wiley-Blackwell.

Registered Office
John Wiley & Sons Ltd, The Atrium, Southern Gate, Chichester, West Sussex,
PO19 8SQ, United Kingdom

Editorial Offices
350 Main Street, Malden, MA 02148-5020, USA
9600 Garsington Road, Oxford, OX4 2DQ, UK
The Atrium, Southern Gate, Chichester, West Sussex, PO19 8SQ, UK

For details of our global editorial offices, for customer services, and for information
about how to apply for permission to reuse the copyright material in this book please
see our website at www.wiley.com/wiley-blackwell.

The right of Jack S. Kahn to be identified as the author of this work has been asserted
in accordance with the Copyright, Designs and Patents Act 1988.

Library of Congress Cataloging-in-Publication Data

Kahn, Jack S.
   An introduction to masculinites / Jack S. Kahn.
      p. cm.
   Includes bibliographical references and index.
      ISBN 978-1-4051-8179-2 (hardcover : alk. paper) – ISBN 978-1-4051-8178-5
(pbk. : alk. paper)   1. Masculinity.   2. Men–Psychology.   I. Title.
   BF692.5.K34 2009
   155.3'32–dc22

                                                                    2008032183

A catalogue record for this book is available from the British Library.

Set in 10 on 12.5 pt Palatino by SNP Best-set Typesetter Ltd., Hong Kong
Printed in Singapore by Ho Printing Pte Ltd

1   2009

Brief Contents

Contents

Preface

Introduction

During the last thirty years, there has been tremendous growth in the amount of academic inquiry dedicated to understanding men in their experiences *as men*. This growth is seen as largely due to a growing awareness of the problems that men face in trying to understand what it means to be masculine. The number of courses studying masculinity and gender has risen and is continuing to rise. Recently, there have been numerous articles in popular media detailing particular men's issues, including men's issues with violence and difficulties in achieving success in higher education (these concerns are covered in this text).

When I first began teaching courses in this area, I was intrigued by all of the fascinating information but often had trouble finding a source that could help my undergraduate students begin the exploration of this field. This was a primary motivator for creating this book, an introductory text that includes information orienting the reader to basic issues within the field of masculinities. The text highlights debates within the field about the definition of masculinity, the origin/location of masculinities, and the crisis in men and masculinity. In addition, it gives the reader a context and structure by which to critically understand and evaluate information about men and masculinities.

While this text is geared toward an undergraduate and/or introductory audience, it certainly could be used in other avenues. *An Introduction to Masculinities* provides an overview of the field with enough background information to reintegrate necessary concepts from other disciplines (such as psychology, sociology, and gender/women's studies) to take the reader on a step-by-step exploration of the field of masculinities.

In addition to presenting content that is approachable for under-graduates, I also wanted to present tools that would encourage them to think critically about the information. My own background and training in feminist and contructionist thinking, two areas well known for encouraging critical thinking, helped to set the tone for this text. This incorporation allows the insights garnered by various thinkers to assist us in understanding the diverse worlds of men while simultane-ously reminding us to be critical of the information.

Text Overall Structure

An Introduction to Masculinities is designed to be an introduction to several areas of interest pursued by scholars in this field. It is not an all inclusive summary of ideas, nor a summary of all of the rich and diverse research findings in this area of study. Rather, it is intended to provide many of the major themes that permeate this body of work and provide a framework to assist readers in better understanding and evaluating material in masculinities. Without such a framework, it is often difficult to grasp new information and be critical about it.

Chapters 1 and 2 orient the reader to basic issues within the field and set the context by which the rest of the text will be critically exam-ined. Chapter 1 begins by addressing the difficulties of defining mas-culinity. It then introduces the reader to different types of feminist theory and argues how various feminist perspectives can assist us in our exploration of masculinities. Chapter 2 specifically discusses how systems of patriarchy affect men and addresses how social privilege influences men in a variety of ways, including the studying of this topic.

After these introductory chapters the text begins with theories about how researchers define masculinity (chapters 3 and 4). As you will see, there are many ways to discuss masculinities. Before one can really debate findings about men's experiences and lived lives, one must understand how researchers come to define what it is they are studying. This becomes *very* important when researchers attempt to get overall impressions of what we are learning in a field. In other words, if we attempt to summarize the research findings in a particular area, what might we find? If researchers think about masculinity in different ways, might they come up with different results when examining it?

As an illustration, an interesting research review by Moore and Stuart (2005) found that, when examining masculinity as a predictor of partner violence, the definition of masculinity used by various researchers affected whether or not masculinity had an impact on predicting whether violence might occur in a relationship. Not only was it important to see that masculinity had some relationship to partner violence, but that only certain ways of defining masculinity had an impact. This seems particularly important since violence is such a major concern for all genders (see chapter 8).

Different researchers think about masculinity differently. Not surprisingly, participants in studies do as well. Hammond and Mattis (2005), for example, found with a sample of African-American men that fifteen different factors accounted for ways in which the men in the sample made sense of what masculinity is (including such things as responsibility, autonomy, spirituality, moral rectitude, and family-centeredness). This illustrates how important it is for us to understand the complex ways in which diverse people will come to understand masculinity for themselves.

Following a review of some of the major definitions of masculinity are several ideas about where masculinity "comes from" (or its "location"). Because masculinities are studied by people from a variety of academic disciplines (anthropology, sociology, psychology, women's studies, queer studies, etc.), scholars have very different ideas about this question. This text includes several major theories in this regard.

The first reason for including this information is that it comprises a major body of work and area of investigation in this field. The question of how infants grows up and eventually concern themselves with masculinity has long fascinated scholars. Is it something people are born with? It is a function of particular childhood experiences? Is it something people learn or are socialized into? Who is in charge of that socialization and how is it that they dictate (a) what masculinity is, (b) who may try to achieve it, and (c) whether or not people are in compliance with it? Does it evolve within individual humans, within our societies, within our stories and ideas, or in some complex interaction? These questions and others are embedded within discussions of the locations of masculinities. An additional reason for including information about the location of masculinities is to better understand the last section of the text. This section includes a summary of some of the current problems that men face (chapter 8), which is followed by theories about the source of, and solution to, those problems, referred to as the crisis in men and masculinity (chapters 9 through 11).

To better understand why this section is useful, an example in another context may be useful. Say, for example, that a student in one of my classes is struggling with academic motivation. Once we have defined what we mean by academic motivation (perhaps by including information about classroom attendance, assignments completed, interest in major, personal values, etc.) we begin to investigate how this came to be. We might come up with several plausible reasons that led to this current state (ranging from economic struggles, discriminative practices by professors, lack of social skills and difficulty making friends, having interests in other pursuits, lack of interest in academic pursuits, etc.). Understanding which of these reasons (if any, or in what combination) can help us better understand the impact of academic motivation on this student and give us ideas about what we might do about it. Similarly, the inclusion of ideas about the location of masculinities helps us to better understand and evaluate concerns and struggles people are having, how they may connect to masculinities, and how that may suggest ideas proposed to assist men. By better understanding where masculinity comes from, one can better understand the ways in which masculinities are affecting us and how we might make changes to improve peoples' lives.

The inclusion of this final section on men's problems and the crisis of men and masculinities serves two purposes. The first is to expose readers to some of the research findings about men's struggles. This is a major area of interest among scholars, particularly those who are invested in outcome research that can assist in improving men's lives. *An Introduction to Masculinities* aims to encourage readers to investigate the rich research that exists beyond this text. The second purpose is to present the fundamental struggles within the field. The crisis of men and masculinity is a very controversial topic and is often a source of much tension within the field. In many ways, this struggle among experts to understand problems men experience and to examine the sources of those conflicts and suggest solutions mirrors the very phenomenon that we hope to understand. We struggle with defining and understanding masculinity in many of the same ways that the participants in our research inquiries do. Exposure to these views will educate the reader to these very real tensions within the field and lead to further knowledge and connection with others attempting to understand and improve our lives.

Text Layout

Each chapter in this text includes several resources to assist you as you learn about this field. The chapters provide personal anecdotes in an effort to make the material more accessible. These examples also take the form of a longer feature provided throughout the chapter called "Making Connections". The hope is that these examples will assist you to understand these concepts in more depth and see how various psychosocial issues may impact masculinities in a more complex way. These illustrations may be personal anecdotes or research examples, and exemplify an **intersectional approach**. Intersectional approaches work to (a) identify how different social categories interact (such as race, age, religion, etc.), and (b) assist us in understanding how they contribute to our interest in masculinities.

Terms that may not be familiar to all readers are highlighted (in bold). Because this field is influenced by many other schools of thought, it often uses language that is common within those other disciplines. Definitions of these terms can be found at the end of the text in a glossary called "Masculinities Terms".

At the end of each chapter, a section called "Review and Questions to Ponder" is provided to help you better understand the main chapter ideas as well as the relevancy of these issues to your own life. These questions will also help generate content questions which may be used by an instructor as homework or exam questions.

The book also includes short biographies of some of the researchers and scholars – professionals who currently work in areas that impact masculinities – whose ideas have helped to shape each chapter. One intent of *An Introduction to Masculinities* is to highlight some of the well-known scholars who are shaping the ideas and knowledge in this field, and whose work provided core content for this text. When possible, contact information is provided to enable you to learn more about them, their research, and future projects.

Finally, the "References" section at the end of the book lists all the sources used to compile each chapter. While these are comprehensive, they do not include every piece of work relevant to the topic.

I encourage you to look at these sources and others more carefully, as there is much interesting information to learn about in the field of masculinities.

Summary

An Introduction to Masculinities is intended as a tool to be used to better understand major ideas concerning the definition, location, and crises of masculinities. Equipped with this knowledge, I hope you will be inspired to seek more information about masculinities, and that you will be able to understand and critically evaluate that information.

Acknowledgments

This book could not have been possible without the support of several wonderful people. Kevin Henze was the first person to read and edit original drafts of this text and provide feedback and care. For that I am very grateful. I benefited immensely from the help of Kathy Russell and the library staff, the psychology department, and the Dean's Office at Curry College, who helped in immeasurable ways. I was also fortunate to have received feedback from various professionals in the field, including Fiona Mills, Jason A. Laker, Elizabeth Hope, Jim Doyle, Michael Addis, and Jim O'Neil, who provided extremely thoughtful and useful suggestions to strengthen and tighten early drafts. Thank you also to my research assistant, Benjamin Brett, who assisted with referencing. In addition, the editing work of my wife Jacqueline Denmon was crucial to the completion of this manuscript. The members and allies of the Boston chapter of the National Organization for Men Against Sexism served as a constant source of support. Finally, I am extremely grateful to Executive Editor Chris Cardone and Publishing Coordinator Constance Adler at Wiley-Blackwell, and freelance Project Manager Janey Fisher, all of whom were incredibly helpful, insightful, and supportive of this project.

1

Overview

Introduction

Throughout the course of most of our educational experiences, the accomplishments of men have been a major topic of focus. Whether through the teaching of theories, research, or history, tales of men's contributions to culture and society have dominated our learning (Connell, 1989; Hearn, 2004; Kaschak, 1992; Sen, 2005). Most of us have learned of contributions by scientists such as Sir Isaac Newton and Copernicus; writers such as William Shakespeare and John Steinbeck; and political leaders such as Abraham Lincoln and Thomas Jefferson. The majority of the men we have learned about have been of European and middle-class backgrounds, leaving out the important contributions of **working-class** men and **men of color** (Bushweller, 2004; Iseke-Barnes, 2005). And while there has been some progress in the inclusion of more diverse voices in our curricula, our educational experiences have been dominated by stories of the contributions of men (Campbell, 2007; Connell, 1989; Hearn, 2004; Tietz, 2007; Tuwor, 2007).

> **Who's Who in Masculinities Research: Ellyn Kaschak, Ph.D.**
>
> Ellyn Kaschak has been Professor of Psychology at San Jose State University since 1974, where she has also been the Chairperson of the graduate program in Marriage, Family and Child Counseling and Director of the University's Family Counseling Service. She is one of the founders of the field of feminist psychology, which she has practiced since its inception some thirty years ago,
>
> *Continued*

and has published numerous articles and chapters on the topic, as well as the award-winning *Engendered Lives: A New Psychology of Women's Experience.*

Website: http://www.ellynkaschak.com/

This text, however, is not focused on men's historical contributions to our world. It is an introduction to the ever-growing field of masculinities. This field seeks to understand people's experiences of masculinities and the social and historical ways in which this phenomenon affects and is affected by human action. This is a relatively new area of exploration (Connell, 1989; Kimmel & Messner, 2001; Levant, 1996; Whitehead & Barrett, 2001). Scholars in this area are interested in the lived lives of men and others that grapple with masculinity and hope to understand how people view themselves and their their place in the world as a function of their negotiation of masculinities. Masculinities theorists try to understand both the challenges and triumphs that people experience.

Masculinity is defined in this text as the complex **cognitive, behavioral, emotional, expressive, psychosocial,** and **sociocultural** experience of identifying with being male. More specifically, this text will use the term **masculinities**, assuming that there are multiple ways in which people may experience the world of masculinity (Addis & Cohane, 2005; Amaya, 2007; Bambert, 2005; Paulsen, 1999; Silverstein & Rashbaum, 1994; Wetherell & Edley, 1999; Whitehead & Barrett, 2001). While not all people in this field take this perspective, because this text reflects multiple definitions of what masculinity means, where it comes from, and the various ways in which it may contribute to the lives of people who identify as men, the use of the pluralized term will often be warranted. Masculinity is referred to as a psychosocial phenomenon with a recognition that social and **relational** experiences play a crucial factor in the development and **negotiation** of the worlds of men (Harrison, 2005; Mahalik et al., 2001).

Masculinity as a Construct

Studying masculinities as a subject can be difficult. This is partially because it is an example of what **social scientists** call a **hypothetical**

construct. Social scientists often study intangible phenomena that do not have a directly observable or measurable basis. For example, a very popular topic for **psychologists** (one of several kinds of social scientist) to study is self-esteem. Some people think that the construct of self-esteem can help to explain many of the things that people do or experience (Luo & Hing-Luan, 1998; Russel, Crocket & Shen, 2008). But self-esteem itself is not something that can be viewed under a microscope or weighed on a scale. It isn't a tangible physical substance the properties of which are largely agreed upon. If you want to ask someone out to dinner, you can't borrow self-esteem from *someone else* to make *you* feel more confident (although there have probably been times when you've wanted to)!

We may use the hypothetical construct of self-esteem to explain why someone may behave in certain ways. So if a person has a low opinion of themselves, doesn't have a lot of friends, and experiences anxiety around others, we may say it's due to the effect of low self-esteem. But self-esteem isn't a tangible or observable thing; it's a way of explaining a cluster (or group) of related experiences. A hypothetical construct therefore refers to a conceptual way of explaining something we cannot directly observe or measure but assume is made up of a cluster of human experiences that may include behaviors, thoughts, or emotions.[1]

Masculinity is a hypothetical construct because, in and of itself, it cannot be directly observed or measured. So, not surprisingly, social scientists do not all agree as to what we actually *mean* by masculinity. What aspects of human action and psychological and or social experience(s) should we focus on? Is masculinity something only experienced by people who are genetically defined as male, or can others experience masculinity? Is masculinity an identity, a set of behaviors, a cluster of characteristics? Is it stable and consistent across situations or **contextual**? Is it a psychological, social, or historical phenomenon? These are all questions that researchers in the field are studying, researching, and debating (and are discussed in more detail in chapters 3 and 4).

Not only do people disagree about what it is we are supposed to be studying when we study masculinity, but whatever masculinity *is* seems to be different in different cultures. Different cultures have varied

---

[1] Some definitions of hypothetical construct only include the observable aspects of human beings, our behavior.

expectations and beliefs about masculinities. For example, comparing European cultures to the United States can yield some interesting differences. While traveling in Italy in 1996, I noticed that many men kissed each other on the cheek as a sign of friendliness. This is not something I have seen many men do in the United States, where I suspect it would be viewed as "not-masculine" by many men.

On the same trip, I tried to buy a packet of blades for my razor. I usually buy razor blades that are designated for women, as they often come with aloe and other moisturizers that men's razors do not have. The blades I intended to purchase were across the counter and I had to request them from the clerk. After several interchanges, I realized she would not sell them to me. "These are for ladies." "Yes, I know. That's what I want." "These are for ladies," Finally, I said they were for my wife and she let me purchase them. Clearly cultures view gender differently and have varying ideas about the way gender works and what kinds of behaviors and items are appropriate and for whom. Furthermore, those views vary between people in the same culture and across different situations.

Beliefs about gender vary not only across and within cultures but also over time. Throughout every culture's history, expectations regarding the acceptability and meaning of human behavior has changed (Harvey, 2005). For example, until the end of the 18th century, it was very common for European men of upper-class status to wear powdered wigs as a symbol of their prominence (King, 2002; MacLeod, 2000; Pendergast & Pendergast, 2004). While some men in specialized roles can be found wearing wigs as a symbol of authority (such as some chief justices in Canada), it is much less acceptable for men to do so in the 21st century, and in fact many men suffer humiliation and harassment as a result of making these kinds of fashion choices, particularly if they are perceived as being feminine (Broad, 2002; Mirehya, 2005).

Researchers also have different **models** about what masculinity is, where it comes from and how we should study it. A model can be thought of as a way of organizing complex information in order to make it easier to understand. Because much of life has multiple facets to it, models help us by organizing information in a way that makes it more accessible.

Many people use small-scale models of large complex phenomenon (houses, airplanes, cars, dolls, etc.) in order to get a better view of the phenomenon and perhaps explain how it works. Today, much of this is also done online. For example, some clothing stores will have programs on their websites that allow you to see what a particular piece of clothing might look like (e.g., www.macys.com). Sometimes the model helps you see the clothing in a way that is different than actually wearing it, because you can observe it in a way you could not in real life. Since we can't always have direct access to certain stores or clothing (and even when we do it can be pretty overwhelming), these web-models allow us to get a general idea about fit, color, etc.

The web-models that are used are of course created by people. These people make assumptions about a whole host of social variables (body size, gender, class, etc.) that pertain to potential customers who might decide to wear the clothes. They even make assumptions about the kinds of computers that might be used to access the website, what browsers people might be using, how their monitor will interpret color, etc. This means that different websites will display information differently as different models will come across differently based on a variety of factors based on these assumptions. So if three programmers made three models for the very same store, they might design very different ways of displaying clothing on the site.

We do the same kind of thing in the social sciences. We try to take complex phenomenon in the real world and explain them in ways that is organized and conveys a certain logic, structure, and approach. The study of masculinity is no exception. We try to explain masculinity with various models. These models were built during different time periods and in different situations from a variety of cultural perspectives. These different models are explored in chapters throughout this text.

Each model of masculinity contains a variety of assumptions. These assumptions concern what the researcher holds to be true about human nature and how they view what masculinity is, where it comes from, and where it is going. Because this field has such diverse contributors from various disciplines we find ourselves with many different ways of studying masculinities. This makes it imperative that we are aware of those assumptions and can be critical of their interpretations.

Feminisms

The field of masculinities uses **feminist models** to critically study its content. It might seem odd that a field dedicated to masculinities would employ feminist theory and research to understand the phenomenon of masculinity. You might wonder how an area of study that predominantly reflects women's writing can be helpful in studying others. In fact, the use of feminist theory and research makes a lot of sense, once you learn about the tools that feminism has to offer us in this investigation (Connell, 1995; England, 1999; Kimmel, 1998; Pateman, 2000; Soban, 2006; Whitehead & Barrett, 2001).

Why Feminism?

There are several reasons why employing a feminist perspective can be illuminating in our study of masculinities. While the reasons are many (and one could certainly write a whole text *just* on this topic), we will highlight a few here.

One of the contributions of feminist scholarship is to give credit where credit is due. Throughout history, people who have made important contributions to culture are often not visible to the majority. This is particularly true when those people are women and/or **people of color**. Feminist theorists put gender on the map for us to study (Enns & Sinacore, 2005). They have helped others to see how the way in which we make sense of gender socially, historically, psychologically, and biologically contributes greatly to the ways in which we understand human beings.

Who's Who in Masculinities Research: Carolyn Enns, Ph.D.

Carolyn Zerbe Enns is Professor of Psychology at Cornell College, where she teaches a wide range of undergraduate courses in psychology and women's studies. Her scholarly interests include multicultural feminist perspectives on psychotherapy and pedagogy, feminist therapy in Japan, and identity development among international students. She has published approximately fifty articles and chapters on topics that focus primarily on gender, pedagogy, and feminist theory and therapy. She is the author of *Feminist Theories and Feminist Psychotherapies: Origins, Themes, and Diversity*, and the co-editor (with Ada Sinnacore) of *Teaching and Social Justice: Integrating Multicultural and Feminist Theories in the Classroom*.

Website: http://people.cornellcollege.edu/cenns & cenns@ cornellcollege.edu

Who's Who in Masculinities Research: Ada Sinacore, Ph.D.

Ada Sinacore is the Program Director for the Counseling Psychology program in the department of educational and counseling psychology at McGill University. She has published many articles and book chapters involving feminism, gender, multiculturalism, and identity. She is the co-editor (with Carolyn Enns) of *Teaching and Social Justice: Integrating Multicultural and Feminist Theories in the Classroom* (2005).

Email: ada.sinacore@mcgill.ca

In addition, as you will soon learn, feminist scholars have been instrumental in highlighting how issues of **marginalization** affect our lives (Enns & Sinacore, 2005; Kronsell, 2005; Sinacore & Enns, 2005). In other words, some people have been denied access to full participation in culture as a result of their belonging to specific social groups. It is believed that this social exclusion affects people in multiple ways. Feminist research has often focused on women's experience in this regard. The process by which people are marginalized, however, can be applied to various social groupings (such as race, age, religion, etc.). Feminists have helped us understand not only the process of that marginalization, but the many ways in which it contributes to our lives (Kaschak, 1992; Sinacore & Enns, 2005). Understanding this process can also lead to some interesting insights about people's lives.

This focus on having marginalized experiences has also contributed to feminist scholars having a critical view of knowledge (Kronsell, 2005). In other words, one of the "advantages" of being outside of something is that it can give you unique ways of looking at it. For example, if you have ever moved from one home to another in a new neighborhood (or city, state, country, etc.), you may notice aspects of your new neighborhood that many locals do not. This is because, as an outsider, you notice certain aspects of the environment in ways that people who are "used to it" often do not. Similarly, feminist analysis provides us with wonderful tools for evaluating beliefs, ideas, and perspectives in ways that many often overlook (Kronsell, 2005).

Finally, feminists (and ideas influenced by feminism) have contributed much content to the field of masculinities (Connell, 1995;

Kimmel, 1998; Whitehead & Barrett, 2001). As you will see, the concepts that have been gleaned from feminist analysis are used both directly and indirectly in the field. In other words, at times feminist theory is given appropriate acknowledgement and credit and other times it is used without citing the feminist origin of the type of analysis. Ironically, even **anti-feminist** thinkers sometimes employ feminist analysis without even realizing it.

Types of Feminism

There are several different types of feminism (Enns & Sinacore, 2005). Feminist theory and research is done in every area one might study at a college, including anthropology, sociology, information technology, biology, economics, and psychology (Hrdy, 1997; Jefferson, 2002; Rosser, 2005). This means that there are feminist anthropologists, feminist economists, feminist biologists, and so on. Each type of feminism gives us a unique and useful way to explore the world of masculinities.

But what are feminists concerned with, and what is a feminist model? All feminists are interested in understanding and bettering the lives of women and others who are marginalized (Sinacore & Enns, 1995). As stated, to be marginalized means that your experiences and worth as a person is not seen as equal to or as valid as others in the **dominant culture** in which you live, and that the culture actively supports the marginalization.[2] The marginalization becomes **institutionalized** when basic societal systems (governments, religions, businesses, families, etc.) support and perpetuate the marginalization.

Countries that withhold the right to vote, own property, or marry based on belonging to some social category (such as being **gay**, **lesbian**, or **transgendered**) reflects the marginalization of those who are denied these rights. People who identify as belonging to these marginalized communities currently struggle with modern marginalizations that can affect all areas of the human experience, including political, familial, economic, social, and psychological avenues of our lives. Feminists have been active in understanding, resisting, and changing these marginalizations (Kronsell, 2005; Sinacore & Enns, 2005).

---

[2]   Think of this as a metaphor for a sheet of newspaper. The "dominant" story is on the front page while the "less important" information is in the margins.

Feminist models vary with respect to their understanding of the causes of marginalization and ways of changing it (Sinacore & Enns, 2005). Each model stresses certain ideas and de-emphasizes others. By examining different feminist models, some useful tools for understanding and studying masculinities can be identified. This text will include a brief summary of **liberal, cultural, socialist, women-of-color feminism/womanism**, and **radical feminisms**. These are certainly not the only types of feminisms, and the descriptions below are simplistic summaries of these very rich and detailed schools of thought. However, this brief review will assist us as we lay the groundwork for the overarching perspective of this text.

Liberal Feminism

Liberal feminism focuses on the acquisition of and access to **cultural resources**. The term cultural resource is used here to refer to a social tool that is used to enhance one's ability to adapt and live within one's culture. For example, education, a job, healthcare, and the ability to vote and own property could be considered cultural resources. In general, liberal feminists believe that all aspects of our social system (e.g., economic, governmental, educational, vocational) are worthwhile pursuits and that all people should have equal access to them (Enns & Sinacore, 2005). The problem is that women and other marginalized people are often prohibited from these resources or discriminated against within institutions (Enns & Sinacore, 2005; Rosser, 2005).

For example, since the founding of the United States, women have not had a strong presence in Congress in terms of their official representation. In the 110th Congress (2007), women represented approximately 16 percent of the congress (73 in the House and 16 in the Senate) (Amer, 2007). This is the largest proportion in the history of the country, but clearly, as 51 percent of the general population, women are under-represented.

A liberal feminist model is useful in that it helps us to see what cultural resources and institutions women (and others) have been denied and what steps can be taken to address this **gender gap** to make equal access available (Enns & Sinacore, 2005; Rosser, 2005). Liberal feminists don't want to change the overall way in which we live, but rather hope to make cultural resources more accessible to people who have not historically had access to them.

As stated, liberal feminism is concerned with access to cultural resources. While men vary in their access to cultural resources due to other factors about them (individual factors, personal history, class, race, age, sexual orientation, etc.) the question here is whether there are resources denied to them solely as a function of sharing the social identity of men. One cultural resource is *femininity*. In other words, in many cultures, men are often asked to deny and repress human behaviors associated with being feminine (Levant 1996; Pleck, 1976, 1989). A liberal feminist perspective is employed when researchers in this field try to understand what the particular aspects of femininity *are* in any given culture and then try to understand the adaptive problems associated with denying aspects of oneself that are associated with those characteristics. In a sense, the liberal feminist perspective focuses on understanding the impact of the denial of the right/opportunity to access aspects of femininity in any given culture.

Cultural Feminism

Cultural feminism, rather than focusing on the rights and opportunities of people, has focused on aspects of gender that have been integrated into the culture. Cultural feminists believe that there are significant differences between genders that make them unique and distinct social groups (Enns & Sinacore, 2005). The difficulty for cultural feminists is that many of the differences associated with women have been under-valued, ignored, or harmed.

For example, women are often viewed as being more emotional than men (Furnham et al., 2004; Mirgain & Cordova, 2007; Simon & Nath, 2004). Rather than recognizing this relational way of connecting to others as something adaptive, the term 'emotional' often carries with it ideas of irrationality or weakness (Foley, 1993; Hercus, 1999). This gives people the message that when something is more prevalent among women, it is often discussed as a liability (Enns & Sinacore, 2005). Cultural feminists want to better understand the qualities they believe make women unique and work toward positively integrating those qualities into all aspects of culture (Enns & Sinacore, 2005).

Cultural feminism asks us to consider whether (a) there are aspects and characteristics of masculinity that are unique to men, and (b) those aspects are viewed disparagingly by the culture. One of the primary ways that the field of masculinities has explored this question is by beginning to research and understand the diverse voices of men. In the past, men have been viewed as such a homogeneous group, and it has been difficult to ascertain what unique qualities they carry (Levant, 1996; Pleck, 1976, 1989). Cultural feminist approaches have assisted us in investigating these qualities and understanding the various ways in which men make sense of themselves as men.

Socialist Feminism

Socialist feminism, unlike liberal and cultural feminism, focuses on economics as a force that ultimately sets the stage for the ways in which people will understand and interact with one another. Socialist feminism sees capitalism as a system that does not hold within it the potential to include women equally. With an emphasis on history and economics, and borrowing from various writers such as Karl Marx, Leon Trotsky, and Ché Guevara (Jimenez & Vogel, 2005; Serra, 2005), socialist feminists argue that an economic system based on competition, which ultimately values financial gain over human worth and dignity, cannot foster an egalitarian role between people since by definition it does not seek a form of democratic partnership (Enns & Sinacore, 2005). This inequality will then affect our various roles as a function of gender and have a likely negative impact on women in particular (Serra, 2005). Socialist feminists are also interested in how issues of race, class, and nationality play into economics and help us better understand the marginalization of women and others (Enns & Sinacore, 2005).

For example, when jobs are moved (outsourced) from one country to another country, members of the original country often complain that they are losing work (Newman, 2005). One reason that outsourcing occurs is because companies often can increase profits by hiring workers in some countries with lax labor laws that allow workers to receive wages far below that of the original country (Newman, 2005). Socialist feminists believe that such an economic practice could never be one in which women could gain equality with men, since human interest and value is seen as secondary to financial gain (Sinacore & Enns, 2005). Socialist feminists have focused on these kinds of issues and how they have contributed to our understandings of gender, gender roles and the marginalization of women and others.

Socialist feminism has been helpful in viewing both the barriers that many men have in the world of work and how that interfaces with their understanding of what it means to be a "man." Many cultures stress the importance of work as a primary source of identity for men (Johnston & McIvor, 2004; Nonn, 2004). If these same cultures pit men of various backgrounds against one another for sustainable incomes, they not only create difficulties for them financially, but also as "men" since they rely so much on these connections for sources of identity. For example, a recently retired acquaintance of mine told me, "Now that I am no longer providing for my family, I am nothing." Sadly, many men experience this kind of disconnection once they leave their working worlds. Socialist feminist thinking offers insight into how that kind of psychological experience can develop in a competitive work world where income becomes a primary indicator of manhood, particularly since many men will never have equal access to work that fits this criteria for being "men."

Women-of-color Feminism/Womanism

Women-of-color feminisms (or womanist feminism/theory, womanism, Black feminist thought) are similar to socialist feminism in their emphasis on understanding the role of social group membership and economics in women's lives (Rosser, 2005; Sinacore & Enns, 2005). In particular, the emphasis has been on the role of race and racism and its impact on women of color, identity formation, and marginalization (Morardi, 2005; Rosser, 2005).

....

Making Connections: Is Machismo Macho?

Within many Latino communities the use of the term "machismo" has often been a source of controversy. Machismo (or being "macho") is often associated with being bullying, paternalistic, and violent towards others (Cranford, 2007; Stobbe, 2005). Machismo in some Latin cultures has been described as a type of dominant masculinity in which men control women through various means and justify that power differential through cultural and historical practices (Cranford, 2007; Stobbe, 2005). Men's norms and ways of being become central and dominant through the machismo behavior of men (Cranford, 2007; Stobbe, 2005).

Some authors, however, have suggested that men can show leadership qualities in their families with caring, respect, and dedication without being paternalistic and sexist. They argue that the desire to protect and provide for one's family can be done in ways that illuminate the importance of family members, rather than demonstrating their inferiority (González-López, 2004). For example, some families may have **sex-role differentiation** in that they expect that different sexes have different roles, but that the importance for each role is equal (González-López, 2004). This is the kind of question womanist thinking helps us to explore. By questioning White norms, investigating cultural meanings, and emphasizing relationships amongst members of a community, womanists help us understand the complex ways in which masculinities are manifested. The way in which people convey the meaning of the term machismo may carry very specific cultural cues that say much about the way we think about gender throughout various cultures.

Scholars such as Alice Walker, bell hooks, and Patricia Hill Collins have helped to form some of the major tenets of womanism. Womanism encourages one to (a) understand that for many women, identity with race is more significant than identity with gender; (b) realize that not all women have the same levels of marginalization; (c) value one's own ideas and experiences as sources of knowledge, rather than what is expected by the **cultural norm**; (d) celebrate the **spiritual** and relational components of being a woman; (e) embody a commitment of caring and responsibility to women of color; (f) recognize the various meanings that concepts like freedom, patriarchy, and relatedness can have in different cultures; and (g) continue to value relationships with men (Banks-Wallace, 2000; Barrett & McIntosh, 2005; Carlton-LaNey, 1997; Morardi, 2005; Ossana, Helms, & Leonard, 1992; Sinacore & Enns, 2005).

Womanism has given a voice to women of color who have identified with various feminist models, but have felt marginalized by a dominant voice of White, middle-class women feminists (Barrett& McIntosh, 2005; Sinacore & Enns, 2005). It has provided a vehicle by which women of color can recognize the connection between race and gender and create conversations that serve to value women's experiences and criticize **oppressive** systems without **dehumanizing** men (Banks-Wallace, 2000).

Womanism has also had an influence in the field of masculinities. Womanist thinking has several applications, including the interface between racial and gender identity, the focus on self-empowerment, and the importance of relationships between men and women. In particular, the use of White male norms for studying men in general has come into question. Womanist thought has helped masculinity theorists and researchers to better understand the connections between racial and gender identity and begin to explore diverse men's experiences within various communities from their own perspectives.

Radical Feminism

The last feminism we will discuss is radical feminism. Radical feminists have made many important contributions in recognizing how our understanding of gender affects all human activities (Enns & Sinacore, 2005; Kaschak, 1992; Rosser, 2005). In fact, we will spend more time and detail on this section, because so many of the themes here will permeate this text.

A major assumption of radical feminists is that gender is at the forefront of all that we do as human beings, and that thinking about gender is the primary way in which humans make sense of the world (Enns & Sinacore, 2005; Kaschak, 1992). Our choices of dress, job, relationship partner, what we eat, how we move, even how we sleep is affected by the ways in which we make sense of gender (Kaschak, 1992; Rosser, 2005), leading to what the noted feminist clinical psychologist Ellyn Kaschak refers to as our **Engendered Lives** (Kaschak, 1992).

In particular, Kaschak points out that our views about gender have been dominated by a **masculinist epistemology**, one that has been dominated by men's values and ideas (Uhlmann & Uhlmann, 2005). She defines masculinist epistemology as "systems of knowledge that take the masculine perspective unself-consciously as if it were truly universal and objective. Despite claims to the contrary, masculine epistemologies are built upon values that promote masculine needs and desires making others invisible" (Kaschak, 1992, p. 11).

For example, prior to the 1970s, most books, research articles, and other information written in the field of psychology were written by men (Kaschak, 1992; Luepnitz, 1988; Prilleltensky, 1994). There were very few critiques of psychology evaluating the impact of a field dominated by men researching men and making claims about *human* behavior (Kaschak, 1992; Luepnitz, 1988, Rosser, 2005). Psychology as a discipline: (a) often did not include women in their research samples, but suggested they were discussing human behavior; (b) often viewed women as atypical or abnormal when they differed from men (rather than different or unique); and (c) considered men's behavior as normal and their scientific methods as neutral and objective, rather than as models by men for studying men (Kaschak, 1992; Luepnitz, 1988; Rosser, 2005). In this respect, aspects of radical feminism can be considered what is now called a **postmodern feminism**[3] in that it emphasizes that the ways we use to discover what we think are true are **socially constructed**[4] (Sinacore & Enns, 2005). For this reason, radical feminism seems to be a progenitor to what is today referred to as **social constructionism**.

There are many different models for understanding the concept of being socially constructed (Edwards, 1997; Raskin, 2002), but for our purposes here, when we say something is socially constructed, we mean that to understand what is true we have to examine the **cultural/historical context** that exists when the information is gathered. In other words, at any given point of time, we have different meanings for different human experiences. Those meanings are influenced by what is happening, in history and in the culture, who is in charge of describing what is happening and how they go about describing it (Tappan, 2000). For example, if you read information about terrorism in the last hundred years, you may find that the meanings of what terrorism is, who commits it, and what its impact has been, may vary as a function of being written at different time periods, in different cultures, and by different people (Lipton, Grannam & Beinin, 2003; Nuzzo, 2004).

By questioning the ways in which we examine and understand the world, radical feminists literally demand that we view the world in alternate and **transformative** ways. This is perhaps one of the most powerful contributions of radical feminism: the critical eye of radical feminists extends to everything we do and opens the doors for new

---

[3] Other terms used are poststructural and postpositivist; it just depends what academic area you are studying (sociology and philosophy generally referring to those two). In psychology you will see both postmodern and constructivist/constructionist/social constructionist used with each term emphasizing different ways of thinking about this general idea.

[4] Construct means to build. So social construction can be thought of as building the truth using the social truths of that particular time and place. Deconstruction is the opposite, which is tearing down something by looking at its social parts.

ways to view the world (Enns & Sinacore, 2005). In fact, as you will see, radical feminism has helped us to look at the concept of gender and masculinities in ways that require us to consider whether traditional ways of thinking about them (e.g. that only two genders exist, that only people born biologically male struggle with masculinity) are in fact, useful in describing the complexity of human experiences relevant to gender.

This radical reconfiguring of *ideas and knowledge* leads to a radical reconfiguring of our *living* our lives. Radical feminists (akin to socialist and womanist feminists) have been at the forefront of questioning the very structure of the systems we live by. Unlike liberal feminists, radical feminists believe that the problems that people face will require an active restructuring and revamping of all of our cultural institutions (family, religion, criminal justice system, etc.) (Enns & Sinacore, 2005). Ultimately we may need to radically alter the ways in which we live our lives if we wish to work toward a truly egalitarian world.

....

Making Connections: Of Course Women Are Depressed

Researchers in psychology recognize that women are significantly more at risk to be diagnosed with major depression than are men (Bergdahl, Allard, Alex, Lundman, & Gustafson, 2007; Husky, Mazure, Paliwal, & McKee, 2008; Luo & Hing-Luan, 1998). In trying to answer the question "Why are women more depressed than men?" a radical feminist might turn the question on its head, asking, "Why aren't even *more* women depressed than what we are seeing in the statistics?" With rates of violence against women rising (Efetie & Salami, 2007; Erlanger, 2006; Hearn, 2004; Jackson & Petretic-Jackson, 1996), increasing numbers of women and children in poverty (Huang & Pouncy 2005; Shackelford, Weeks-Shackelford, & Schmitt, 2005), and the large proportion of single mothers not receiving child support (Huang & Pouncy, 2005; Shackelford et al., 2005) it's a wonder that the statistics aren't higher.

Radical feminists with knowledge of research on lesbian relationships might also point out that some studies have indicated that lesbian women report the most satisfaction in relationships when compared to gay male and heterosexual couples, suggesting that further analyses of these couplings should be investigated to understand why women are not as depressed in these relationships (Kurdek, 2004; Rothblum, 2004; Schreurs, 1994). Understanding the unique strengths of these relationships could assist in re-examining the ways in which other couples relate with one another.

....

Radical feminism provides a key perspective for our investigation of masculinities. Social constructionist thinking, an important area in masculinities, with its emphasis on history, power, and the investigation of who has the ability to define the world for others, has also been influenced by radical feminism. Much of the critical thinking in this field is influenced directly or indirectly by radical feminist analysis.

Integration

In summary, what these feminisms have in common is their agreement that women are under-represented in the social world, that they are undervalued, and that their voices and perspectives are not viewed as important as men's. The major areas that these models highlight include how people are impacted socially and psychologically by their (a) access to cultural resources; (b) understanding of what it means to be gendered; (c) class and class identity; and (d) race and racial identity. Ultimately, there is a recognition that in order to evaluate these issues we must pay attention to how we define what we are studying and recognize who is doing the studying and how the researcher's voice might affect the truths that are discovered.

Each feminist model points to different elements that can help us in our exploration of masculinities. Because men are not a monolithic group with similar characteristics and access to cultural resources, they too are affected by the same phenomenon as others. For example, all of the concerns feminists have about women can be applied to men. However, men are not affected in the same way as women, and therefore part of this field's mission is to understand the similarities and differences in the way in which people are affected by these various issues of marginalization.

One significant difference in this regard is the overall disparity in power that men carry as a group in comparison to women (Connell, 1995; Enns & Sinacore, 2005; Kaschak, 1992). This difference in power, both in comparison to women and amongst men, is discussed in the next chapter and helps set the basic contextual stage for our investigation of masculinities.

Summary

This chapter introduced the reader to the field of masculinities and to many of the basic questions that researchers and scholars are concerned with. Several different types of feminism were introduced and argued to be useful in the studying of masculinities.

The remainder of this text exposes the reader to the core issues within the field of masculinities. These issues include an overview of popular models of masculinities, theories about the origins of masculinities, and an exploration of the "crisis in men and masculinity" and three perspectives as to the origins of that crisis. This exposure will assist the reader in the investigation of other readings in this field that may provide the ample background to fully appreciate the rich and detailed explorations into the world of men.

Review and Questions to Ponder

1. What is the difference between studying men and studying masculinity?
2. Why do we use the term masculinities? Can you give an example to explain?
3. What is a construct? Why is masculinity a construct?
4. Can you think of other examples of constructs you have learned about in other classes? What are they?
5. What do we mean by a model? How do they relate to constructs? How do assumptions relate to models?
6. What are the basic interests of feminist models?
7. What does it mean to be marginalized? Can you think of examples of marginalization?
8. What do we mean by dominant culture?
9. What is the basic concern of liberal feminism? What would this model like to see changed about culture?
10. What is the basic concern of cultural feminism? What would this model like to see changed about culture?
11. What is the basic concern of socialist feminism? What would this model like to see changed about culture?
12. What is the basic concern of woman-of-color feminisms? What would this model like to see changed about culture?

13. Do you think it is possible to be macho without being paternalistic? Why or why not?
14. What is the basic concern of radical feminism? What would this model like to see changed about culture?
15. What do we mean by engendered lives? Can you think of examples of this idea?
16. What is a masculinist epistemology?
17. What is postmodern feminism? What do we mean by social construction?
18. What is meant by deconstructing the social and historical context of a situation?
19. Do you agree with any of the concerns of feminist models? Which ones? Do you consider yourself a feminist or womanist?
20. Were you surprised that feminist models are used to study men? Why? What are potential advantages and disadvantages to doing so?
21. What do you think about the argument that women are more depressed than men because they have more difficult social circumstances than men to live with?

2

Social Context and Masculinities

Chapter 1 briefly introduced the field of masculinities and the goal of investigating the psychosocial lives of people who identify as being men. It gave us an overview of many of the basic themes in the field. The chapter also highlighted the importance of feminist theory as it applies to our investigation of masculinities.

Social Structure and Organization

This chapter is concerned with setting the social context of our investigation. As mentioned in chapter 1, social context refers to the social and situation-specific realities that influence how people view themselves and interact with others (Kaschak, 1992; Fisher, Hauck, & Fenwick, 2006; Murray & Greenberg, 2006). In other words, to make sense of any particular psychosocial experience, we will need to know when it happened, where it happened, to whom it happened, who described how it happened, and a host of other factors that might influence what that experience was like for those involved. For example, a man expressing his concern for another person could be interpreted and experienced differently if that 'other' were an adult male as opposed to a young child. He may be understood differently if he expressed concern at home, at work, or at a rock concert. He may be understood differently if the person to whom he expressed concern were of a similar or different racial group, nationality, and so on. Many variables ultimately contribute to the context and meaning of any given psychosocial event.

Our specific interest here is in how social context affects men, how they view themselves as men, and how this may influence their interaction and relationships with others. The specific social context interest of this chapter is in what **sociologists** call the **social structure** of a society (Turner, 2006).

Every human group has some form of organization within it. This organization consists of **social institutions** which have designated roles to ensure a society's survival (Roy, 2006; Stearns, 2006; Turner, 2006). Each institution operates under certain rules that both define what a particular institution *is* and what its relationship is to other institutions. For example, most societies have institutions such as government, education, and religion that all play a part in the functioning of any given society (Stearns, 2006). Each operates within a set of rules that guides the institution. The institutions and their relationships to one another make up the social structure of a society. Understanding ways in which various institutions are created, maintained, and interact can be thought of as an investigation of a particular society's social structure, something in which many sociologists and other social scientists are interested.

One example of a social structure you may be familiar with is a **monarchy**. Monarchy literally means "ruled by one" and it is often associated with kings, queens, and other hereditary rulers (Bell, 2006; Constantine, 2006). Monarchal cultures have a relatively small set of people that are the designated rulers. In this social structure, this small group of people is arranged in a hierarchy where one person ultimately has the supreme say (typically the king or queen) (Bell, 2006; Constantine, 2006). The monarchy ultimately decides what the cultural institutions will be, who will lead them, who will benefit from them and how. While monarchies are significantly less common today than they were in the past, they are often represented in stories and fairy tales like "The Lion King" and "Sleeping Beauty" (Disney, 1999; Levine, 2003).

One might wonder why others who are not members of the powerful elite group allowed (or allow) the **nobility** to have so much control over the well-being of society. One contributing factor to a ruling group's reign is the belief that such people are entitled to rule over others because of their membership in a more important or superior social class (Hurwich, 2003). In a very basic way, all members of monarchal cultures believe that some people are destined to be in the position of ruling and others of following.

Monarchies were much more common in the past, yet several still exist today. Thailand and the United Kingdom for example, still have monarchies, yet their power is very limited. Saudi Arabia had a monarchy until 1992, and since that time has been examining the role of its constitution, Muslim law, and how they interact with the role of the royal family (Bell, 2006; Nevo, 1998; Sivaraksa, 2002).

Over time, social structures change as human cultures change. People question not just how each society is organized, but whether that organization is best for that society, and in particular, for *whom* in that society. In the film *Monty Python and the Holy Grail*, a peasant farmer asks King Arthur what gives him the right to be the king. The king explains that the Lady of the Lake gave him the holy sword Excalibur, which, when wielded, would give him the right and privilege to be a sovereign ruler. The peasant replied, "Strange women lying in ponds distributing swords is no basis for a system of government. Supreme executive power derives from a mandate from the masses, not from some farcical aquatic ceremony" (Python, 1976). While this is clearly meant to be entertaining, it raises the important issue of examining who is in power and how it is that they get to be there. This type of thinking has led to many nations moving away from monarchies to other forms of social structure and organization.

Patriarchy and Masculinities

Patriarchy

One form of social structure that exists commonly today is **patriarchy**. Patriarchy refers to a kind of social system in which the social structure is literally ruled by men. Not surprisingly, there are different views on what patriarchy *actually* means and how it has affected our lives. We will use the definition proposed by renowned sociologist Allan G. Johnson (1997). He has defined **patriarchal cultures** as those that are (a) **male dominated**, (b) **male identified**, and (c) **male centered**.

Who's Who in Masculinities Research: Allan G. Johnson, Ph.D.

Allan G. Johnson is writer, teacher, and public speaker who has worked on issues of privilege, oppression, and social inequality since receiving his Ph.D. in Sociology from the University of Michigan in 1972. He has worked with more than 170 schools and

Continued

organizations in 34 states. He has written several texts including
The Forest and the Trees: Sociology as Life, Practice, and Promise and
The Gender Knot: Unraveling Our Patriarchal Legacy.

Website: http://www.agjohnson.us

Male dominated means the cultural institutions of a given society
are over-represented by men (Johnson, 1997). As discussed briefly in
chapter 1, most modern cultural institutions (governments, educational
systems, businesses) are dominated by and controlled by men.
Historically, men have also actively prevented women from participating in these institutions (such as voting, home ownership, and
higher education) (Johnson, 1997). And while women are entering and
reshaping institutions today more than ever before in history (Kahane,
1998; Kantrowitz & Juarez, 2005; Ossana, Helms, & Leonard, 1992;
Wilson, 2004), we have a long way to go before women are equally
represented in cultural institutions (Erickson, 2007; Johnson, 1997;
Kantrowitz & Juarez, 2004; Wilson, 2004; Watanabe, 2007). And even
when the number of women increases and begins to equal that of
men in certain vocations, they make significantly less money for the
same positions and are very unlikely to be in positions of authority
in their respective fields (Huffman & Cohen, 2004; Johnston, 2002;
Petrzelka, 2005; Price, 2007; Smith, 2002; Watanabe, 2007; Weeks &
Wallace, 2007).

To say that patriarchal cultures are male identified means that people
utilize male **norms** to determine the value or worthiness of human
behavior (Johnson, 1997). Perhaps one of the most famous examples of
this in the field of psychology occurred when Carol Gilligan criticized
her mentor Lawrence Kohlberg's theory of morality, suggesting that
his emphasis on abstract notions of justice was a male standard and
that women who use a relational style of care to determine morality
would be viewed as morally inferior by this model (Gilligan, 1982;
Page & Tyrer, 1995; Woods, 1996). While research has been mixed in its
ability to determine differences based on this criticism (Jaffee & Hyde,
2000; Page & Tyrer, 1995; Woods, 1996), Kohlberg's theory is a good
example of male identification, in that it makes a male perspective seem
invisible or neutral.

Male identification has often led us to view what men do as normal and good, and what others do as abnormal and wrong (Johnson, 1997; Kaschak, 1992). Men are seen as objective, which is good; women are seen as subjective, which is bad. Men are rational and logical, which is useful; women are emotional and irrational, which only leads to problems. Men are strong, women are weak. Ultimately what is meant by these constructs has largely been determined by men who portray women as substandard and inferior (Johnson, 1997; Kaschak, 1992).

Finally, by male centered, we mean that what the members of the culture largely focus on are the activities of men (Johnson, 1997; Kahane, 1998). Patriarchal cultures keep men and men's ways of being at the center of attention and others in the margins. As Johnson (1997) explains, "If you want a story about heroism, moral courage, spiritual transformation, endurance, or any of the struggles that give life its deepest meaning and significance, men and masculinity are usually the terms in which you must see it" (p. 9). In short, men become the center of attention through cultural institutions that are dominated by men advocating for men's perspectives.

The media, for example, a cultural institution, often portrays men as active people and the main characters of the story, while women are more often than not secondary to the storyline. Among the 2005 Academy Awards nominees, it was exciting to see a film with a female protagonist, *Million Dollar Baby*, win. However, 80 percent of the nominees had male protagonists, and 100 percent of the directors and cinematographers who were nominated were men. Women were better represented in categories involving art, lighting, and set design (Academy of Motion Picture Arts & Sciences, 2005). This is not surprising to feminists concerned about women in media, who indicate that when women are better represented in number, they are often in more expected traditionally feminine roles, particularly those that emphasize sexuality and what goes on in the background rather than the foreground (Sobel, 2005).

Privilege

Patriarchy is related to what social scientists call **privilege**. Peggy McIntosh, a well-known researcher at Wellesley College, has written much about this topic and provided a useful metaphor of privilege as an "invisible knapsack" to help us better understand this concept (McIntosh, 1990, 1993, 2000). According to McIntosh (1993), "privilege

> **Who's Who in Masculinities Research: Peggy McIntosh, Ph.D.**
>
> Peggy McIntosh is the Associate Director of the Wellesley College Center for Research on Women in Massachusetts. She is Founder and Co-director of the United States S.E.E.D. Project on Inclusive Curriculum (Seeking Educational Equity and Diversity). In 1988, she published the ground-breaking article, "White Privilege and Male Privilege: A Personal Account of Coming to See Correspondences through Work on Women's Studies." In addition to having two honorary doctorates, she is the recipient of the Klingenstein Award for Distinguished Educational Leadership from Columbia Teachers College.
>
> Website: http://wcwonline.org/content/view/653/214

is like an invisible weightless knapsack of special provisions, maps, passports, codebooks, visas, clothes, tools, and blank checks" (p. 3).[1]

Privilege can be thought of as an unearned social granting of a route to accessing cultural resources (Donnelley, Cook, Van Ausdale, & Foley, 2005; McIntosh, 1993; Penterits, 2004; Pewewardy & Severson, 2003). Privilege is described as having both **positive advantages** and **negative advantages** (McIntosh, 2000). When, as a function of belonging to a community or society, certain social resources are made available to you (such as safety, affordable housing, nutrition, healthcare, and so on), you are then receiving positive advantages of privilege. These are considered positive because these kinds of privileges can help communities sustain themselves by ensuring that all people are granted access to resources they need to survive (McIntosh, 2000).

However, when these kinds of social needs are granted to you solely because of some social characteristic (gender, race, class) they begin to have *negative* advantages (Donnelley et al., 2005; McIntosh, 1993; Penterits, 2004; Pewewardy & Severson, 2003; Schacht, 2003). These are considered advantages because *some* people still benefit from them.

---

[1] McIntosh is specifically referring to White privilege here but applies the concept to male privilege as well.

They are negative in that some groups do not have equal access to these resources and are therefore **discriminated** against. As a function of this negative advantage, tension increases between social groups and reinforces **hierarchical relationships** amongst them (Schacht, 2003). Over time, human groups become so used to these differences that they begin to view them as a function of the natural order or a 'god-given right' rather than as the function of an unjust social system (Connell, 1995; Johnson, 1997; Johnson, 2001; Kimmel, 1998).

This text is primarily concerned with *male* **privilege**, which means that, as a function of being or presenting as male, certain opportunities, activities, and resources are made more accessible to you than to others (Johnson, 1997; McIntosh, 1990, 1993). The field of masculinities also explores **racial privilege, class privilege**, and **heterosexual privilege**, in which all refer to the same concept with different **social character-istics** as the reason for the privilege.

Privilege is sometimes hard to understand, particularly for people who benefit from it the most (Branscombe, 1998; McIntosh, 1990, 1993; Johnson, 1997). Since privilege is such a normal part of many peoples' experiences, they can't imagine how it could be any different. To help illustrate this, I created a list of my own privileges much like the one Dr. McIntosh created, to help understand some of the privileges that many men share (see Figure 2.1). Because many of us live in cultures

Figure 2.1: Statements of Male Privilege

> The following statements were based on McIntosh's *Questions of White Privilege* (1990, 1993). After I contacted Dr. McIntosh, she suggested that I try to create a list of privileges I have experienced as a man, or experiences of privilege that other men have shared with me.
>
> See how many of these you say yes to in order to understand feelings of male privilege. Each of these won't apply to everyone equally (A few of these questions are geared more toward heterosexual identified people, etc.), but see if it helps you understand the concept a bit better. The more you answer 'yes', the more privilege you are likely to have.
>
> 1. If I spend time solely with people of my own gender, it is rarely questioned or thought of as abnormal or an attempt at separatism.
> 2. I rarely think about safety when I am in a parking lot or when it is dark outside.

3. I have seen myself as having the primary income in my family and therefore my partner will make career choices around mine since I will logically earn more.
4. People usually don't take into account whether what I wear is appropriate.
5. People don't usually keep track of who might be coming to visit me in my home/apartment/residence hall room.
6. I can refer to media sources and see people of my gender widely represented in leadership positions.
7. When I learn about history or literature I am mostly shown people of my gender and their contributions.
8. I can be sure that my children will be given curricular materials that demonstrate the important contributions of my gender.
9. I can be pretty sure of having my voice heard in a group in which I am the only member of my gender.
10. I can go into a CD store and count on finding the music of my gender represented by people who primarily market their musical ability, not just the way they appear.
11. If I have children, I can assume that I don't need to spend as much time with them as my partner and that most people will consider that normal.
12. I am not likely to be stopped and asked at a store whether my credit cards are mine or my spouse's.
13. People have never questioned whether the choice of my last name represents some aspect of my personality.
14. I do not tend to worry about whether a person on a date will try to get me to do something I don't want to.
15. I do not tend to worry whether having children in the future will affect future employers' thoughts about me.
16. I do not spend much time thinking about what order I would like to do things in life (having children, having a career, etc.).
17. I tend not to worry about the proportion of body hair I have on my body.
18. I am not usually seen as a representative of my gender.
19. People expect me to advocate for my self-interests and when I do otherwise it is seen as odd.
20. I can be pretty sure that when I ask for someone's supervisor, they will be of my gender.

that emphasize individuality and also carry privileges, it is sometimes hard to see them. For example, a White man who sees himself as successful in his career may be able to recognize his own contributions to that success, but may experience difficulty recognizing the institutional procedures that have both assisted him and prevented others from gaining access in that fashion (Davies-Netzley, 2002; Farough, 2003; Hall, 2004).

It is important to understand the concept of **entitlement** as it relates to privilege. Having male privilege leads men to believe that cultural resources belong to them in some natural or unquestioning way (Kimmel, 1998). Entitlement often comes from an ignorance of the privileges that exist, a denial of these privileges, and a belief in righteousness and superiority over others (Kimmel, 1998).

For example, Kimmel (1998) points out that when people emigrate from other countries to the United States some Americans may exclaim, "They are taking *our* jobs," without questioning what is meant by *our*. With the exception of Native Americans and African Americans, the United States' population exists as a function of immigration. Phrasing employment opportunities as "our jobs" is a form of expressing entitlement and privilege in that vocational resources are thought to be owned by a particular group and this ownership is not based on any criteria but some abstract notion of rightness or worthiness (Johnson, 1997; Kimmel, 1998).

As a function of living in a patriarchal culture, men have access to certain privileges that others do not. This is not always obvious to them, usually because they have never really understood how it came to be that most institutions are represented by men and advocate for men's interests. This can lead to a kind of entitlement in which men believe they deserve those privileges because it is the way things are or the way they were meant to be. This is perhaps similar to the way in which monarchal nobility justify being in positions of power.

Patriarchal social context becomes very important to our discussion of masculinities because many Western nations meet the above definition of patriarchy. Members of those nations who identify as men both receive the benefits of patriarchy and struggle to define what masculinity is within that social system. This entitlement affects all of the basic endeavors within any society, including the studying of masculinities. But not all men are privileged by patriarchy in the same way.

Hegemonic Masculinity

So how do men **negotiate masculinity** in a patriarchal culture? R. W. Connell, an important contributor to the field of masculinities, devised the construct of **hegemonic masculinity** to help explain the relationship between patriarchy and privilege, and how men make sense of masculinity in different social contexts (Connell, 1995, 2001; Johnson, 1997). Before explaining what hegemonic masculinity is, a brief introduction to systems theory can help us better understand how hegemonic masculinity can be used to investigate masculinities.

> **Who's Who in Masculinities Research: R. W. Connell, Ph.D.**
>
> Raewyn Connell holds a university chair in Sociology at the University of Sydney. She is a senior editor of the journal *Theory and Society* and is on the editorial board of five other social science journals. Her teaching fields include research methods, social dimensions of education, and gender issues. Professor Connell has contributed several foundation texts to this field, including *Masculinities* and *Gender and Power*, and is the author or co-author of twenty-one scholarly books and more than a hundred papers in social science journals.
>
> Email: r.connell@usyd.edu.au

Hegemonic Masculinity as a Systems Theory

A **system** is defined as a collection of interdependent individual parts that accomplishes something greater than any individual part alone (Goldenberg & Goldenberg, 1991; Winton, 1995). Sometimes, in order for a system to remain stable or retain what systems theorists call **homeostasis** (which means a balanced state), the individual parts sense when other parts are damaged and try to compensate (Goldenberg & Goldenberg, 1991; Winton, 1995). Systems generally resist change and seek homeostasis even when individual parts are damaged in the process. In systems terms, this is called a **negative feedback loop**. In summary, when a part of the system **deviates**, other parts of the system react by self-correcting to establish homeostasis (Goldenberg & Goldenberg, 1991; Winton, 1995).

Our human body can be thought of as a system (Windelspecht, 2004). I learned this lesson all too well during a visit to my doctor's office several years ago. I came in reporting a terrible backache. She did some initial tests and then asked me the question that no one wants to answer: How much do you exercise? I fibbed a bit, but clearly I was not exercising much. She explained that my backache was not due to weak back muscles or a spinal injury, which I had assumed, but to my legs! Evidently, because my leg muscles were weak from lack of exercise, my back muscles were overcompensating in order to allow me to stand up straight. So while I was clearly in pain, my back would continue to work too hard until I addressed the lack of mobility in my legs (which I did by the way, and I am doing much better). From a systems perspective, the weakness in my legs was compensated for by my overworking back muscles so that I could stand up straight (maintain homeostasis). My back muscles were involved in a negative feedback loop; despite their soreness (damage), they continued to overcompensate.

Hegemonic masculinity, a theory informed by radical feminism, asserts that people will act in ways that reinforce male privilege by supporting conformity to an idealized version of masculinity, even when it may not be in their best interest, in order to maintain the system of patriarchy (Cheng, 1999; Connell, 1989; Connell, 1995; Hearn, 2004; Jefferson, 2002; Johnson, 1997; Kimmel, 2003; Kimmel & Messner, 2001; Levant, 1996; Whitehead & Barrett, 2001). Understanding patriarchy through the lens of systems theory, we know that, when parts of the system deviate from patriarchal ideals, other parts will compensate to facilitate conformance of the deviant parts to the expected norms. The systems metaphor, while not perfect here, can help us to understand how parts in a system may sometimes behave in ways that seem contradictory in order to maintain the system. This seeming stability sometimes comes at a cost to its members (see chapter 8).

Hegemony, as originally coined by political theorist Gramsci, works by coaxing, rather than forcing people to abide by social norms (Connell, 2001; Speer, 2001). Hegemonic masculinity suggests that men comply with social norms of masculinity by subordinating women (referred to as **external hegemony**) and marginalizing men (referred to as **internal hegemony**). Men comply in order for the system of patriarchy to continue with both advantages to men as a group and dire consequences to its individual members (Demetriou, 2001; Hearn, 2004; Peralta, 2007; Wetherell & Edley, 1999).

We can think of the process of hegemonic masculinity operating from both larger sociological and individual psychosocial perspectives. Hegemonic masculinity can take place at the level of male-dominated institutions that create policies that subordinate women (Barrett, 2001; Kronsell, 2005). Hegemonic masculinity can also take place on the playground, where boys tease and harass girls and boys who "act like girls." Parents can contribute by reinforcing these masculine ideals at home (Messner, 2004).

People engage in all kinds of behaviors (ranging from name calling to literally killing other men) to make sure other men act like "real men" (Albury, 2005; Connell, 1995; Hall, 2004; Kimmel, 1998; Peralta, 2007; Phillips, 2005). These negative feedback loops give information to deviant members in order to perpetuate the system of patriarchy. Hegemonic masculinity suggests that all members of a society try to get men to conform to its view of the "right" way to be masculine, even if it has negative repercussions for individuals. The ways in which men do this is informed by their varying access to male privilege.

Examining only the specific behaviors of individual men will not help us fully understand the problem. If my doctor had only examined my back without an appreciation of my body as a system of interrelated parts, my back might still be aching today. Similarly, if we only look at the individual behaviors of men, without an appreciation of how such behaviors relate to the system of patriarchy, we are destined to miss important influences on men's lives.

Components of Hegemonic Masculinity

While men receive privilege from patriarchy, not all men receive it in the same way (Connell, 2001, hooks, 2003; Kimmel, 2003; Paulsen, 1999). To help understand this hegemonic process, Connell (2001) suggests that hegemonic masculinity includes four types of relations that are hierarchical: **Dominant masculinity**, **Complicit masculinities**, **Marginalized masculinities**, and **Subordinated masculinities**.

Dominant masculinity refers to the idealized and socially expected ways of being male (Connell, 2001; Paulsen, 1999; Smith, 2007). Connell (1995, 2001) argues that Dominant masculinity in Western nations emphasizes competition, wealth, aggressiveness, and heterosexuality. Men who are well represented in the culture and hold wealth and class privilege would be primarily able to negotiate masculinity within this realm. This idealization becomes symbolized in a male-center__ culture through various institutions such as the media, family, religion, and education (Harvey, 2005; Speer, 2001). Movies like *XXX*, programs such as *TNA Wrestling*, and music performers like Pantera and 50 Cent embody this ideal when they present themselves in ways that reinforce aggression and violence (Oppliger, 2004). By being bombarded with these images and symbols throughout our lives, we begin to adopt dominant masculinity as the way men *are*, rather than the way we have **socially constructed** them (Harvey, 2005; Peralta, 2007; Speer, 2001).

....

Making Connections: 50 Cent's Dominant Masculinity

In this excerpt from the track 'Make Money by any Means' from his *Power of the Dollar* CD, hip-hop artist 50 Cent states:

> You can call me player yeah, but I ain't playing fair (Uh huh)
> Takers say I'm the hottest thang comin' this year (No doubt, ha ha ha)
> In the hood niggas know, how I handle my problems
> I walk up close, and I fo', fo' revolve 'em
> Don't make me run to you, put the gun to you
> Have yo ass on Phil Donahue explaining what the fuck I done to you
> Thug niggas in the street saying I'm sunning you
> Dude I'll smoke you and every motherfucker under you
> (http://display.lyrics.astraweb.com:2000/display.cgi?50_cent%
> 2E%2Ethe_power_of_the_dollar%2E%2Emake_money_by_
> any_means)

This passage is indicative of the dominant masculine ideal discussed in chapter 1. It includes aggression and a focus on competition and entitlement. If you traverse 50 Cent's Sony website (http://www.50cent. com/) you will encounter imagery and material in that fashion, including language and imagery that is blatantly sexist toward women.

Using hegemonic masculinity, however, might help us to view this differently. 50 Cent grew up in a poor, working-class family in the borough of Jamaica, Queens, New York. He was raised without a father,

Continued

and his mother was killed when he was still a young man. His youth was filled with crime and fear (http://www.50cent.com/).

As a working-class Black man in a racist society, he did not have anything approaching the access to cultural resources that other men do. The concerns of urban Black men are often ignored in this country, and the difficulty they face obtaining gainful employment and the bias of the law enforcement and criminal justice system makes it very hard to "be men" when employment is so closely tied to masculine identity. A man like 50 Cent would be primarily struggling with both marginalized and subjugated masculinities in a culture that has not demonstrated a concern for the plight of African American men.

Viewing 50 Cent's concerns within the framework of hegemonic masculinity can perhaps better explain his outrageous persona. This explanation is not meant to exonerate the blatant violence and sexism that 50 Cent portrays in some of his work, but to try to understand this via hegemonic masculinity. And unfortunately, akin to many men, rather than denouncing the system that puts him in this place, he exaggerates it, presumably because he lacks any tools or cultural support to do otherwise. And this has worked. He has gained major financial success as a result. In this respect, he gains access to dominant masculinity.

But 50 Cent is not alone in contributing to the symbols of dominant masculinity. Who else is complicit and stands to gain from his personae? Sony record executives, producers, background singers, and many others in the industry gain by being affiliated with this persona. People who purchase his CDs, t-shirts, books, and other paraphernalia are also complicit. All who participate keep the system going and benefit from it. And so all of us can contribute to this dominant form of masculinity.

This brief analysis was meant to help you apply the concept of hegemonic masculinity. It does not suggest that a human being can so easily be understood in such a brief description. And certainly 50 Cent is only one of many men who represent an aspiration to dominant masculinity. His struggle can be viewed as one all men endure to different degrees and in different ways within a patriarchal culture.

Ironically, the majority of men will not be able to attain this type of masculinity (hooks, 2003; Kimmel, 1998; Peralta, 2007; Smith, 2007). Most men will not meet the physical, personality, class, race, or economic prerequisites for the dominant ideal (Cheng, 1999; hooks, 2003).

In the United States, for example, the top 5 percent of Americans earn 21 percent of the income in the country, while the bottom 20 percent earn only 4 percent of the national income (Schwarz, 2004). And while the chances of being poor or working class are 1 in 10 for White men, they are 1 in 4 for Black and Latino men (Mantsios, 2003). So while all men are surrounded by a context of dominant masculinity, not all men are equally dominant in their ability to access cultural and economic resources. Yet attainment of dominant masculinity is often an aspiration of men across various groups (Connell, 2001).

Complicit masculinity refers to masculinity that in and of itself is not dominant, but supports dominant masculinity (Connell, 2001; Paulsen, 1999; Sargent, 2005). This would include participation in aspects of masculinity that conform to dominant masculine norms in hopes of receiving rewards for being like the dominant group, while recognizing perhaps at some level you will never be primarily in the dominant sphere. Complicit masculinity is more widely available to men as a group because potentially all men can benefit from privileges of the hegemony whether directly or indirectly (Connell, 1995; Johnson, 1997; Smith, 2007).

In the seventh grade, a friend of mine told me a story that is a great example of complicit masculinity. The walls of his room were covered with posters of male heavy metal artists. One day as he sat in his room, his father came in. His father began to chastise him for having pictures of men all over his walls and began calling him derogatory and heterosexist names (i.e., What are you, gay? A faggot?) in order to emphasize that it was not acceptable to hang posters of men in his room. Soon after this incident, my friend ordered a Playboy calendar poster that featured mini-photos of the Playmate models from the previous year, and hung them on his wall. The next time his father came into his room, he congratulated my friend for this choice, while his mother sat in confusion. From her perspective, this did not seem to be something her son would do.

In the context of coercion and humiliation, my friend complied with masculinity. By hanging the Playmate posters, he alienated his mother and participated in the **objectification** of women in order to keep his father from harassing him. This young man would not likely (both due to age and other characteristics) be able to achieve many direct benefits of dominant masculinity, but he could benefit from it through complying with a more dominant male's wishes, even at a cost to others and himself. Boys and men find themselves in this conundrum often. Men can receive what Connell (2001) refers to as a **dividend**, or advantage, from patriarchy; even when men do not always benefit directly from patriarchy, they can benefit by being complicit with it.

Marginalized masculinities refer to groups that are on the outskirts of dominant masculinities as a function of identifying with a social grouping that is not dominant (Connell, 2001). These masculinities could be based on ethnic, religious, or racial identifications. They are marginalized in that their interests and perspectives are often not taken into consideration by the **dominant culture** (Connell, 2001; Phillips, 2005).

For example, when I was worked with an **African Latino/a Asian Native American (ALANA)** student group at a university in the northeast, one concern voiced by students was that the university bookstore did not purchase hair products they could use. It never occurred to the buyer for the bookstore that people would need different types of hair products. The products that were purchased were primarily for White students. In this way (and in many others), the ALANA students' experience was marginalized as a function of not belonging to the dominant racial group. No one thought to ask them or to include their needs.

From a masculinity perspective, dominant masculinity often reinforces the idea that men should not be concerned about these kinds of beautification issues, although attitudes regarding these kinds of issues do change over time (Dunbar, 1999).[2] However, some social groups (such as in some African and Latino-American communities) do attribute attention to hair as an aspect of masculinity and racial awareness and pride (Buddington, 2001, Johnson, 2001). Not only does this concept not exist within the dominant sphere, but it is actively accentuated for some men when the dominant group does not provide the products necessary for hair care and ultimately for an aspect of self-identification. In this way, men who care about their hair must be "less than men." Therefore, marginalized men have the potential to be men if they lose their "deviant" masculine identities.

Subordinate masculinities refer to experiences that are not only marginalized but also **subjugated**, meaning that these aspects of masculinity are viewed as denigrated forms of masculinity and not viewed as being legitimately what men do. For example, gay men are sometimes

---

[2] Ironically, in many cultures, it is when men lose their hair that hair seems to become a stronger symbol of the lack-of dominant masculinity.

characterized as being flamboyant and expressive in their behavior, which some view as being more feminine (Gleitzman, 2003; Voon, 2007). Men displaying dominant masculinity often view more "feminine" behavior as being "unmanly," and harass and humiliate gay men when they express themselves in this way. Gay masculinity can be viewed as a subordinate masculinity, as not only is it marginalized, but it is also, as a whole, rejected as being a part of masculinity and is often denigrated (Connell, 1995; Voon, 2007). Subordinated men essentially are viewed as "not men."

One of the best illustrations of hegemonic masculinity I can think of happened in one of my courses, ironically a course in masculinity. The course had approximately 30 students in it, and about half of them were male. I noticed in the beginning of the course that only a handful of men, and perhaps two women, actively participated in the class. What was interesting was that the men's participation was extremely "politically incorrect." They said things with fervency about women and gay men (such as the idea that women were incapable of playing sports or succeeding in business and several derogatory remarks about gay men). The attitudes themselves didn't surprise me; the fact that they were said with such assuredness in a social setting did.

These attitudes represented external hegemony. Whenever issues were brought up to illustrate any strengths of women, or diversity amongst men, the same handful of men seemed invested in demonstrating that these statements were absolutely not true. The statements did not go unnoticed. Two women in the course actively argued with them, while the rest of the class was silent.

What was interesting about this was that I knew several of the other men in the class, and knew that they did not agree with some of the ridiculous statements being espoused. But none of them said much. In fact, when one male student attempted to give examples of women who possessed extraordinary skills, the dominant group was quick to dismiss the student and the suggestions. After a few of those interactions most men remained silent.

This example illustrates internal, external, and complicit hegemony. Men who deviated from the way that the dominant men in the course were defining masculinity were shot down or belittled for their contributions. Men who differed from the way the dominant men defined "men" were thought of as less than men, or not men. And while this dynamic continued, most men in the course kept quiet and accepted their dividend of safety from the callous remarks of the men who were representing dominant masculinity.

Throughout the course, the dynamic did change (with a lot of interventions from me), particularly after a discussion of the irony of learning about hegemonic masculinity while it was occurring in the course. But the whole class represented a struggle in which dominant attitudes tried to prevent alternative ideologies from existing.

Connell's framework allows for the possibility that all men are affected by a psychosocial struggle with all four layers of hegemonic masculinity simultaneously. Different men will have different options in their struggles due to their social group belonging and individual experiences, but ultimately all men will struggle with all levels as they make sense of masculinities within a patriarchal culture and across a variety of situations. While this model is very useful as an over-arching guide, it ultimately cannot address the individual and unique ways in which men develop, grow, and even resist patriarchy.

As men develop and become more conscious of this struggle, they can make choices and affect the ways in which they navigate these spheres of masculinities throughout their lives (Finley, 1996; Kimmel, 1998). This can then impact the modern state of patriarchy. This is important to consider, since people often assume that all cultures are patriarchal, and that things have "always been this way" which is not necessarily the case (Connell, 1995; Johnson, 1997).

Resisting Patriarchy

While patriarchy has been the dominant form of rule in most nations, it is not the only way that human beings have organized themselves (Johnson, 1997). The Iroquois Native Americans, for example, are known to have had a very democratic form of government; one that was far advanced compared with many modern systems in terms of women's representation in social life. Clan mothers, important tribal leaders, were responsible for choosing who would represent their interests at political meetings with the confederacy (Ackerman & Klein, 1995). Modern systems of democracy (particularly in the United States) are said to have been influenced by the Iroquois, though tragically not mimicking their inclusion of women (Ackerman & Klein, 1995).

Some scholars believe that many pre **Judeo-Christian** cultures were more egalitarian than they are today (Szarycz, 2001; Vogel, 2003). For example, archeologists studying the remains of ancient cultures argue that the fact that women are displayed prominently in art, pottery, and other cultural resources suggest that they may have been more revered and that while their roles were often gender-specific, the role itself was viewed as more equal than they seem to be in patriarchal cultures of today (Anderson, Balme, & Beck, 1995; Bolger, 1966; Gero, 2001; Tulloch, 2004).

Cultures exhibit far greater license than this in selecting the possible aspects of human life which they will minimize, overemphasize, or ignore. And while every culture in some way **institutionalized** the roles of men and women, it has not necessarily been in terms of contrast between the prescribed personalities of the two sexes, nor in terms of dominance or submission. (Mead, 1963, p. vi).

Historically speaking, not all cultures have been patriarchal, and cultures have changed from being more to less patriarchal over time (Johnson, 1997). With growing numbers of women entering the public sphere in a variety of contexts (government, education, religion, etc.) it is possible that, as representation becomes more equal, the system may change (Johnson, 1997; MacInnes, 2001). Past and present cultural changes suggest that individual people who negotiate within patriarchy can adapt and change themselves nevertheless (Johnson, 1997; Paulsen, 1999).

It is important to highlight that all men struggle with these issues and some men struggle against them. While all men may benefit from patriarchy, some men struggle against it and try to work toward both systemic and individual change that will lead to a more just world for all people.

....

Making Connections: W. E. B. Dubois' Profeminism

One of the most well-known men to advocate for women and a "grand vision" for society is William Edward Burghardt (W. E. B.) DuBois (Brown & Fee, 2003; Deegan, 2001; Okoampa-ahoofe, 1997). Dubois has been described as "the most brilliant and influential African American intellectual of the 20th century" (Brown & Fee, 2003, p. 274). After earning a Ph.D. at Harvard, DuBois wrote several texts examining the connection between slavery and African American life (Deegan, 2001).

Continued

He was a co-founder of the National Association for the Advancement of Colored People (NAACP) and was an extremely influential writer, sociologist, and activist (Brown & Fee, 2003).

One of the grand visions associated with DuBois is **Pan-Africanism** (Brown & Fee, 2003). Pan-Africanism is a movement to assist people of African nations to become more self-sufficient (and in some cases totally separate from non-Africans) and united to their African brothers and sisters of other nations (Rucker, 2002). DuBois' work helped African American people in the United States see the connection between American slavery and oppression of the descendants of Africa, and their shared plight with all Africans at the hands of White people, who continued to subjugate them in a variety of ways (Rucker, 2002). He established the first Pan-African Congress in 1919, in hopes of working toward the goal of unifying peoples of Africa and the African Diaspora and ending imperialism (Rucker, 2002).

DuBois interest in Pan-Africanism grew from his efforts to fight White supremacy in the United States (Rucker, 2002). While he was an intellectual, he was also an activist committed to women's lives (Deegan, 2001). One of his most well-known connections to White supremacy and working alongside women was his work at the Hull House of Philadelphia between the years of 1896 and 1898 (Deegan, 2001). Hull House was co-founded by sociologist Jane Addams and Ellen Gates Starr as a community home to provide shelter and assistance to the people, particularly the women and children, of Philadelphia (Deegan, 2001). The application of sociological methods to the understanding of poverty and social change were crucial elements of this endeavor (Deegan, 2001). DuBois, an Assistant Professor at the University of Pennsylvania, was assigned to work and live at the house. He interviewed 5,000 residents of Philadelphia to better understand what life was like for the urban poor, and to develop assistance for them in the community. This work was important both for the people of Philadelphia, the Hull House, and for the disciplines of sociology and community psychology, as it exemplified *applied* social science as one that uses the methods of the disciplines to work with people to bring about change in their communities (Deegan, 2001).

Initially, DuBois was concerned about accepting the Hull House position as it essentially had come about after his realization, soon after completing his PhD, that his White male colleagues in prestigious academic institutions did not seem to advocate him as a professor (Deegan, 2001). But his experience at Hull House was an important connection for him. He came to see how he had been disregarded as a sociologist, much like the women leaders of Hull House (many of whom were White). He maintained friendships with many of the women he worked with and described the experience as an important one (Deegan, 2001). While some have claimed that DuBois did not adequately recognize the work of women's contributions in his work (particularly by not acknowledging the activist contributions of Black women), he is still regarded as an important historical profeminist man (Waite, 2001).

Some men have adopted feminist ideology and activism into their work, resulting in the controversial use of the term feminist to describe them. Some women (and others) have been resistant to this usage, largely out of concern that men will usurp another human activity, and because of the inherently paradox in being in a position of power while claiming to try to denounce it (Austin-Smith, 1992; Douglas, 1994; Duelli Klein, 1983; Dworkin, 1987; Kahane, 1998; Lingard & Douglas, 1998). As a function of this controversy around men's involvement with feminisms, men have opted to use different terms to refer to themselves and their feminism. The terms reflect the varying ways in which men attempt to resolve apprehensions and criticisms as well as their own understanding of what it means to be a feminist.

Harry Brod, a Professor of Philosophy and Humanities, differentiates between **pro-feminist** (with hyphen) and **profeminist** (without hyphen). The term pro-feminist is used by men who wish to express support for feminism. Typically, it is used by men who primarily see feminism as something that women identify with and do (Brod, 1998). These pro-feminist men may subscribe to many of the tenets that women feminists do (such as being pro-choice, supporting equal pay for women, even adopting socialist or radical principles that are consistent with feminist principles); however these men view feminism as an activity for women (Brod, 1998).

Who's Who in Masculinities Research: Harry Brod, Ph.D.

Harry Brod is a Professor of Philosophy and Humanities at the University of Northern Iowa, and holds a Ph.D. in Philosophy

Continued

from the University of California at San Diego. He has over twenty
years of teaching, writing, and activism in the academic study of
masculinities and has contributed to several texts including his
most recent book *White Men Challenging Racism: 35 Personal Stories*
(co-authored with Cooper Thompson and Emmett Schaefer) and
his next co-edited text: *Brother Keepers: New perspectives on Jewish
masculinity* (co-edited with Rabbi Shawn Zevit).

Email: harry.brod@uni.edu.

Others, like Brod, have suggested that, while this is well-intentioned,
the term pro-feminism distances men from feminism in a way that does
not acknowledge their responsibility in allying with women to end
oppression (Brod, 1998). "The problem as I see it, however, is not that
'pro-feminism' brings men too close to the women's movement, but
rather the opposite, that the hyphen leaves too much space between
the 'pro' and the 'feminism'" (Brod, 1998, p. 207). For this reason, some
men have adopted the term *profeminist* to indicate both a respect for an
ideology that is grounded in women's experiences and a recognition
of the connection men must have with feminism (Brod, 1998). It is
intended to express a commitment not implied by pro-feminism. While
it is unclear whether men with these differing sentiments consistently
adhere to the grammatical distinction, the difference does seem to
represent varied perspectives on this issue.

These men have advocated that to call oneself a feminist is to take
over another sphere of women's lives, and that the term profeminist
implies advocating without dominating (Brod, 1998). In fact, some men
originally referred to themselves as **anti-sexist men** in order to convey
a position without usurping the term (Clatterbaugh, 1997; Dekeseredy,
Schwartz, & Alvi, 2000; Stoltenberg, 1993).

The terms liberal and radical profeminist have been used to draw
distinctions within the profeminism camp (Clatterbaugh, 1997). **Liberal
profeminism** has been associated with the incorporation and celebration of qualities associated with women (and hence similar to cultural
feminism), while **radical profeminism** stresses the dismantling of
patriarchy as its intended goal (Clatterbaugh, 1997; Vicario, 2004). Some
radical profeminists would not recognize that such a distinction
between liberal and radical profeminism exists, as radicals define

profeminism as having at its root an analysis of power and power relationships, and therefore to some radicals, liberals are not feminists (Clatterbaugh, 1997; Kahane, 1998).

While the hyphen/non-hyphen distinction seems to capture two different types of alignments with feminisms, they do not appear to be actively used by men who have these varying viewpoints. In other words, in my own experience, I have met men who seem to subscribe to these two different philosophies, but have never heard anyone actually argue the use or non-use of a hyphen. This is an academic way of distinguishing between two different positions, rather than a way actually used within activist communities (at least to my knowledge).

Finally, some men will use the term feminist with no qualifications. There are at least two reasons for using the term feminist as opposed (or perhaps in addition) to profeminist. The first is that any qualifications (pro with hyphen or sans hyphen) seem to imply a form of **binary** essentialism, in that only women can really *be* feminists (Digby, 1998, Gutterman, 2001; Hopkins, 1998).

> To categorically denounce men becoming and being feminist however, is not only an essentialist argument, but such a position falls into a trap set up by patriarchy itself. That is, the reality that patriarchy tries so hard to "ontologically" imprint into each of our brains is that we live in a dichotomous, binary, world. (Schacht & Ewing, 1997, p. 168)

Adopting the term feminist as a privileged man has the potential to be subversive in the ways in which we have defined and understood gender and gender identity.

Utilizing the term feminist is also an acknowledgement of the personal and political insights feminism gives to all willing to listen, learn, and change (Smith, 1987). Claiming the name and identifying it is an acknowledgement for some that feminism, while largely created by women, has insights that can benefit all people. This issue of men incorporating feminism is discussed in more detail in chapter 11.

Adopting a particular label of feminism is not the only way of rebelling against dominant forms of patriarchy. People engage in all kinds of behaviors, discussions, and actions that promote social change and suggest ways of living that are in contrast with the hegemony. Connell's model is very useful in examining the ways in which people attempt to keep the system of hegemony maintained, but has a harder time explaining resistance to this system.

Resistance and Hegemonic Masculinity

An interesting survey research study by Johansson and Hammarén (2007) illustrates both the process of hegemonic masculinity and the recognition of ways that people may resist it. The researchers were interested in understanding how young Swedish students view pornography through the lens of hegemonic masculinity. Pornography can be seen as a vehicle for male dominance, in that it often portrays men in a stereotypically dominant heterosexual role (strong, muscle-bound, virile, and coitus-centered) while simultaneously objectifying and subjugating women and non-dominant forms of masculinity (Johansson & Hammarén, 2007).

After analyzing responses to a survey tapping into attitudes about pornography, the results found that, while most men had positive attitudes toward pornography, 22 percent had negative attitudes toward pornography, and 20 percent believed that it was denigrating to women. "Today we see, among men, considerable resistance to various traditional male behaviors and rituals" (Johansson, & Hammarén, 2007, p. 66). These attitudes represent resistance to dominant masculinity.

In addition, the authors suggest that this depiction is much more complicated than it may first appear. Not only are some resisting pornography that supports male dominance (all genders), but others are resisting the idea that all forms of erotica must support hegemony (Johansson & Hammarén, 2007). Another form of resistance may also come in the creation of erotic materials that have a very different kind of impact on a variety of diverse consumers (Johansson & Hammarén, 2007).

It is important to learn about the social context in which we all live, and it is equally important to remind ourselves that individual human experiences cannot be understood by merely understanding broad, sweeping social influences. Therefore, we must seek to understand the difference between men as a social group and the beliefs, values, and behaviors of individual men. In other words, while men as a social group may hold certain power and privilege, and sub-groups within groups of men may have differing access to dominant masculinity and strive toward complicity for the homeostasis of the gender system, this will not necessarily predict the lived lives of individual men.

Within each social system are individual people with unique histories, lives, and struggles. Some will conform to dominance, others will dissent. Regardless of their intent and stated values, all men will struggle with elements of dissent and conformity to dominant masculinity, and will do so imperfectly and inconsistently as they make sense of who they are as human beings.

Summary

This chapter discussed the importance of examining social structure as it applies to the study of masculinity. In particular, we discussed patriarchy and how patriarchal systems lead to privilege and entitlement for men who exist within them. We then discussed hegemonic masculinity and emphasized that not all men benefit from patriarchy in the same way. Finally, we emphasized that social systems change and that, while patriarchies have been in existence for a long time, people of all genders are resisting and hoping to make them more just. One such method of resistance comes in the form of men adopting and learning from feminist ideology. This reminds us to be cognizant of both psychosocial realities and individual experiences. Throughout your exploration of masculinities you will learn of the many ways that men resist dominant ideologies in order to discover their authentic selves.

Review and Questions to Ponder

1. What do we mean by social structure/organization?
2. What is a social institution?
3. What is a monarchy?
4. What is meant by "noble breeding"? How does it relate to the concept of dominant masculinity (discussed below)?
5. What is patriarchy? How is it male dominated, identified, and centered? Can you think of examples of this?
6. Do you think the country you live in as a whole is dominated by patriarchy? Why or why not?
7. What do we mean by privilege? What are the positive advantages? Negative advantages?
8. Can you think of examples of male privilege? White privilege? Class privilege? (Try using Table 2.1 for ideas.)
9. What is entitlement? How does it relate to privilege?
10. What is hegemonic masculinity?

11. How do general systems concepts like homeostasis and negative feedback loop help explain hegemonic masculinity?
12. Can you think of other examples of how popular artists display and struggle with dominant masculinity? Can you think of any who try to resist it?
13. What is the difference between external and internal hegemony?
14. What are dominant, complicit, marginalized, and subjugated spheres of masculinity? Can you think of examples of these?
15. What is a dividend of patriarchy?
16. Are all cultures equally patriarchal? Can you think of cultures that are more matriarchal or more egalitarian? What about subcultures in your country?
17. Why is the term "feminism" controversial for men to use?
18. What is the difference between pro-feminism, profeminism, and feminism as a label for men?
19. Besides DuBois, what other men have you learned about who have advocated for women? If you can't think of many, do you think that is because there are not many, or that we haven't been taught much about them? If the latter is the case, why might that be? What is the difference between liberal and radical profeminism?
20. Do you believe men can be feminists? Why or why not?
21. What other ways might men resist patriarchy besides aligning with feminism?
22. What is the difference between viewing men as a group and men as individuals?

3

Difficulties of Definitions and Masculinity as a Social Construct

Chapters 1 and 2 comprised the first section of this text, which introduced the basic issues within the field of masculinity. The next section of the text is intended to provide an overview of the diverse ways researchers define and explain **masculinities**; it is divided into three chapters, each with several subsections. This chapter is divided into two primary subsections. The first subsection describes difficulties in defining masculinities. The second subsection overviews social models for describing what researchers believe masculinity is and includes concerns about those theories. Chapter 4 describes psychological models of masculinity and chapter 5 describes interactive models of masculinity. Both chapters conclude with concerns about those views.

Difficulties in Defining Masculinity

Perhaps one of the most important and complicated tasks for us in the field of masculinities is defining what exactly it is that we are studying. Most people seem to have a general idea of what masculinity is. If you ask someone what a "man" is like, you often get a series of adjectives such as strong, independent, logical, dominant (many which may correspond with dominant masculinity). While on the surface it may seem that we are speaking about the same phenomenon, as it turns out, defining masculinity can be a very complicated process (May, 1986; Paulsen, 1999; Silverstein & Rashbaum, 1994; Wetherell & Edley, 1999; Whitehead & Barrett, 2001).

Studying exactly what we *mean* by masculinities can be very difficult, since researchers often do not provide definitions, and when they are given, they are often unclear (Abdullah, 2005; Good, Borst, & Wallace, 1994; Green, 2000; Hoffman, 2001; Spence & Buckner, 2005).

This leads to confusion when reading and learning about this field, because people use so many different terms and often use them inconsistently (Good et al., 1994; Green, 2000; Hoffman, 2001; Spence & Buckner, 1995). There are several potential reasons for this differential use of terms. We turn now to one of them that constitutes a problem in all social sciences.

Studier Studied

Human beings are incapable of studying human processes without implicating themselves. Such is the case for masculinity theorists and researchers. People interested in this field are often the studier and the studied simultaneously. We cannot step outside ourselves to study masculinities (Connell, 1995). This means as we explore masculinities, choose what areas we believe are important to study, make assumptions we believe to be true, and ultimately choose language to describe our knowledge, we are unable to do so without implying truths about ourselves.

In other fields, this issue may not be as much of a problem. A **botanist** may be very passionate about a **hypothesis** she has; however, her study's results do not have direct implications on how she views herself as a person. In the social sciences, what we learn is a summary of the way we see ourselves and our potential as human beings. As we research and learn about ourselves, how do we understand our pains, struggles, and triumphs and portray them in a way that is accurate, understanding and critical? This basic problem seems to be a major factor in the multiple definitions of masculinity (Fausto-Sterling, 1999; Frable, 1989; Good et al., 1994; Green, 2000; Hoffman, 2001; Levant, Cuthbert, & Richmond, 2003; Pleck, 1976; Pleck, Sonnestein, & Ku, 1993; Spence & Buckner, 1995). While the "studier studied" phenomenon results in several specific disagreements within the field, we will focus on two that are important for this text: a) the *focus* when defining masculinities; and b) the *meaning* of normalcy and how it applies to the study of masculinities.

Questions of Focus

As discussed in chapter 1, cultural definitions of masculinity differ across time (Harvey, 2005; Hofstede, 1998). In and of itself this is not necessarily a problem. For example, when researchers conduct studies, they could clarify that their results reflect certain ideas common to a particular time and place in order to give us a context to understand the material. In order to do that, they would have to first define specifically what is meant by the construct for that study and how that reflects current cultural standards. This becomes a problem, however, when people study different aspects of masculinity without making it clear what they *mean* by masculinity and thereby assume it is common knowledge or obvious to the reader, which, as you will see, it is not.

Human beings are very complex creatures. We have an elaborate **neurological** system that allows us to process and interpret **sensory information** in a variety of ways (Kirshner, 2002; Pogun, 2001). These **experiences** are often divided into categories that we think affect one another. Some basic aspects of the human experience social scientists focus on are **biological**, cognitive, **affective**, learned, and expressive, with the later including **kinesthetic**, sexual, and language-based types of expression (Weiten, 2004).

The question then becomes on which characteristics of human experiences do we focus to understand masculinities? Do we focus on a) the biological contributions to our experience (hormonal, neurological, genetic); b) the ways that people may think (attitudes about the world, gender, themselves); c) the ways people experience emotion; d); the ways that people behave (their observable actions); e) the roles or situational ways people behave; f) the different ways that people express themselves; or g) a combination of these things? And which ones? And is masculinity a purely psychological experience? Is it a social phenomenon? Or some sort of interaction? Is it something only men with certain biological characteristics experience? Such questions of focus have been answered differently by masculinity researchers who have used different characteristics of human experience (and combinations) to measure the same construct of masculinity (Mahalik, Good, & Englar-Carlson, 2003). The characteristics and definition one focuses on determine one's understanding of masculinity and a whole host of other factors that are believed to be related to the construct. Margaret Mead (1963) exemplifies the importance of focus when comparing two unique tribal cultures – the Arapesh and the Mundugumor peoples of New Guinea:

> The Arapesh believe that painting in colour is appropriate only to men and the Mundugumor consider fishing an essentially feminine task. But any idea that the temperamental traits of the order of dominance, bravery,

aggressiveness, objectivity, malleability, and inalienability associated with one sex (as opposed to the other) is entirely lacking. (pp. xiii–xiv)

So when comparing these two cultures in terms of gender, **role definitions** (specific behavioral tasks associated with a social role) would differentiate them (as people who paint *or* fish) but **traits** (or **characteristics**) (dominance, bravery, etc.) would not. So the role definition would suggest that people have important differences, and the trait definition would suggest that they are very similar.

Clearly, the question and debate for scholars in the field of masculinities is which way of describing masculinity speak to uniqueness as experienced by those who identify themselves as men. This is very important to consider, as any particular person might be similar to a group of people utilizing one definition of masculinity, but not with another. What might that say about an experience of masculinity? Is it a normal experience? It seems that what masculinity means depends on what counts as masculine (and who gets to count it). The studier who studies masculinity not only determines the focus of inquiry, but can also define what is thought of as normalcy.

The Meaning of Normalcy

While the concept of normalcy is common in the social sciences, it is not always used consistently. This inconsistency stems from the difference between an understanding of what people *actually* do (called **descriptive norms**) and what some people think they *should* do (called **sociocultural** or **prescriptive norms**). These terms are used interchangeably, which is not only confusing to learners but also makes it appear that sociocultural norms are the same as descriptive norms, when in fact they may not be and often are not (Connell, 1995; Thompson & Pleck, 1986; Thompson, Pleck, & Ferrera, 1992). In other words, the way that some expect other people to be does not necessarily match the way they actually are. In the study of masculinities, diverse experiences with masculinities suggest that a lot of prescriptive norms are not only inaccurate, but harmful (Mahalik et al., 2003; Pleck, 1995). For example, a common descriptive norm for boys is that in general all boys are good at sports. The truth is, as in any activity, boys' skills vary in relation to sports. But because this descriptive norm is often expressed as a prescriptive norm, boys evaluate their self-worth on the assumption that all boys excel at this activity (Bowker, Gabdois, & Cornock, 2003;

Daniels & Leaper; 2006; Swain & Jones, 1991). This can lead to much self-doubt for young boys who utilize this activity as a primary way to determine their self-worth (Bowker et al., 2003; Swain & Jones, 1991).

If men's experiences are quite diverse from one another, then the concept of a norm or "average experience of men" really doesn't explain much about individual men. As we learn about the contributions of racial, ethnic and cultural identities, sexuality, religious beliefs, class, and a host of other variables to the experiences of masculinities, we may discover that statements that begin with "Most men . . ." are not really accurate. In fact, whether masculinity is a phenomenon only experienced by people who identify as men has been a major aspect of this concern.

So what might make one think that there is not a clear norm (or set of **norms**) by which to examine masculinities? First, some argue that our binary way of thinking about gender is inaccurate and does not reflect the diverse identities that exist among people (Grinnel College, 2001; Kimmel & Messner, 2001; Messner, 1995). In other words, is it accurate that there are only two **genders** or **sexes**? Some argue that gender is also dynamic and is something that develops over time (Hyde, Kranjik, & Skuldt, 1991). Others argue for the situational differences in our gender expression (Edwards, 1997; Potter & Wetherell, 1987; Wise & Stake, 2002). And still others are exploring what is often called a **relational self**, suggesting that our identities are always in flux as we are interacting with one another in social contexts (Bergman & Surrey, 1993; Gergen, 1999; Harré, 1998). Many in the field of masculinities have questioned the assumption that gender is universal, binary, consistent and stable and are critical of whether any type of "normal" masculinity exists (Edwards, 1997; Fausto-Sterling, 1999).

Masculinities researchers find themselves with disagreements about what normalcy means as well as multiple definitions of masculinity. There is not always an acknowledgement that these differences exist. In order to better understand this diverse understanding, we now turn to examine some of these definitions of masculinity.

Approaches to Defining Masculinity

Knowing some of the tangles involved in defining masculinity will assist as you try to understand different views on masculinities. We will now explore a few popular models for explaining what masculinity is.

We begin here with social models and then turn to psychological and interactive models in the following chapters. Each model is followed by concerns people have expressed about that perspective. Not all of the different ways of defining masculinities (nor all the concerns and debates about the models) are represented in this text, but several of the common methods are included. We will begin with two social views of masculinity – gender role theories and masculinity as power.

Masculinity as a Gender Role

Before exploring the **gender role** model of masculinities, we must first understand the difference between sex and gender. We use the term sex when we are referring to a biological way of differentiating between human beings (Franklin, 1988). Gender, on the other hand, refers to general social and cultural beliefs on the part of individuals and societies about people and what differentiates them (Franklin, 1988; O'Neil, 1981). These social and cultural beliefs about gender determine societal expectations about people's thoughts, feelings, and behaviors, otherwise known as gender roles (Franklin, 1988).

Sex, gender, and gender roles

There are several biological factors that are used to differentiate human beings by sex including **anatomical**, **physiological**, and **hormonal** factors. The most commonly used biological criteria, however, are the **sex chromosomes** (Franklin, 1988). The majority of humans are born with two patterns of sex chromosomes. XX is the chromosomal pattern for females and XY for males (Franklin, 1988). While the majority of people are born with these patterns, there are a variety of other combinations that exist. For example, some people are born with the pattern of XXY, which is described by the field of medicine as **Klinefelter's syndrome**. These people are typically referred to as men with an extra X chromosome due to the presence of testicles. Common physiological differences that people with this pattern struggle with are infertility, developmental delays, typically less than average intelligence scores on tests, and overall muscle weakness (Geschwind & Dykens, 2004; Polani, 1969).

People born outside the expected pattern of sex chromosomes are often considered to possess a **syndrome**, rather than as belonging to a legitimate sex that exists outside of male or female. This is largely due to the binary way we think of sex, as well as a specific focus on the physiological and psychological struggles that are often common to people with these sex chromosome combinations.[1] Describing this situation as a syndrome might make sense if one views the number of people with this genetic combination as rare; however, many of these alternate patterns are more common than one might think. Klinefelter's syndrome, for example, is found in approximately 1 out of 500 men (ranging from 1 in 500 to 1 in 1,000) (Geschwind & Dykens, 2004). People who have less common sex chromosome patterns and less common sexual reproductive anatomical features are sometimes called **intersexed** and can teach us a lot about the way we think about masculinities.

While our chromosomal sex seems to be an important contributor to the experience of human beings, we are also psychosocial animals who have expectations and create social rules about the various ways in which we interact with one another (Johnson, 1997). One way of studying our socialness is by examining our **social roles**. In any society, there are social roles or positions that have certain expectations associated with them that tell you how to interact with others in particular situations (Johnson, 1997). It is as if society writes a script with different parts and then one learns how to play the part. So your expected behavior, cognitions, and emotions as a friend may differ from those as an employee or sister, but each role requires certain types of human expression (Johnson, 1997).

Social roles are sometimes applied to the concept of gender. As noted above, gender, refers to general social and cultural beliefs about the ways in which individuals and societies think about males and females and what differentiates them (Franklin, 1988; O'Neil, 1981). Gender role and sex role are both terms used by social scientists somewhat interchangeably and sometimes inconsistently (O'Neil, 1981). Some authors differentiate between the two (Franklin, 1988; Mahalik, Cournoyer, DeFranc, Cherry, & Napolitano, 1998); however, for this text, we will use the term gender role. Gender role is the term used to refer to the specific ways in which a particular culture has expectations about the ways in which people's behaviors, thoughts, and feelings should be (Connell, 2001).

---

[1] It is the presence of these struggles that often justifies its classification as a syndrome. However, if you look at all of the physiological and psychological struggles that are linked to the chromosomal pattern of XY it can begin to look like a syndrome as well (see the Crisis section of this text).

Making Connections: Playing Your Part

One way to think of a gender role is as a role in a play. Gender role is used specifically to denote your pre-written part as a gendered person in any particular social situation. And as theorists interested in gender will emphasize, many cultures seem to link gender to just about everything that we do.

For example, I remember once going out to dinner at a microbrewery in California with a group of women in my Masters program. After we ordered drinks with one server, a different server brought them to us and sat a beer in front of me. I hadn't ordered the beer, but he assumed that I did because he expected this behavior due to his understanding of the male gender role and his experiences as a server. Men drinking beer is an expectation of the male gender role and women drinking a "softer" spirit is an expectation of women's gender role (Strate, 2004). Obviously, this server didn't know how gender roles played out in my Masters program!

The idea is that we make assumptions about the way people "are" based upon our social expectations about their gender and the gender role for the culture in which we live. Sometimes our assumptions are based on our own experiences, which have adaptive value. In the example above, the server likely meets a lot of men that order beer and therefore acted in that regard. This will work sometimes, but will fail when interacting with those who are outside expectations on that particular behavioral norm.

Gender role approaches

Most societies categorize gender role into two predominant types, male and female, also expressed as the phenomenon of masculinity and femininity (Franklin, 1988). The most common approach to under-standing and evaluating gender roles in the social sciences is called the **global approach** (Franklin, 1988). The global approach assumes that there is a general set of social expectations about being masculine or feminine (Connell, 1995; Franklin, 1988). This set of expectations is assumed to be carried with people as they interact with others in the environment. Popular books such as John Gray's (2004) *Men Are from Mars, Women Are from Venus: The Classic Guide to Understanding the Opposite Sex* take advantage of people's belief in this global approach. People assume they can just learn what the global differences are between the two most common sexes and learn how to react to them. As John Gray explains:

> We have forgotten that men and women are supposed to be different, as a result, our relationships are filled with unnecessary friction and conflict. Clearly recognizing and respecting these differences dramatically reduces confusion when dealing with the opposite sex. When you remember that men are from Mars and women are from Venus, everything can be explained (Gray, 2004)

Gender role models as a whole explore differences across men by examining social positions of men (men in roles at work, family, and in relationships) and by defining what characteristics men are expected to have in any culture to play the role of a "man" (Cazenave, 1984; Franklin, 1988). All of these models assume that there are particular norms (both sociocultural and descriptive) that are **universal** in that all men struggle with them as they make sense of masculinity (Franklin, 1988; Thompson & Pleck, 1986). We will discuss two different global role models for understanding masculinity: Deborah David's and Robert Brannon's (1976) **Blueprint for Manhood** model and Robert Moore and Douglas Gillette's (1990) **Archetypes for Masculine Energies** model.

The Blueprint for Manhood

The Blueprint for Manhood model was proposed by David and Brannon in 1976. This commonly cited gender-role model proposes that there are four major masculine themes with which men struggle to maintain the gender role of men (David & Brannon, 1976; Kimmel, 2003; Thompson & Pleck, 1986). These can be thought of as benchmarks against which all men are measured (Kimmel, 2003). Not achieving each benchmark can result in problems for men and for others (Franklin, 1988).

Who's Who in Masculinities Research: Deborah S. David, Ph.D.

Deborah David, psychologist, has written over thirty articles, books and papers on areas concerning gender. She has taught undergraduate courses at Brooklyn College.

Who's Who in Masculinities Research: Robert Brannon, Ph.D.

Robert Brannon is an Associate Professor at Brooklyn College in the Psychology Department. He has been active at the college's Center for Sex Role Research and has focused his interests in areas such as sex objectification, male role issues, rape, and domestic abuse.

The first, and thought to be the most influential, theme is called "**No Sissy Stuff**". This refers to the idea that being a man involves figuring out what women do and not doing whatever that is (Kimmel, 2003; Thompson & Pleck, 1986). This way of thinking reinforces the idea that people belong in separate groups (i.e., that there are two *opposite* sexes) (Furby, 1983). For example, many heterosexually identified men seem to express discomfort around men who are gay identified. **Homophobia/heterosexism** toward gay men is an example of the No Sissy Stuff theme since the marginalization of gay men by other men is rooted in the rejection of all things perceived as feminine and threatening to the "role" of masculinity (Kimmel, 2003; Stoltenberg, 1989).

The second theme is called "**Be a Big Wheel**". This refers to men needing to feel that they are in charge of situations. This theme suggests that masculinity involves dominance and power over others in the forms of wealth, status, physical space, etc. (Kimmel, 2003; Stoltenberg, 1989). The Big Wheel aspect of masculinity can range from being a leader, bullying children on the playground, or the sexual exploitation of others (Pronger, 1998; Stoltenberg, 1989). Not achieving Big Wheel status often results in men feeling powerless and despondent (Franklin, 1988).

"**The Sturdy Oak**" constitutes the third masculine theme. This theme involves a need to be independent and self-reliant, like the oak tree, unaffected by the weather and conditions around it as it tries to remain standing. It also includes control over one's emotions in order to be seen as reliable (Franklin, 1988). One can see this theme by viewing men at work, as they are described as distancing themselves psychologically from problems and from others (Bernard, 1989). While being able to separate oneself from difficulties can be adaptive, men who fully embody this theme do not seem to know how to experience emotion and have difficulty maintaining relationships (Berger, Levant,

McMillan, Kelleher, & Sellers, 2005; Franklin, 1988; Levant, 1998) (see chapter 8).

The final theme is called **"Give'em Hell"**. This theme involves the need to be courageous and a risk-taker, even when it may not be in one's best interest (Kimmel, 2003). Men subscribe to this theme in varying ways. Some may hold to an ethic of perseverance, while others may resort to violence at the peril of themselves and others in order to ensure their alignment to this masculine ideal (Bernard, 1989).

David and Brannon (1976) suggest that no particular man would likely be able to achieve all these four themes. However, the assumption is that all men compare themselves to, and attempt to achieve, these masculine benchmarks. Connecting this to the concept of hegemonic masculinity, one can see how this model provides specific requirements for idealized dominant masculinity that most men are unable to achieve.

Archetypes for Masculine Energies

While some authors gravitate to a role theory to explain masculinities, they disagree as to what constitutes the masculine role (Franklin, 1988). They also disagree as to whether masculine roles are purely harmful, or harbor beneficial qualities as well. While theorists like David and Brannon (1976) suggest that the core-requisites of being male are inherently harmful to men and all people, other theorists have attempted to see how masculine themes with which men may struggle have potential to be both harmful and beneficial, depending on how they are enacted in the world. Two such theorists are Robert Moore and Douglas Gillette. Their model is based in psychoanalytic and Jungian approaches to understanding human beings (Gilbert, 1992). The psychoanalytic framework and some basics of Jungian psychology are discussed below in order to understand Moore's and Gillette's (1990) model and how it might be viewed as a social role model.

Who's Who in Masculinities Research: Robert L. Moore, Ph.D.

Robert L. Moore is a psychoanalyst and consultant in private practice in Chicago and also serves as a Distinguished Service

Continued

Professor of Psychology, Psychoanalysis, and Spirituality at the Chicago Theological Seminary. His work on neo-Jungian theory and its application to masculinity and the formation of the self has been very influential and has contributed to the growth of other movements interested in spirituality and masculinity.

Who's Who in Masculinities Research: Douglas Gillette

Douglas Gillette is a mythologist known for his text; *Shaman's Secret: The Lost Resurrection Teachings of the Ancient Maya* as well as several titles with Robert Moore. Gillette has focused his work on understanding cross-cultural spirituality and how that contributes to the formation of the self.

Jungian psychology, based on the works of famous psychoanalyst Carl Jung, is rooted in Freud's **psychoanalytic theory** and based on the examination of the balance of our **conscious** and **unconscious** energies (Satinover, 1986). Freud (and others) postulated that the human mind (or **psyche**) can be thought of as having a **pre-conscious**, conscious, and unconscious sphere (May, 1986). The pre-conscious sphere refers to stored information that could be accessed, but is not currently being processed (such as stored memories). The conscious sphere involves the current processing of information, essentially what is in the mind at any current time. The unconscious is the aspect of the mind that contains drives, instincts, memories, and aspects of memory for which the conscious mind is generally unaware (Burger, 2004; Weiten, 2004). Our personality can be thought of as developing via a conflict between our unconscious (unknown) motivations and desires, and our conscious wants and needs (Burger, 2004; Freud, 1963).

Jungian theorists are interested in examining this conflict and finding ways to be more in touch with things outside of our awareness (Moore & Gillette, 1990; Wehr, 1987). In particular, there is an interest in understanding the role of the unconscious and its effect on the way we understand ourselves and the world (Gilbert, 1992; Steinberg, 1993; Wehr, 1987).

According to Jungian theorists, within the unconscious sphere resides the **collective unconscious**. The collective unconscious is a storehouse of **archetypal energies** (Gilbert, 1992; Hopcke, 1999). Archetypal energies can be thought of as symbolic cultural prescriptions or images for aspects of culture that are transmitted over time (Gilbert, 1992; Hopcke, 1999). These images include influential roles such as mother, father, man, hero, and woman, among others, that have been passed down over centuries of human life (Moore & Gillette, 1990; Gilbert, 1992; Youmans, 2004). Archetypal energies are contrasted with a person's personal past, which involves their own life history. So Jungian theorists contend that everyone carries common energies passed down over the centuries from which we can draw when interacting in the world (Gilbert, 1992).

Jung originally argued that all humans have two major struggles in their psyche; these are referred to as the animus and the anima (Connell, 1995; Hopcke, 1999; Shimoda & Keskinen, 2004). The **animus** (or **persona**) (also referred to as masculine energy) is formed through psychosocial interactions in the environment (Connell, 1995; Satinover, 1986). Animus is the part of our psyches that guides us to connect to others and to use our uniqueness to enhance our own lives and those with whom we connect. It is described as similar to the concept of our social role or social self (Satinover, 1986; Steinberg, 1993).

The **anima** (or **shadow**) (also known as feminine energy) is formed by repressing energy into the unconscious (Connell, 1995; Hopcke, 1999; Satinover, 1986; Shimoda & Keskinen, 2004). Anima is the part of us that utilizes characteristics that are unique aspects of self as a means of emotional self-protection, sometimes at the expense of others (Satinover, 1986; Steinberg, 1993). Jung (1971) describes the anima as "a factor of the utmost importance in the psychology of a man wherever emotions and affects are at work. She intensifies, exaggerates, falsifies, and mythologizes all emotional relations with his work and with people of both sexes" (p. 120).

More modern interpretations of Jung's work suggests that the shadow is not equivalent to femininity, but rather represents what is "less known" by that particular sex. So for men the anima is more in shadow and for women the animus is more in shadow. This is suggested to change over time as the person develops and incorporates more of this shadow into their psyche (Hopcke, 1999).

Moore and Gillette (1990) use the above-mentioned basic assumptions from Jungian psychology to outline major archetypal energies of masculinity. Their model includes a number of archetypal masculine energies, but here we focus on four: **king**, **warrior**, **magician** and **lover**.

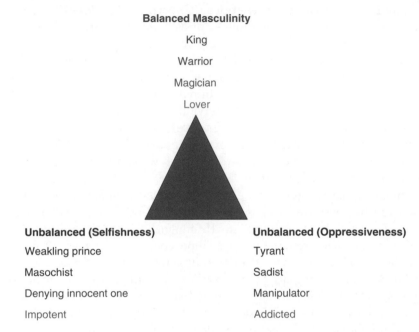

Balanced Masculinity

King

Warrior

Magician

Lover

Unbalanced (Selfishness)   **Unbalanced (Oppressiveness)**

Weakling prince   Tyrant

Masochist   Sadist

Denying innocent one   Manipulator

Impotent   Addicted

Figure 3.1: Moore's and Gillette's (1990) Archetypes for Masculine Energies

Each archetypical energy can be represented as an upright isosceles triangle, as they have the potential to be balanced or to be at one of two unbalanced poles (Gilbert, 1992; Moore & Gillette, 1990). The unbalanced (or shadow) energies represent extremes of survival, the **exploitation** of others and **narcissistic self-protection** (Gilbert, 1992) (see figure 3.1).

King

The king can be thought of as similar to David's and Brannon's (1976) "Be a Big Wheel." The king is described as a courageous and thoughtful leader when balanced, but punishing and oppressive when guided by shadow. As noted by Moore and Gillette (1990), "the mortal man who incarnates the king energy or bears it for a while in the service of his fellow human beings . . . is almost an interchangeable part, a human vehicle for bringing this ordering and generative archetype into the world" (p. 50). When unbalanced, the king becomes a **tyrant**, harshly punishing others or a **weakling prince**, not taking responsibility for leading (Gilbert, 1992; Moore & Gillette, 1990).

Certainly, one can think of many male leaders who might embody the 'king' image, such as men like Mahatma Gandhi, Malcolm X, or Cesar Chavez, who utilized positions of leadership for justice and change (Freedberg, 2007; Krishna, 2007; León. 2007, Reitman, 2007). The king archetype emphasizes that leading others is not merely the result of personal charismatic qualities but is purposeful in the betterment of others.

Warrior

The warrior is probably most similar to David's and Brannon's (1976) "Give 'em Hell." The warrior is the part of the masculine psyche representing drive and energy. When the warrior is balanced it can result in men being productive, responsible, and satisfied. Moore and Gillette (1990) note that, "the characteristics of the warrior in his fullness amount to a total way of life . . . Aggressiveness is a stance toward life that rouses, energizes, and motivates. It pushes us to take the offensive and to move out of a defensive or "holding" position about life's tasks and problems" (p. 79). When guided by shadow a warrior can become a **sadist**, who gains self-worth through putting others down, or the **masochist**, who makes choices to harm themselves, which results in immobilization (Gilbert, 1992; Moore & Gillette, 1990).

The warrior archetype is often represented as the 'action-hero' in movies such as the *Die-Hard, Rambo* and *Rocky* series (Peyser, 2005; Weiner, 2006; Woods, 2007). However, the warrior could really be any man who takes risks and acts aggressively to accomplish something. This could be a man who quits an oppressive job or one who advocates for his children in a way that demonstrates pursuing righteousness at any cost.

Magician

The magician involves spirituality, wisdom, and self-reflection (Gilbert, 1992). When balanced, the magician can be a source of guidance, assistance and creativity. As characterized by Moore and Gillette (1990), "the magician energy is the archetype of awareness and insight, primarily, but also out of knowledge of anything that is not immediately apparent or commonsensical" (p. 106). When guided by shadow, it can lead to being a **manipulator**, using personal skills to gain interest from others, or a **denying innocent one**, one who utilizes a quasi-independence to gain attention from others (Gilbert, 1992; Moore & Gillette, 1990).

The magician is much like the wise father or grandfather who often knows you better than you think they do. They also exhibit patience when others are unable to utilize their wisdom due to their own development and place in life. The magician archetype is often embodied as an influence that may not always be at center stage but whose presence is integral for others' growth. Yoda from the *Star Wars* series is a wonderful illustration of this archetype.

Lover

The lover is the aspect of the male psyche that connects to and cares for others. When balanced, the lover forms intimate and caring connections and is described as not only the "joy of life" archetype, but also the archetype that connects men to the pain of others through legitimate interpersonal connection (Moore & Gillette, 1990). When guided by shadow the lover archetype can result in the **addicted lover** who derives all self-worth through others or the **impotent lover** who lacks the ability to connect intimately with others (Gilbert, 1992; Moore & Gillette, 1990).

The lover archetype emphasizes that men have important relationships in their lives. These relationships are with romantic partners and with friends to whom they are dedicated. These men also love themselves, accept who they are and wish to share that uniqueness with others (Moore & Gillette, 1990).

While Moore's and Gillette's archetypes for masculine energies model was not originally proposed as a traditional "role model" approach, its emphasis on cultural prescriptives is analogous to traditional role models' focus on universal norms. Their model also allows for understanding how individual men might struggle with these prescriptions, given that no man can fit them perfectly – a reality to which Youmans (2004) speaks:

> I have come to see my relationship with employers as part of an unconscious search for a father to replace the one I missed as a boy. I project both the archetypal father who will love me, and an archetypal king whom I can serve. Inevitably as they fall off the pedestal I put them on, I become discouraged, and I distanced myself from them, and ultimately from myself. The process of individuation, which leads toward the development of a unique mature personality includes the integration of our shadows. (p. 107)

Concerns with Gender Role Theories

While the concept of a gender role may seem like a plausible way to study masculinities, there have been some major concerns with the use of "role" as it applies to gender. The first concern is that of a general misapplication of the concept of social roles (Johnson, 1997). As discussed, roles are suggestions of how one is expected to be, given the social position in which one is located (Johnson, 1997). So one may be in the role of a student, a friend, or a brother. Each role may call for different ways of approaching a situation. Certainly you would not act the same way with your professor that you act with your siblings or friends. According to Johnson (1997), in order for the concept of role to make sense one would have to be able to answer the question, "What role are you playing right now?" (p. 66).

The terms masculine (male) or feminine (female) do not refer to a specific role in the same way that terms like student, friend, or brother do. While we play roles that are linked to beliefs about gender, we are never *predominantly* in the role of male or female (Johnson, 1997; Spence & Buckner, 1995). Johnson (1997) suggests that to understand this concern one can imagine the issue of role playing with other identity-related social groups. Can you imagine saying something like, "I am in the role of an Asian American right now"? This does not mean that issues such as gender and race have no impact on the way we think of ourselves and the way we behave; rather, it suggests that thinking of race and gender as purely social roles does not seem to fit what is meant by roles (Johnson, 1997).

Another concern with gender role theories relates to our discussion of the different uses of normalcy. Scholars have argued that this confusion between descriptive and prescriptive/socio-cultural norms has merely been a way to support dominant masculinity in a binary view of gender (Connell, 1995; Furby, 1983). In other words, by saying that men *should* be a certain way according to social roles, without providing information about whether they really *are*, we merely reinforce the actualized ideal of masculinity and marginalize those who presumably do not fit this ideal (Connell, 1995; Demetriou, 2001; Johnson, 1997; Spence & Buckner, 2005). As cultural feminists would emphasize, this way of viewing gender may hide unique aspects of gender as a function of the specificity of the role definitions. For example, several role theories suggest that men who do not fit within the norms are **deviant** or **pathological** (Connell, 1995).

It is important to note that the role theories presented here do not necessarily suggest this. They claim that these are prescriptives with which all men struggle with imperfectly. David and Brannon, in particular, suggested that masculine norms are rather unhealthy ideals (Connell, 1995; Franklin, 1988). Neither claims that men will fit the model perfectly. However, while men may struggle with gender role expectations, the focus on role misses the diverse experiences of men. Any presentation of roles limits our ability to view masculinities, because it is a product of the specific prescriptives given in the model and not an understanding of unique experiences outside of the proposed norms. In other words, even if we agreed on the specific themes of a particular model (which is doubtful) we would only learn about masculinity as it relates to that theme and miss experiences of masculinity that are related to a variety of other experiences.

Making Connections: Stereotyping and Gender Roles

Gender role stereotypes can help illustrate one of the problems with using the construct of gender roles to describe masculinities. A gender role stereotype is a belief that all members of a particular gender *do* act in consistent and predictable ways. A common gender role stereotype, for example, is that boys are very independent and don't need their parents as much as girls do (Pollack, 1995; Silverstein & Rashbaum, 1994). In fact, research shows that young boys in the United States (under three) seem to need more attention from their parents than do girls and are generally less resilient than girls in many ways (Hayslett-McCall & Bernard, 2002; Pollack, 1995; Silverstein & Rashbaum, 1994).

What is interesting about gender role stereotypes is that they are often based on gender role expectations, or prescriptive norms. That is to say, they are not necessarily based on what people actually do. The stressing of independence, for example, may represent more of a value than an observation. Not all societies value independence in their children, and in fact, the construct is defined very differently by different people (Harrington & Liu, 2002; Kagitcibasi, 2005).

Cultural values tend to contribute to how people expect themselves and others to be and thus may lead to what we observe. In short, gender role expectations may inform cultural values and contribute to a gender self-fulfilling prophecy. Cross-cultural research suggests that people in different societies have very different experiences of interdependence. For example, Harrington and Liu (2002) found that native Maori children of New Zealand stress interdependence and collectiveness more than their peers from European families. In addition, Kitayama and colleagues (2000) found that Japanese and American college students' experiences of emotion were related to cultural views of dependence and interdependence. Japanese students were more likely to equate positive emotions with interdependence and interpersonal engagement than their US counterparts (Kitayama, Markus, & Kurokawa, 2000). So, some cross-cultural research suggests that autonomy and individualism are not essentialized traits that all human beings are destined to embody. On the contrary, the degree to which people are interdependent is much informed by cultural context. This is important to underscore, since such seems to be the case with gender role expectations as well.

While gender role expectations exist in all cultures, the degree to which individual members negotiate those expectations is varied. In a context of hegemonic masculinity, gender role stereotypes reflect dominant masculinity in that they represent an idealized version of masculinity, but not necessarily the way people actually are. So one problem with the concept of gender role occurs when authors use it without clearly explaining the difference between prescriptive norms of gender and gender roles (what is expected as compared to what is observed). Arguably, gender roles themselves can lead to stereotypes about behavior, which often do not reflect actual experiences of people.

Such non-consideration of experience has been a major criticism of Moore's and Gillette's (1990) model. Their model implies not only that there is a way that men *should* be, but in fact a way that men simply *are* (Kimmel & Kaufman, 1995). Moore and Gillette view masculinity as though there is a natural or "true essence" of masculinity (referred to as **mature**/adult/**deep masculinity**). In referring to the archetypal masculinity themes, Moore and Gillette (1990) claim they are "hard wired subsections of our genetically transmitted psychic machine" (as quoted by Kimmel & Kaufman, 1995, p. 25). These **essentialist** assumptions cause concern among those who view masculinities as ever-changing and adapting across cultural contexts (Levant et al., 2003). Essentialist descriptions of male and female become particularly problematic when they equate masculinity with knowingness and femaleness with unconscious and irrational dark energy, as Jung often did (Connell, 1995; Satinover, 1986).

In referring to the **mythopoetic men's movement's** (a movement largely influenced by Jungian ideas: see chapter 9) interest in Jungian psychology, Kimmel and Kaufman state a concern often promoted by radical feminists (1995), "The men's movement, therefore, misses one of the central insights of social science – that gender is a product of human action and interaction and our definitions of masculinity and femininity are the products of social discourse and social struggle" (p. 25). Moore and Gillette (1990) recognize that patriarchy as a system is harmful to people, describing it as "a reflection of the immature masculine" (p. xvii); however, they do not see how patriarchy has informed *our very definitions* of masculinity and femininity (Kimmel & Kaufman, 1995). Ultimately, by assuming that gender is binary and universal, there is no room to explore the real ways in which it has differed cross-culturally and continues to be constructed differently by different people (Kimmel & Kaufman, 1995; Connell, 1995; Levant et al., 2003).

There have been attempts at addressing and bridging these concerns especially in relation to Jungian and mythopoetic perspectives (Barton, 2000; Wehr, 1987). Authors interested in Jung's work have acknowledged Jung's general negative portrayals of women and femininity and his over-reliance on data and symbols (archetypes and mythology) that often represent *men's* views of culture[2] (Rowland, 2002; Wehr, 1987). There has also been an acknowledgement of Jung's view of the psychology of women being based on his own experiences with what he considered femininity, not on research and collaboration with women (Rowland, 2002; Wehr, 1987). These authors have attempted to utilize Jungian insights and ideas and integrate them with perspectives that can empower people, rather than perpetuate stereotypes and misogyny (Rowland, 2002; Wehr, 1987).

Masculinity as Power

While the concept of gender role is a popular way of understanding and exploring masculinity, it is not the only social way of understanding this phenomenon. In chapter 2, we discussed how patriarchy and

[2]   In addition to his describing femininity as weak and irrational, at one point Jung literally wrote about whether or not women had souls (Wehr, 1987).

privilege affect the experiences of masculinities. One of the main themes of that discussion was that in patriarchal cultures our social and psychological experiences are affected by our access to social privileges. Some models of masculinity view patriarchy not just as the context in which men struggle with making sense of masculinities, but as *equivalent* to masculinity.

Such models can be understood through feminist standpoint theory. This theory was originally rooted in work by Karl Marx and Georg Lukács and then expanded upon by Nancy Hartsock and various feminist writers, such as Patricia Hill Collins, a Professor of Sociology at the University of Maryland (Changfoot, 2004; Collins, 1989, 1997; Hekman, 1997; Kronsell, 2005; O'Leary, 1997). While the theory is focused on the usefulness of feminist analysis, rather than an explanation of masculinity, its basic premises can help tie together a model described here as "Masculinity as Power." The basic concept of feminist standpoint theory includes an understanding of people's **social positions** relative to social privilege and then an understanding of the results of that position (Kronsell, 2005).

Who's Who in Masculinities Research: Patricia Hill Collins, Ph.D.

Patricia Hill Collins is a social theorist whose research, scholarship and activism have examined intersecting power relations of race, gender, social class, sexuality and/or nation. Her award-winning books, such as *Black Feminist Thought: Knowledge, Consciousness, and the Politics of Empowerment, Race, Class, and Gender: An Anthology* (2004), edited with Margaret Andersen, have been extremely important contributions to this field. She is currently a Distinguished University Professor within the Department of Sociology at the University of Maryland, College Park. In 2007, she was elected the 100th President of the American Sociological Association, the first African American woman to hold this position in ASA's 104-year history.

Email: pcollins@socy.umd.edu

As discussed previously, in patriarchal cultures, men have social power over others in a variety of institutions (Johnson, 1997; Kaschak, 1992; O'Leary, 1997; Uhlmann & Uhlmann, 2005). Through their entitled position of being dominant and centralized, men view their experiences and needs as normal (Connell, 1995; Johnson, 1997; Kaschak, 1992; Prilleltensky, 1994; Uhlmann & Uhlmann, 2005). Marginalized others then view their own experiences as abnormal (Connell, 1995, 2001). In feminist standpoint terms, these social positions designate men as **subjects** of the world and women as **objects**, **others**, or outsiders (Uhlmann & Uhlmann, 2005). The general relationship between men and women is seen as analogous to a master-slave relationship (Changfoot, 2004).

However, being an "other" gives women a unique perspective on the dominant group as they often see things to which the dominant group is blind, because the dominant group often does not notice their own behaviors and impact on the world (Changfoot, 2004; Collins, 1989, 1997; Hekman, 1997; Kronsell, 2005; O'Leary, 1997; Uhlmann & Uhlmann, 2005). Being on the outside necessitates that women (and others who are marginalized by race, ethnicity, etc.) understand both what men are like and what women are like, in order to learn how to adapt. The insiders do not need to do this, because the world was prepared with their interests in mind (Changfoot, 2004; O'Leary, 1997; Uhlmann & Uhlmann, 2005). As Hekman (1997, p. 345) suggests, "the ruling group's vision is partial and perverse and the vision of the oppressed exposes the 'real' relations amongst humans." In fact, proponents of this theory have suggested that the "outsider" is the only person who has a vision of the actual social reality (Changfoot, 2004; Hekman, 1997; Kronsell, 2005).

Perhaps some of you have had a similar experience beginning a new job. I have found that, when I start a new job, I sometimes notice things about the environment that others don't. For example, I was a faculty member at a college in which there were no street signs. Granted, it was a small college, but there were streets but not one street sign in sight. I remember mentioning this to some faculty who said they had not noticed this lack of signage! This seemed particularly peculiar to an "outsider" but it never bothered people who had worked at the college for a long time, because *they* knew where everything was.

This is similar to the focus of feminist standpoint theory. The dominant group often does not recognize the needs of others because they assume their own needs are everyone's needs. The "other," however, is both negatively affected by being on the outside and acutely aware of aspects of the dominant group, about which the dominant group is largely unaware. Being masculine by this model is essentially occupying this dominant position of power and assumes that men, like the faculty member at that school discussed above, have no ability to view what is real given their dominant and "normal" position.

Masculinity as power suggests that *all* aspects of men's being are affected by this social position (Changfoot, 2004; Hekman, 1997). That is, all men's behaviors, cognitions, and emotions are a function of being in this position of power (Changfoot, 2004; Sattel, 1989). In order to maintain dominance, men adopt a persona that keeps them in this position. If we consider the "stereotypical male" traits, such as aggressiveness, competitiveness, distance, lack of emotion, and non-communicativeness, we can see how these traits could aid a man in maintaining his dominance. As Sattel (1989, p. 352) notes, "to effectively wield power, one must be able both to convince others of the rightness of the decisions one makes and to guard against one's own emotional involvement in the consequences of that decision; that is one has to show that decisions are reached rationally and efficiently." For this reason, according to feminist standpoint theory, men's experiences in the world are more ideological than based on relations with others in the real world (Changfoot, 2004; Hekman, 1997).

One of my students once gave me a wonderful example of this phenomenon. In attempting to form a relationship with his father after years of contentious interactions, my student finally told his father what he wanted. "All you ever do is talk about world events. Why don't you ever ask me about my life, my partner, my job, my wishes and dreams? You don't know me at all!" To that the father replied, "But your opinions about politics and the world *are* you, I would never even think of asking those other questions, it would never occur to me." The father in this scenario defines himself based in ideology and abstractions in areas that are largely governed by men's ideas and perspectives rather than viewing himself in the "real" world of relationships.

As long as men remain distant, ideological, and detached from others, their positions of power are secure. And since that position is normal to them, they often do not perceive it as being powerful, or being an advantage. It is just normal. As a result, men see other people as extensions of their dominance. Pleck (1989, p. 25) captures this view when noting that "men's patriarchal competition with each other makes us see women as symbols of success, as mediators, as refuges, and as an underclass".

Concerns with the masculinity as power model

Social theories in general tend to stress the deterministic nature of social expectations and downplay the potential for active responses to environmental demands. While most agree that social forces clearly set constraints, many believe that humans are also active in this process. In other words, social forces may set the stage, but they don't *cause* us to behave in certain ways (Bandura & Bussey, 2004; Kelly, 1963). As actors we may stray from their lines, sometimes asking the director to change or eliminate certain scenes. We as actors may even quit performing because the character does not seem true.

The masculinity as power model also views men as a monolithic group passively accepting and benefiting from their elite positions of power. As discussed in chapter, while men benefit from patriarchy, not all men do in identical ways, nor do they seem to universally and passively accept social demands on them as men (Johnson, 1997; Kimmel & Messner, 2004; Paulsen, 1999). Furthermore, not all women accept a passive role. In fact, many women are active in resisting and changing their position (Changfoot, 2004; O'Leary, 1997; Uhlmann & Uhlmann, 2005).

Indeed, one of the main criticisms of feminist standpoint theory is its misuse of the concept of position (Hekman, 1997; Kronsell, 2005). Position is not equivalent to biological sex. According to the theory, it is position that makes men "masculine" and women "feminine". In other words, position determines dominance, so theoretically speaking, if circumstances were different, women could be dominant (and then could be like "men are now").

A related concern of feminist standpoint theory is its self-contradictory premise about what constitutes "reality." According to the theory only women can know what reality *truly* is, but the theory also contends that there is no objective reality to know since it is defined by positions of power (Changfoot, 2004; Hekman, 1987; Kronsell, 2005; O'Leary, 1997). The theory essentially claims there is no reality to know, but that women know what that reality is (Changfoot, 2004). Feminist theorists have been addressing this paradox by extending the theory and moving away from viewing diverse women's experiences as being "correct" or "superior" to viewing them as important and unique or alternative to the dominant male reality (Changfoot, 2004; Hekman, 1997; O'Leary, 1997).

Summary

While social theories have shed an important light on our understanding of masculinities, other social scientists have looked to theories that include a more psychological and active role of individuals in our negotiation of masculinities. These models provide for more uniqueness in experiences within masculinities across diverse men. The next chapter will include theories that focus on that perspective.

Review and Questions to Ponder

1. How are masculinity and femininity typically defined?
2. What is the "paradox" for men studying masculinities?
3. What is meant by the "focus" of masculinity? How might that focus differ across researchers? Why would it matter?
4. What is the difference between prescriptive and descriptive norms?
5. What is the problem in identifying a norm for masculinities?
6. What is the difference between sex and gender?
7. What is meant by considering the possibility of multiple sexes?
8. What is a social role? What social roles are you involved with in your life?
9. What is a gender role? What aspects of the current gender role do you see in yourself? What aspects of you are different than the gender role?
10. What are the four aspects of David's and Brannon's model for masculinity? Can you give examples of each?
11. What is the difference between the pre-conscious, conscious, and unconscious spheres of the mind?
12. What is Jung's concept of the collective unconscious?
13. What are archetypes?
14. What are the animus and anima?
15. What are the four masculine energies of Moore's and Gillette's model? Can you give examples of each?
16. In what ways are Moore's and Gillette's model similar to David's and Brannon's? In what way are they different?
17. How does gender not fit with the concept of a "social role"?

18. How are social roles argued to support dominant masculinity? How does this relate to David's and Brannon's model?
19. How is essentialism related to the concept of the gender role? How does cross-cultural research present a particular concern?
20. What are general concerns with the concept of gender role?
21. What are some concerns with Moore's and Gillette's model?
22. How have Jungian theorists incorporated feminist concerns in their work?
23. What is the basic premise of the masculinity as power model?
22. What is feminist standpoint theory?
23. What does it mean to say that men are subjects and women are objects/others by this perspective?
24. What are concerns with viewing masculinity as power?

4

Psychological and Interactive Models of Masculinity

The last chapter began with an explanation of the difficulties scholars have when trying to define masculinity. It then discussed social constructs for masculinity and ended with concerns about social models that tend to view behavior as monolithic and predetermined by social forces. This chapter emphasizes psychological views of gender and masculinity, first highlighting the trait approach to masculinity. It then explores two interactive models for masculinity which arose from criticisms from other models. By the time you have completed this chapter, you will be better prepared to investigate the next section of the text, which examines theoretical approaches to explain the *origins* of masculinity.

The Trait Approach

The trait approach to describing masculinities relies on understanding the concept of **gender identity**. In comparison to gender role, gender identity is the term used to refer to how individuals make sense of their own way of being gendered (Franklin, 1988; Meissner, 2005). People sometimes use the term **internalization** to refer to the process by which people take ideas about the external world (in this case gender roles) and incorporate them to their own identity (Connell, 1995). It is theorized that once gender-roles are internalized, they become an aspect of a person's **self**. Accordingly, gender identity reflects an aspect of the self, in particular one's own expectations and beliefs about one's own gendered behavior in the world (Franklin, 1988).

Gender identity theory (as it refers to men) has been referred to as the **Male Sex Role Identity Paradigm** (MSRI) (Pleck, 1995), an approach to masculinity that first became popular in the 1970s (Connell, 1995;

Pleck, Sonnestein, & Ku, 1993). MSRI is based on an assumption that there is a normal or expected sex role for people and that one's gender identity is dependent upon internalizing sex-role-related norms (Connell, 1995; Epstein & Liverant, 1963). The model also assumes that there are no negative consequences for men and women who adopt the expected norm (Pleck et al., 1993).

One common method of measuring a person's gender identity has been the **self-report scale**. Self-report scales assess hypothetical constructs via participants' responses to a series of **forced-choice questions** that are then compared to established **norms**. Researchers interested in gender identity work to gather information about how men and women view themselves as identifying with gender, which is often defined in a binary way (male *or* female).

Scales with questions pertaining to gender are thought to measure the characteristics or traits that uniquely differentiate males from females (Pleck et al., 1993; Spence & Buckner, 1995). There are two approaches to measuring traits. **Nomothetic** approaches to measuring traits assume that people have the same traits but to various degrees (Meier, 1994). The **idiographic** approach assumes that there may be some traits that are inherent to specific people (or groups) which ultimately defines their uniqueness (in this case gender uniqueness) (Meier, 1994). A nomothetic view of gender would suggest that all humans have the same traits but that differences in proportions of certain characteristics would distinguish different gender groups. The idiographic view would argue that separate gender groups carry unique characteristics that the others do not possess.

What both approaches have in common is a **positivist** view of defining masculinity. The positivist view assumes that masculinity can be defined by the way it is measured and the results of such measurement (Connell, 1995). A major tenet of positivistic approaches is the **reliable** and **valid** measurement of underlying constructs. Many positivist approaches define constructs (or imply their definitions) by the **items** (questions) that are included in their measurement methods (Meier, 1994). So rather than describing what masculinity is, they will generate items for a scale and suggest that whatever the norm on the scale is "is" masculinity. By definition this view portrays masculinity as an average or prototypical set of characteristics associated with men.

There is an abundance of research on trait models of masculinity. In this chapter, we will cover the basic conceptual differences between them, but please see the works cited in the reference pages to learn more about their ideas and research findings. Much of the information about the trait models summarized below comes from Dr. Janet Spence, a recently retired researcher from the University of Texas at Austin; in particular a piece written with her colleague Camille Buckner is used to help organize this extensive literature (Spence & Buckner, 1995). Three categories of trait-based models are discussed, representing different approaches for studying trait models of masculinity. The categories are referred to here as unifactor, two-factor, and three-factor models for gender (Spence & Buckner, 2005).

Who's Who in Masculinities Research: Janet Taylor Spence, Ph.D.

Janet Spence is a Professor Emeritus of Psychology at the University of Texas at Austin. She has spent over fifty years as a contributor to psychology (in fact she has been a fellow in the American Psychological Association for nearly that long). She is well known for her work in gender as well as anxiety and task performance. She has recently retired from academe, but will continue her work as the editor of *the Annual Review of Psychology.*

Unifactor Models

Unifactor models (often called M-F tests) were popular views of gender in the social sciences prior to the early 1970s (Epstein & Liverant, 1963; Hoffman, 2001; Lenney, 1991; Pleck et al., 1993). They view gender as existing on a continuum with masculinity on one end and femininity on the other (Hoffman, 2001; Lenney, 1991; Spence & Buckner, 1995). This gender continuum assumes that masculinity and femininity are opposites and that a person's experience with gender is somewhere along the continuum (Lenney, 1991; Spence & Buckner, 1995).

Perhaps the most popular example of a unifactor gender model is the Male/Female **scale** of the widely used Minnesota Multiphasic Personality Inventory (Hathaway & McKinley, 1943; Lenney, 1991). Each question on the scale is assumed to differentiate between male *or* female, representing the assumptions of a bipolar continuum of opposites (Spence & Buckner, 2005). Answering a true/false question as either true or false would mean you were either more like one gender or the other. The implication of this idiographic scale, as well as the model in general, is that if a person is biologically male and identifies along the female continuum, then they are experiencing some type of potential pathology (Spence & Buckner, 1995). There has been much debate about the use of the MMPI M-F scale, as responses to this subscale are of dubious reliability and questionable validity (Johnson, Jones, & Brehms, 1996).[1]

Unifactorial views of gender are often seen in popular culture. A satirical piece by Tierney in *Forbes Magazine* (Tierney, 1995) entitled "5 things you should never say to the opposite sex" reveals some of the stereotypical concerns of the "opposite" sexes. For example, a few of the concerns revolve around sexuality and are pointed toward women. Women are cautioned not to reveal any past promiscuous behavior and men are cautioned not to mention her past. It is also suggested that men do not make light of the need for birth control (especially if she is young). "Do we really need to worry about birth control *at your age*?" (p. 135). Keeping in mind that these are warnings of what *not* to say, these admonitions illustrate expectations about the sexes that are quite opposite. Women are (a) responsible for birth control; (b) not supposed to be sexual (or at least to be quiet about it); (c) younger than their partners (which could be really problematic with the intention here being very unclear as to this difference in age); and (d) heterosexual (perhaps the one thing they have in common here). Those interested in unifactor models believe that, while the sexes are opposite, members of each sex do not like to admit this fact and thus get irritated when these kinds of stereotypes (as the warnings here indicate) are launched against them.

Two-Factor Models

In contrast, **two-factor models** view masculinity and femininity as two separate constructs rather than endpoints on a gender continuum. Two-factor models generally assume that gender is split into masculinity and femininity, that these are separate constructs that differentiate men from women and that they are marginally related at best (Spence & Buckner, 1995). The goal for this view is to then determine which characteristics are dominated by masculinity and which by femininity.

---

[1]   The people who originally took the Femininity scale of the MMPI to establish the female norm were 13 gay men, who arguably experienced a masculinity loaded with all kinds of marginalizations (Hoffman, 2001).

Spence & Buckner (1995) discuss the Personal Attributes Question-naire (PAQ) as a good example of a tool to measure a two-factor model of gender. This questionnaire, which was originally created by Spence and colleagues (Spence, Helmreich, & Stapp, 1974), contains items representing **socially desirable** stereotypes associated with mas-culinity and femininity (Lenney, 1991; Choi, 2004; Ward, Thorn, Clements, Dixon, & Sanford, 2006). This is not to suggest that undesir-able characteristics of men and women are nonexistent. Rather, the focus on socially desirable stereotypes was purposeful, because when people are evaluating gender, they might be less likely to acknowledge a negative characteristic, particularly of their own gender (Lenney, 1991). Recognizing this, the scale is said to measure an *aspect* of gender not a global gendered concept (Choi, 2004; Lenney, 1991; Spence & Buckner, 1995; Ward et al., 2006).

Since the creation of the PAQ, Spence and Buckner (1995) have suggested that the constructs be re-categorized as measuring **expressiveness** and **instrumentality**, rather than femininity and mas-culinity. Expressiveness indicates an ability to communicate and under-stand others, while instrumentality refers to behaviors that promote action and goal-seeking in the environment (Choi, 2004; Spence & Buckner, 2005; Stake, 1997; Ward et al., 2006; Wise & Stake, 2002). By re-categorizing them in this way, the hope was to break the assumed causal link between men and instrumentality and women and expres-siveness, since the scale allows for self-reporting in either direction (e.g. men who are expressive or instrumental or some combination of both). The exploration of these two factors has been a popular pursuit of psychologists who believe these traits can predict behaviors in a variety of situations and settings (Choi, 2004; Wise & Stake, 2002).

The two-factor model assumes that, while men will have primarily masculine traits and women will have primarily feminine traits, either sex could carry some traits of the other. This is commonly conveyed when people use the term "my (fill in the blank with gender) side" to refer to the part of oneself that reflects the sex of which you are not. So when a man is crying, he is showing his feminine side (pre-sumably a feminine characteristic) and if a woman is standing up for herself, she is showing her masculine side (presumably a masculine characteristic).

An interesting article about changes at the Best Buy electronics chain entitled "Best Buy gets in touch with its feminine side" illustrates this quite well (Fetterman, 2006). In 2006, Best Buy made a conscious effort to make the space more "women friendly." "The "feminization" of the consumer electronics business is underway" (p. 01b). They have made aisles wider for baby carriages, toned down the music and lights, and trained their sales staff to focus on how electronics can fit into people's lifestyles and the appearance of one's home (Fetterman, 2006). The store still carries all the gadgets and games popular with men, however, and will in no way become "feminine." This was conveyed by Julie Gilbert, the Vice President of Best Buy, when she assured Best Buy customers, "We are not going to paint the stores pink" (p. 01b). The two-factor view of gender allows for men (or male spaces) to be influenced by femininity and still remain consistent with the presumed unique needs of the different sexes.

Concerns with Unifactor and Two-Factor Models

Criticisms of unifactor theories of gender have existed since the early 1970s. A critical and commonly cited article by Constantinople (1973) addressed many of the major problems with a unifactor conceptualization of gender (Lenney, 1991; Hoffman, 2001; Spence & Buckner, 2005). The basic premise of a unifactor model is that men and women are separate groups with opposite characteristics, yet such a premise did not seem to be logically or empirically sound. Men and women may be different in some ways, but viewing those differences as *opposite* does not seem to make much sense. Given any characteristic, it is possible that men and women may differ from one another. But to consider that difference as being an opposite does not seem to adequately describe the way men and women actually are. So, as a nomothetic view might suggest, women may stereotypically be more emotionally expressive than men, but considering women as "emotional" and men as "distant" does not to really describe the diversity both within and among groups of people.

In addition, these models as a whole also implied that the more one was similar to the expected social role in terms of characteristics, the healthier one would be, with little research to support that claim (Pleck et al., 1993; Spence & Buckner, 1995). Just because a biological male checks off characteristics that other biological males check off does not necessarily mean those characteristics are necessarily good. It is just an indication that they are common. We often forget that just because something is normal (or common/expected) does not mean that it is necessarily adaptive or beneficial.

The two-factor model certainly solves this "issue of opposites." However, there have been concerns with this model as well. If masculinity and femininity are separate categories, then items on a test that measure masculinity should **correlate** with one another and not with those that measure femininity (and vice versa). If a person who identifies as male is taking a two-factor scale, they should generally respond to items meant to measure masculinity in one way and those meant to measure femininity in a different way. However, research is mixed in its ability to consistently find traits that will do this (Hoffman, 2001; Lenney, 1991; Spence & Buckner, 2005). From an idiographic perspective, identity scales have had difficulty identifying traits that distinguish masculine and feminine constructs (Spence & Buckner, 2005). Instrumentality and expressiveness are perhaps a compromise; however, they are not global gender measures; they lack a consensual definition; and research is mixed in finding actual differences across men and women (Hermann & Betz, 2004; Stake, 1997; Stake, 2000; Wise & Stake, 2002).

Many of the self-report identity models also call their measurement scales "role measures" (Spence & Buckner, 2005). By referring to them in this way, the implication is that self-reported characteristics and roles are the same thing, which they are not (Spence & Buckner, 2005). Role refers to expected values, whereas identity refers to how one perceives oneself. But if items on a test only reflect expected roles, it makes it appear as if we are measuring masculinity when we are really measuring whether people see themselves similar to the role as proposed by the researcher's scale (Pleck, et al., 1993; Spence & Buckner, 2005). In fact, some authors have preferred the use of the term **gender role orientation** to suggest that, while gender roles are socially associated with sex-linked characteristics and all of us look toward gender roles to understand social expectations, our behaving in the world is not biologically determined, but rather socioculturally reinforced (Muris, Mesters, & Knoop, 2005).

Many two-factor theories, like unifactor role theories, can serve to reinforce dominant views of masculinity by assessing the characteristics that reflect researchers' beliefs about gender and sex role requirements (May, 1986; Minter, 1999; Pleck et al., 1993; Spence & Buckner, 2005). Instead of measuring characteristics that may really differentiate these social groups, the majority of two-factor theories have simply come up with trait-like questions to correspond to gender-role norms, leaving us unaware of how people actually are (Pleck et al, 2003;

Spence & Buckner, 2005). This would be a major concern for cultural feminists who are interested in the ways in which we describe people and how we may value some characteristics more than others (by simply placing those items on a scale and leaving other items off).

In order to illustrate this problem, I often give students a sheet of paper with a list of musical artists who would be considered slightly out-of-fashion. I then ask them to choose their favorite. They begin to protest the question, but I ask them to simply mark one answer. I then give them the results in percentages and suggest that I am going to make that information known to the public (which of course is embarrassing given who I have chosen to pick from). Similarly (although not identically) the problem with identity models based on self-report scales is that many reflect the ways in which experts believe that people *should* be, rather than truly tapping into who they are.

For that reason, some authors prefer to use other methods (such as qualitative interviews) to avoid that concern. For example, Hibbins (2006) found some very interesting aspects of masculine identity with a sample of Chinese male migrants in Australia. One theme explored was how interest in sports seemed to be linked more to expanding social contacts and an appreciation for how men involved in sports could advance financially, rather than to an identification with a male sports archetype. For these men what made participation in sports masculine was that it could lead to financial security and taking care of others. These kinds of nuances are sometimes more easily accessed with research methods that avoid a presumed definition (such as a scale) prior to the investigation.

The Androgyny Model (a Three-Factor Theory)

In the early 1970s, Sandra Bem, now a Cornell University researcher, revolutionized gender research by proposing that masculinity and femininity were not the only gendered ways of being available to people (Auster & Ohm, 2000, Lenney, 1991; Spence & Buckner, 2005). She proposed the term **androgynous** to refer to a person of either sex who incorporates aspects of maleness and femaleness within them (Bem, 1974, 1981a, 1981b, 1984). In doing so, she offered a new language to people who believed that they did not fall within the typical expected gender role (Stake, 1997). The term also gave people an ideal or aspiration to work toward, as being androgynous is described as being able to be free to make human choices, without being restricted by the

Who's Who in Masculinities Research: Sandra Bem, Ph.D.

Sandra Lipsitz Bem is Professor of both Psychology and Feminist, Gender, and Sexuality Studies (FGSS) at Cornell University, where she also served for many years as the Director of FGSS. She did theoretical and empirical work on gender and sexuality from the early 1970s until the mid 1990s, the culmination of which was a book entitled *The Lenses of Gender*, published in 1993. Five years later, she published a second book, a memoir entitled *An Unconventional Family*. In the late 1990s, Bem retrained as a clinical psychologist and now has a small private therapy practice specializing in trauma.

Website: http://www.psych.cornell.edu/people/Faculty/slb6.html

gender roles of one's community. So if I identify as a male, but am comfortable crying and nurturing others (presumably traits associated with femininity), I might view myself as androgynous rather than "not a man" or "feminine." This model could be considered a three-factor trait theory since it proposes a third factor that has specific characteristics associated with it.

One example of androgyny can be found in the recent resurgence of so-called "boy bands." Now, of course, there are many bands with all male members, but the boy band has a definitive style (Jamieson, 2007). The boy-band image typically portrays young, attractive (presumably heterosexual) men who are interested in fashion and singing and dancing to music that is often associated with being more feminine. Their androgynous nature is argued by some to have been a major influence on young people. "The Backstreet Boys were the most popular manufactured boy band in the world, and as such influenced the sexual development of millions of young women and men" (Jamieson, 2007, p. 245).

Sandra Bem's Bem Sex Role Inventory (BSRI) is a widely used scale for measuring gender identity (Auster & Ohm, 2000; Konrad & Harris, 2002; Lenney, 1991; Stake, 1997; Peng, 2006). The scale contains a series of questions developed to assess typically masculine, feminine, or neutral traits (Auster & Ohm, 2000; Lenney, 1991). Each BSRI respondent receives a score indicative of how many masculine, neutral, and feminine items they responded to (Bem 1974, 1981a, 1981b, 1984). The overall responses can be examined to see if the person is mostly masculine, feminine, neither, or combined (androgynous) (Auster & Ohm, 2000; Bem, 1974; Konrad & Harris, 2002; Lenney, 1991).

The BSRI has been used to examine gender in a variety of situations (Auster & Ohm, 2000; Peng, 2006; Spence & Buckner, 1995; Stake, 1997). And while there are many other measures available, it is still cited as an extremely useful test (Stake, 1997; Ward, 2000). Its utility is due in part to its broader recognition of how people identify with gender and the notion that biological males and biological females might both experience gender similarly through their relating to androgyny (Stake, 1997). In offering this concept, Bem was one of the first psychologists to begin to truly differentiate sex from gender and gender role from gender identity.

Concerns with the Androgyny Model

While Bem's original work was quite revolutionary, it still contained some assumptions that sat poorly with various researchers. Some were concerned with the scale itself. The name of the scale is sex *role* inventory, yet it contains items with trait-like adjectives and is often used as a measure of identity (Spence & Buckner, 2005). The scale seems to confuse endorsement of roles with traits and characteristics, which is common for these kinds of approaches (Spence & Buckner, 2005).

The scale and model also propose a binary between men and women in suggesting some traits *are* "masculine" and others *are* "feminine" and ultimately does not allow for differences to represent different ways of being masculine or feminine or some other way of being gendered. Differences get interpreted as not belonging (or belonging to androgyny), rather than as diverse expressions of masculinity or femininity (Minter, 1999; Pleck et al., 1993; Spence & Buckner, 1995). This concern was addressed in Bem's Gender Schema Theory (see chapter 6).

....

Making Connections: Ignoring Differences

Perhaps an example using race will help to explain this concern. Imagine this scenario (based on an actual event) between a Black woman and White man. The woman's male friend was telling her a story about some kids he had seen on the train and then he said something like, "Well, you know how Black people can be on the train." She (my friend) said something like, "Um, I'm Black and I don't act that way on the train." Her friend replied, "Yah, but you aren't *really* Black." After questioning him, she learned that he did not think of her as being "really Black" because she did not live up to the normed expectations of the way Black people "are." In other words, the way she dressed, spoke, and behaved were not "Black" according to her friend. And by saying she wasn't Black he also implied that she was more "White." She looked him right in the eyes, rolled up her sleeve, pointed to her skin and said, "Uh, *I'm Black*, OK?"

This is a complicated scenario to explain (and I am sure much more complicated for the two who lived through it). The man in this situation was arguing that there was *a* way to be White and *a* way to be Black and that he was an expert in describing that difference. He was guilty of an unfortunately common behavior: When people act outside of the expectations we have of their social groups, we think of them as being "different" or "not a member of that group" rather than questioning our expectations of that group in the first place. The Black woman in this scenario was not able to be seen as a "real" Black woman, presumably, because she did not fit into the way that he defines what being Black means.

Similarly, when thinking about Bem's original binary way of conceiving androgyny, there is an assumption that there is a way to be masculine and a way to be feminine and that men can be "feminine" and that women can be "masculine" which she called androgynous. If we discover, for example, that many men cry in sad situations, Bem might have called that androgynous, since we assume that crying is a feminine characteristic. But that is erroneous. It does not mean they are exhibiting a *feminine* characteristic, it means that they are displaying a masculine one, since it is observed in men; we resist viewing crying as related to being masculine because of the binary way we think about gender. When women cry, we say it's feminine; when men cry we say they are acting in a feminine way because we assume that crying is feminine, even though we can see men doing it right in front of us.

....

Gender identity as a construct has largely been evaluated through the use of a researcher-designed self-report scale. These criticisms may be more of a concern for the way in which gender identity is measured, rather than the concept itself. In other words, the idea that people have different ideas about what it means to be gendered in any given culture and that this "identity" may influence the way they understand themselves and interact with others, may still hold merit. This recognition of the potential usefulness of the concept has influenced the development of other ways of understanding masculinity.

Interactive Models

Interactive models have arisen out of criticisms of trait-based theories and other psychologically based theories of gender (Lucke, 2003; Spence & Buckner, 2005). Interactive models assume that there is substantial diversity in the ways in which people make sense of gender and what it means to be a gendered person. These models explore an interaction between social context, role expectations and stereotypes in the culture and people's own development and unique experiences (Lucke, 2003; Pleck et al., 1993; Spence & Buckner, 1995). Masculinity by this model is not within a person, but a process of grappling with one's own current views of expected cultural norms (Lucke, 2003; Pleck et al., 1993). We will explore two interactive models here: Masculine Ideology and a Social Constructionist View of Gender.

Masculine Ideology

A good example of a multi-factor theory is that of Joseph Pleck, who is a Professor of Human Development and Family Studies at the University of Illinois at Urbana-Champaign. Pleck devised the **Masculinity Ideology** approach to studying masculinity (Levant et al., 2003a; Pleck et al., 1993). This approach understands masculinity not as traits inherent in the person, or a role to play, but rather as an ideology or attitude about gender (Addis & Mahalik, 2003; Chu, Porche, & Tolman, 2005; Pleck et al., 1993). Specifically, masculinity ideology focuses on attitudes towards the ways men are, attitudes about the way men should be, and the unique internalizations of those norms (Chu, Porche, & Tolman, 2005). The goal of this model is to establish how attitudes about gender norms can predict future behaviors of men (Pleck et al., 1993).

Who's Who in Masculinities Research: Joseph H. Pleck, Ph.D.

Joseph H. Pleck is Professor of Human Development and Family Studies at the University of Illinois at Urbana-Champaign. Pleck has published numerous articles on men and masculinity with a particular focus on gender role conflict. His groundbreaking books *Men and Masculinity* (co-authored with Jack Sawyer) and *The Myth of Masculinity* were very influential in the formation of this field. He has presented Congressional testimony in support of the Family and Medical Leave Act, and has been an advisor to the National Research Council's Panel on Employer Policies and Working Families and to the Family and Work Institute's National Survey of the Changing Workforce. His recent interest has been on fathers and fatherhood.

Email: jhpleck@uiuc.edu

Typically, masculinity ideology is assessed by examining **traditional masculinity ideologies** and **non-traditional masculinity ideologies** (Fitzpatrick, Salgado, Suvak, King, & King, 2004). Traditional ideologies are those which seem to fit within current male norms, whereas non-traditional ideologies are those which run counter to current male norms (Fitzpatrick et al., 2004). Another approach is to assess perceptions of female norms and their relationship to men and male norms (Fitzpatrick et al., 2004). Understanding these various perspectives is important because a person can have conflicting attitudes about gender norms (Chu et al., 2005).

In a sense, Pleck's model combines role models and identity models by examining the relationship between them with a suggestion that what gender is *is* the way in which we view gender in any given sociocultural context (Pleck et al., 1993). In fact, scales have been devised based on David's and Brannon's (1976) Blueprint for Manhood to determine attitudes about the male role as defined by their role theory (Thompson & Pleck, 1986). In addition, other male role norm scales have been devised examining many factors involving attitudes toward male norms (Berger, Levant, McMillan, Kelleher, & Sellers, 2005; Fitzpatrick et al., 2004). Researchers have noted that role norms differ across communities, so the same concept can be applied to other populations by understanding dominant role norms, norms within marginalized communities, attitudes about these norms and how those attitudes interact and predict other outcomes (Abreau, Goodyear, Campos, & Newcomb, 2000; Levant et al., 2003a). This research has led to an increased understanding of the problems that men face as a result of conforming to these dominant roles (see chapter 8).

The masculine ideology approach avoids problems associated with roles and traits. Unlike measures that presume assessment of roles and traits, which, as noted above, are often biased by researchers' definitions, the masculine ideology approach focuses on attitudes toward masculinity. It also completely avoids binary views of gender, as the model does not claim to measure identity (Pleck et al., 1993). The masculine ideology approach also recognizes that attitudes and norms can change over time, so it avoids making universal assumptions about the "correct" way to define or experience masculinities.

An interesting study by Levant and colleagues (2003b) investigated whether masculine ideology differed between men and women, European and African Americans, and whether or not those ideologies were related to **alexythymia**, a syndrome which involves difficulties with the experience and expression of emotion. The study found that women endorsed a significantly less traditional ideology than men. European Americans also endorsed a less traditional ideology (this was less significant amongst men) than African Americans. And, finally, men who expressed more traditional masculine ideologies also scored significantly higher on scales measuring alexythymia (Levant et al., 2003b).

This is a unique aspect of this model in that it recognizes that conformity to gender roles is not necessarily healthy. In fact, Pleck was one of the first scholars in the field to recognize and push us to understand how conforming to gender role norms has negative consequence for men (Pleck et al., 1993) (see chapter 8).

Concerns with Masculinity as an Ideology

Concerns about this model come largely from social constructionists and feminists. Social constructionists have critiqued Pleck's model in the past, noting that it does not address issues of power, which is an important aspect of many social constructionist perspectives (Pleck, 1995). In other words, this approach (to some) does not address *who* gets to decide what the dominant norms are and *how* they become

viewed as norms. Feminist models certainly concur with a social constructionist critique that models of masculinity absent issues of power
do not adequately assess masculinity (Connell, 1995).

In addition, for some social constructionists, Pleck's model does not
adequately address how gender norms are really *dominant* masculine
gender norms that may not reflect the masculinity attitudes of marginalized men. And while scales such as the Male Role Attitudes Scale
address power issues in relationships (Pleck et al., 1993) they include
attitudes about *dominant* gender norms rather than attitudes about the
norms of other male sub-groups. While a growing body of research has
explored the experience of marginalized men (e.g., Abreau et al., 2000;
Levant et al., 2003a, 2003b), some have claimed that the model of
masculine ideology does not account for differing access to privilege
as an aspect of masculinity that affects masculinity norms to which
marginalized men are compared (Kimmel & Messner, 1989). For
example, if a Latino-identified man is taking the Male Role Attitudes
Scale, it may measure his view about some dominant male norms that
certainly affect his experience of masculinity. However, the scale would
not access his views of masculinity norms within the Latino community, which may differ from, and interact with, dominant norms of
masculinity.

The use of self-report scales may also be basically incompatible with
a theoretical perspective that de-emphasizes norms and seeks to understand unique experiences. Much of the work on understanding gender
from a social constructionist perspective is utilizing and emphasizing
the unique construction of masculinities and viewing masculinities as
performance rather than identity (Cornwall, 1997; Edwards, 1997).

A Social Constructionist Model

There are several different theories that fall under the "constructionist"
umbrella (Raskin & Bridges, 2002; Strong, 2004). This section will
present a brief overview of what makes social constructionist models
different from other models. We will then focus on how a social constructionist model can explore gender and masculinities.

Understanding Constructivism

In order to better understand the constructivist perspective, Raskin and
Bridges (2002) suggest dividing the **philosophy of science** into three

periods: the **pre-modern**, **modern**, and **post-modern**. The philosophy of science can be defined as the rules and assumptions that sciences make in order to pursue their goals. The pre-modern philosophy of science stressed **rationalism**, the idea that one could arrive at scientific truths by using "pure logic and reason," and **introspection** (Aune, 1970; Raskin & Bridges, 2002). Philosophers like René Descartes were known for this perspective (Aune, 1970). The modern era of science stressed the use of **empiricism** to study observable facts in order to arrive at answers referred to as **objective truths** (Raskin & Bridges, 2002). British philosopher John Locke was known for this approach (Benjamin, 1997). He suggested that we must use our senses to gather information we can observe in an objective way, rather than rely only on knowledge.

Post-modern philosophy is grounded in a concern with the objectivity of the information gathered from our senses. The basic assumption is that humans uniquely gather information from their senses and describe it in different ways and that what we really have access to is **constructed truth**, not an objective truth (Gergen, 1999; Raskin & Bridges, 2002). Philosophers such as Immanuel Kant and Michel Foucault are known for advocating this perspective (Aune, 1970; Foucalt, 1965, 1995; Uhlmann & Uhlmann, 2005).

Constructivist literally means to build. People build realities, rather than being affected by objective external realities. Constructivists believe it is impossible to define any objective external reality because of the kinds of creatures we are and the way we interact with one another. This is to suggest neither that predictions about human behavior are impossible nor that we are unaffected by the world around us (Raskin & Bridges, 2002). Sometimes people think that constructivists are suggesting that whatever we believe to be true is true, like some kind of magic. When introducing constructivism, I sometimes tease my students by making an argument for my constructing myself as a bird and then pretending that I can fly and therefore I should jump out the window. And since I believe it is true, it must be so. This is not what constructivism claims.

In order to get a better grasp of constructivist thinking, I like to use the example of color perception, because it is a physiological example which seems pretty "objective," but is also one that can help us understand the basic idea of constructivist models. If you look at the clothes you are currently wearing and stop to think how they get their color your first answer is probably from the dyes that are used in the fabric (Lustig, 2001). If you were trying to understand this phenomenon, you could certainly do experiments with different dyes, different fabrics, and so on, and find all kinds of interesting things about the various physical qualities of these items that contribute to their color (Lustig, 2001).

However, you would be missing two other contributors to the fabric's color. The first is the light that shines on it. Light from the sun (or lamps) shines on objects and contributes to their color (Bund & Do, 2005). This means that if the light from the sun changes, the color changes. Or, if you observe the fabric in different light, the color looks different. So the kind of light that illuminates an object affects the way the color looks to you (Weiten, 2004).

The second contributor is us. More specifically, the way our eyes are configured allows us to have the experience of color (Galambos, Juhász, Lorincz, & Szilágyi, 2005). Scientists suggest that it is the cones in our eyes that interpret light (Galambos et al., 2005; Weiten, 2004). Therefore, if the cones in your eyes changed, the color of light would seem different as well. This is of course true for people who experience **color vision deficiency** (those who are "color blind"), who have a variety of differences in the way their cones interpret signals (Pardo, Perez, & Suero, 2004).

This is a great metaphor for a constructivist view. To a constructivist, the color of your outfit is not *in* your outfit. It exists due to a specific combination of factors that allow color to exist. If any of those factors change, the color changes. People who are not constructivists would say the "real" color looks "different" in different situations. Constructivists say that there is no "real" color, only an experience of color that shifts as the factors that contribute shift; thus color can be viewed as being constructed. So for this reason, constructivists do not tend to have a model for explaining masculinity or gender, but rather a method for exploring social phenomenon. Because the basic belief is that masculinity is socially and historically constructed, no model would be useful for very long, as human experiences are always changing.

Certain themes help constructivists in exploring masculinity. We focus here on a **social constructionist** model for exploring masculinities, one of the many constructivist models available (Raskin & Bridges, 2002). Social constructionists stress that the constructions of truths happen in a social context (Gergen, 1999). A social constructionist perspective asks us to **deconstruct** knowledge. Sinnacore and Enns (1995, p. 44) define deconstruction as "showing how reality is created rather than something that exists in a 'natural' or true state, and showing how reality is defined by hierarchies of power."

Social Constructionism Applied

Social constructionism is a type of constructivist theory that has a particular focus on the social factors that give meaning to our experiences (Raskin & Bridges, 2002). So when social constructionists think about gender (or in our case, masculinities) they do not focus on some specific issue inside of a person (such as an in-depth exploration of brain function or gendered beliefs). Social constructionists strive to identify all the factors that affect the way in which we investigate, categorize, and discuss gender. They also wish to understand how our own experiences affect that interpretation. Like radical feminists, they wish to include an exploration of power and understand who gets to determine what "counts" as being the truth (in this case what masculinity "is") and how that affects others (Brickell, 2005; Gergen, 1999; Kimmel & Messner, 1989). So what masculinity is at any given moment is a product of all of those factors and, like color, could shift with a shift in any factor. Social constructionists often use the phrase **doing gender** or gender as performance rather than gender identity or gender role because they view gender as a socially active and constructed activity (Brickell, 2005; Cheng, 1999; Cornwall, 1997; Nye, 2005).

Michael Messner, a Professor in the Department of Sociology at the University of Southern California, outlines three different factors that can be considered when doing an analysis of social constructing (Messner, 2004). These factors are the **interactional level**, **structural context**, and **cultural symbol**. The interactional level refers to the actual behaviors in which people engage that signify they are "doing gender" (Messner, 2004). The structural context refers to understanding aspects of that particular situation that contribute to the ways in which people interact (Messner, 2004; Nye, 2005). Finally, cultural symbol refers to the meaning that the overall culture assigns to those behaviors (Messner, 2004).

Who's Who in Masculinities Research: Michael Messner, Ph.D.

Michael Messner is a Professor of Sociology and Gender Studies in the Department of Sociology at the University of Southern California. He is particularly interested in the sociology of sports and has published several recent pieces in that area, including *Paradoxes of Youth and Sport* (2002), and *Taking the Field: Women, Men, and Sports* (2002). He has been President of the North American Society for the Sociology of Sport, and has conducted research on gender in sports media for the Amateur Athletic Foundation of Los Angeles, and for Children Now.

Website: http://www.usc.edu/schools/college/soci/people/faculty1003528.htm/

For example, Messner (2004) discusses an analysis of a children's soccer ceremony in which several teams from the Los Angeles area gather. In this fascinating account, Messner traces some of the behaviors of participants from the naming of teams to interacting with others. One all-girl team calls itself the "Barbie Girls." During the ceremony, some of the boys responded to the all-girl team with chants of "No Barbie! No Barbie! No Barbie!" while simultaneously displaying interest and excitement about the "Barbie Girls" (Messner, 2004). This is the interactional level, the observed behaviors of the people involved.

In order to understand the meaning of the chanting, one must explore the structural context. Messner provides information about power and the structure of the soccer ceremony (how is it laid out, who plans it, who are in positions of power, and so on). This is because social constructionists pay particular attention to whose voice conveys knowledge (Chan, 2000; Cheng, 1999; Sampson, 1993). Like radical feminists, social constructionists believe that it is important to examine who is in positions of authority to determine what gets to count as good, appropriate, and normal. Social constructionists pay particular attention to the marginalized voices in human activity in order to learn about diverse experiences and ways of understanding the world (Sampson, 1993). So, for example, while the event was attended by all genders, it was primarily organized by men and men were in primary roles of leadership (Messner, 2004).

Finally, all of this exists in some historical and cultural space. There are many cultural symbols relevant to understanding gender here, in particular the meaning of the Barbie doll. At this level of analysis, information is provided regarding the current historical and cultural meaning of the behaviors (such as the sport, soccer, family, the Barbie doll, and so on). For example, the Barbie doll, while consistently a popular toy, has undergone significant physical and cultural changes since its inception in 1959 (Harper, 2000; Reid-Walsh & Mitchell, 2000). And while the doll has represented White standards of unattainable beauty it has also represented empowerment for girls in the differentiating them from boys and boys' interests (Reid-Walsh & Mitchell, 2000).

The way gender takes shape here is a combination of multiple factors and is specific to this situation (Messner, 2004; Nye, 2005). The analysis continues by examining how these cultural symbols, power dynamics, and specific behaviors give information in which the boys express interest and disdain for femininity and in how girls use traditional notions of femininity for recognition and power in a very male-oriented space (Messner, 2004). As Messner (2004, p. 98) noted, "The most fruitful approach is not to ask why boys and girls are so different, but rather to ask how and under what conditions boys and girls constitute themselves as separate, oppositional groups." So what gender or masculinity "is" from this view has to do with the way gender takes shape as a function of multiple factors in a given social space and time.

Concerns with Social Constructionism

This section has presented a basic introduction for understanding a social constructionist model for exploring masculinities. For simplicity's sake, it has been presented as a uniform theory which does not represent the rich detail available in this area (Raskin & Bridges, 2002). Regardless, much like all of the models presented here, concerns have been presented about this approach to studying masculinities. We will focus on two concerns: the emphasis of power and the neglect of content.

Some authors have suggested that while an analysis of power is necessary for understanding gender dynamics, it should not be the only aspect on which we focus (Pleck, 1995). Social constructionist models have been critiqued for viewing power as the sole driving force behind gender and ignoring other aspects (Pleck, 1995). While the focus on marginalized communities has been very important, it has implied to some that that "dominant men" have a common experience of masculinity, without adequately assessing the heterogeneity of experience amongst "dominant men" (Pleck, 1995). There continues to be a general point of disagreement amongst people in this field as to how much (if at all) the construct of power should be included in the analysis of masculinities.

The second concern is one of content. Social constructionist perspectives have been applauded for providing frameworks and tools for analysis, but chastised for the lack of content produced from their research (Nola, 2004). By being careful to point out the uniqueness of masculinities, they have been accused of ignoring overlapping themes. As Pleck (1995, p. 25) notes, "in their effort not to mischaracterize *any* particular issue as affecting all men, these writings give little acknowledgement of specific issues that affect *any* men."

Summary

This chapter reviewed several models for describing masculinity. We began with trait theories that view masculinity as an endpoint on a continuum or a collection of unique characteristics. This evolved into a presentation on androgyny, suggesting that gender could be understood as more than two categories. We then explored masculinity as a type of ideology. Finally, we ended with considering masculinity as a type of social construction. In each section, we considered concerns from various theorists about these ways of viewing masculinities and gender.

Now that you have an exposure to different models for masculinities, you likely get a sense of the very different ways that people have approached the exploration of this topic. Each model reflects different assumptions about who men are and what masculinity and gender means to the researchers exploring this topic. These differences will continue into the next chapter, where we will review several models that attempt to explain where masculinity "comes from." Many of these models are based on what we have discussed in this chapter but are presented in a separate chapter to make the information easier to comprehend.

Review and Questions to Ponder

1. What is meant by gender identity?
2. What does it mean to internalize gender identity?
3. What is a self-report scale?

4. What is a trait?
5. What is the difference between nomothetic and idiographic investigation of traits?
6. What is a positivist view?
7. What is a unifactor model for studying masculinity?
8. What is a two-factor model for studying masculinity?
9. How is Best Buy used as an example to support the two-factor theory? Can you think of other examples?
10. What is the difference between expressiveness and instrumentality? Do you see yourself as being more one than the other or a balance of both?
11. What are problems with trait theories for studying masculinity?
12. How are trait theories argued to support dominant masculinity?
13. What is androgyny?
14. How does androgyny connect to essentialism?
15. How are "boy bands" an example of androgyny? Can you think of other modern examples?
16. How does ignoring differences within groups support the idea of separate groups?
17. What is meant by an interactive model for studying masculinity?
18. What are traditional ideologies? Non-traditional ideologies?
19. What is a masculinity ideology? How does this approach for studying masculinity avoid some of the problems of other methods?
20. What is the social constructionist concern with research using the masculinity ideology as a model for masculinity?
21. What are the pre-modern, modern, and post-modern eras of science?
22. What does it mean to deconstruct something?
23. How does the constructivist view generally differ from others in this text?
24. Do you view yourself as a constructivist? Why or why not?
25. What is meant by gender as a performance or doing gender?
26. Describe Messner's three approaches of understanding gender (interactional, structural, cultural symbol) and give an example of how each would be accomplished.
27. What are concerns with the social constructionist model?

5

Origins and Locations of Masculinities

Social Models

Locations of Masculinities: "How It Happens"

The previous section of this text discussed models for examining what masculinity "is". In this section, we turn to theories about where it "comes from." Generally, the process of gender formation is referred to as **sex typing**, or **gender identity/role development**, which involves the incorporation of the behaviors, thoughts, emotions and self-concept expected of one's gender (Bem, 1984).

There are multiple ideas about this process from various fields, including psychology, sociology, anthropology, women's studies, and queer studies. While many of these fields discuss the social context of patriarchy as one in which men and others negotiate gender, there are many views about how humans who are "men" become "masculine," and how such varies by cultural context. As I am sure you can imagine, because people think of masculinity differently, they have varying views as to how to discuss its **location**. I am using the term location here to emphasize that the way theorists describe how masculinities manifest (how they "happen" or how they "develop") differs greatly.

This section of the text is divided into three chapters that cover three different approaches to describing the location of masculinities. We will focus first on social models of masculinity, which include evolutionary, behavioral and social learning approaches. We will then cover psychological models, focusing particularly on psychoanalytic theory, psychodynamic theory, and gender schema theory. We will conclude this section with a discussion of the conformity to gender norms model, an interactive model for understanding location of masculinities, and wrap up with an examination of masculinity as discourse and as an aspect of relational self. While other models of masculinity location exist, we focus here on several commonly discussed in the masculinities field. Most of these models are about gender (in that they discuss issues relevant to all people), but we concentrate here on their implications for masculinities. The descriptions that follow are condensed versions of these very rich models. Please consult the works in the reference section to learn more about them.

Social Models

Social models are those which rely on an analysis of the social environment and an understanding of how that environment affects individuals within it. Social models range from those that view the environment as solely responsible for our experiences, to those that strongly emphasize its impact. We will explore three social models as they apply to the study of masculinities: the evolutionary, behavioral, and social learning approaches.

Evolutionary Psychology

There are several areas in the social sciences that examine biological contributions to gender, such as **physiological psychology** and **evolutionary sociology**. Researchers in these areas study the connections between human **anatomy** and **physiology** such as hormones, genetics, and brain structure and their relationship to psychological and sociological phenomenon (Hamilton, 1995; Pogun, 2001).

One field interested in these kinds of connections is evolutionary psychology. Evolutionary psychologists, formerly known as sociobiologists, are interested in understanding how our experiences serve **adaptive value** in terms of our survival (Fischer & Rodriguez Mosquera, 2001; Gannon, 2002; Ickes, 1993; Van Leeuwen, 2001). Influenced by Charles Darwin and other evolutionary thinkers, researchers in this field explore physiological and social contributions to our adaptive behavior (Ickes, 1993; Imwalle & Schillo, 2004). The basic assumption is that, over time, traits or characteristics that help us adapt to our current environment will be genetically encoded, whereas those that are of maladaptive value will slowly be deselected from our genetic code (Ickes, 1993; Miller, Putcha-Bhagavatul, & Pederson, 2002).

Who's Who in Masculinities Research: Linda Gannon Ph.D.

Linda Gannon is an Emerita Professor of Psychology at Southern Illinois University Carbondale. She is the author of *Menstrual Disorders and Menopause and Women* and *Aging: Transcending the Myths*. She is also Associate Editor of the *Psychology of Women Quarterly* and *Psychology, Evolution, and Gender*.

A fundamental assumption of evolutionary psychology is an **essentialized/** naturalized relationship between biological sex and gender (Ickes, 1993). Masculinity, then, is something that biological males are born with and that is displayed through social aspects of relating and adapting to the world (Ickes, 1993). For evolutionary psychologists, masculinity is what comes from the natural biological aspects of being male and femininity is the result of the biological uniqueness of being female.

One of the primary methods evolutionary psychologists use is **comparative research**, which involves comparing other species behavior to humans in order to learn more about the species and apply that information to human behavior (Gannon, 2002; Smuts, 1995). Evolutionary psychologists tend to use non-human primates in their research (particularly chimpanzees) since they are genetically similar to humans[1]. While there is much to compare, this brief summary includes information on mating behavior and parental investment.

One particular area that evolutionary psychologists study is **mating behavior** (Miller et al., 2002). Mating behavior refers to the ways in which animals go about attracting and finding mates (Murai, 2006). Evolutionary psychologists often study the mating behavior of non-human primates to draw comparisons to human mating behavior. The goal is to observe mating behaviors of primates, relate that behavior to humans, and demonstrate how those behaviors make sense considering an evolutionary model of survival and adaptation. This can then be applied to other areas of human life, as it is assumed that mating behaviors set the basic tone for our behavior based on sex differences

---

[1] The term non-human primate is used here since humans are a type of primate. The chimpanzee is approximately 97.5 percent genetically similar to human beings (Guterman, 2005).

(Miller et al., 2002; Smuts, 1995; Van Leeuwen, 2001). This model specifically focuses on understanding the roles of males and females in adaptation, understanding attraction and what behaviors are engaged in to attract mates.

Attraction is assumed to be necessary in order to increase the likelihood of sex between male and female primates. The process of **sexual selection** involves examining how attractiveness relates to this mating behavior (Gannon, 2002). The most attractive members of the species are seen as the ones most likely to create viable offspring. The most attractive female to mate with should be seen as one who is youthful and nurturing and capable of producing children (Buss, 1994; Ickes, 1993). The most attractive male should be the one who has the most access to survival, wealth, power, and status, one who is older and more likely to be in charge (Buss, 1994; Ickes, 1993). Therefore, we would expect that older males with more status would be most interested in younger females who are interested in securing resources to care for their children (Buss, 1994).

Sexual selection is also theorized to affect what types of behaviors males and females use to attract mates. In order for the species to survive, a male primate's driven evolutionary goal is to impregnate as many females as possible (Miller et al., 2002; Van Leeuwen, 2001). With the high proportions of fetal deaths amongst our ancestors, male primates' drive to **copulate** increased the chances that females would bear viable offspring. Females, on the other hand, are driven to be more careful about these choices. If females do not choose males that are the most desirable, they are likely to produce less desirable offspring (Miller et al., 2002). They are also prohibited from frequent **procreative** behavior, due to spending much of their **fertile** lives pregnant and obviously unable to conceive in that state (Van Leeuwen, 2001). Therefore, females are more selective of who they mate with, whereas males are interested in mating with as many females as possible (Ickes, 1993; Miller et al., 2002; Van Leeuwen, 2001).

Eventually, mating behavior leads to the birth of offspring. Parental investment refers to the kinds of behaviors that animals are involved with to ensure the survival of their offspring (Bercovitch, 2002; Miller et al., 2002). According to the evolutionary model, male and female primates play necessarily different roles in order to ensure survival (Bercovitch, 2002; Miller et al., 2002; Van Leeuwen, 2001).

Because the female's primary role is often viewed as involving nursing and taking care of children, they presumably adopt characteristics that ensure the survival of their offspring. Since they are also involved in the feeding process right from the beginning they are physically tied to their children and provide them with warmth and comfort (Ickes, 1993). In addition, females also learn behaviors to keep the attention of their mate, in order to draw his attention to the care of his children (Ickes, 1993).

Males, on the other hand, whose primary role has been described as providing food and protection, develop skills to enhance that role (Ickes, 1993; Smuts, 1995). Males develop competitive and aggressive tactics to protect against predators and to establish power and status within the group (Ickes, 1993). In terms of their social behavior, then, males as a whole have been described as power and status seeking and women as closeness and solidarity seeking (Bercovitch, 2002; Fischer & Rodriguez Mosquera, 2001; Ickes, 1993; Smuts, 1995; Van Leeuwen, 2001).

Evolutionary psychologists utilize this kind of information to explain differences in behavior between men and women (Gannon, 2002). Stereotypically, men are often described as "dogs" or "players" unable to control their sexual desires (Buss, 1994). Women, on the other hand, are often stereotypically described as being interested in men who meet very specific criteria in terms of money, power, and prestige, hence the feminine "gold-digger" stereotype (Van Leeuwen, 2001). To evolutionary psychologists, these stereotypes represent an extension of survival techniques passed down to us from ancestors. Some of the ills of our society (such as men's aggression, violence, competition, rape, territoriality, social dominance, etc.) have even been explained as having an evolutionary root (Connell, 1989; Fischer & Rodriguez Mosquera, 2001; Gannon, 2002; Smuts, 1995; Van Leeuwen, 2001). This model is considered so seriously by some researchers that they suggest that rape prevention on college campuses should include teaching men about the evolutionary predispositions to this behavior (Gannon, 2002).

Perhaps one modern saying that best captures the premises of evolutionary psychology is "Don't hate the player, hate the game." This statement captures many of the assumptions of evolutionary theory. The idea is that men (presumably) are destined to be players and therefore hold no responsibility for their behavior. If we want to be angry we should focus it on the unfortunate game that involves the roles we play in order for the species to survive and adapt.

In summary, this model sees masculinity as determined by our evolutionary destiny. In fact, evolutionary psychologists would not likely use the term "masculinity," because it assumes separateness between sex and gender. The task for evolutionary psychologists has been to observe differences between men and women and to tie those differences into survival-related theories, particularly those related to sexuality. While this model certainly seems to provide a logical understanding of where gender differences in behavior comes from, there are some concerns with this view.

Concerns with the evolutionary view

While many concerns of evolutionary psychology exist, five are discussed here. A major concern with evolutionary psychology is the **methodology** used to provide data to support the model. Some social scientists have questioned whether evolutionary psychology can include itself as a "science," since it violates a basic principle of science: **empirical** testing of observable phenomenon (Gannon, 2002; Van Leeuwen, 2001). Certainly, we can measure current behaviors of men and women. We can also do experiments on a variety of animals to test cause-and-effect relationships about current behavior.[2] We can show how the results of these current behaviors might link to the basic ideas of evolutionary psychology, but it is impossible to directly test that possibility, because the theory is used to explain something that happened in the past and we cannot directly observe past processes in the present (Gannon, 2002; Van Leeuwen, 2001). Gannon (2002, p. 176) furthers this point, noting that evolutionary psychologists "neglect to adequately test hypotheses and assumptions, and, consequently, theories- even those that are testable or falsifiable." Furthermore, current differences between men and women and amongst animal species can be explained by a multitude of other theories, many of which directly test experimental hypotheses (Fischer & Rodriguez Mosquera, 2001; Gannon, 2002; Van Leeuwen, 2001).

Some of the basic premises of evolutionary theory are also being questioned within the field. For example, evolutionary biologist Joan Roughgarden recently published a text documenting over 300 **vertebrate** species exhibiting both male and female sex organs, homosexual behavior, sex changing, and other behavioral patterns,

---

[2] While according to the American Psychological Association we are ethically permitted to do so, it is also controversial within our field as to how much (if any) experimental research with animals should be conducted. See Herzog (2005) for a historical treatment and current assessment of this controversy.

challenging the assumption of an essentialist sexual binary in the animal kingdom (Roughgarden, 2004). Many humans also engage in sexual activity without any desire for producing offspring and also display diversity in their sexual and gender identities (Ellis & Eriksen, 2002; Roughgarden, 2004).

In addition to the theoretical aspects of the model, another concern relates to the data selected to prove the argument (Fischer & Rodriguez Mosquera, 2001; Gannon, 2002; Van Leeuwen, 2001). Several authors have suggested that evolutionary psychologists utilize data that supports their speculations, but leave out that which does not (Fischer & Rodriguez Mosquera, 2001; Gannon, 2002; Van Leeuwen, 2001).

Hrdy (1997) suggests that no other primates besides humans exhibit a pattern of older males investing energy in younger females for mating. In fact, when opportunities exist, male non-human primates choose elder females the majority of the time (Hrdy, 1997). Yet evolutionary psychologists frequently disregard such evidence, saying instead that men are destined to be dominant and prefer younger women. In addition, research on the Bonobo (or Pygmy Chimpanzee, described as our closest living relative) has revealed some fascinating social group interaction, suggesting the species to be relatively egalitarian, with females often being in dominant positions of power (Vervaecke, Vries, & Elsacker, 1999). Leaving out this kind of contrasting information, (particularly with primates) leaves some skeptical about this approach, particularly when it is argued to provide evidence about human behavior.

Much of our modern human behavior also does not seem to support the model. First, men and women seem to exhibit many behaviors that are contrary to individual survival and survival of the species. It is difficult, for instance, to see how elevated risk-taking and harmful behaviors of men toward women and one another are adaptive and/or increase the likelihood of reproductive success (Pollack, 1995; Van Leeuwen, 2001) (see chapter 8). While reproduction seems to be a logical motivator for mating behavior, the motivations of humans appear to be much more complex. As Gannon (2002, p. 184) suggested, "the assumption that reproductive success is the prime motivation for human behavior is contradicted by the fact that men are not lined up for miles to donate to sperm banks."

A final concern is the blurring of the concepts of sex and gender, which is certainly not unique to evolutionary psychology (Connell, 1989; 2001; Johnson, 1997). When we see men exhibiting a behavior, "maleness" is not necessarily at work. Taking for granted for a moment that the descriptions of male behavior by evolutionary psychologists are accurate and common, that does not imply that they are natural. Believing they *are* natural is an example of fusing the observation of a common behavior with a seemingly necessary biological explanation (Connell, 2001; Kimmel & Messner, 1989; Kronsell, 2005). When such fusing takes place, "what is normative (i.e. what is prescribed) is translated into what is normal and the mechanisms of this transformation are the assumed biological imperative" (Kimmel & Messner, 1989, p. 4).

We would rarely do this with other psychological constructs. For example, Catholicism is a very commonly practiced religion for Latino cultures (Hunt, 2001). Meaningful rituals and belief systems exist within the Catholic religion, and logical arguments could connect the adaptation of Catholicism and practices therein as adaptive for Latino people (Hunt, 2001). However, one would find it odd to espouse a pre-disposition to Catholicism or religiosity gene in people of Latino origin in comparison to those of other origins. The practice of religion is rooted in historical and cultural adaptive practices, which may be influenced by biological mechanisms, but the two are not equivalent. This confusion is related to what some evolutionary psychologists argue is missing (even from many evolutionary psychologists) – recognition of survival's *total dependence* on the cultural context to which humans adapt (Smuts, 1995).

In conclusion, while some see an integration of these concerns (Smuts, 1995), others claim that evolutionary psychological theories have merely reinforced gender stereotypes, and provided a justification for patriarchy and men's control over women (Connell, 1989; Hrdy, 1997; Van Leeuwen, 2001). Ultimately, to some, evolutionary psychological models of gender can be viewed as supporting a complicit masculinity that emphasizes an idealized version of masculinity over diverse masculinities men experience. "The sociobiologists' pre-history is speculative, their anthropology highly selective, and the mechanisms of selection and inheritance simply imaginary" (Connell, 1989, p. 177).

Behavioral Approach

Behaviorism, a subfield of psychology, grew out of major concerns with the field as a whole (Schwartz & Lacey, 1982; Stevenson & Haberman, 1998). In particular, behaviorists are concerned that in explaining human behavior, psychology has relied too heavily on internal constructs for explanations, rather than specifically observable phenomenon (Schwartz & Lacey, 1982; Stevenson & Haberman, 1998). John Watson, one of behaviorism's founders, claimed that if psychology wanted to refer to itself as a science, then psychology should literally abandon its study of the mind and focus only on what is observable about the human experience, human behavior (Watson, 1913, 1919).

So behavioral psychologists, in their understanding of masculinity, focus on the actions of boys and try to predict and understand what motivates their behavior. Behaviorists focus on the effects of the environment and the ways in which environmental stimuli **condition** us to behave in certain ways. Behaviorism in many ways is consistent with evolutionary psychology in that it examines the relationship between traits and characteristics of animals and the ways in which those traits assist in conditioned adaptations to various environments (Stevenson & Haberman, 1998). So behaviorists by definition don't really study masculinity. They try to understand and predict the behaviors of boys and men. In order to understand how behaviorism works, we need to re-examine some basic behavioral concepts.

Edward Thorndike, a pioneer of behaviorism, introduced the concept of **trial and error learning,** which is a helpful introduction for the basic model of behaviorism (Burger, 2004; Schwartz & Lacey, 1982; Skinner, 1953). Trial and error learning begins with the idea that all animals are born with certain traits that help them adapt to the environment (Thorndike, 1911). Once in a particular environment, animals will begin a series of practice behaviors, some of which will be adaptive, some of which will be unsuccessful (Thorndike, 1911). They will do this until they figure out which of those behaviors will be most suited to help them in that environment. Essentially, animals learn how to adapt to the environment through interaction with it. As an animal and environment interact, learning occurs and an animal's initial characteristics are modified (Burger, 2004; Schwartz & Lacey, 1982; Thorndike, 1911).

Beginning a college career for many students is a similar situation. The transition to college, particularly for first-year traditional-age students, is a time of much stress and change (Adreon, & Durocher, 2007; Urani, Miller, Johnson, & Petzel, 2003). The college environment, with its new demands and choices, make it very difficult to adapt (Adreon & Durocher, 2007; Urani et al., 2003). Eventually, students find ways in which their own characteristics and skills can help them adapt. Students come in with a variety of characteristics and utilize them to adapt to the environment. Some students may be more social and comfortable interacting with others to learn. Others will seek private spaces for self-reflection. To a behaviorist, the characteristics themselves are not "good" or "bad," but some are more able to be used successfully to help one to adapt in certain environments.

This provides a useful metaphor for the behavioral model. All animals have characteristics that allow them to adapt and survive in various environments. Each animal utilizes different characteristics to adapt to a particular environment. In order to learn what methods are available, the animal tries a host of behaviors until one leads successfully to a desired outcome. The behaviors that are necessary are relative to the specific environment.

Applying the aforementioned behavioral concepts to gender, it is argued that all areas in the environment carry information about expected **gender-specific demands**. These messages can be portrayed by various aspects of culture, including the media (television, movies, radio, the Internet, literature, etc.) (Hurtz & Durkin, 2004; Pike & Jennings, 2005; Tirodkar & Jain, 2003). In addition to the media, we find the same kinds of messages in sports (Glassner, 1989; Messner, 1989), video games (Beasley & Standley, 2002; Dietz, 1998), religions (Morgan, 1987), parenting styles (Pollack, 1995) and community organizations, such as the Boy Scouts (Hantover, 1989; Pryke, 2001).

Gender, to a behaviorist, is a process in which humans adapt themselves to these conditioned gender-specific environmental demands. All cultural institutions (the media, family, religions, etc.) provide the environmental information about the expected male gender role. Boys, in the maze that is their life, through trial and error learning, find behaviors that are more likely to help them adapt to those environmental demands. Eventually, through trial and error, they find the latch that helps them adapt to a particular situation. The environment contributes to boys' adaptation through two primary pathways: classical and operant conditioning.

Classical conditioning

Classical conditioning, often associated with Russian scientist Ivan Pavlov, examines how physiological reflexes can be shaped by the environment (Burger, 2004; Schwartz & Lacey, 1982; Weiten, 2004). Classical conditioning relies on examining the relationship between stimuli and responses. A **stimulus** is anything that can cause an effect in the environment. A **response** is a reaction to a particular stimulus

(Burger, 2004; Schwartz & Lacey, 1982). If someone blows on your eyelid and it closes, the blowing is the stimulus and the closing is the response.

There are both **unconditioned** and **conditioned** stimuli and responses. Unconditioned literally means "not learned," or automatic. Conditioned means "learned." In other words, there are some stimuli that automatically cause an expected natural reaction and others that will cause a reaction, but only after they have been learned. So there are unconditioned stimuli, conditioned stimuli, unconditioned responses, and conditioned responses (Burger, 2004; Schwartz & Lacey, 1982).

Pavlov demonstrated classical conditioning in research experiments exploring canine behavior and salivation (Burger, 2004; Schwartz & Lacey, 1982; Weiten, 2004). Pavlov remarked that dogs naturally salivate when food is presented to them. So in that case, the presentation of food is called the unconditioned stimulus, and the salivation, the unconditioned response because salvation comes naturally to them when presented with food (Pavlov, 1927). However, we can also condition the dog to salivate by the food with another stimulus (Burger, 2004; Pavlov, 1927; Schwartz & Lacey, 1982). When pairing we present another stimulus (in the famous example, ringing a bell) with the food. If we do that enough times, presenting just the bell will lead to salivation. In Pavlov's experiment, the bell was the conditioned stimulus, and the salivation that resulted a conditioned response, because the dog's salivation to bell ringing had to be learned. So pairing the unconditioned stimulus of food and conditioned stimulus of the sound of the bell resulted in a conditioned response of salivation (Burger, 2004; Pavlov, 1927; Weiten, 2004).

In addition to the pairing of unconditioned stimuli and conditioned stimuli to get a conditioned response, one can also pair conditioned stimuli with each other. Behavioral psychologists have demonstrated this in experiments where an unconditioned stimulus (say food) is paired with a sound and then the sound is paired with a bright light (Burger, 2004). Eventually, you can get the animal to exhibit any conditioned responses that the original unconditioned stimulus provoked by pairing the conditioned stimuli with one another repeatedly (Burger, 2004). This is called **second-order conditioning** (Burger, 2004; Pavlov, 1927; Weiten, 2004).

Now consider all of the stimuli that we're are constantly exposed to that link gender to a variety of areas of our lives. We see men and women engaged in various activities over and over which conditions us to view those activities as paired to gender. This pairing occurs in many ways. For example, the average American family watches fifty-two hours of television per week in which they are exposed to a multitude of commercials with information about the ways in which advertisers would like us to behave (de Heer, Bloem, Paijmans, & Sofie, 2004; Hurtz & Durkin, 2004; Pike & Jennings, 2005; Tirodkar & Jain, 2003). Messages about gender are in train terminals, on t-shirts, in conversations at school, at home, just about everywhere we go.

....

Making Connections: Conditioning Sexual Arousal

Experimental research has shown that the conditioned pairing of stimuli can be accomplished rather quickly (Pavlov, 1927; Thorndike, 1911). Consider the topic of sexuality and arousal and trying to understand what leads to sexual attraction.

Hoffman and colleagues (2004) conducted a study examining whether they could pair stimuli to sexual arousal in both a conscious and subliminal condition. In brief, heterosexual male- and female-identified participants were brought into a laboratory with equipment attached to their genitals to measure arousal. They were shown film clips of heterosexual sexual activity (the assumed unconditioned stimuli) and simultaneously shown photographs with photos of an abdomen of the other sex (conditioned stimuli) or a gun (conditioned stimuli). The photographs were presented to them in trials when they could see them and in trials when they were presented **subliminally**. The study found that they could elicit conditioned sexual arousal in men from both the photograph of the abdomen and that of the gun both consciously and subliminally (Hoffman, Janssen, & Turner, 2004).

The implications are that the stimuli that we are unconsciously exposed to can condition us. Because we are often not aware of all of the stimuli in the environment, it is easy to assume that behaviors we observe are "natural" simply because they are commonly viewed. When we see men acting in ways that perhaps reflect dominant masculinity (see chapter 1) we may view these in an essentialized way, as a natural extension of "being male". From a behavioral perspective, these characteristics have been *learned*, often without the conscious knowledge of the learner.

....

I have noticed a recent example of this phenomenon for commercials for a phone-company that emphasize their unlimited minutes plan. One commercial in particular has a young girl (probably about age 12) on the phone with her boyfriend. Another commercial from the same company shows a young girl of the same age also engaged on the phone in a variety of conversations. The message of the commercial is that, since girls will be on the phone for so long (with their boyfriends in commercial number one), you should have an unlimited plan. What is interesting is that I suspect we will never see a commercial with the boy on the phone. Even though in the first commercial the girl is presumably speaking to a boy, we won't see a boy on the phone. Seeing these kinds of commercials over and over gives us messages about the differences between the genders. In this case, girls are portrayed as "hyper-communicators." From the classical conditioning model, the idea is that boys learn masculinity through being repeatedly conditioned by the major elements and stimuli of our social world.

Operant conditioning

Operant conditioning, based largely on the work of B. F. Skinner, has been a very influential model in the social sciences (Schwartz & Lacey, 1982; Stevenson & Haberman, 1998). Skinner, drawing conclusions about human behavior from research primarily on pigeons, rats and other non-human animals, focused on environmental responses to behavior, rather than just the pairing of stimuli (Burger, 2004; Schwartz & Lacey, 1982). The two primary environmental responses Skinner concerned himself with were reinforcements and punishments.

Behavioral psychologists define a **reinforcement** as anything in the environment that increases a behavior (Skinner, 1953). There are two types of reinforcement: positive and negative. People often think of the words positive and negative to be evaluations equivalent to good and bad. They are not. Positive here means "to add" and negative means "to subtract." When we say **positive reinforcement**, we mean that the environment is adding something that increases an animal's behavior. When we say **negative reinforcement** we mean the environment is taking something away which results in an increase in behavior (Burger, 2004; Skinner, 1953).

Research provides examples of the efficiency of operant conditioning of gendered behaviors. Simple verbal conditioning can provide an environmental conditioner. By praising gender-expected responses by boys and girls in a classroom, a teacher can increase their conformity to gender role norms in a fairly brief time (Alegre & Murray, 1973; Epstein & Liverant, 1963). This is considered *positive* reinforcement because something is *added* by the environment (the praise) to *increase* a behavior (conforming to gender norms). It is not necessarily positive in the sense that it is "good," as conformity to gender norms can lead to problems as well (Mahalik, Locke, Theodore, Cournoyer & Lloyd, 2001; Pleck, Sonnestein, & Ku, 1993).

Punishment, on the other hand, is exactly the opposite. **Punishment**, to a behavioral psychologist, is anything in the environment that decreases a behavior (Burger, 2004; Skinner, 1953). There are also two types of punishment: positive and negative. When we say **positive punishment** we mean that the environment is adding something that decreases an animal's behavior. When we say **negative punishment** we mean the environment is taking something away that results in a decrease in behavior. If a parent takes away a boy's dinner for crying in order to condition a masculine gender expectation, that would be considered negative punishment because something is taken away (dinner) resulting in a decrease in behavior (crying) (Burger, 2004; Skinner, 1953).

To understand how operant conditioning works, let us consider the relationship between physical violence and gender. In the last ten years, psychologists have become increasingly concerned with children's violence toward one other (Tapper & Boulton, 2005). In particular, while girls' violence has been increasing, the vast majority of perpetrators of physical violence are male and the vast majority of victims are also male (Pollack, 1995, 1998; Tapper & Boulton, 2005; Wencelblat, 2004). To a behaviorist, this situation must be examined by understanding the environmental responses that maintain violence.

Tapper and Boulton (2005) investigated the ways in which children between the ages of 7 and 11 responded when violence occurred throughout the school day. A sample of students wore wireless microphones and video cameras that were switched on and off during the day. The results of the study found that positive reinforcement from male peers reinforced aggression in boys. When perpetrators acted aggressively, other boys laughed, shouted, and encouraged the aggression. In fact, peers are said to provide support for aggression the vast majority of the time with little intervention to end aggression (Leadbeater, Banister, Ellis, & Yeung, 2008; Schad, Szwedo, Antonishak, Hare, & Allen, 2008; Tapper & Boulton, 2005).

A behavioral psychologist would look at the ways in which a particular culture reinforces certain behaviors. Behaviorists would argue that boys and men are reinforced for behaviors that meet the culture's standards and punished for those that do not. All of the various systems of the culture such as family, peers, and education act in ways that encourage boys to engage in some behaviors and avoid others (Pollack, 1998). So not only are there automatic pairings of stimuli, but the environment is constantly and continually reinforcing and punishing behaviors in order to assist boys in adapting to the acceptable status quo. Ultimately, boys and men learn to behave in a masculine way through the ways in which they are conditioned by the environment through reinforcement and punishment.

The behavioral model has provided us with much understanding of how certain behaviors can be learned in the environment. It has also provided various tools for changing behaviors in a variety of settings, including schools, mental health centers, and home environments. This model, which really does not address "masculinity," but rather complex behavior patterns of boys and men as conditioned responses to environmental demands, has been called into question by various psychologists.

Concerns with behavioral models

Many scholars in this field more than likely see contributions from social models as important in understanding masculinities. However, there are several concerns with models that adopt a purely social perspective to evaluate masculinities.

Environmental models neither allow for the diversity of masculinities nor for the resistance of power to be a potential aspect of an identity (Hekman, 1997). In other words, environmental models do not account for men who non-conform to norms of masculinity despite environmental demands. Men as a group may hold positions of dominance, but as individuals often do not, due to other social characteristics and personal experiences (Connell, 1995). If men become aware of these environmental influences, it is argued that men can make choices about being a man which then become a part of what masculinity is and must include attempts at resisting dominant masculinity (Connell, 1995).

Another major concern with environmental models is their tendency to view human behavior as relatively passive and essentially determined by the environment. Skinner, a **radical behaviorist**, believed just that (Skinner, 1971). Radical behaviorism, similar to evolutionary psychology, focuses on the necessary adaptation to a particular environment and how powerful the demands of that environment can be. Skinner believed that we do not make choices, but that in fact our choices are made for us (Skinner, 1971). In philosophy, this is known as a disagreement about **determinism** and **freewill** (Wilks, 2000). While that debate is very complex, it concerns whether or not we are able to control our own destinies or whether destinies control us.

Environmental theories tend to stress the deterministic nature of the environment and downplay the potential for active responses to environmental demands. While most agree that environmental forces clearly set constraints for behavior, many believe that humans are also active in this process. In other words, environmental forces may set the stage, but they don't *cause* us to behave in certain ways (Bandura & Bussey, 2004; Kelly, 1963).

Social Learning Theory

Much like most areas in the social sciences, behaviorism has been adapted by people who believed that the basic model was useful, but needed amendments particularly in its adherence to some of the concerns presented previously. One such person was Albert Bandura, who believed that much of what behaviorism has to offer is useful, but that it leaves out certain kinds of learning (Bandura, 1977; Bandura & Bussey, 2004; Bussey & Bandura, 2004; Dowd, 2004; Weiten, 2004). Bandura added a **cognitive** component to behaviorism. He suggested that the way we *process information* as it relates to environmental demands is an important aspect of behaviorism (Bandura, 1977; Bandura & Bussey, 2004; Weiten, 2004).

Who's Who in Masculinities Research: Albert Bandura, Ph.D.

Albert Bandura is considered to be one of the pioneers of behaviorism and is known as the developer of social learning theory. He has published numerous books and articles on this topic and others. He is a Professor at Stanford University where he currently is interested in the basic mechanisms of human agency through which people exercise control over their level of functioning and events that affect their lives. These mechanisms are studied in the areas of sociocognitive development, affect regulation, health promotion and disease prevention, organizational functioning, and collective action for social change.

Bandura's model of **social learning theory** emphasizes how people learn by observations of others and themselves in the social environment (Franklin, 1988; Weiten, 2004). One of the main ideas of this model is that sometimes people learn behaviors even when they are not directly rewarded or punished for them (Bandura & Bussey, 2004; Weiten, 2004).

··

Making Connections: Modeling Objectification

I have an early memory of an event that is a good example of social learning. It is an unfortunate one in that it was one of many events in my life when I began to learn how to **objectify** women. I can't remember exactly how old I was (I'd guess about age 11), but I remember the incident well.

I was with a group of boys at school recess, talking, when one instructed us to check out one of the girls with a "great ass." He was pointing to a group of girls that were all standing in a circle. I had no idea what the criteria was for a "great ass" but I played along as if I knew what he was talking about. All of the boys participated in this objectification, even though some of us did not even know (yet) what the specific normative requirements for body size were, or, in particular, the size and shape of a girl's bottom.

This led to a series of interactions in which I tried to learn what a "great ass" was and how I was expected to behave in the presence of one. One could not ask one's peers what you were supposed to already know, so I observed others in many different situations until I could both understand what was meant by a "great ass" (which was always on a thin White girl) and how I was intended to act (stare, make comments under my breath or out loud, etc).

This is of course also a form of complicit masculinity. The adaptive value for this conformity was camaraderie with my male classmates. The cost was my relationships with these particular girls and my own continued learning of **sexism** through modeling.

··

Bandura contended that people will be more motivated to learn and imitate behavior when the person doing the behavior is viewed as more similar or desirable and when the person doing the behavior is also rewarded for doing so (Bandura & Bussey, 2004). He referred to this idea as **modeling**. Modeling works through three primary processes: **attentional**, **retentional**, and **reproductive** (Bussey & Bandura, 2004; Franklin, 1988).

Attentional processes include two types of modeling: **direct** and **symbolic** (Franklin, 1988). Direct modeling occurs when a person directly observes a behavior (Newcomb, Huba, & Bentler, 1983). Symbolic modeling occurs when a behavior is viewed or represented in some medium, but not directly observed (Henry, 1987; Maibach & Flora, 1993). If I see a man in the park holding hands with his son, I would experience direct modeling. If I read a newspaper article, see a movie, or watch a TV show about a man and view a man and his son holding hands, I would experience symbolic modeling. In the above examples, my ability to pay attention to stimuli in the environment leads toward adaptation (Franklin, 1988). Paying attention to one's environment facilitates the first step of modeling, namely learning the rules and variability of a particular behavior in different situations (Bussey & Bandura, 2004).

Retentional processes of modeling refer to a person's ability to retain and remember past information about the appropriateness of behavior. Representation of past learned information takes two primary forms: **imaginal** and **verbal**. Imaginal representations are images in one's mind that represent behaviors. Verbal representations represent the actual words used to describe and communicate the behaviors to others that reinforce the behavior (Franklin, 1988).

Reproductive processes of modeling refer to the individual's ability to follow through on what they have learned (Hasher & Griffin, 1978; Lott & Maluso, 1993). In other words, just because you have paid attention to certain behaviors, and have ideas about them, doesn't mean you will follow through with those behaviors. You must be able to physically begin the behavior, monitor it in a social setting, and refine it if necessary (Lott & Maluso, 1993). Essentially, one must practice the behavior to learn how to refine it and under what specific contexts it is appropriate (Bussey & Bandura, 2004). For example, in the **objectification** example above, boys learn that these kinds of conversations typically occur in groups of one's peers and not with parents or in mixed-gender groups.

Social learning theorists see these processes as fundamental in the acquisition of gender and gender-typed behavior (Roopnarine & Mounts, 1987). Social learning theory understands gender acquisition as occurring through exposure to numerous examples of gendered behavior in the world and associating certain behaviors with men and others with women (Lott & Maluso, 1993). A process of **triadic reciprocal causation** explains gendered behavior by focusing on personal (biology, beliefs), behavioral (behaviors), and environmental effects (stimuli and reward processes) (Bussey & Bandura, 2004; Gamber, 2006). So in addition to being conditioned, rewarded or punished by the environment, one learns gender through observing what others do, seeing how they are regarded in the environment, and eventually adopting and practicing that behavior, which is then responded to by the environment in a continual interaction (Gamber, 2006; Lott & Maluso, 1993).

An unfortunate example of triadic reciprocal causation could be seen in Jakarta, Indonesia, in 2006, where a nine-year-old boy was killed by other male friends imitating moves they had viewed in "smackdown style" American wrestling (Fitzpatrick, 2006). The boys engaged in play behavior that symbolized the wrestlers they looked up to, and the imitation of these figures brought reinforcement and camaraderie in the peer group. Since the horrific incident, the country has been grappling with censoring television and trying to derive consequences for those who continue to imitate the behavior since the incident (Fitzpatrick, 2006). Ironically, the social welfare minister who was publicly and outspokenly outraged by the incident was criticized for being a poor model himself, as his own family had been shirking responsibility for a mudslide disaster at a mine that they owned (Fitzpatrick, 2006).

Social learning theory can be used to explain much of what we observe in our gendered behavior. We observe men in a variety of settings throughout the day. Masculinities, from a social learning perspective, are developed through a continual process of boys observing, internalizing, enacting, and modifying what are believed to be masculine behaviors. This means that one's own experiences of negotiating masculinity will be dependent on the stimuli to which one is exposed. Of the theories discussed thus far, social learning theory is the first to allow for a diverse experience of masculinities, since it allows for differing environments contributing different models and also emphasizes individual processing of those models (Bussey & Bandura, 2004).

Concerns with social learning theory

The major concern with early work in social learning was a presumed determinism between stimulus and imitation. In other words, the implication reflects the old adage "Monkey see, monkey do." If boys view similar models acting in ways that they identify with, they will imitate them. This is of course is not always the case. It seems that imitation is clearly one way of adopting gendered characteristics, but blind obedience to what we observe does not seem to capture the complex ways in which gender happens, especially since not all behaviors are imitated in every case.

While the modern social learning models have identified internal processes as having an impact on our learning masculinities, they have not (as a rule) provided an explanation for how those internal processes work. In other words, the **intra-psychic** experience of individuals as they internalize information about models has been less of a focus. Rather than focusing on those concerns explicitly here, we will turn to understanding the workings of the cognitive process in the next chapter of this text.

Summary

This chapter presented three social models to explain the position or origin of masculinities. We began with a review of evolutionary psychology, then discussed behaviorism, and finally reviewed social learning theory. Each model has particular strengths and limitations in explaining the acquisition of masculinities from a largely social influence. The limitations noted highlight the disadvantage of largely environmental models and provide fuel for other ideas about gender and masculinities. In the following chapter we will turn to models that focus more on the inner-workings of the individual psyche and how that contributes to masculinities.

Review and Questions to Ponder

1. What is evolutionary psychology and what is the basic premise behind this model?
2. What is comparative research?
3. What is mating behavior?
4. What is parental investment and sexual selection? How are they related to attraction?
5. What are some concerns with evolutionary psychology and its explanation of the development of masculinity?

6. What concerns do behaviorists have about the field of psychology?
7. What is trial and error learning?
8. What are gender-specific demands?
9. What are conditioned/unconditioned stimuli and responses? What is pairing? Can you give examples of them as they relate to the behavioral explanation of masculinity?
10. What is higher-order conditioning? Can you give examples of it as it relates to the behavioral explanation of masculinity?
11. How can something like sexual arousal be conditioned? What other human behaviors are conditioned? Can you think of any that are gender-specific?
12. What is positive/negative reinforcement/punishment? Can you give examples of them as they relate to the behavioral explanation of masculinity?
13. What are concerns with environmental models for explaining masculinity?
14. What is meant by determinism versus freewill?
15. Peers can reinforce violence through reinforcement. Can you think of other gender-specific behaviors that are reinforced by the environment?
16. How does Bandura's social learning theory explain the development of masculinity?
17. Explain modeling and its three parts: attentional, retentional, and reproductive processes.
18. What is direct modeling? Symbolic modeling?
19. What are imaginal representations? Verbal representations?
20. What does it mean to say that social learning theory uses a triadic reciprocal causation to explain how it works?
21. How is social learning theory similar to behavioral models? Different?
22. Can you think of other examples of gender-specific social modeling?
23. In what ways do you think social models adequately explain the location of masculinities? In what ways are they incomplete?

6

Origins and Locations of Masculinities

Psychological Models

In the previous chapter we discussed social models for explaining the location of masculinities, focusing particularly on evolutionary, behavioral and social learning approaches. These models all share a general emphasis on external influences to the individual to explain how one "becomes" masculine. This chapter covers psychological models and focuses on internal explanations for the location of masculinity. Psychological models look to unique experiences within the individual as the primary influences on masculinity, rather than those outside of individual people.

This chapter covers three psychological models: psychoanalytic theory, psychodynamic theory and gender schema theory. While these three models are commonly used to explain the psychological origins of masculinity, they are not the only models available. However, reviewing them will give you a basic understanding of a psychological approach to explaining the location of masculinity. Each of the three models is described, then followed by model-specific concerns.

Psychoanalytic Models of Masculinity

Freud's Psychosexual Model

The psychoanalytic model of understanding masculinity has been perhaps one of the most influential models for explaining sex-typed differences in personality (Bem, 1984; Maguire & Dewing, 2007; Roopnarine & Mounts, 1987). Many of our modern discussions about masculinity come directly or indirectly from assumptions rooted in the psychoanalytic intra-psychic model, which emphasizes the inner processes of the mind. What follows is a concise summary of Freud's basic arguments regarding the origins of masculinity. This summary is followed by several alternative intra-psychic models that consider feminist concerns and analysis.

Sigmund Freud, considered the father of psychoanalysis, was trained as a physician with a biological and essentialist view of human nature (Colman, 2001; Ullian, 1977). By this view, gender is essentially *determined* by one's **sex** but is *formed* through interactions within one's family. This concept is explained in Freud's text *Civilization and Its Discontents*, in which he describes the basic premise of psychoanalytic theory and the framework for understanding the development of personality and gender (Freud, 1961).

From a psychoanalytic perspective, human beings are born comprised primarily of instinctual urges that are contained in their **id**, the unconscious sphere of the mind (Christiansen, 1996; Freud, 1963). These instinctual urges include **libido** (sexual), **thanatos** (aggression), and **eros** (life) (Burger, 2004; Freud, 1963). These basic instincts are the "animal" aspects of ourselves that serve the function of individual survival. They deal with motivations for self-preserving behavior, with no regard for others (Burger, 2004). I often joke with my classes about imagining a newborn infant waiting to cry, because he is concerned about waking a parent. Newborns don't do this because presumably they are driven purely by their capacity to react with instinct to the environment. According to psychoanalytic theory, without proper social interactions from the family, the infant's mind would remain in this uncivilized state (Burger, 2004).

Parents are responsible for the **socialization process**, so that this infant can develop other parts of the mind to help it survive in human society (Freud, 1963). Not getting its instinctual needs met causes **anxiety** in the infant, but the parents (particularly the mother) can help the infant learn how to control that anxiety through socialization (Burger, 2004; Freud, 1963; Hurvich, 1997; Smith, 1997). The strongest instinct, according to Freud, is the libido, and therefore the struggle to control that instinct became the basis for personality development (Freud, 1963). Through a series of **psychosexual stages**, the child learns how to balance its instinctual needs by using other developing spheres of the mind including the **ego** (reason, logic, memory) and **superego** (ethics, concern for others) (Burger, 2004; Christiansen, 1996; Freud, 1963; Kissen, 1992). Thus it is the struggle in the early years of life between what the developing infant instinctually craves and the social demands of society that set the stage for the development of a child's personality and gender (Burger, 2004; May, 1986; Roopnarine & Mounts, 1987).

In my introductory psychology class, I often give an example of this phenomenon by asking if anyone is hungry *and* has not eaten. Several students raise their hands. I then ask them *why* they are in class, rather than fulfilling this instinctual need. Many of them respond, "We *have* to be here." I then respond by opening the door and making sure they know they do not *have to* be there. We then discuss what aspects of ego (wanting the material for the exam, for example) or superego (not wanting to disturb other students) help them make the decision to control their instinctual need. So those who choose to stay presumably have developed ego and superego to control their instincts and participate in human culture.

As stated, the mind's structure develops in stages. The psychosexual stage that is of most importance to our understanding of masculinity's location is the **phallic stage** of development, which takes place around age five (Burger, 2004; Tyson, 1982). Observing young boys at this stage, one can see that, if fortunate, they often have very close attachments to their mothers (Silverstein & Rashbaum, 1994). Freud believed that this attachment can be described as an **Oedipus complex**, in which a young boy's libido forms an unconscious sexual crush on his mother (Burger, 2004; Christiansen, 1996; Deachan, 1998; Tyson, 1982).

While people often have difficulty with this concept, if one thinks about it, the first close and intimate connection one has is with one's parents or primary caregivers. Many of you can likely remember when you were very young and inseparable from a parent. Some of my students who work in preschools often share stories of children screaming at the top of their lungs when they are dropped off at school. Freud believed that it was only natural for children to feel this kind of intimacy toward their parents; they just had to learn to eventually put their energy (which he thought was rooted in unconscious sexual feelings) in a more appropriate place, or toward other interests and relationships (Burger, 2004; Christiansen, 1996; Deachan, 1998; Tyson, 1982).

While simultaneously experiencing this sexual desire, boys recognize that their mother already has a partner, their father. They begin to feel **castration anxiety** around their father, which is an unconscious fear of being castrated due to sexual feelings about their mother (Burger, 2004; Christiansen, 1996; Colman, 2001; Satinover, 1986; Tyson, 1982). The boy realizes that he is in a competition with his father that he is sure to lose. Eventually, according to the model, the boy must break this bond with his mother, identify and learn to be like his father, and transfer the sexual libidinal energy to other activities in his life and eventually to girls and women (Blazina & Watkins, 2000; Deachan, 1998; Satinover, 1986; Tyson, 1982).

This process is what forms masculinity. To Freud, the breaking-away from the mother was the defining characteristic of masculinity: a boy learn how *not* to be like his mother by imitating his father (Deachan, 1998; Kissen, 1992). This practice has been described as a **disidentification** with mother and a **counteridentification** with father (Christiansen, 1996; Diamond, 2004; Kissen, 1992). The disidentification is to separate all femaleness from maleness. The identification with father has been described as counteridentification, since during the initial castration anxiety boys learn to both identify and compete with their fathers and other men (Diamond, 2004).

Freud saw masculinity as a literal detaching and separation, which represents the kind of relational style we often see in boys and men. Qualities such as independence, detachment from emotions, and the discomfort with "all things female" are seen as rooted in this process. In fact, the development of the superego was argued to be dependent on this detachment because, according to Freud, justice and objectivity requires an ability to suppress and separate one's emotions (equated with femininity) from situations (Kissen, 1992; Satinover, 1986; Ullian, 1977). Ultimately, Freud argued that boys have better-developed super-egos because of their break from their mothers, which does not happen with girls (May, 1986; Ullian, 1977).

Following Freud's psychosexual model, several alternate models were derived. Several scholars took the basic premise outlined in Freud's work and amended, changed, and updated areas that they believed needed to be improved. These **neoFreudians** (or **neoanalysts**) included several famous psychologists such as Alfred Adler, Erik Erikson, and Carl Jung (Roopnarine & Mounts, 1987). For our purposes, we will discuss the contributions of an early pioneer, Karen Horney and a more recent contributor, Nancy Chodorow.

Horney's Masculine Dread

Karen Horney, a prestigious analyst and medical doctor, is well known for being one of the first people to challenge Freudian thought, particularly as it relates to women (Deachan, 1998). One of her major criticisms was rooted in the recognition of culture's influence on the developing infant (Deachan, 1998; Horney, 1966; Paris, 2000). Horney's recognition of a social context in familial relations helped steer the direction of psychoanalytic work from a solitary focus on the mother as a satisfying object of infantile needs to understanding the infant–mother relationship (Deachan, 1998; Paris, 2000).

Horney postulated that infants possess a **basic anxiety** that is separate from the anxiety that is experienced as a result of unmet instincts. This basic *social* anxiety results from "the feeling a child has of being isolated and helpless in a potentially hostile world" (Horney, 1966, p. 41). Controlling this anxiety becomes a primary part of the development of the infant's personality (Horney, 1966).

One aspect of this basic anxiety relates to gender. Horney agreed with Freud that boys and men displayed a fear of the feminine, which she referred to as a **masculine dread of femininity** (Deachan, 1998; Horney, 1968). She described the dread as not being simply an unconscious fear, but a deep-seated unconscious **misogynistic** loathing of anything associated with women (Deachan, 1998; Horney, 1968). In her work, Horney cited information from various cultures to demonstrate this loathing (Deachan, 1998; Horney, 1968; Paris, 2000). For centuries, in cultures all across the world, men seem to be obsessed with controlling women and making them appear inferior to them, which, according to Horney, is a manifestation of masculine dread. Horney was essentially arguing that patriarchal cultures seem to have been prevalent for much of human history and that patriarchy was rooted in men's dread of women.

Horney believed that men's historical dread of the feminine was specifically related to the Oedipus complex (Deachan, 1998; Horney, 1968). When the boy developed unconscious sexual urges for his mother and began to behave on them, his mother would reject the boy's attention in this regard. This early rejection results in a **narcissistic injury** to the male child (Deachan, 1998; Horney, 1968). The boy, acting only out of natural impulse, is rejected and made to feel shame in his natural behavior. The boy, attributing her rejection to a literal rejection of his small, unsatisfying penis, experiences a **psychic trauma**. Psychoanalytic theory in general sees the shaming of instinctual behavior as the root of psychic trauma and the cause for later psychological problems (Deachan, 1998; Horney, 1968).

Following narcissistic injury, the boy separates himself from his mother and develops a narcissistic psychological defense around his identification as a man and feelings about his penis. Masculinity then becomes the combining of independence from mother with a narcissistic defense of **grandiosity** and self-importance, as well as an unconscious need to dominate and control women (Deachan, 1998; Horney, 1968). This becomes exacerbated when men realize that the one aspect of being human that they cannot possess is the ability to give birth. Men then unconsciously associate their inability to birth with feelings of rage. Horney refers to this as **vagina or womb envy** (Deachan, 1998; Horney, 1968).

Research also supports the contention that fear of the feminine has a significant impact on men. For example, Jakupcak and colleagues (2005) were interested in whether men's fears of emotion would help us understand men's anger and aggression as much as their own sense of their masculinity. The study found that mens' fear of emotion was significant in understanding men's overt hostility, expression of anger, and ability to control it (Jakupcak, Tull, & Roemer, 2005). Men who reported greater fear of emotion had significantly more difficulty with all three of these concerns.

In Horney's view, this helps to explain why men as a social group seem to be so obsessed with controlling women, especially women's sexuality and reproduction. It also helps explain men's obsession with the viability of their penises (Colman, 2001). Men's obsession with their penis and sexuality becomes a defense against early separation and rejection from an unconscious instinctual desire for a woman (i.e., their mother), which they could not possess (Deachan, 1998).

I remember many examples of feminine dread growing up. Music, in particular is an area that always stood out. When I was younger, it was common to refer to certain styles of music as being "gay" (pop music was often in this category). What this really meant was that it was *feminine* in that is was expressive and full of feelings other than anger. The very idea of liking music that was "gay" seemed repulsive because it was not masculine. This masculine dread exhibited itself in the use of heterosexist language that demeaned certain musical genres and non-heterosexual lifestyles.

Horney's views have been important to the development of psychoanalytic thinking. In particular, her emphasis on the cultural contributions to child development has influenced and helped analytic thinkers understand gender in a cultural context. She also helped scholars recognize mothers as people with whom a child's early relationship is extremely important. This recognition prompted others to further explore the infant–mother relationship.

A Psychodynamic Model of Masculinity

Chodorow's Psychodynamic Model

In recent years, psychoanalytic thinkers increasingly turned their attention to understanding the dynamics of attachment in child–parent relationships (Deachan, 1998; Hayslett-McCall & Bernard, 2002). While Horney (among others) revolutionized psychoanalytic thinking by stressing the relationship of intra-psychic occurrences with familial and cultural influence, Nancy Chodorow, a scholar at the University of California at Berkeley, is recognized for turning our attention to the importance of attachment as it relates to gender development (Diamond, 2004; Meissner, 2005; Pollack, 1995). Her model can be viewed as a **psychodynamic model**, one that focuses on the ways that current relationships are affected by the ways in which our childhood relationships occurred (Burger, 2004; Goldberg, 1993).

Who's Who in Masculinities Research: Nancy Chodorow, Ph.D.

Nancy Chodorow is a Professor of Sociology at the University of California at Berkeley. She has a full-time private practice as a psychoanalyst and psychotherapist in Cambridge, MA. Dr. Chodorow has written several texts including *The Reproduction of Mothering, Feminism and Psychoanalytic Theory, Femininities, Masculinities, Sexualities: Freud and Beyond* and *The Power of Feelings: Personal Meaning in Psychoanalysis, Gender, and Culture.* She is also the author of numerous articles on comparative psychoanalytic theory and technique, sexuality, the psychology of gender, and the history of women in psychoanalysis.

Chodorow's psychoanalytic model emphasizes humans' inherent need for attachment in the forming of a healthy self and the development of gender awareness (Chodorow, 1978, 1990; Hayslett-McCall & Bernard, 2002). Chodorow included these ideas in the formulation of an alternative model of psychoanalytic gender development. While her model applies to boys and girls, we will focus on the aspects related to the development of masculinity.

Chodorow's model recognizes the contributions of culture *and* social context to the ways in which children attach to their parents (Chodorow, 1990; Deachan, 1998; Meissner, 2005). Before examining the developmental issues theorized to affect the genesis and unfolding of masculinity, it is important to describe the specific social context in which children struggle to find their identity, according to Chodorow.

In many Western nations, parenting is done primarily by women (Chodorow, 1990; Pollack, 1998; Shackelford, Weeks-Shackelford, & Schmitt, 2005). Research shows that even when couples include a father, he is often not involved in the parenting process to the degree the mother is (Huang & Pouncy, 2005; Shackelford et al., 2005). While there are multiple reasons for this (men not viewing "domestic work" as part of the male gender role or within their responsibility, the culture not supporting men for being nurturing, etc.), the outcome is the same in most cases – that women primarily raise children (Chodorow, 1990; Pollack, 1998; Shackelford et al., 2005).

Given that mothers basically raise children, boys' first primary attachment is usually with their mother (Chodorow, 1978; Hayslett-McCall & Bernard, 2002). The mother forms attachments and relationships with her children under different assumptions. Mothers view sons as "my child who is not like me" due to their sex difference (Chodorow, 1978; Meissner, 2005). This sets up a strange pattern for young boys in that, as they get older and need to separate physically from their mothers, they also do so in a way that "rejects the feminine" due to being of a different sex. This experience of necessary rejection presumably does not happen with girls, since separation will not require that type of process (Chodorow, 1978; Meissner, 2005).

This presents an interesting paradox for mothers, as all infants need connection to another person, but mothers are encouraged to be responsible simultaneously for both nurturing boys and pushing them away (Chodorow, 1978; Pollack, 1995, 1998; Hayslett-McCall & Bernard, 2002). Certainly women have been informed by various aspects of the culture that assert that boys need to be autonomous and independent from their mothers in order to achieve masculinity (Hayslett-McCall & Bernard, 2002; Pollack, 1995, 1998). Mothers get mixed signals from culture and from their young boys, and boys have to achieve a masculine sense of self by separating and seeing themselves as different from their mothers (Hayslett-McCall & Bernard, 2002; Meissner, 2005; Pollack, 1995, 1998).

As children are nearing the Oedipus complex, mothers begin to act in ways to encourage boys to separate from them (Chodorow, 1978; Hayslett-McCall & Bernard, 2002; Pollack, 1998). They essentially push their boys away at a time that is critical for them to form basic aspects of the self related to relationship-building such as empathy and communicativeness (Chodorow, 1978; Meissner, 2005). While boys still crave attention from others, they are encouraged to play with their toys and be "productive" in this **state of detachment** (Hayslett-McCall & Bernard, 2002; Meissner, 2005; Pollack, 1995, 1998). Early in their development, then, boys are denied a basic human need for connection and forced to have to make sense of this rejection (Chodorow, 1978; Pollack, 1998). Mahler and McDevitt (1982) discussed the idea that one's self cannot become autonomous and independent without first having been fully connected to another. Boys are argued to have never had this early connection, which results in an early **gender trauma** referred to as a "traumatic abrogation of the early holding environment" (Pollack, 1995, p. 41) (see chapter 10).

Fathers are involved in this trauma as well. Fathers, as a function of being men, and having suffered from the gender trauma themselves, may not have the skills to attach well to their children and therefore may not be psychologically available to give their children the attachment opportunities (Pease, 2000; Pollack, 1995). At times, fathers are also physically absent from parenting (due to their spending time at work or other outside activities) (Huang & Pouncy, 2005; Levant, 1997; Shackelford et al., 2005). They may also chastise their sons for being too dependent on their mothers, or chastise their partner for encouraging a close relationship between mother and son (Chodorow, 1978; Diamond, 2004; Hayslett-McCall & Bernard, 2002).

I have observed parents do this with young boys as young as two. In fact, I think one of the most ironic statements I have heard parents say to their boys is "don't be such a baby." Often that statement is made when they *are* just babies, the stage where all children are very much just learning the basics of human life.

The result of this premature detachment contributes strongly to basic aspects of masculinity (Chodorow, 1978; Hayslett-McCall & Bernard, 2002). Boys and men are often described in terms of what they *do*, as opposed to how they *are* in relationships with others. Such a focus on doing activities is said to stem from the displacement of mother–son relating with activities in the world. Boys' early sense of self is literally connected to activities instead of another human being, which becomes a struggle that continues throughout adulthood, as men may make choices for work, career, or finances over their families and relationships (Hofstede, 1998).

Boys also develop gender-specific psychological characteristics as a result of this phenomenon. They develop a general distance from others and seem to have difficulty understanding others and communicating with other people (Pollack, 1998). Such interpersonal distance manifests from a **defensive autonomy** in which men deny experiences of pain and hurt from others because they never developed a healthy whole self (Pollack, 1998). They are both unaware of their own experiences and the experiences of others because they were never given a chance to develop these skills as children (Pollack, 1998).

Chodorow suggests that this problematic situation could be averted if we changed the ways in which we rear children. If parenting were done in a more **egalitarian** fashion by including father as a primary provider of child care, it would help boys and girls learn how to separate without having to disidentify with their mothers (Chodorow, 1978). They would be separating from authority as opposed to separating from a particular sex. This would require major structural changes in our culture, but such changes are argued to harbor benefits for all involved. Mothers would not be burdened with the primary task of rearing children; fathers would recognize the importance of their contributions to their children's development; girls could be encouraged to be more autonomous; and boys would not be faced with disidentification with their mothers. This, of course, would have to occur within in a cultural context that recognizes the importance of these early relationships for boys and encourages them to make the transition from their relationship with their mothers to positive relationships with others that increase their autonomy and encourage their future connectedness (Diamond, 2004).

Concerns with Psychoanalytic and Psychodynamic Models

There have been several concerns with the psychoanalytic model for explaining masculinities. These concerns are not unique to the explanation of masculinities but apply to this model as a whole. The three we will focus on here are the basic assumptions about gender; the focus on the unconscious; and the lack of attention to the effects of the environment.

As stated, psychoanalytic models are essentialist models (Christiansen, 1996; Colman, 2001). This means they see gender as a natural extension of sex. In fact they view our **psychological experiences** as a direct function of our differing genitals and their unconscious representations (Colman, 2001). Such a view results in a binary way of understanding sex and gender expression, which can result in dismissing unique experiences of masculinities.

....

Making Connections: Whose Disorder Is It?

Gender identity disorder is a **diagnosis** given to people who experience significant psychosocial concerns as a function of a disparity between their biological sex and their identifying with, and wishing to be, another gender (Bryant, 2006; Richardson, 1999). Some argue that clinically the diagnosis makes sense when it identifies *significantly* extreme personal struggles with an identity that is in conflict with social norms (Bryant, 2006; Richardson, 1999). Others argue that this personal experience is always within the context of a culture and that it is a dominant view of gender as binary that sets the stage for such discordant experiences (Bryant, 2006; Mintner, 1999; Newman, 2002).

In other words, psychologists may not consider that gender identity disorder cannot exist within a person as a "disease," since the very existence of it is dependent upon the current prescriptive norms for gender (Newman, 2002). Classifying something as a disorder that is so dependent on cultural norms is in stark contrast to the definition of **mental disorder** in the first place. As noted in the **Diagnostic and Statistical Manual** used by mental health providers:

> Neither deviant behavior (e.g., political, religious, or sexual) nor conflicts that are primarily between the individual and society are mental disorders unless the deviance or conflict is a symptom of a dysfunction in the individual. (American Psychiatric Association, 1994, p. xxii)

More importantly, the consideration of nonconforming gender identities as "disorders" contributes to pathologizing people, making them

Continued

feel alienated and disconnected from others (Newman, 2002). This is not to suggest that no one suffers extreme amounts of discomfort as a result of having experiences that are outside of the prescriptive norms of their culture. But mental health providers' continuing consideration of this phenomenon as a psychological, as opposed to cultural, disorder may not be a solution that leads to the understanding and empowerment of diverse masculinities (Newman, 2002).

Psychoanalytic models have been chastised for lacking in their explanation of homosexuality and transgender experiences, except perhaps when these experiences have been portrayed as pathological (Connell, 1995; Prilleltensky, 1994). While Freud viewed homosexuality as an acceptable and alternate way of life,[1] he did not directly address it much in his major works (Christiansen, 1996; Prilleltensky, 1994). The majority of those who followed him unfortunately published much work pathologizing homosexuality (Prilleltensky, 1994). Freudian psychoanalytic theory can be thought of as a role theory of dominant masculinity in this sense, because it argues the ways in which analysts believe men *should* be but not how diverse they actually *are* (Spence & Buckner, 1995).

Psychoanalytic theory also focuses much of its attention on the unconscious mind. While this has resulted in fascinating explanations for human experiences, it has been an extremely difficult perspective from which to do research. Because much of the emphasis in psychoanalytic theory is on unobservable constructs, it is hard to measure whether the descriptions of these constructs are real. Even in research that measures very specific tasks related to attachment, or research that documents specific behaviors that boys may be having trouble with, it is difficult to connect these observations with psychoanalytic explanations such as the Oedipus complex. So while we might view boys as being more distant than girls or more interested in activities than in relationships, it is hard to test *why* that might be so, if we rely exclusively on intangible constructs.

Models like Chodorow's and others that focus on attachment circumvent concerns of other psychoanalytic theories. Chodorow focuses less on the unconscious and more on the observed relationships between

[1] In fact, Freud viewed all people as born bisexual and then developing into heterosexuality or homosexuality as a function of the resolution of the Oedipus complex (Christiansen, 1996).

parents and their children, thereby alleviating a reliance on unobservable constructs to explain causes. In fact, much research has demonstrated the negative effects of early detachment of boys and linked that detachment with a variety of problems including delinquency, drug use, crime, and violence (Hayslett-McCall & Bernard, 2002; Pollack, 1998; Schwartz, Waldo, & Higgins, 2004). Such research sheds light on relationships between attachment and a variety of experiences, but does not necessarily identify the *causes or origins* of masculinity, nor why the social situations that affect the experiences of masculinity take place in the first place.

Finally, while there has been recognition of environmental influences on development, there has not been much specific work within psychodynamic theory explaining *how* larger systems affect the specifics of early relationships (Luepnitz, 1998). To some (like radical feminists and social constructionists), theories that focus on the intra-psychic and family relationships may be a good starting place, but need to address and include the role of systems, an analysis of power, and an understanding of the ways in which the environment affects the ways in which families interact (Kaschak, 1992; Luepnitz, 1998). For example, issues such as access to healthcare, poverty, dealing with racism, domestic abuse, etc., can greatly affect family dynamics (Kaschak, 1992; Luepnitz, 1998). Without an in-depth analysis of systems, we ignore issues of power that affect the ways families function, children develop, and ultimately the meaning of gender (Connell, 1995; Johnson, 1997; Kaschak, 1992; Kimmel & Messner, 2004; Luepnitz, 1998; Prilleltensky, 1994).

Gender Schema and the Cognitive Approach

Walter Mischel, Lawrence Kohlberg, Jean Piaget and many others contributed to the beginning of what is now referred to as the **cognitive revolution** in psychology (Dowd, 2004; Miller, 2003; Proctor & Vu 2006; Weiten, 2004). A hallmark of the cognitive revolution is the recognition of human information processing. Cognitive psychologists have suggested that human information processing is equally important to (or perhaps more important than) environmental conditions in understanding and predicting human experiences (Dowd, 2004; Miller, 2003; Proctor & Vu, 2006). In other words, the way we think about events may be more influential than the events themselves. The cognitive revolution gave birth to a number of cognitive approaches. Here, we will first review the basics of information processing in order to better understand **gender schema theory**. Following a presentation of these models, concerns with cognitive psychology are addressed.

Information Processing

Jean Piaget, a noted cognitive psychologist, explained that human adaptation to the world occurs by way of behavior and cognition (Burger, 2004). We **assimilate** new information constantly as we navigate our day-to-day experience (Piaget, 1954). Cognitive thinkers view humans as approaching the world as scientists do, gathering data through the various sense organs, which ultimately are processed in the mind and used to help us adapt to the world (Burger, 2004).

This assimilation can be understood via the information processing model. Information processing can be thought of as occurring in a series of steps (Barbera, 2003; Bem, 1984; Derry, 1996; Roopnarine & Mounts, 1987). These steps fall into four categories: **attention**, **encoding**, **storage** and **retrieval**. Discussing them in order creates a bit of a false impression, as the process by which these steps occur is nearly simultaneous and incredibly fast (Weiten, 2004). But putting them in steps can help us better understand each component's particular application to the cognitive model as related to gender and masculinity.

Attention concerns the ability to focus the senses on a particular stimulus of interest (Roopnarine & Mounts, 1987; Weiten, 2004). The world is filled with a variety of sensations that are constantly available for our attention. Cognitive scientists view attention like a filter that places stimuli of interest at center and non-relevant stimuli (referred to as **noise**) in the background. The information we acquire about gender and masculinity begins with the stimuli on which our senses are focused.

This information is then encoded so that the brain knows what kind of information it is. The assumption is that, in order for the brain to work effectively, it must organize all of the information it is assimilating by coding information. There are many categories of information to which to pay attention (sights, sounds, etc.) as well as types of those categories. Giving information a code is like a label to help the brain know what kind of information it is.

This is similar to labeling music by genre. When new music becomes available to an Internet music site, they are coded so that listeners can find them easily. Otherwise, when you searched for punk you might get hip-hop, heavy metal, blue-grass, or Celtic music. The proposition that our brain codes information makes sense, because typically we are able to retrieve information fairly readily, suggesting perhaps that it is well organized. Similarly, as you are assimilating information from the world, you are coding some of it as being related to gender and some of it as not being related.

Once information is encoded, it is stored and made available for retrieval (Roopnarine & Mounts, 1987). Various subsystems are involved in this process, which include **sensory memory**, **short-term memory**, and **long-term memory** systems (Gruber & Goschke, 2004; Pearson, Logie, & Gilhooly, 1999; Weiten, 2004). While we will not go into the specifics of these areas here, the basic idea is that information we have assimilated is related to when we were presented with the stimuli. Some information we assimilated is from many years ago, while some is from a few minutes ago.

Cognitive psychologists acknowledge that automatic learning occurs through conditioning as well, but a cognitive model focuses on conscious aspects of ourselves for which we have access. This is the primary difference between a behavioral and cognitive model in psychology. Unlike behavioral models, cognitive models stress that humans are active in selecting stimuli to pay attention to and that this affects the way in which they engage the world (Bandura & Bussey, 2004).

But how is information we assimilate stored in our memory systems? Information is stored in our memory systems in what are referred to as schemas. **Schemas** can be thought of as a network of organizations that categorize and guide an individual's perceptions of the world (Barbera, 2003; Bem, 1984; Derry, 1996; Lemons & Parzinger, 2007). The schema serves not only to organize information that has been assimilated, but also to help anticipate future events (Barbera, 2003; Bem, 1984; Derry, 1996). The schema can be thought of as a collection of social categories of information that has some similarities to others but is also unique to us. Cognitive psychologists also believe that these schemas are organized in such a way to facilitate our use of them in the most adaptive way in a variety of environments.

....

Making Connections: the Personal Computer

I often use the metaphor of a personal computer (my apologies to Mac users) when explaining schemas to students. Your computer has several

Continued

components, but let's focus on the monitor and hard drive. What is showing on your monitor can be thought of as your conscious mind. It is what you are currently processing.

Now, if you look at the contents of your hard drive (perhaps by clicking on 'my computer' in Windows) you will see that it is separated into sections. It shows you the different drives on your computer including your hard drive(s). If you double-click on your hard drive, you will notice two things. First, there are hidden folders. These are folders that your computer manufacturer wants to keep out of your awareness, because they are concerned that, if you start messing around with them, you will find yourself in trouble (and they are often correct about this!). Now you may be thinking: "I don't see any hidden folders." That is because they are hidden. There is something you can do to reveal them, but you will have to consult your PC manufacturer for that much information! We might think of the hidden folders as the unconscious mind.

Now, the folders that are shown on your hard drive are the schemas. When you buy a new computer, most people have similar folders on their computer (program files, downloads, and so on) because many of us use the same operating system (Windows). But as you use your computer, download files, delete programs, or create documents, etc, your folders change. Your folders begin to look different from one another. These folders can be thought of as schemas. They contain information about various aspects of the way your computer functions.

The specific programs and organization of your computer will become more and more unique to you over time. This is not to say you don't have a generally similar computer to other people, but that over time yours has taken on a specific look and feel because of your interaction with it. Much like the model of cognitive psychology, all humans begin with similar (but not identical) brain structures. Over time, we assimilate (download) new information and organize it on our brain (hard drive) through schemas (folders) which contain all the unique information about our lives.

The basic idea is that when we are in a particular situation in the world we "call up" various schemas to help us navigate that social situation (Barbera, 2003). The schemas help us to predict the way others may behave in that situation, as well as to give us ideas about how to respond and contribute (Barbera, 2003; Bem, 1984). Throughout that interaction we may access other schemas that might be necessary, or even adapt our current schemas to help us survive in the future (Barbera, 2003; Bem, 1984). This process of **adaptation** works through **equilibration**, which emphasizes our fluctuatation between **disequilibrium** (when our schemas do not seem to be adaptive) and **equilibrium** (when our schemas are adaptive). Schemas exist to organize all kinds of information in our lives, but the schema that is of most importance to an understanding of masculinity's location is the gender schema.

Gender Schema Theory

Based on thirty years of work and significant contributions to the field of psychology, Sandra Bem's gender schema theory has been widely used and researched (Barbera, 2003; Hudak, 1993). Much of the research on this theory has incorporated the Bem Sex Role Inventory (BSRI), which, as mentioned, is one of the most widely used pen and pencil inventories of gender (Lenney, 1991). The basic premise of gender schema theory is that all human beings have a gender schema, or basic template for gender, that they use to interpret information about themselves and the world (Bem, 1984). Consistent with the general assumptions of information processing and schema theory, the importance of the gender schema for interpreting events varies between individuals (Barbera, 2003; Bem, 1984). Some people will rely heavily on the gender schema to interpret the world, whereas others will perhaps not rely on their gender schema at all. This variance stems from what Bem calls **gender-schematic processing**.

Information for our gender schemas comes from our interactions in a cultural context (Bem, 1981a, 1984). Western culture (and historically most cultures) tend to divide people into two sexes with two distinct genders (Bem, 1981a). These two genders are then assigned differing characteristics presumed to be sex-linked to those genders (Bem, 1981a, 1981b, 1984). The assumption is that there is a cultural norm for gender from which we draw our interpretations and experiences of gender, which are organized within a binary perspective (Bem, 1981a; Kelly, 1963). However, the way in which we interpret and experience gender will vary across people depending on their own unique experiences in the world (Bem, 1984).

The overall culture may give meaning to the schemas, but ultimately the way in which people internalize this information affects how they view themselves (Bem, 1981a, 1984; Scherer & Petrick, 2001). Gender schemas are not just guides for interpreting social events, but also serve as guides to evaluate ourselves (Bem, 1981a). Ultimately, our self-worth can be strongly affected by the ways in which we evaluate how we meet the expectations of our gender schemas (Bem, 1981a, 1984).

This self-evaluation is often within the context of **social comparison**, whereby we evaluate others via our self-schemas (Miller, 1984). Bem suggested that concepts of social learning theory (as discussed previously) are important components underlying the formation of our gender schemas (Bem, 1981a, 1984). We are affected by the ways in which we observe others making sense of gender and gendered behaviors.

People can be thought of as being gender schematic (or sex typed) or **gender aschematic** (non-sex typed) in their use of the gender schema (Bem, 1981a, 1984; Lobel, Rothman, Abramovitz, & Maayan, 1999). Those who are gender schematic can be categorized as **masculine, feminine, cross-sexed** or **undifferentiated**. By referring to someone as masculine or feminine in their gender schematic processing, the assumption is that the person utilizes stereotypical views about their own sex in the ways in which they interpret and interact with the world (Bem, 1981a, 1984). If a person is referred to as having a cross-sexed schema, they are seen as a person who is of one sex, but utilizes the gender schema of the other sex to interpret the world (Frable, 1989). Undifferentiated is used to refer to someone who does not appear to have sex-typed gender schemas but still incorporates some gendered information in their interpretation of the world (Lobel et al., 1999).

Androgynous individuals are those who are aschematic in their processing and accordingly do not employ gender schematic processing to interpret events in the world. They are viewed as people who have incorporated aspects of both men and women into their overall being (Bem, 1981a, 1984). The assumption is that those who are androgynous do not see gender-related characteristics as very important in understanding the ways that others behave (Bem, 1981a, 1981b). This is not to suggest that androgynous people believe gender is unimportant or that they are apathetic to, or deny the existence of, **sexism**, only that, when they interact with others, they view people more fluidly and openly (Bem, 1984).

People often misunderstand Bem's concept of androgyny. For example, the satirical television show *Saturday Night Live* had an on-going character (who later appeared in a film in 1994) called "Pat," who, by an average TV viewer's impression, was of ambiguous gender

(Thorpe, 1994). Pat was described as being androgynous. Now while Pat *could* be androgynous, Pat's blending of gender in appearance is not a criterion for androgyny. Androgyny refers to incorporating traditional male or female characteristics regardless of your sex and does not mean you are genderless but rather that you are more flexible in your gender expression. So someone like Oprah Winfrey could be called androgynous. She has characteristics associated with femininity (communication, nurturance, expressiveness) and those associated with men (independence, willfulness, strength). In addition, she does not seem to rely on her own sex as a barrier to how she views her own (or others') potential. In contrast, the terms **androgyne** and queer/ **genderqueer** are terms used today to refer to people who do not identify with gender at all or do so in a more fluid and variable manner (Mayo, 2007).

Research suggests that understanding one's gender schema can assist in understanding many of our perceptions and behaviors. Let's consider the area of work. Research has shown that sex-typed individuals pay attention to the sex of job applicants more than their aschematic peers (Frable, 1989). People working in teams also seem to think of their teams in different ways depending on their views of appropriate gendered characteristics (Scherer & Petrick, 2001). The idea is that our gender-schema will predict the ways in which we interact with others.

Gender schema theory understands masculinity as a collection of ideas about gender and ourselves. To be masculine means to hold or agree with traditional notions of masculinity that one has learned in one's culture. The way in which masculinities develop is through our complex interactions in various environments in which we build and rebuild schemas to try to understand our world and our place within it. Some people will rely more on gender as a primary schema to evaluate the world (as radical feminist theory has suggested), while others will rely less on their gender schema as a primary interpretive lens.

Concerns with Cognitive Psychology and Gender Schema Theory

While the overall cognitive approach has provided useful models for understanding the origins of masculinities, concerns have been expressed about them. These concerns pertain to assumptions of the cognitive model and the gender schema theory itself. We will include three primary concerns here: binary views of gender; interpretations of the Bem Sex Role Inventory; and issues of power.

Some have criticized cognitive psychology and schema theory for binary assumptions about gender. While the model is theoretically open to individual interpretations and schemas about gender, it sometimes proposes this flexibility in seemingly narrow ways. Even concepts like androgyny and cross-sexed, while allowing for flexibility, do so by viewing flexibility as a mix of "male" and" "female" rather than the potential to be some other gender. Cognitive psychology as a model is not necessarily at odds with this claim, but any attempt to measure schemas by proposing what will count as "male" or "female" beforehand presupposes a certain type of schema that may not in fact be the one used by all people.

Authors have suggested the likelihood that people's gender-self schema and schema for others are not necessarily the same (Crane & Markus, 1982; Signorella, 1999; Spence & Buckner, 1995). It is also possible that, as a function of gender, what the schema looks like will also vary (Crane & Markus, 1982). So, when measuring gender-schema, if we use the same scale for sex-typed individuals we may miss specific aspects of schemas that are not shared amongst each sex – this has constituted a significant criticism of interpretations from the Bem Sex Role Inventory (Crane & Markus, 1982). As a counterpoint to these criticisms, some researchers have devised ways of assessing a diversity of gender schemas, such as gender schema for general attitudes and age-related developmental differences in schemas (Katz, Silvern, & Coultier, 1990; Lobel et al., 1993; Signorella, 1999; Spence & Buckner, 1995). Others have argued for a multidimensional approach to gender schemas like that detailed in **self-schema theory** (Scherer & Petrick, 2001; Tenenbaum & Leaper, 2002).

Finally, while not theoretically incompatible with issues of power, cognitive models do not explicitly address the social context in which people form their schemas. In other words, cognitive psychology models describe a process by which individuals assimilate and interpret information about gender, but do not typically explain how the available information itself is affected by who is in control of that information. The recognition that schemas are formed within culture begins this discussion, but without recognizing the social struggle to *define* and defend what gender is, cognitive psychology may be missing an important element of gender formation.

A major concern for feminists and social constructionists in this field is understanding how humans struggle to make sense of gender's *meaning*, given their unequal access to that struggle (Connell, 1995; Kimmel & Messner, 2004). A dear friend of mine once said, "I didn't even know I was oppressed until I was in college." This was not meant sarcastically. She had never assimilated certain beliefs or interpretations of her experiences with gender because they had never been offered to her and hence were not available for assimilation into her gender schema. Clearly, cognitive psychology models offer a rich understanding of gender construction. But, as my friend's experience suggests, cognitive psychology models would become more integrative with a recognition of social context and power (Gelman & Taylor, 2000; Kantrowitz & Ballou, 1992).

Summary

This chapter presented three psychological models to explain the location of masculinities. We began with a review of psychoanalytic theory. We then discussed psychodynamic views and information processing/gender schema theory. Each model has particular strengths and limitations in explaining the acquisition of masculinities. The noted limitations highlight the disadvantage of the purely psychological models and provide fuel for other ideas about gender and masculinities. In chapter seven, we will turn to interactive models that focus on understanding how the individual psyche and social influences work together to contribute to masculinities.

Review and Questions to Ponder

1. What are the basic instincts of the id?
2. How is the idea of conflict used by Freud to explain the formation of gender?
3. What is socializing? How is it related to anxiety according to Freud?
4. What are the id, ego, and superego?
5. What is the Oedipus complex?
6. What is castration anxiety and how does it relate to masculinity?

7. What is disidentification/ counteridentification? Can you think of examples of this in your own life or others that you know?
8. How did Horney's model for masculinity differ from Freud's? What was similar?
9. What is basic anxiety?
10. What is masculine dread? Can you think of examples of it?
11. What is a narcissistic injury and how does it relate to a significant psychic trauma in boys according to Horney?
12. What is vagina/womb envy?
13. What is meant by a psychodynamic model?
14. What is attachment theory and how does it connect to the formation of masculinity?
15. What is gender identity disorder? What is potentially harmful about using this concept?
16. How does Chodorow's model compare to Horney and Freud's? What is similar? What is different?
17. What is the state of detachment and how does it relate to gender trauma?
18. How do mothers and fathers contribute to gender trauma in boys?
19. What is defensive autonomy?
20. What are some general concerns with the analytic explanation for the formation of masculinity?
21. What did Piaget mean by "assimilate" as it relates to information?
22. What is meant by a cognitive information processing model to explain masculinity?
23. What is meant by attention, encoding, storage, and retrieval?
24. What is a schema?
25. What is equilibration?
26. What is disequilibrium/equilibrium? Can you give an example of this process?
27. What is a self-schema?
28. What is the basic premise of Bem's Gender Schema Theory?
29. What is meant by gender schematic processing?
30. What is a sex-typed vs. non-sex typed schema?
31. What is a cross-sexed schema?
32. What does it mean to be undifferentiated in relation to a gender schema?
33. Can you think of examples of how gender schemas affect perceptions and behaviors?

34. What does it mean to be androgynous in relation to a gender schema (according to Bem)?
35. Why is the cognitive model argued to be the first model that genuinely allows for the idea of masculinities (vs. masculinity)?
36. What are some concerns of the cognitive explanation for the development of masculinities?
37. What are some concerns with gender schema theory in particular?
38. How does self-schema theory differ from gender schema theory?

7

Origins and Locations of Masculinities: Interactive and Social Constructionist Models

The previous chapter focused on psychological models for explaining the location of masculinities and included a psychoanalytic, psychodynamic, and cognitive approach. These models all share a general emphasis on internal influences to explain how one "becomes" masculine. This chapter covers an interactive model and two social constructionist models. The interactive model includes both social and psychological phenomena as influences on masculinities. The social constructionist models question some basic assumptions about **self** and apply those concerns to the understanding of the location of masculinity. What these models share in common is their view of masculinity as a process that is affected by various aspects (Ickes, 1993; Mahalik, Good, & Englar-Carlson, 2003b).

This chapter includes the conformity to gender role norms model, gender as discourse, and gender as an aspect of relational self. These are three fairly modern approaches to explain masculinities. Of the models presented in this text, they are the least likely to use the term "origin" in understanding the "source" of masculinity, as you will soon learn. The explanation of each model included here will conclude with a discussion of the concerns about that particular model.

Conformity to Gender Role Norms

James Mahalik, a Professor of Psychology at Boston College, has recently devised a thorough and well-researched interactive model of masculinities called the conformity to gender role norms model (Mahalik, Burns, & Syzdek, 2007; Mahalik et al., 2003a; Mahalik, Talmadge, Locke, & Scott, 2005; Mahalik & Rochlen, 2006). Mahalik's

Who's Who in Masculinities Research: James Mahalik, Ph.D.

James R. Mahalik is Professor and Training Director in the Department of Counseling, Developmental, and Educational Psychology at Boston College. He is a fellow of the American Psychological Association in the Society of Counseling Psychology and the Society for the Psychological Study of Men and Masculinity. He has spoken nationally and authored numerous articles and chapters related to understanding the sources of gender role conformity and how it affects developmental, psychological, relational, and physical well-being for individuals, families, and communities.

Website: http://www.bc.edu/schools/lsoe/facultystaff/faculty/mahalik.html

Email: Mahalik@bc.edu.

model combines several elements of other models discussed in previous chapters. It incorporates an overarching theme of Connell's hegemonic masculinity model and recognition of diverse norms in marginalized and subjugated masculinities (Mahalik et al., 2003a). The model incorporates Pleck's emphasis on the importance of exploring attitudes about role norms (Mahalik et al., 2003a, 2003b, 2005, 2007). It includes an evolutionary recognition that conformity to gender role norms can be adaptive (Mahalik et al., 2003a, 2003b, 2005). It also integrates Bem's conceptions that nonconformity to male norms can also be health promoting (Mahalik et al., 1998, 2003b, 2005). Finally, it involves behavioral, cognitive, and emotional components (Mahalik et al., 2005).

This model views masculinities as an interactive process, rather than an identity or collection of behaviors, since it is an on-going negotiation between men and the culture at large (Mahalik et al., 2003a, 2007; Mahalik & Rochlen, 2006). Masculinity, according to the conformity to gender role norms perspective, is a process by which people struggle with degrees of conforming or non-conforming with ever-changing norms of masculinity. Mahalik and colleagues outline this process as including five major components: **sociocultural influences, norm communication, group and individual factors, extent of conformity,** and **effects of conformity** (Mahalik et al., 2003a, 2005; Mahalik & Rochlen, 2006).

Psychosocial Influences

Mahalik and colleagues begin with the premise that norms exist in a sociocultural context (Mahalik et al., 2005). Similar to Bem, Pleck, and others, they suggest that cultural groups develop different expectations about gender (Mahalik et al., 2003b, 2005). In addition, Mahalik stresses that the norms that exist reflect the attitudes, values, and beliefs of the most dominant groups. Similar to Connell, Mahalik argues that these dominant norms affect all men, but in different ways, due to individual men's social position in relation to the dominant norms (Mahalik et al., 2003a, 2003b).

Some of the norms theorized to reflect the dominant group are reflected in the conformity to masculine norms inventory. Eleven major norms are included in this scale, (which are listed in Box 7.1). This paper-and-pencil inventory is based on a recognition of the strengths of other inventories that emphasize conflict and stress resulting from conformity to norms (including O'Neil's and Pleck's scales) and dominant themes as suggested by theorists such as David and Brannon (Brannon, 1976; Mahalik et al., 2003a). The intent of Mahalik and colleagues has been to derive a scale that includes norms reflective of

Box 7.1: Norms Reflecting Conformity to Norms Model

Winning
Emotional control
Risk-taking
Violence
Dominance
Playboy
Self-reliance
Primacy of work
Power over women
Disdain for homosexuals
Pursuit of status

current norms in the United States that are capable of differentiating men from women (Mahalik et al., 2003a).

Norm communication

Once dominant norms have been established, it is important to understand how they become internalized by men. **Social role theory**, an area of social psychology, provides the background for Mahalik's in-depth application of norm communication to masculinities (Ludlow & Mahalik, 2001). Borrowing from social role theory, Mahalik and colleagues (2003a) cite three major types of norms that are reinforced in different ways: **descriptive**, **injunctive**, and **cohesive** norms.

Descriptive norms. Descriptive norms, as discussed in this text, refer to norms regarding what is observed as a common behavior (Ludlow & Mahalik, 2001; Mahalik et al., 2003a). Descriptive norms are largely internalized by the observation of others in a variety of social contexts. This includes the observation of what men do, but also what others do. In a culture that often views men and women as binary opposites, men learn what they are supposed to do by following descriptive norms of men and what not to do by viewing descriptive norms of others (Mahalik et al., 2003a).

Injunctive norms. Injunctive norms are similar to prescriptive norms. These are norms that deal with expectations of how one is *supposed* to behave or act and often come with consequences when violated. As Cialdini and colleagues suggest (1991), "Injunctive norms are expectations about how people are supposed to behave. Thus, they provide guidelines as to behaviors that are likely to elicit disapproval or shame" (Cialdini, Kallgren & Reno, 1991). These norms include all aspects of human expression, such as our opinions, feelings, whom we partner with, and how we behave in the world (Mahalik et al., 2003a).

The inclusion of injunctive norms is important as our conformity (or nonconformity) to injunctive norms has very different consequences than our responses to descriptive norms (Harrison, 2005). When a descriptive norm is violated, it is likely that we will see an effect of surprise from others (Harrison, 2005). For example, on the comedy series *Seinfeld*, one episode had several people eating candy bars with a knife and fork (Ackerman, 1994a). This might be seen as a violation of a descriptive norm, as our observations of others in the world suggest that we typically see people eat candy bars with their hands. When an injunctive norm is violated, however, it often results in negative consequences that may have more of an impact on our sense of self.

On the same television series, a quote from one of the characters, George Costanza, can illustrate injunctive norms: "Bald men with no jobs and no money who live with their parents don't approach strange women" (Ackerman, 1994b). In this quote, George not only highlights some of the "shoulds" of masculinity (head of hair, work, capital, independence, autonomy, and heterosexuality), he says it in such a way that implies his affective response to these dilemmas, which bring him much concern.

··

Making Connections: Masculinity on Seinfeld

Imagine a diner with two men sitting next to each other discussing their goals in life. On this episode of *Seinfeld*, Cosmo Kramer and George Costanza discuss Kramer's view of George's worth as a person and as a man who is violating injunctive masculine norms.

> KRAMER: You're wasting your life.
> GEORGE: I am not! What you call wasting, I call living! I'm living my life!
> KRAMER: OK, like what? No, tell me! Do you have a job?
> GEORGE: No.
> KRAMER: You got money?
> GEORGE: No.
> KRAMER: Do you have a woman?
> GEORGE: No.
> KRAMER: Do you have any prospects?
> GEORGE: No.
> KRAMER: You got anything on the horizon?
> GEORGE: Uh . . . no.
> KRAMER: Do you have any action at all?
> GEORGE: No.
> KRAMER: Do you have any conceivable reason for even getting up in the morning?
> GEORGE: I like to get the *Daily News*!
> (Ackerman, 1994c)

··

Cohesive norms. Cohesive norms are norms that are tied to popular people within a culture. So these norms are the norms of influential and powerful people that others look up to and often wish to emulate (Ludlow & Mahalik, 2001; Mahalik et al., 2003a). Cohesive norms are important to include in considering masculinities, particularly with adolescents, who seem to be greatly influenced by these kinds of norms (Ludlow & Mahalik, 2001).

A discussion of descriptive, injunctive, and cohesive norms helps us understand some of the uniqueness we may see in men in terms of their level of gender role conformity (Ludlow & Mahalik, 2001). By understanding norms in a nuanced way, we can see how men could conform to some norms and not others. While there are different motivations for conforming to each norm, men may conform to them in unique ways. Appreciation of descriptive, injunctive, and cohesive norms underscores the importance of understanding whether men believe they do conform or should conform to particular masculine roles and whether such beliefs are context-dependent. Clearly, the conformity to gender roles model provides us with a broader picture of the variety of norms that affect the context of masculinities (Ludlow & Mahalik, 2001).

As an example, Burn & Ward (2005) were interested in whether there was a relationship between heterosexual college men's endorsement of traditional masculine norms and relationship satisfaction with women. They found that the more men endorsed traditional views of masculinity, the less satisfied they were in their relationships. Perhaps not surprising, the strongest predictor was the desire to be a "playboy." Interestingly, not only were men who endorsed traditional masculinity less satisfied but their partners were as well. In fact, women were also less satisfied in relationships with men who they perceived as conforming more closely to masculine roles (Burn & Ward, 2005). This study is a good example of how the negotiation of norms of masculinity can be understood as they affect areas of men's lives.

Group and individual factors

The group and individual factors component of Mahalik's model suggest that, in addition to understanding the dominant social context and types of norms available to which men can conform, we must also understand how our belonging to various social groups affects our conformity, as well as our unique individual experiences. **Social groups** here refer to groups from which we derive an important aspect of our identity, and **individual factors** refer to specific individual experiences that may affect the ways in which we interpret norms (Mahalik et al., 2003a).

For example, Mahalik and colleagues (2003a) cite racial identity as a potential individual factor that could influence the way in which we internalize norms. They also suggest that social groups we belong to have their own norms, but individual men still make sense of the interaction of dominant norms and group norms (Mahalik et al., 2003a). It is important to recognize both the groups we belong to that could influence this conformity and also our own internalization and struggle with these group norms.

In the gay male community, for example, it has been argued that a **polygamous sexuality** is the norm in some gay communities (Aoki, 2005; Bouhnik, 2006; Jensen, 2004). This means that the norm for gay men in some communities is the expectation that relationships are dynamic, open, and not bound to one partner. A man who identifies as gay who wishes to be in a monogamous relationship may struggle with dominant norms of heterosexuality and how that ties into norms of masculinity and a particular gay communities norm of polygamy, which can result in a double-marginalization for some gay men (Jensen, 2004). And while that norm does not exist for all gay communities, all gay men, regardless of their own preferences, must decide when to conform or not conform to varying norms. This will be more complicated by the existence of norms of other groups they may identify with (such as class, race, etc.).

Extent of conformity

Ludlow and Mahalik (2001) suggest that the extent of this conformity struggle can be expressed as people who are **extreme conformers or nonconformers** and **moderate conformers or nonconformers**. Extreme conformers and nonconformers are rigid in their struggles in that they conform (or do not conform) regardless of the outcome of their behavior. On the other hand, moderate conformers are more flexible and adapt to situations more readily (Ludlow & Mahalik, 2001).

Ultimately, the factors described above affect the extent of men's conformity. While these categories may be helpful in explaining some people's conformity, Mahalik emphasizes that it is not a question of whether a person does or does not conform, but rather the degree to which one conforms in a variety of settings (Mahalik et al., 2003a). Rather than viewing all men as categorically conformers or non-conformers, Mahalik argues that the extent of conformity will vary across the different norms and be internalized uniquely by different men (Mahalik et al., 2003a).

Effects of the conformity

By examining the variety of norms we have discussed, and the ways they are internalized by unique people who are members of various social groups, we can have a better understanding of how men's struggle with conformity effects them and their lives with others. According to Mahalik and colleagues, male role norm research has resulted in a better understanding of the ways that male norms can harm men, but has not clearly articulated their interactive and adaptive value (Mahalik et al., 2003a). To address this lopsided view, Mahalik suggests that we understand whether the degree of conformity or nonconformity is adaptive or not adaptive and whether such conformity comes at a cost or benefit to others (Mahalik et al., 2003b, 2005).

The degree of conformity and nonconformity toward these norms requires that the cognitive, behavioral and emotional consequences related to particular conformity and nonconformity outcomes be assessed (Mahalik et al., 2003a, 2005). As Mahalik and colleagues (2003a, p. 5) suggest, "We believe this broader assessment is important as one man may behaviorally comply with a certain masculinity norm but not conform affectively or cognitively to it, whereas another man may internalize the same norm and conform behaviorally, affectively, and cognitively to it." Clearly, the degree of conformity may differentially affect our experiences with masculinities.

For example, as a man who identifies as a feminist, I have had several experiences throughout my life of gender role norm violations. All men who identify as feminists violate norms, yet all do not have the same *internalized experience* of role violation. One frequent discussion amongst male feminists concerns our male friends, how to respond to sexist remarks and behaviors that we observe and to what extent we support sexism by maintaining relationships with people who we feel are not in support of other genders. Some men are very comfortable confronting their friends on their sexism and even breaking ties with sexist men. Others have a harder time and struggle emotionally when they are confrontational with other men. This, of course, also affects them cognitively in different ways and how they make sense of a feminist identity and their own role as a man. So, while feminist men might engage in a similar nonconformity (confronting sexism), their own experience with that norm may be quite different.

Concerns with the Conformity to Norms Model

This model for viewing masculinities is fairly new, and research continues to provide updates and connections to a variety of areas (Mahalik, Locke, Theodore, Cournoyer, & Lloyd, 2001). There has not been much active criticism of the model, which may be partly because of its newness, but perhaps also a testament to its inclusion of many factors. One can imagine sources of concern might come primarily from those with monolithic understandings of masculinity, including those who view gender as an exclusive intra-psychic experience and those who view gender as situationally dependent and as a form of social action.

Models that incorporate systemic contributions sometimes come under fire by psychologists who do not see how it connects to individual intra-psychic experiences. This model includes neither a focus on family history nor on the contributions of parenting to the development of, and struggle with, masculinities. Parenting could certainly be included as an aspect of the environment that contributes to norm formation, but its lack of explicit focus could be a deficit for psychologists with a family systems/developmental focus.

While it is described as a social constructivist model (Addis & Mahalik, 2003) some doing work in the area might question some of the methods used to understand the model. While advocating and recognizing that masculinity is a process that is "created and confirmed by men" and is "something that is actively done in specific contexts rather than a property of individuals" (Addis & Mahalik, 2003, p. 9), the research on this model has largely been through the use of forced-choice **self-report scales**, which to some social constructionists violate the basic assumptions of constructivist theories (Potter & Wetherell, 1987). Rather than viewing specific situations in which people actually **construct** gender, men are asked to rate themselves on a host of dimensions believed to be related to masculinities and then are compared to a norm (or "average" response of men as indicated by the mean responses on scale **items** or **subscales**) based on those dimensions. To some, this does not allow us to see the unique ways in which people "do gender" nor how various *actual* situations contribute to them doing so. As noted by Potter and Wetherell (1987, p. 40), "in surveys

or opinion poll research, restriction arises from collecting a very constrained selection of participants' discourse on one discrete occasion
... The expression of flexible opinions tailored to the context and
inconsistent responses are ruled out by the response format."

In addition, the model presumes that masculinity is a phenomenon
only experienced by men and leaves out the possibility that other
genders may also negotiate masculinities. Recently, there has been an
upsurge in the interest in exploring masculinities as experienced by
people who identify as women and/or queer. This is not to suggest
that the model could not be adapted in this way, but it currently does
not address this phenomenon (McCormack, 2006; Rifkin, 2002).

The Social Constructionist Approach

While the models we have discussed in this text vary in many ways,
they do have one thing in common. They assume that masculinity is a
relatively stable phenomenon that primarily occurs within a person, a
society, or some interaction between the two. While some of the previously discussed models recognize that masculinity changes over time,
they tend to suggest that at any given moment masculinity is relatively
stable and can be defined and understood in this way.

Not all experts in this field view masculinity this way. Some believe
that it is less important to know what masculinity "is" or where it
"comes from" and more important to know how people understand
what masculinity is, who gets to decide that, how we learn about that
and what impact that understanding has for us. In other words, to
some it is more important to understand the process by which people
define and explain masculinity than to derive a definitive definition of
what masculinity "is." In fact, these theorists would say that what
masculinity "is" is ultimately the way in which we come to understand,
define, measure, and react to it.

An example of this general perspective can be found in the work of
Albert Ellis, one of the founders of cognitive therapy, who emphasized
that it was ultimately the way that people interpret events that had an
effect on our experiences (Ellis, 1989). This was in stark contrast to his
colleagues, who emphasized the environmental impact on phenomena
such as stress and depression. Ultimately, people's experiences are a
function of the way they interpret the world and themselves, not a
product of some external objective force (Ellis, 1989).

One perspective that views masculinity this way is the social constructionist perspective. As discussed in previous chapters, there are many forms of constructionist thinking (Raskin, 2002). What these theories all have in common is a rejection of theoretical approaches that believe humans can understand and describe reality in some **objective** way. The social constructionist assumption is that through our own experiences we essentially "build" realities in which we live. To understand where masculinity "comes from" in this perspective, we must study the processes in which humans engage to define, explain, and then react to what masculinity is assumed to be. We will be exploring this constructing via two primary approaches: gender as discourse and the relational self.

Gender as Discourse

Social constructionists are particularly interested in the way in which we use language to describe what we construct. This is sometimes known as the study of **hermeneutics**. Hermeneutics gets its name from the Greek god Hermes, the messenger of the gods (Boyles, 1994). People interested in hermeneutics want to understand the ways in which messages are delivered and conveyed, which they think has a large impact on the way we experience the world (Raskin, 2002; Speer, 2001).

....

Making Connections: Language Can Create a Reality

Paying attention to the language people use can help you better understand the ways in which they are attempting to understand you and themselves. For example, I remember once having a phone conversation with a male friend about my not having any children. We ended the conversation with him saying something like, "Well that's cool, you are just being selfish right now." I responded in the affirmative and hung up the phone.

When I got off the phone, I began to think of the use of the term selfish in that context. Selfish is a word that has (at least) two meanings of which I am aware: To do something for oneself, or to do something at the expense of someone else for oneself. This use of this term in the conversation (as well as the added *right now*) implied that this choice

Continued

was at the expense of others (an unborn child or society perhaps) and could (or should) be remedied.

I would not view my non-behavior as selfish and would certainly view it as a relationship concern rather than an individual choice for me to be making. So a specific behavior (or non-behavior in this case) could take on very different social meanings depending on how language is used (and by whom and in what context). By constructing my non-behavior in this way, this man was able to portray his own choices in a way that were perhaps "better," "more ethical," or "more altruistic" than mine. Language ultimately is argued not just to convey information about the world but also to reflect the ways we view each other in our social interactions (Edwards, 1997). There are, of course, a variety of methods used to examine how language contributes to people's experiences of masculinities.

Who's Who in Masculinities Research: Derek Edwards, Ph.D.

Derek Edwards is a Professor of Psychology at Loughborough University in Leicestershire, UK. His interests are in the analysis of language and social interaction in everyday and institutional settings. His books include *Common Knowledge* (co-authored with Neil Mercer), *Ideological Dilemmas* (with Michael Billig and others), and *Discourse and Cognition*.

Website: http://www.lboro.ac.uk/departments/ss/staff/edwards.htm/

Gender theorists have been active in exploring the relationship between language and gender for the last 30 years (Nichols, 2002; Stokoe & Smithson, 2001; Sunderland & Litosseliti, 2002; Winter & Pauwels, 2006). In the 1970s, the primary objective was to understand gender uniqueness in speech styles (Stokoe & Smithson, 2001; Sunderland & Litosseliti, 2002). This interest typically focused on how this uniqueness reflected presumed deficits, dominance, or differences between genders (Stokoe & Smithson, 2001; Sunderland & Litosseliti, 2002). In addition, the examination of **gender-bias** in language was also a dominant theme in early research in this area (Sunderland & Litosseliti, 2002).

Feminist theorists in particular have also been interested in the role of language (Gill, 1995, Nichols, 2002; Winter & Pauwels, 2006). These theorists have explored ways in which language has been used to reinforce a gender binary (Sunderland & Litosseliti, 2002); concerned themselves with how language essentializes presumed differences between people; and highlighted the ways in which language frequently portrays women as inferior and perpetuates the oppression of women (Gill, 1995).

For example, Foley and Safran (1994) were interested in exploring whether two editions of popular learning disabilities (LD) textbooks had gender-biased language differences. One textbook was written by a female author and the other by a male author. The study revealed that the male author used male pronouns seven times more often than female pronouns, while the female author had no significant different in her use of gender-based pronouns (Foley & Safran, 1994). Analyzing language such as this can help us understand how certain concerns become highlighted through their presence and others marginalized by omission (such as those of girls or others who do not identify as being male *or* female).

Discursive psychology

A relatively new theoretical perspective called **discursive psychology** is a popular social constructionist way of exploring language (Hepburn & Wiggins, 2005; Nichols, 2002; Speer, 2001; Wetherell & Edley, 1999). It combines methods from several approaches and has been influenced by feminist ideologies (Gill, 1995; Speer, 2001). It involves an in-depth **qualitative** examination of the actual language people use to convey their meaning and works to understand how that use of language shapes the significance of people's social relationships (Hepburn & Wiggins, 2005; Nichols, 2002; Wetherell & Edley, 1999).

Riley (2003) suggests that this approach involves three major ideas. The first is that examining and understanding consistent uses of language can help us understand the way a social group is constructing something. In other words, listening carefully to the language people use when describing something and noticing how they respond can help us understand the way in which they form an understanding of what is occurring. Second, language is not just a neutral tool for describing events, but is used to actively convey information about the relationships between people who are interacting. This then has implications for the way the world is interpreted by participants. Finally, **power** also plays a part in these discussions, so that some views are held to be more truthful and genuine than others (Riley, 2003).

An important feature that underlies this approach and differentiates it from others is that the researcher is assumed to approach each situation in which they hope to understand how gender (or whatever phenomenon they are interested in) is uniquely being created within a *particular instance* (Hepburn & Wiggins, 2005; Speer, 2001; Stokoe & Smithson, 2001). That is, the researcher is interested in individual instances of meaning, as opposed to applying general categories of meaning to various situations. In discussing **conversational analysis**, a technique in this area, Stokoe and Smithson (2001) explain: "Rather than seeking to impose categories on the analysis of discursive data (such as 'gender' or 'power') the focus is on what members orient to in their discussions" (p. 13). In other words, researchers assume they don't know what gender "is" or "means" for any particular event until the event happens and is socially constructed (Speer, 2001; Stokoe & Smithson, 2001; Tan & Tan, 2006).

When analyzing language, Potter and Wetherell (1987) suggest that three levels guide this approach. The first is an analysis of **function**, which refers to the question "What is the result of having used a specific kind of language? How does the use of language affect the participants?" The second issue is **variation**. People often use language differently in different situations. How is language being used here? For example, they may use language that implies a gendered cause in one situation and one that is genderless in another (Edwards, 1997). This is because language has a different function in each context. Finally, the interpretation of language is used to **construct** individuals' perceptions of the world (Wetherell & Edley, 1999). This type of analysis then seeks to understand how the variety of language we use has different functions in different situations and helps shape our constructions of the world.

Discourse and masculinity

The basic premise of this approach rests on an understanding of the way in which humans gather information, attribute its source, communicate about it, and ultimately are affected by that conceptualization (Nichols, 2002; Speer, 2001). In any social interaction between people, they will engage in various behaviors. Some of those behaviors will be linked to different social phenomenon, including masculinity. Someone may do or say something that prompts the other to say, "Well you feel that way because you are a man." What results will be a social constructing of the linking of those previous ideas/behaviors to "masculinity." Any human behavior or belief could be viewed as being linked to masculinity, but it is the ones that are, the manner in which they are, and the result that is what masculinity *becomes* in a particular social context. So masculinity, from a discursive perspective, can be viewed as a process in which humans engage in a social discourse about what masculinity is, and react to it, and to each other.

An important concept used in this approach is the idea that people negotiate masculinity (Riley, 2003). Rather than "being" male, people who identify as men are viewed as engaging in a social interchange with others, in different situations, to make sense of what it means to be masculine. This negotiation process is an on-going process that occurs in one's life, in many situations, and with diverse people (Riley, 2003).

Discursive analysts have reconsidered many concepts in the masculinities field, including the concept of hegemonic masculinity (see chapter 2) (Speer, 2001). From this perspective, hegemonic masculinity is not a stable state from which men garner masculinities, but a fluid process in which people can negotiate multiple masculinities simultaneously (Speer, 2001). Men can be male in different ways in different situations depending on the social context. In fact, as Susan Speer, a researcher in conversational analysis, has claimed, "It is not simply the degree of alignment with (what is constructed as) masculinity, that changes, but it is also participants' definition of masculinity that changes" (Speer, 2001, p. 126).

Who's Who in Masculinities Research: Susan Speer, Ph.D.

Susan A. Speer is a Senior Lecturer in Language and Communication in the School of Psychological Sciences at the University of Manchester, UK. Her research focuses on topics and debates at the intersection of feminism and conversation analysis. Her work includes *Gender Talk: Feminism, Discourse and Conversation Analysis*. She is currently Principal Investigator on the ESRC-funded

Continued

project Transsexual Identities: Constructions of Gender in an NHS Gender Identity Clinic, which forms part of the Identities and Social Action Research Programme (http://www.identities.org. uk/). She is currently collaborating with Elizabeth Stokoe on an edited collection, Conversation and Gender, for Cambridge University Press.

Website: http://www.psych-sci.manchester.ac.uk/staff/121358

For example, I was recently privy to an interesting conversation about masculinity with a group of people on a conference call. A young man, who happened to be in the military, made a statement that went something like this: "I am so loving this smell. I know this is kinda girly, but I just cleaned my carpets and used this new carpet freshener and my whole house smells like flowers. It's great." Following the statement, one of the people on the phone replied, "Well, I wouldn't have thought it was so girly, if you weren't so excited about it." This statement set the tone for the rest of the phone call, in which the expression of interest or excitement was linked to this comment and to femininity. People on the phone who I assume identified as men would say, "Well, I don't mean to get all girly on you, but I think that is a great idea."

The original statement had a lot of potential to evoke multiple responses. For example, the fact that he was cleaning his house could have been a subject of concern to those who view that activity as "women's work". His exuberance and choice of activity could also have been praised or attributed to other factors. Perhaps his cleanliness could be linked to his military training and viewed as a function of being orderly. Clearly, language has the potential to be used in multiple ways, depending on the participants and the specific social context (Edwards, 1997; Riley, 2003; Speer, 2001).

Masculinity as discourse does not view masculinity as having an origin in social or psychological phenomena. Instead, it views it as a process that is negotiated by participants in various contexts. This negotiation largely occurs through the use of language. The way that language is utilized by participants results in a socially constructed meaning for masculinity which has ramifications for the ways in which we engage those who are understood to identify as men.

Masculinity as Relational Self

The previous model focused on how the use of language can be viewed as a tool for constructing masculinity in social contexts. While language is often an important issue for social constructionists (Raskin, 2002, Edwards, 1997, Riley, 2003), it is not their only focus. Another common focus has been that of identity and how we go about making sense of what it means to be who we are. In other words, how do we socially construct the self?

The construct "self" is a popular notion in the social sciences (Andersen & Chen, 2002; Cross & Morris, 2003). While the term is commonly used, it is not always agreed upon what "self" is (Cross & Morris, 2003). For this text, we can think of the self as cognitive ability, which includes a capability to interpret the world, reflect on and recognize one's consciousness, and plan for and contemplate the future. The self is sometimes viewed as a verb rather than a noun, as it implies an ongoing process or ability, rather than an object (Chen, Boucher, & Tapias, 2006). The assumption is that this process of self allows us to make sense of who we are and our place in the world. Our self then influences the way we express ourselves and behave in the world. It is often argued that self is a uniquely human phenomenon, although some researchers believe that other primates such as chimpanzees and orangutans (and perhaps other species) have some capacity for self as well (Bower, 2005; Heyes, 1994).

The concept of self is rarely discussed as a solo entity (Cross & Morris, 2003; Evans, 2005). It is usually discussed in relation to other concepts of our psychosocial experience. Popular notions such as self-esteem, self-efficacy, and self-awareness emphasize the idea that the self has some connection to the social world (Evans, 2005). In other words, in our attempts to make sense of who we are, we do so through our multiple interactions in the social world.

While the theory presented here is considered "modern," the idea of the self being social is not (Andersen & Chen, 2002; Chen, et al., 2006; Evans, 2005). Aristotle wrote about the social self as early as 330 BC (Evans, 2005). William James, one of the founders of the discipline of psychology, once said that people have "as many different social selves as there are distinct groups of persons about whose opinion he cares" (as cited in Chen et al., 2006, p. 151)

Cooley (1902) was another important contributor to writing about the self as a social phenomenon. Cooley conceptualized the **"looking glass self"**, which emphasizes that the way in which we view ourselves is largely influenced by how the social world defines us. There is certainly some implicit logic in the understanding that, whatever the self *is* or *does*, it does so in the presence of others. Therefore, when I am trying to figure out who *I* am, I do so while in the presence of others and thus must compare them to me. This form of **social comparison** is a necessary process of the self, whether done automatically/unconsciously or actively. For example, as Evans (2005, p. 78) proclaims, "No one is 'fat' or 'thin' except with some reference to some standard or 'ideal' weight."

This type of analysis has influenced researchers to develop the concept of a **relational self**. It will probably come as no surprise that there are many different models to define and explain how the relational self works (Andersen & Chen, 2002; Avsec, 2003; Cross & Morris, 2003; Gabriel, Renaud, & Tippin, 2007). For the purpose of this text, we will view the relational self as an on-going process of understanding who we are and our place in the world through our various relations to other selves. We will also draw much on the work of Dr. Susan Cross, a Professor of Psychology at Iowa State University, who has written much about this perspective. The idea is that who we are will change as a result of the different relationships and situations we are in. Rather than having a "self," we have multiple relational selves who are engaged differently by different people in different situations (Andersen & Chen, 2002; Cross & Morris, 2003; Gabriel et al., 2007). This conceptualization fits well under the social constructionist umbrella as it assumes that we continually both define and are defined by others in various social contexts.

Who's Who in Masculinities Research: Susan Cross, Ph.D.

Susan Cross is a Professor of Psychology at Iowa State University. She has written numerous articles about the relational self, which originally grew out of her work and interest in cross-cultural psychology. She also works closely with graduate students in supervision, particularly those who are interested in her theoretical approach. She is currently working on issues related to self and relationships in Asia; culture and emotion in the US and Asia; threats to honor and their implications for well-being and retaliation in the US and Turkey.

Email: scross@iastate.edu.

Markus and Cross (1990) described three ways in which the self can be viewed as relational. The first way is when others' behaviors, emotions and feelings are believed to be one's own. This is often discussed by developmental psychologists as a process called **mirroring**, in which parents and significant others infuse children with their own view of them which ultimately becomes children's views of themselves (Frolund, 1997). Second, people evaluate themselves as they compare themselves to others in what social scientists call social comparison. Finally, the self can be viewed as relational in that certain aspects of who we are only exist when in the company of certain people. This may be why we feel so strongly about certain people; they "bring out" certain aspects of us when in their presence (Markus & Cross, 1990).

One debate within this perspective is whether relational selves have some sort of consistency (in that individuals have some consistent group of selves from which to draw), or whether the self is socially enacted in a unique way in novel social situations (Fosshage, 2002). Those who advocate for some kind of consistency use the term **relational-self construal** to emphasize how our sense of self is relative to the quality of our relationships with other people (Cross & Morris, 2003; Gore, Cross, & Morris, 2006). In other words, the strength of our relational selves is dependent on the nature of those real-life human relationships (Cross & Morris, 2003). These relationships form the basis of the relational selves from which we draw in all social situations (Cross & Morris, 2003; Gore et al., 2006). It is also assumed by this view that our relational self-construal varies amongst people. In other words, while all selves are social, the importance of the relational aspects of self vary for different individuals (Cross & Morris, 2003; Gore et al., 2006).

For masculinities, not only are there multiple masculinities across people but within them as well. These various forms of masculinity would be re-enacted differently depending on a variety of factors, such as the similarity of new relationships to established ones (Andersen & Chen, 2002), and the importance of specific relationships for sense of self (Avsec, 2003; Cross & Morris, 2003).

One example that highlights this perspective is apparent in online gaming. I was introduced to online gaming about two years ago and find it fun and fascinating as a psychologist. The Internet presents all kinds of interesting opportunities for presentation of self, as well as fodder to analyze gender and the relational self.

One game that I have been interested in is set in a fantasy world and involves coordination and communication with a group of people, forming strategies, and planning acts of pillaging "evil doers." The game itself is a Massive Multiplayer Online Role-playing Game (MMORPG). McBirney (2004) suggests that these kinds of games present people with the opportunity to engage in at least three selves: (a) the real self; (b) the online identity; and (c) the identity of the character one portrays in the game. One may also have an online identity on a website or forum pertaining specifically to the game. These four selves interact in unique ways depending on the nature of the game, specific players who may be online at any given time, and the changes over time that affect all selves involved in this process.

Presumably, when engaging in this activity, I draw from a masculine self that is connected to strategic thinking, adventure, and fantasy. This masculine self has a relational past with others in my life who have informed this kind of masculinity within me.

When I tell people who know me well how much I enjoy this game, they are often surprised. This is because I do not seem to them like the "type of person" who would enjoy games that involve violence. If you stood in my home office and listened to me giving directions to others about how to overthrow an Ogre King, you might find yourself quite shocked! And certainly I have dedicated my real-life pursuits to quite the opposite. With a traditional view of the self and masculinity, this engagement might be seen as an inconsistency, at best, or perhaps a sign of unconscious hostility and/or potential problems to come!

If my sense of masculinity is relational and flexible, then the concept of inconsistency does not fit. The kind of masculinities I draw from to play this game are perhaps different than the kind I draw from when I interact with students or my friends. It may be different from the kind of masculinities I draw from when I go on a march to support women's rights or when I make an important connection with someone I love. In other words, perhaps I have many masculine selves that are engaged differently in different situations. In fact, researchers are beginning to explore and understand the "plasticity" of self that can be achieved through the use of such games (McBirney, 2004).

In summary, masculinity as a relational self views masculinity as being diverse across men as well as within men. This means that within all men there are various forms of masculinity to draw from to apply to different situations. The strength and utility of these various forms may be influenced by our past and current relationships to others, as well as the meaning these relationships have in our lives.

Concerns with, and Paradoxes within, Social Constructionist Models

Social constructionist models for exploring masculinity do not focus on an origin of masculinity, but rather try to understand how masculinities are socially constructed by various people in various situations. There are many different models within this framework and much argument about the way in which this constructing occurs (Coulter, 2004). In particular, whether there is some "self" that has some potential for consistency or whether self is completely renegotiated in different contexts seems to be a subject of disagreement within the field (Andersen & Chen, 2002; Avsec, 2003; Coulter, 2004; Cross & Morris, 2003).

One concern regarding social constructionist approaches relates to their arguing for a lack of consistency for constructs like masculinity due to the ever-changing nature of social context. And while the arguments do seem very plausible, we do appear to experience consistency in our lives. Previously in this chapter, I gave an example about my engagement in an online game. I suggested that perhaps I have masculine selves that are put to use differently in different situations. At the same time, I find some interesting consistencies with my real life in my engagement in this game. For example, I pulled together several other players and devised a rewards strategy that would distribute rewards in a more equitable way, rather than through sheer luck or popularity. This is a process I try to engage in regularly in my real life and could be hard to explain from an approach that relies on social context, situation-specificity, and the ebbs and flows of human interaction.

One of the fundamental paradoxes these approaches leave us with concerns the research methods used to employ them. Whether the focus is discourse or the self, the criticisms social constructionists have about our understanding of participants' worlds and constructions of masculinity also apply to the researchers themselves. In other words, the researchers' use of discourse in defining and understanding a study or perhaps their own relational selves will affect the social construction of the research (Speer, 2002). This is viewed as a strength of this approach to some in the field, but to others it creates doubt about the overall usefulness of research conclusions.

Another paradox relates to feminist concerns and social constructionist approaches like conversational analysis. Since the approach does not make presumptions prior to understanding gender, it cannot make assumptions about power and domination, which are often concerns of feminists. However, many who do this work believe that examining the role of power and domination in language is an important element of language analysis (Stokoe & Smithson, 2001). One cannot have assumptions about gender and power and *not* have assumptions about gender and power simultaneously (Stokoe & Smithson, 2001). Finding a common ground for this concern has been an interest of many in this field (Gill, 1995; Speer, 2002; Stokoe & Smithson, 2001).

While these approaches present fascinating issues to explore and are resulting in innovative methods for doing research (Speer, 2002), to some the aforementioned paradoxes make it difficult to have any sense that these investigations have pragmatic value. If in fact researchers are as diverse as the participants for whom they wish to understand/ co-construct social meaning, how do we ultimately have any sense of what constructs like masculinity mean when this not only changes as a function of participants and social context, but also as a function of the context in which they are investigated? How can we have a sense of what any human constructs mean if they are in this constant change of flux? Social constructionist approaches have been critiqued for the analysis being so relative to historical, temporal and social factors that they leave people with questions about their pragmatic application. This major concern is being addressed by social constructionists who believe that there are many applications for this kind of thinking (Maguire, 1995; Riley, 2003; Speer, 2001).

Summary

This chapter focused on both an interactive model to explain the "origin" of masculinities and two social constructionist models. These perspectives highlight the idea that masculinity is not something within a person or within a culture or social setting, but exists as a function of the interaction amongst these elements. These models (particularly the social constructionist) also advocate for an understanding of the researcher's role in negotiating masculinity with participants.

The past seven chapters have focused on theoretical models for explaining the social context in which men live, the definition of "masculinity," and explanations for where masculinity "comes from."

Knowing these different perspectives is important in this field because they are at the base of our work and understanding of men's lives. As you read and learn more about diverse men throughout your studies, this information can help you ask yourself questions like: (1) What does this author mean by men and masculinity? (2) How does this author consider issues of power and equity when evaluating men's lives? (3) What kinds of assumptions does this author make about where masculinity comes from and how might that affect their conclusions? Authors who draw their perspectives from psychoanalytic, behavioral, evolutionary, or social constructionist perspectives will go about this task in diverse ways. Knowing these differences can empower you to make sense of their assumptions and intentions.

Review and Questions to Ponder

1. What is the basic premise of the conformity to gender role norms model?
2. What are the components of the conformity to gender role norms model?
3. What are descriptive, injunctive, and cohesive norms?
4. Can you think of examples of different norms?
5. How do social groups and individual factors contribute to the experience of masculinity according to Mahalik?
6. What is extreme/moderate conformity/nonconformity?
7. Can you think of examples in the media that point out current social norms?
8. What are concerns with the conformity to masculine norms model?
9. What is hermeneutics?
10. What were some of the early interests in gender and language?
11. What have been traditional interests of feminists with language?
12. What is discursive psychology?
13. What are the three main ideas stressed in discursive psychology?
14. What are the three levels of language analysis?
15. Can you think of ways in which language is used to support certain ideas of gender (like the example concerning gender in textbooks).
16. What does it mean to negotiate masculinity?

17. What are problems with the traditional notion of hegemonic masculinity from a discursive psychological perspective?
18. How does the concept of negotiating masculinity differ from others in the text?
19. What do we mean by saying that the self is social?
20. What is a looking glass self?
21. What is social comparison?
22. What is the relational self?
23. What are three ways the self can be viewed as relational?
24. In what other ways might the internet/social networking provide opportunities for relational selves?
25. What is the debate regarding whether relational selves have some consistency?
26. What are concerns with the social constructionist model?

8

Men in Crisis

The first seven chapters of this text presented a variety of ideas about masculinities' definition, social context, and source. Researchers have varied perspectives on these ideas, which provide the field with exciting and healthy debates. These kinds of debates are very common in the social sciences. It can seem rare to find information that is generally agreed upon, particularly when a field is made up of so many diverse people who bring their unique experiences to their analyses.

There is one area in the study of masculinities that has some consensus, however. This is in the recognition that men as a social group are faring poorly in many different ways. This has been described as a **crisis for men** (Jefferson, 2002; MacInnes, 2001). This is not to suggest that there is something inherently wrong with people who identify as being men, but rather that men as a social group are experiencing problems at a rate disproportionate to their numbers and with a uniqueness that seems to be a part of the lived world of men (Jefferson, 2002; MacInnes, 2001).

Understanding these problems is sometimes confusing as experts refer to both a crisis for men and a **crisis of masculinity**. This chapter will deal with the crisis for men, which refers to problems that men are experiencing. The crisis of masculinity identifies confusion as to what masculinity entails as being at the heart of these problems.

Typically this research includes people who both biologically and psychologically view themselves as male. This is not to suggest that transmen and/or genderqueer folks do not struggle with similar concerns, only that research on the crisis in men has tended to focus less on these identities. Three views on the crisis in masculinity are found in chapters nine, ten, and 11.

The research literature describes several crisis areas. Three of these crisis areas are discussed in this chapter: higher education, violence, and health/health-seeking. The bulk of the research included here summarizes concerns in the United States; however other nations are also discussed. In the three chapters that follow, three arguments concerning what researchers believe cause these problems and what should be done to change them is presented. While many experts agree that men are in crisis and there is a crisis in masculinity, they do not agree as to the definition, cause, or cure for these crises (Jefferson, 2002).[1]

Problems with Men

Higher Education

Education has been changing throughout the last 50 years in the United States. More students are attending college today than they ever before (Leppel, 2002; Özden, 1996). With the country's emphasis on the importance of a college education and statistics that demonstrate a significant income difference for people who graduate from college, it behooves us to ensure that all people have access to higher education and that barriers that prohibit student access to, and completion of, their college degree be addressed (Banerji, 2004; Leppel, 2002; Özden, 1996; Sibulkin & Butler, 2005).

One primary issue preventing students from completion has been the rising cost of education (Banerji, 2004; Carlson, 2008; Cox, Korth, 2008; Leppel, 2002; Nathan, 2005). The cost increase has been particularly high in recent decades, even when inflation is taken into account (Banerji, 2004; Carlson, 2008; Cox et al., 2002; Korth, 2008; Leppel, 2002, Nathan, 2005). This increase in costs has been particularly hard for working-class families and people of color, particularly Latinos, who, unlike other marginalized people, do not seem to be making significant gains in enrollment (Banerji, 2004; Beattle, 2002; Weiher, Hughes, Kaplan, & Howard, 2006).

While the real and primary concern of finances and other variables contribute to students' difficulties, researchers have identified another concern, which until recently was not identified as a concern whatsoever. This newfound concern, as you may have guessed from this

---

[1] Not all scholars believe a crisis in masculinity exists and that other variables (such as poverty, discrimination, etc.) are better predictors of problems people may be experiencing.

chapter's focus, is being male. Indeed, it seems that being male may be an even better predictor of college self-withdrawal than other variables (Leppel, 2002; Phoenix, Frosh, & Pattman, 2003; West, 1999).

In the United States today, approximately 58 percent of all men apply for college, which is significantly higher than the past, but is significantly lower than the proportion of women, which is closer to 64–67 percent (Baum & Goldstein, 2005; Pollack, 1998). This trend has been increasing disproportionately every year since 1988, except in the year 1995 (Baum & Goldstein, 2005). In terms of actual enrollment, men and women also enroll at differential rates. For community college, the rate is close to 40 percent men and for four year colleges closer to 45 percent, resulting in women representing higher proportions of college students (Baum & Goldstein, 2005; Chronicle of Higher Education, 1995; Dickey, Asher, & Tweddale, 1989; Evelyn, 2002; Marcus, 2000).

Research demonstrates a trend that begins even before high school which may be contributing to this differential enrollment by sex. Beginning in the eighth grade, girls tend to demonstrate higher aspirations for college than boys, and consistently perform better than boys, which is quite a difference from 30 years ago (Marcus, 2000; Pollack, 1998; Su, 2006; Tyre, Murr, Juarez, Underwood, & Wingert, 2006). This is not to suggest that young women do not struggle with feelings of self-doubt and lowered expectations (e.g., Mayo & Christenfeld, 1999), only that such disproportionate feelings in boys seems to be new and equally discouraging.

While boys' overall aptitude does not seem significantly different from girls', as evidenced by research on the Scholastic Aptitude Test (SAT), males tend to perform more poorly in every area of academic pursuit except in areas of math and science (Mau & Lynn, 2001). Boys represent the bottom quartile of Grade Point Average (GPA) in high school (Baum & Goldstein, 2005). Boys also take part in fewer extra-curricular activities associated with collegiate life, which results in their being less competitive (Mau & Lynn, 2001). These may be factors in differential enrollment and acceptance rates for boys, as they are less competitive for college as a group (Marcus, 2000; Pollack, 1998; Su, 2006).

Once enrolled, men are also much more likely to have academic problems in college (Evelyn, 2002; Goldman, Blackwell, & Deach, 2003; Marcus, 2000; Tyre et al., 2006). Men's reading, formal writing, and communication skills are consistently lower than women's throughout their education (Garden, 2006; Pollack, 1998; Tyre et al., 2006;

West, 1999). Similar to earlier educational experiences, men's GPAs are significantly lower than women's, in all areas except math and science (Evelyn, 2002; Felder, 1994; Kinloch, Frost, & MacKay, 1993; Tyre et al., 2006; West, 1999). Women's performance is also more predictive of **persistence** than is males'. In other words, statistically speaking, one can predict whether women will complete college largely by knowing information measuring success (such as GPA), but for men success does not always predict persistence (Leppel, 2002). Research also finds that men are more likely to be on academic probation and more likely to be dismissed from college (Evelyn, 2002; Fasko, Grugg & Osborne, 1995; Goldman et al., 2003; Isonio, 1995; Kus-Patena, 2004; Oklahoma State Regents, 2000; Tyre et al., 2006).

When faced with difficulties, men are also less likely to seek assistance from resources on their college campuses. While men need more services than women, they under-utilize what is available when compared to women (Gowdy & Robertson, 1994; Hudson, 1988). Research shows that women represent 60–70 percent of those who use academic support services regardless of the need to do so (Evelyn, 2002; Hudson, 1988).

Men are also less likely to graduate from college. Approximately 70 percent of men who attempt a college degree eventually obtain one (Arenson, 2004; Beattle, 2002; Cross & Slater, 2000; Sibulkin & Butler, 2005). Women are much more likely to complete a college degree. In two year colleges, 30–40 percent of the people that receive associates degrees are men (Evelyn, 2002; Chronicle of Higher Education, 1995). In 4-year colleges, the numbers increase, but still show a problem for men. Approximately 40–46 percent of graduates receiving bachelor's degrees are men (Chronicle of Higher Education, 1995; Evelyn, 2002; Tyre et al., 2006).

Men of color are at an even higher risk of not completing college, with only 46–47 percent of those who initially enrolled graduating with undergraduate degrees (Arenson, 2004; Beattle, 2002; Charles, Roscigno, & Torres 2007; Cross & Slater, 2000; Sibulkin & Butler, 2005). This is important to consider, in light of the fact that the majority of students leave of their own accord, as opposed to being forced to leave by the institution. Only 15–25 percent of students are asked to leave college (Leppel, 2002). Readmissions are also substantially disproportionately female (Green & Hill, 2003; Kinloch et al., 1993). In sum, the majority of students who leave college and do not graduate are men who are not required by the institution to leave.

In terms of the reasons they pursue college educations, the overall intent seems to be different for women than for men. Women, on average, see college as a place for learning and engaging in academic behaviors (Archer, Pratt, & Phillips, 2001; Green & Hill, 2003; Mickelson, 2003). This is consistent with research that finds that women value **intrinsic work dimensions** more than men (Ovadia, 2001). Men, seem to stress the practical and necessary aspect of college as a means to an end (Archer et al., 2001; Beattle, 2002). Higher education seems to present a social climate in which there is much unknown to all students, including the link between how current behaviors will lead to productive gains (Archer & Hutchings, 2000; Archer et al., 2001). This is a potential cause of anxiety for any student, but can be especially problematic when the primary reason for going to college is focused on productivity and the future.

In addition, research is beginning to suggest that higher education and behaviors associated with a traditional college education (reading, writing, analysis, classroom learning) are associated for many men with femininity and with "middle-class" values (Archer et al., 2001; Lasane, Howard, Czopp, & Sweigard, 1999). "Men are afraid they will be in class, holding hands, and singing *Kumbaya*" (Shelley in Evelyn, 2002, p. 33). There seems to be a resistance in viewing traditional college activities as a potential part of men's identity as well as a vehicle for changing one's identity (Archer et al., 2001; Lasane et al., 1999; Scher, Canon, & Stevens, 1988). This potentially creates a conflict between some faculty and male students who may have very different agendas. Educators often stress the importance of a college education to transform the way one views the world, while many men may be viewing it as a means to a personal and practical end. This is not to suggest that *all* men view college only in practical terms. Proportionally, however, men seem to advocate for this more often, and appear to be struggling more in the college environment (Archer et al., 2001; Evelyn, 2002; Nathan, 2005; Reese & Dunn, 2007; Scher et al., 1988).

....

Making Connections: Men in My Courses

Men's overall poorer performance in college is something I can unfortunately relate to. As a college professor, I noticed this trend prior to

Continued

reading and learning about it for this text. In the first-year classes I teach, the proportion of men and women seems to be about equal. However, by mid-term examinations, almost 90 percent of the students who are at risk of failing my courses are men. The young men whom I deal with as a group seem to present a "macho" attitude about doing work in my courses, taking advantage of extra help, or asking for assistance. They seem to be more comfortable failing the course than getting help or engaging in the course in a way that would improve their grades. I have had many wonderful male students (some of whom I am still very close to), but overall, many men do seem to shy away from "typical" college behaviors such as reading, homework, analysis, and class discussion.

Some faculty have responded to this problem by arguing that we need to "masculinize" the classroom by providing more hands-on activities, and more "action-oriented" assignments that will engage men (Evelyn, 2002). There are some advantages to this approach. Viewing the problem this way honors the way in which men may be approaching the world and asks professionals to accommodate the needs of their students. In this regard, it is similar to research on **learning styles** that suggest that the more we understand the ways in which people learn, the more prepared we can be to offer diverse ways to engage and teach them (Reese & Dunn, 2007; Tileston, 2005).

I believe there is some value in this position. If we can think of ways that will be more likely to engage students, we should try them. However, what I am noticing is that these alternative methods are sometimes *replacing* traditional methods, which I do not believe is good for students (regardless of whether they are male) in the long run. Entire "hands-on" majors seem to exist to provide these kinds of "alternate" ways of teaching and learning.

I have also noticed this trend among some students of color, who are often more at-risk of leaving college than their White counterparts (as discussed previously). I have had multiple conversations over the years with male students of color who struggle both with issues of masculinity as well as with discrimination and racial and ethnic identity. Not only are the behaviors associated with college viewed as feminine, they are also sometimes viewed as "White" by some of their peers and members of their community. Because of racism and historical oppression, some young Black men for example, have unfortunately come to view these human activities that have existed across the globe as things that "White" people do, thus making them seem less desirable. Institutional attempts to not require so-called "traditional" learning is a form of racism (and sexism), as they imply that male students of color are not capable of participating equally in these cultural activities. It is an insult to all of our students for the same reason, and I am often discouraged by trends in higher education which seem to be moving in this direction.

Knowing how to read, write, and communicate are skills that are necessary for all people. Men may have more difficulty doing these things for a variety of reasons, and I do not think the solution is to create learning experiences in which they essentially do these things less often. It is important to understand why men are having difficulty in these areas, and to provide as much support as possible for them to excel in these areas to the best of their ability. All of us have areas in which we need to grow, and college should be a supportive place to do that kind of growing, not a place in which we find ways of skirting around our growing edges.

The issue of college identity seems to be particularly difficult for working-class men (Archer & Hutchings, 2000; Archer et al., 2001; Connor et al., 2001). There seems to be a consistent decrease in men's ability to persist in college when one compares two-year to four year colleges (Chronicle of Higher Education, 1995; Connor et al., 2001). While there are many differences between two- and four-year colleges (from cost to mission statements to resources to marketing, etc.), one factor that seems to consistently differentiate them is the greater proportion of working-class students at community colleges (Banerji, 2004; Burd, 2006; Connor et al., 2001; DiMaria, 2006; Evelyn, 2002, Zamani, 2000). People of color, who are largely over-represented in the working classes, are also significantly more at risk for leaving college than their White counterparts, which may reflect even more complex issues of identity and discrimination (Archer et al., 2001; Burd, 2006; DiMaria, 2006; Özden, 1996; Zamani, 2000).

In sum, young men have less competitive portfolios when they apply for college. They apply less often to college and, when they do apply, they seem to demonstrate lowered expectations of themselves. They are more likely to have academic issues, less likely to ask for help, and less likely to complete a college education. Some researchers believe that men's disengagement has to do with masculine identity and the view that behaviors associated with education are feminine and therefore not for men. College life is viewed by some men as a **"risky identity"**, particularly for those men who seem to feel out of place in the higher education setting (Archer & Hutchings, 2000; Archer et al., 2001; Scher et al., 1988). And while men struggle with integrating education into their identity, they have numerous additional social problems.

Violence

Violence is so pervasive, widespread and disproportionately committed by boys and men that it is considered a gender-based epidemic and a general public health concern (Leander, 2002; Miedzian, 1991; Pollack, 1995, 1998). There are differences across cultures in the amount and severity of male violence, but it appears to be present in all nations, and is disproportionately higher in the United States (Brannon, 2005; Miedzian, 1991; Ogunjuyigbe, Akinlo, & Ebigbola, 2005; Reilly, Muldoon, & Byrne, 2004; Rudmin, Ferrada-Noli, & Skolbekken, 2003; Wood, Maforah, & Jewkes, 1998). While it is true that women commit violence and report using relationship violence sometimes at the same rate as men, there is no comparison as to the intensity, coerciveness and severity of violence that men use toward women, each other, and themselves (Courtenay, 1999; Hamberger & Guse, 2002; Russell & Oswald, 2002).

Well-known anti-sexist writer, activist, and producer Jackson Katz has been very vigorous in getting people to acknowledge the link between violence and masculinity (Katz, 2003; Katz, Ericsson, & Talreja, 2000; Katz & Jhally, 2000). The problem that Katz purports is that people are often able to see when other social variables are related to violence (such as race or religious belief), but are quiet when the social variable is gender.

Who's Who in Masculinities Research: Jackson Katz, Ed.M.

Jackson Katz is an anti-sexist educator, author and filmmaker. He has lectured on hundreds of college and high school campuses and has conducted hundreds of professional trainings, seminars, and workshops in the US, Canada, Europe, Australia and Japan. He is the co-founder of the Mentors in Violence Prevention (MVP) program, the leading gender violence prevention initiative in professional and college athletics. He is also the creator and co-creator of educational videos for college and high school students, including *Tough Guise: Violence, Media, and the Crisis in Masculinity, Wrestling with Manhood* and *Spin the Bottle: Sex, Lies and Alcohol.*

Website: www.jacksonkatz.com

In recent years, there have been thousands of news stories, television specials and town meeting discussions of "youth violence," which is perpetrated overwhelmingly not by youths of both sexes but by adolescent males. Last summer, Woodstock '99 featured several rapes and countless sexual assaults by men against women. The festival concluded with a shameful display of wanton destruction by out-of-control males. And yet the discussion afterward blamed it on the "crowd." More recently, when groups of men went on a rampage after the NBA victory of the Los Angeles Lakers, the media focused in again on a "mob" out of control. (Katz & Jhally, 2000, p. 5)

There is much defensiveness in discussing violence as a gender issue, particularly in calling it a problem with men (Courtenay, 1999; Katz et al., 2000; Miedzian, 1991). Miedzian (1991) cites two primary reasons for this. The first is that people often *hear* statements linking men to violence as suggesting that "most men are violent", in contrast to "most violent people are men" (Miedzian, 1991). Due to an often defensive reaction, discussions around this topic often lead to anger and confusion and are feared to cause more divisiveness and strain between people (Miedzian, 1991).

In addition, because men's aggressiveness and violence is unfortunately a part of the way we view the way men "should be" (see chapter 2), it becomes difficult for people to view men's violence as a form of deviance, because at some level, men acting violently is expected (Miedzian, 1991). This difficulty in viewing the link of men to violence is particularly true for men who are not used to self-criticism, since their behavior is often viewed as the norm by which others are compared (Miedzian, 1991).

Defining men's violence is also extremely difficult to do (Bevan & Higgins, 2002; Hamberger & Guse, 2002; Leander, 2002). This is due to several different factors that come from the people collecting data about this issue and from the respondents from whom researchers collect this data. As for the data collectors, the data comes from a variety of different professionals (including psychologists, sociologists, police officers, social workers, therapists, nurses, etc.) who work in a variety of settings (Henning & Feder, 2004). These professionals utilize different methods to collect information and rely on **self-report** and various types of **other reports** which often conflict (Busch & Rosenberg, 2004; Hamberger & Guse, 2002). In addition, when producing data, people do not always discuss whether they used **clinical** or **community samples** (Busch & Rosenberg, 2004). Clinical samples involve people who have come into professional settings seeking help while community samples involve a more general group of people. These factors make it hard to **aggregate** or combine the reports; it is therefore hard to summarize them (Bevan & Higgins, 2002).

At the level of the respondents, there are several reasons why reports of violence may be inaccurate. People who have recently suffered a form of trauma often have cognitive and emotional impairments and may have trouble recalling events (Bevan & Higgins, 2002; Herman, 1992; Jackson & Petretic-Jackson, 1996). When the victim is male, there is often additional shame and embarrassment attached to the victimization, which frequently prevents men from reporting abuse in both gay and heterosexual partnerships (Johnson, 1997). There are often further repercussions for people who report violence to authorities, which may bias the information reported, particularly if the victim is dependent on the perpetrator (financially, etc.), a common pattern in heterosexual violence against women (Kimmel, 2002). For these reasons and others, violence as a whole is believed to be under-reported, making it difficult to get a sense of its occurrence on a widespread basis (Kaura & Allen, 2004).

While difficult to define and measure, I will include information pertaining to two areas of violence: violence against women and violence against men. These sections are meant to describe the phenomena, rather than to summarize the various factors related to them.

Violence against women

Violence against women is so prevalent that it is described as a pandemic problem in the United States (Hearn, 2001; Jackson & Petretic-Jackson, 1996). The most common type of violence against women is committed by a man whom she knows (Aberle & Littlefield,

2001; Dobashi, Dobashi, Cavanagh, & Lewis, 2004; Kimmel, 2002; Leander, 2002). This violence ranges from the subtle to the persistent and can result in long-lasting trauma and death (Hearn, 2001; Kimmel, 2002). Classification of violence against women can be on the basis of frequency, type, relationship to perpetrator, location, and severity, among a host of other factors. For this review, we will include information on domestic violence, intimate partner violence, and rape and sexual assault.

Domestic violence **Domestic violence** is a commonly used phrase, although what is considered to be domestic violence is not always agreed upon by researchers (Bevan & Higgins, 2002; Hamberger & Guse, 2002; Leander, 2002). The basic assumption is that the emphasis of *domestic* is to differentiate this kind of violence from violence that happens outside of one's home (Leander, 2002).

As previously noted, a growing body of research suggests that in terms of incidences of violence, men and women report resorting to violent tactics nearly to the same degree and women sometimes report using physical aggression in relationships more often than men (Busch & Rosenberg, 2004; Hamberger & Guse, 2002; Henning & Feder, 2004; Kaura & Allen, 2004). This data should be interpreted carefully. There are numerous studies showing men reporting much higher incidences of using violence than women (Garcia-Moreno, Jansen, Ellsberg, Heise, & Watts, 2006; Henning & Feder, 2004; Johnson, 2004).

In addition, while self-report of use of physical aggression in some contexts is similar, dissimilarities include the past police records of perpetrators, severity of violence used, and the overall social context. Male perpetrators arrested for domestic violence are significantly more likely than women to hold a police record for other violent offenses and for other criminal behaviors (Busch & Rosenberg, 2004). The severity, persistency, and level of violence are also much more dangerous when committed by men (Busch & Rosenberg, 2004; Kaura & Allen, 2004). Finally, in a patriarchal culture, women are far more likely to be dependent upon their male partner financially, and to be unsafe in the home (Kimmel, 2002). Given that framework, it is estimated that 1.8 million women are physically harmed by their spouses each year (Beneke, 2004). "In established market economics, gender-based victimization is responsible for one out of every five healthy days of life lost to women of productive age" (Heise, Pitanguy, & Germain, 1994, p. ix).

Researchers are now differentiating between **intimate terrorism** and **common couple violence** as categories of domestic violence (Henning & Feder, 2004). Intimate terrorism is used to refer to violence that is frequent, severe, and presents a major health risk for the victim (Henning & Feder, 2004; Johnson, 2004). Common couple violence includes violence that is less severe, less frequent, and does not escalate over time but remains relatively stable (Henning & Feder, 2004; Johnson, 2004). Intimate terrorism is argued to be over-represented by male perpetrators and common couple violence is more likely to approach equal contributions of both partners (Dobashi et al., 2004; Frye, Manganello, Campbell, Walton-Moss, & Wilt, 2006; Johnson, 2006). Overall, nearly 50 percent of women have been victims of some form of domestic violence (Dobashi et al., 2004; Frye et al., 2006; Garcia-Moreno et al., 2006; Hearn, 2001; Leander, 2002).

Intimate partner violence **Intimate partner violence** refers to violence committed in the context of a dating or social relationship (Williams & Frieze, 2005). Unfortunately, research suggests that both severe and lower-level types of violence are increasing in dating situations (Kaura & Allen, 2004). While lower-level violence is more common, both kinds of violence are prevalent in dating relationships (Kaura & Allen, 2004; Williams & Frieze, 2005). For example, in American college populations, between 30 and 60 percent of women report having experienced physical dating violence at least once (Dobashi et al., 2004; Garcia-Moreno et al., 2006; Kaura & Allen, 2004). Fifty percent of women report having been in abusive relationships and one in four report having been in an abusive relationship this year, suggesting that the actual proportion is likely larger (Garcia-Moreno et al., 2006; Hearn, 2001; Tilley & Brackley, 2005).

It is also important to consider the context in which violence occurs. Oppressive dating behaviors can include psychological abuse and other behaviors that intimidate and frighten victims (Bevan & Higgins, 2002; Williams & Frieze, 2005). For example, some male perpetrators use "lower-level" tactics such as pre-stalking (doing research on their potential victims), stalking (surveillance and following potential victims), and persistence (including humiliation, intimidation, and threats) with their potential victims (Williams & Frieze, 2005). These behaviors often increase the effects of aggression (Frieze, 2005; Williams & Frieze, 2005). While not all violence involves stalking behaviors, the psychological factors that accompany physical abuse

both in dating and in the home (verbal aggression, intimidation, humiliation and dehumanization) often become the most difficult for victims
to deal with as their effect can sometimes be longer lasting than the
effects of the physical violence alone (Williams & Frieze, 2005).

Rape and sexual assault   Rape and sexual assault can occur with couples
who are married or who are dating, although the United States did not
legally recognize rape between married couples in all 50 states until
1993 (Bergen, 1996). This type of abuse can occur both in and outside
the victim's home. Discussions of rape and sexual assault are often
presented separately from physical aggression because of the unique
traumatic experiences that are often felt by victims related to forms of
abuse and control (Herman, 1992; Parrot & Zeichner, 2003). Before
presenting the troubling statistics, it is important to understand the
difference between these two forms of violence.

The definitions of **rape** and **sexual assault** vary amongst states and
from federal guidelines (Lyon, 2004; Peterson & Muehlenhard, 2004;
Tracy, Fromson & Else, 2001). Similar to issues of physical aggression
that do not involve sexual assault, it becomes difficult to summarize
what rape and sexual assault mean given the different definitions. In
general, sexual assault is a legal term for any unwanted forced physical
sexual contact (Lyon, 2004). Rape is a specific type of sexual assault
which includes specifically the unwanted penetration into any orifice
(Lyon, 2004). Both sexual assault and rape can be in general classified as
forms of **sexual abuse**. The definition of sexual abuse is often broader,
also involving other kinds of activities that do not need to specifically
involve touching such as verbal intimidation, coercion, or unwanted
sexual attention (Williams & Frieze, 2005). When these behaviors take
place in public work spaces they are often known as **sexual harassment**
(Harlos & Axelrod, 2005). As with other forms of violence, the vast
majority of sexual abuse incidences involve a male perpetrator whom
the woman is dating or an acquaintance of (Aberle & Littlefield, 2001).

The statistics for sexual abuse are staggering (Locke & Mahalik,
2005). Fifty percent of women report having been sexually abused
throughout their lives (Brannon, 2005). For college women, one out of
every three to five women will be sexually assaulted during her college
career (Aberle & Littlefield, 2001; Choate, 2003). However, only 10
percent of sexual assaults are reported to police (Aberle & Littlefield,
2001; Brannon, 2005). Only 22 percent of college women tell their
parents and the majority tell no one at the time of the crime (Aberle &

Littlefield, 2001; Brannon, 2005). The majority of reported assaults are reported to college staff (such as resident assistants) and often don't involve legal representatives outside the school system (Aberle & Littlefield, 2001). Women often do not report these crimes due to fearing retaliation or being concerned that the administration and legal system will not take them seriously (Choate, 2003).

I have served as a representative on college committees and have seen the reality of women's concerns for reporting issues of violence. On one committee we were charged with addressing various aspects of college culture that might make the climate more dangerous for women. We (faculty, staff, and students) compiled a report that addressed issues of lighting, lack of locked doors, and the general absence of consequences for violators. It was clear by the work we had done with women (particularly those who were directly affected by violence) that they did not feel supported or safe on campus. I actually had a conversation with a Director of Residence Life of students who, in response to the committee's suggestions, said that the women were unfortunately mistaken and that despite what they said, they *had* been supported by the college. So regardless of how they felt and the numerous issues the committee raised, the students were simply wrong. This kind of attitude can be common and make it difficult for women to report their concerns.

For example, specific to rape, between 300,000 and 900,000 women are estimated to be raped each year in the United States (Beneke, 2004; Parrot & Zeichner, 2003). And, as stated, the majority of rapists are men that women know, thus the need for the term **acquaintance** or **date rape** (Brannon, 2005; Choate, 2003; Thio, 1998).

Sentencing of convicted rapists is often limited and, in some jurisdictions, rape is not defined as a violent crime (Aberle & Littlefield, 2001). This clearly diminishes the impact of this event on a survivor (Aberle & Littlefield, 2001). This negligence and dismissal contributes to a culture of **blaming the victim**, or making the victim of the crime feel that it is their fault for being harmed (Beneke, 2004; Brannon, 2005; Peterson & Muehlenhard, 2004; Thio, 1998). Blaming the victim begins with a lack of understanding of what rape and sexual assault is (Choate, 2003). One study showed, for example, that, when surveyed, approximately 12 percent of men admit to behaviors that meet the legal definition of rape, but only 7.7 percent of men classify the behavior as rape (Koss, Gidycz, & Wisniewski, 1987). Many men, for example, do not know that if a person is intoxicated, then they cannot give consent to sex from a *legal* perspective (Choate, 2003). Since the legal system views any behavior that would affect a sound mind as a concern for legal consent to *any* social contract, it applies in this context as well (Choate, 2003). This mentality adds to some men's general beliefs that women should be forced into sexual activities against their will because of their suggestive behaviors (ranging from perceived flirtations to style of dress) (Brannon, 2005; Thio, 1998). These beliefs are institutionalized through systems that do not protect women and children (such as the workplace, criminal justice system, etc.) and contribute to what some authors call a **rape culture**, inferring that patriarchal cultures that devalue women and emphasize male violence and aggression create an atmosphere where rape is accepted as normal and justified behavior (Boswell & Spade, 2004; Locke & Mahalik, 2005; Scharrer, 2001a; Thio, 1998).

Blaming the victim is particularly unfortunate, since research suggests that men who have battered or sexual assaulted their partners are significantly likely to have been battered or sexually assaulted themselves, or to have witnessed their fathers or other significant male figure assault their mothers (Bevan & Higgins, 2002; Ewing, 1989; Kaura & Allen, 2004; Thio, 1998). Violence experienced by young boys and men then repeats itself in relationships throughout life (Pollack, 1998). And this violence doesn't stop with women

Violence against men

While women are a major group that suffers from men's violence, they are not the largest group affected by this widespread travesty. The group of people most likely to be victims of male violence is men (Brannon, 2005; Fischer & Rodriguez Mosquera, 2001; Pollack, 1998; Scharrer, 2001b). Men of color are even more affected, with a much higher likelihood of being victims of male violence from other men (Brannon, 2005; Johnson, 1997; Taylor Gibbs, 1989). Much like violence against women, there are several categories of male-against-male violence. We will discuss non-sexual physical violence, sexual and intimate partner abuse, and suicide.

Physical violence   Perhaps the first encounter a boy will have with violence outside the home is at school. Bullying has changed much in the last 50 years in frequency of incidents and in intensity. It can be defined as "repeated unprovoked aggressive behavior in which the perpetrator is more powerful than the person or persons being attacked" (Flouri &

Buchanan, 2002, p. 126). It is very hard to estimate the actual incidences of bullying, due to boys' reluctance to discuss these problems, particularly in the presence of other boys (Isernhagen & Harris, 2003; Phoenix et al., 2003). Given these concerns, the National Association for School Psychologists suggests that 160,000 children per day miss school for fear of being bullied (Pollack, 1998). Isernhagen and Harris (2003) found that 13 percent of boys reported being bullied at least once per week.

Bullies are both physically and psychologically abusive with their victims (Flouri & Buchanan, 2002; Isernhagen & Harris, 2003; Pollack, 1998). Because schools are often strict with their rules, bullies learn covert and indirect tactics to harass others including taunting and humiliation (Flouri & Buchanan, 2002; Pollack, 1998). In addition, bullying may target a person as an individual, or be relational in its social and psychological consequences. In other words, some forms of bullying are intended to merely harass and others to purposefully alienate children from their friends (Flouri & Buchanan, 2002; Isernhagen & Harris, 2003).

Bullying in its most extreme form is referred to as a form of **hypermasculinity** in the research (O'Donohue, McKay, & Schewe, 1996; Parrot & Zeichner, 2003; Rosen, Knudson, & Fancher, 2003; Scharrer, 2001a, 2001b; Toch, 1998). Hypermasculinity involves an exaggerated sense of masculinity similar to Connell's (1995) description of dominant masculinity that is often exhibited in violence towards others (men and women). "Hypermasculinity is characterized by the idealization of stereotypically masculine or macho traits and the rejection of traits perceived as the antithesis of machismo" (Scharrer, 2001a, p. 160). It is related to both physical and sexual aggression towards others (Parrot & Zeichner, 2003).

Hypermasculinity in men is perhaps one of the reasons why gay and transgendered men as a group are a target of **hate crimes** and violence from other men (Johnson, 1997; Thio, 1998). And while many of the factors associated with violence are similar to what female victims experience (i.e., psychological and physical pain, use of threat and exploitation by perpetrators), the shame and guilt male victims feel is also affected by the internalization of dominant masculine norms, making it less likely that they will seek help for these kinds of problems (Thio, 1998).

Hypermasculinity, bullying, and fighting in their extreme form lead to homicide (Courtenay, 1999). Homicide is the second leading cause of death for men aged 15 to 19 and has been increasing for young men in the last 20 years (Fischer & Rodriguez Mosquera, 2001; Pollack, 1998; Portner, 1994; Sabo, 2004). For people of color, the statistics are even more severe. Homicide is cited as the number one cause of death for Black men (Sabo, 2004; Taylor Gibbs, 1989). Men of color are also more likely to live in hazardous areas, to work in hazardous occupations, and to lack access to health care (Kilmartin, 2001; Rehman, Hutchison, Hendrix, Okonofua, & Egan, 2005). Thus, not only are men of color more likely to be in a violent situation, but are also less likely to have access to services to help them after being victimized by violence (Kilmartin, 2001).

Suicide   The last form of violence against men that we will address is suicide. Suicide rates have been increasing for men and have quadrupled in the past 25 years (Allebeck & Allgulander, 1990; Gunnell, Middleton, Whitley, Dorling, & Frankel, 2003; Kaslow et al., 2005; Sabo, 2004; Stillion & McDowell, 2002). It is estimated that between 5,000 and 10,000 men per year complete suicide in the United States, which is the highest of any Western nation (Moller-Leimkuhler, 2003; Murphy, 1998). It is the seventh leading cause of death for men in the United States (Sabo, 2004). And while women attempt suicide more often than men, men are three to five times more likely to complete the suicide (Addis & Cohane, 2005).

....

Making Connections: Natives and Suicide

Native people in several industrial nations have higher than expected suicide rates (Ferry, 2000). In Canada, for example, many regions have suicide rates for Natives that are up to 20 times the national average (Ferry, 2000). In the United States, suicide is 2.5 times higher for Natives than for any other racial group. It is also the second leading cause of death for boys and men between ages 15 and 24 (Gary, 2005; Shaugnessy, Doshi, & Jones, 2004). The first leading cause of death is car accidents that typically involve alcohol (Shaugnessy et al., 2004).

There have been studies conducted to try to understand why Native people are particularly at-risk for suicide. One line of reasoning finds that Native people have a higher incidence rate for many of the factors that correlate with suicide. Some of these individual behavioral

Continued

risk-factors include prior uses of violence, smoking, involvement in the juvenile justice system and alcohol and drug use (Gary, 2005; Shaugnessy et al., 2004). Family factors include family instability, attempted suicide by family members, and multiple home placements (Gary, 2005). Finally, psychological variables such as low self-esteem, hopelessness, and lack of problem-solving skills seem pronounced in Native youth, particularly in boys (Gary, 2005).

Another reason cited is **social disintegration** and **acculturation** difficulties (Gary, 2005). Since Native peoples' first contact with Europeans in the 18th and 19th centuries, European diseases and the genocide of Natives has resulted in the decimation of various Native cultures (Ferry, 2000). Since that time, Natives have largely not been able to reclaim a positive Native identity nor acculturate to other norms (Ferry, 2000). "Many Native people lost their roots, their beliefs, and their value systems very quickly at that time. This led to a loss of self-worth, to diseases, to self-neglect, and suicide" (Avery in Ferry, 2000). Racism towards Native Americans is still a reality in the United States, making issues of acculturation difficult at best (Shaugnessy et al., 2004).

In addition, the establishment of **reservations** to some has essentially led not to self-pride and a renewal of Native culture, but rather to isolated and alienated communities (Ferry, 2000, p. 906). In addition, some critique the tribal government system within the reservations for keeping Native people from making progress (Ferry, 2000). These systems are described as largely hierarchical and ones in which many suffer and few profit (Ferry, 2000).

....

While stereotypically suicide is associated with young men under 24 (the second-highest at-risk group), the highest proportion of men who commit suicide are those who are over 60 years of age, who are ten times more likely to complete suicide (Bould, 2005; Kilmartin, 2001; Stillion & McDowell, 2002). Older men's higher suicide rate is often associated with health-related issues and disabilities that physically and psychologically contribute to men's decisions to end their lives (Bould, 2005). White middle-class men are still the largest proportion of men who complete suicide, but rates have been disproportionately increasing for Black men, Native American men, and men of all racial groups who identify as being gay, bi-sexual, or transgendered (Barlas, 2005; Castle, Duberstein, Meldrum, Conner, & Conwell, 2004; Kaslow et al., 2005; Kilmartin, 2001; McNaught & Spicer, 2000; Parker, 2005; Sabo, 2004; Thio, 1998; Winters, 2003).

Men are also more likely to use more violent means to end their lives (Kilmartin, 2001; Sabo, 2004). For example, men are more likely to use firearms, poison, and hanging than women (Sabo, 2004; Thio, 1998). Men are also more likely to be involved with other activities associated with suicide such as alcohol and drug use (Moller-Leimkuhler, 2003; Preuss et al., 2003). Men also view failed suicide attempts as unmasculine, which motivates future suicide attempts (Canetto, 1995). These themes likely increase the probability that the suicide completes. For example, women often use drug overdose as a method of suicide attempt, which can leave more room for discovery and intervention than a handgun (Moller-Leimkuhler, 2003; Murphy, 1998). The 'failure' on women's part does not seem as likely to represent an additional reason for pursuing future attempts (Canetto, 1995).

The persistency and differences in attempt and completion of suicide also seems related to values associated with dominant masculinity (Moller-Leimkuhler, 2003; Sabo, 2004). The decision to end one's life seems to be related to perceived weakness and vulnerability in men (Sabo, 2004; Preuss et al., 2003). Cultural values that mirror values of dominant masculinity can also predict differences across nations with members of nations adopting values such as individualism and self-reliance (Rudmin et al., 2003).

Sexual and domestic abuse   Perhaps the crime least likely to be reported by boys and men is sexual abuse (Macfarlane et al., 1986). While there seems to be more openness in discussing this issue, overall there is still much resistance in discussing this type of abuse (Macfarlane et al., 1986; Thio, 1998). Rates have been increasing over the last 30 years, although it is not clear whether this is due to more reporting or more incidences. Considering these concerns, it is estimated that at least 10,000 men are raped every year (Thio, 1998). On college campuses 12–48 percent of men report being forced into non-consensual sex. The majority of these cases involve heterosexual couplings in which women use verbal pressure or blackmail rather than violence (Thio, 1998). However, violence is used both by male and female perpetrators, although knowledge of female rapists is scant at best (Thio, 1998).

The majority of men who rape and sexually abuse boys and men are heterosexual in their identity. There are gay men who rape and abuse other men, but the vast majority of men that engage in this type of violent crime are heterosexuals. This is sometimes difficult for people to understand because they assume that if a man is the perpetrator of sexual abuse against another man, then he identifies as being gay. Rape and sexual abuse is a form of power and control, and while some perpetrators also experience sexual arousal, sexual abusers' gratification often comes from the powerlessness and humiliation they view in their victims, rather than sexual satisfaction (Eigenberg, 2000).

Finally, there has been an increased awareness of intimate partner violence amongst gay men (Craft & Serovich, 2005; Thio, 1998). Unfortunately, due to several factors, the extent of violence in gay male couples is only beginning to be understood (Craft & Serovich, 2005). Gay men often don't report violence in their relationships due to not recognizing it as violence and feelings of shame and embarrassment (Craft & Serovich, 2005; Thio, 1998). Gay men have reported that it sometimes takes a long time to determine that they are being abused, because they assume that relationships with other men are intended to include a level of physical roughness, due to the dominant culture's expectations of men (Thio, 1998). However, gay men are believed to be as likely (and in some cases more likely) to be the victims of intimate partner violence.

In conclusion, violence as an issue of masculinity is expressed through men's violence against women, other men, and themselves. Issues of violence affect all of us and violence within the United States has increased to the point that people are referring to it as a national epidemic. All men are affected by this problem, but men of color and men that identify as being gay, bisexual, or transgendered are significantly more likely to be affected by violence and its correlates. But what are the factors that contribute to men's violence? Exploring men's health and health-seeking may shed some light on these issues.

Health Concerns

Men's health has been argued to be in desperate need of attention (Addis & Cohane, 2005; Galdas, Cheater & Marshall, 2004; Robertson & Fitzgerald, 1992). In addition to men's diseases that are specific to physiological and genetic uniqueness of men (Finney-Rutten, Meissner, Breen, Vernon, & Rimer, 2005), men appear to be experiencing health problems at alarming rates that cannot be explained by biological differences alone, suggesting that the differences are due to behaviors and attitudes common to men (Courtenay, 2004; Galdas et al., 2004; Copenhaver & Eisler, 1996). These differences are being understood as a function of being male and beliefs about masculinity (Galdas et al., 2004; Copenhaver & Eisler, 1996; Robertson & Fitzgerald, 1992).

While longevity of life has been increasing over the last 100 years, there is a substantial difference in the proportional longevity of men (Harris, 1989; Stillion & McDowell, 2002). While men live longer today than they did 100 years ago, on average they live 7 years less than women (Addis & Cohane, 2005; Copenhaver & Eisler, 1996; Sabo, 2004; Stillion & McDowell, 2002). The death rate for men is higher on all reasons for death and at all ages for men (Addis & Cohane, 2005; Galdas et al., 2004; Copenhaver & Eisler, 1996). The death rate is also higher in the United States than the majority of Western nations (Stillion & McDowell, 2002). These rates are even more problematic for men of color, who have an even higher proportional death rate than White men (Galdas et al., 2004; Rehman et al., 2005).

One cannot discuss issues of men's health without mentioning risk-taking. Men consistently take more risks than women (Chapple & Johnson, 2005; Courtenay, 2004; Stillion & McDowell, 2002). Men are also seemingly unaware of the consequences of the risks they take in comparison to their female peers (Chapple & Johnson, 2005; Courtenay, 2004; Stillion & McDowell, 2002). Boys and men report being immune to health risks even though they disproportionately engage in risky behaviors that lead to health problems (Courtenay, 2004; Monk & Ricciardelli, 2003; Pollack, 1995, 1998). It is estimated by researchers that 75 percent of men's health problems are related to these risk-taking behaviors (Copenhaver & Eisler, 1996; Kilmartin, 2001).

There are numerous risky behaviors that men engage in that are correlated with health problems. For example, men drink alcohol four times as much as women do and binge drink more often (Copenhaver & Eisler, 1996; Guilamo-Ramos, Jaccard, & Turrisi, 2005; Moller-Leimkuhler, 2003; Monk & Ricciardelli, 2003). By the eighth grade, 19 percent of boys self-report binge-drinking behaviors (Guilamo-Ramos et al., 2005). Boys are also more likely to have alcohol-related illnesses. They are twice as likely to have liver diseases such as cirrhosis (Copenhaver & Eisler, 1996). Men are more likely to drive while intoxicated and not wear seatbelts (Copenhaver & Eisler, 1996). Men also die in alcohol-related deaths twice as often as women (Monk & Ricciardelli, 2003; Stillion & McDowell, 2002).

Men's smoking has increased 250–300 percent in the last 30 years. Men smoke more often and in greater amounts than women, although women have been catching up with men over the last 20 years

(Courtenay, 2004; Gades et al., 2005; Peate, 2005). It is estimated that there are 46.2 million adult smokers and 440,000 premature deaths a year as a result of smoking (Gades et al., 2005). Cancer is a significant cause of men's smoking-related deaths. Men develop lung cancer six times as often as women do (Copenhaver & Eisler, 1996) and in comparison to women, develop mouth and throat cancer at a rate of 2.5 to 1 (Kilmartin, 2001). Other smoking-related illnesses such as bronchitis and emphysema are 3.5 times more likely to occur in men (Kilmartin, 2001). In addition, other disorders particular to men, such as erectile dysfunction, are associated with smoking (Gades et al., 2005; Peate, 2005; Polsky, Aronson, Heaton, & Adams, 2005). It is estimated in the United Kingdom that 120,000 men between 30 and 50 have erectile dysfunction as a result of smoking (Peate, 2005).

Men are also more likely to engage in unsafe sexual behaviors (Kilmartin, 2001; Mustanski, 2008; Stoltenberg, 2000). In 1989, almost 20,000 men between the ages of 25 and 44 died from Acquired Immune Deficiency Syndrome (AIDS) in the United States, in comparison to approximately 3,000 women, which equates to men representing approximately 87 percent of AIDS cases (Kilmartin, 2001). While AIDS-related deaths have decreased proportionally since the late 1980s, by 1997 men represented 75 percent of people diagnosed with AIDS (Center for Disease Control and Prevention, 2005). The most at-risk group is men having sex with men, constituting 42 percent of new Human Immunodeficiency Virus infections (HIV) (Belcher et al., 2005). The increase in women's acquisition of AIDS has also been of great concern and considered a crisis for women (Anderson, 2005).

In addition to interpersonal risk-related problems, men are also more likely to work in dangerous occupations with serious environmental risks that are likely to take a toll on their health (Belcher et al., 2005; Copenhaver & Eisler, 1996). Jobs in which people's lives are at stake (such as the police and the military) are over-represented by men (Bannerman, 1996; Feminist Majority Foundation, 2002; Rogers, 1990; Rosen et al., 2003). Historically, men's disproportionately high representation in such fields has been related to a variety of factors, including prohibitive and discriminatory practices on the part of these institutions (Feminist Majority Foundation, 2002; Rogers, 1990; Rosen et al., 2003). They are fields that would incur much stress for anyone, but are largely over-represented by men. In addition, as discussed, men make choices to deal with their stress that are often not health promoting (Courtenay, 2004). Such stress is taking a toll on men's bodies. Men are more likely to have stress-related problems such as high blood pressure, hypertension, ulcers and heart disease (Galdas et al., 2004; Rehman et al., 2005).

In addition to the physiological consequences to risk-taking, there are also psychological consequences. Men's mental heath has been a major concern for professionals. One mental health concern in particular that has been given much attention is **major depressive disorder**, or what is typically known as depression (American Psychiatric Association, 1994). Eleven million people in the United States are estimated to suffer from depression (Real, 2001). It has been estimated that 6–10 percent of the population will struggle with some form of depression at some point in their lives (Real, 2001).

While some researchers believe that there is a biological predisposition to this disorder, others are concerned about the ways in which clinicians diagnose the disease (Addis & Cohane, 2005; Real, 2001; Wexler, 2006). Depression is a disorder that is overwhelmingly diagnosed in women in comparison to men. The **Diagnostic and Statistical Manual for Mental Disorders** (DSM-IV) (American Psychiatric Association, 1994) relies on the expression of certain types of behaviors in order to give a diagnosis of depression (Addis & Cohane, 2005; Real, 2001). The problem is that men often do not report symptomology or express how they are experiencing the world, which makes the diagnosis inappropriate for a variety of situations in which men likely suffer from depression (Addis & Cohane, 2005; Bould, 2005; Real, 2001; Wexler, 2006). For this reason, it is believed that many men suffer from depression, but may not display depression in the same ways that women do, nor disclose when they do share similar symptoms (Real, 2001; Wexler, 2006). Since mental health professionals often rely on self-report, it may prevent them from detecting problems in men who are often reluctant to discuss problems (Bould, 2005; Real, 2001; Wexler, 2006). And unfortunately, like other arenas of men's lives, getting assistance for mental health concerns is also something with which men struggle (Burke & McKeon, 2007; Oliver, Pearson, & Coe, 2005).

Help Seeking

Not only are men developing health related illnesses at alarming rates, but they are also not doing what needs to be done to alleviate problems. Men are less likely to seek help for nearly every physical and mental health problem, according to Michael Addis, a researcher who studies men and help-seeking behaviors at Clark University (Addis & Cohane, 2005; Addis & Mahalik, 2003). For example, Cook and colleagues (1990) (cited in Galdas et al., 2004) found that 10 percent of men aged 45 to 65 never go to visit their general practitioner and 45 percent go only twice a year. Men report ignoring symptoms and not telling others when they are experiencing pain (Galdas et al., 2004). Sharpe and Arnold (1998) discovered that, when asked if men believed a minor illness could be fought off if you don't give into it, 64 percent of their male sample said yes and 52 percent said they simply ignore symptoms, hoping they will go away. Research shows common patterns across men from various nationalities in this regard (Oliver et al., 2005; Mahalik, Levi-Minzi, & Walker, 2007).

Who's Who in Masculinities Research: Michael Addis, Ph.D.

Michael Addis is currently Professor and Chair in the Department of Psychology at Clark University. Dr. Addis has published over 50 articles and books including *Ending Depression Pne Step at a Time: The New Behavioral Activation Approach to Getting Your Life Back* and *Depression in Context: Strategies for Guided Action*. Dr. Addis's current work focuses on variations in the way men experience, express, and respond to mental health problems. As part of the NIMH-funded Men's Coping Project, Dr. Addis and his colleagues are developing and testing motivational interventions for men suffering from depression, anxiety, and related disorders.

Email: maddis@clarku.edu.

And while several features regarding health-seeking seem common across men from varying nationalities, there also appear to be various factors specific to different cultural groups. For example, Mahalik, Lagan, & Morrison (2006) found in comparing a sample of college students from the United States and Kenya that Kenyan students were more likely to (a) see self-care as being in conflict with masculinity and (b) more likely to believe that fate or luck had more to do with their health than their American counterparts (Mahalik et al., 2006).

Understanding the commonalities and differences across cultural groups is an interest of researchers who hope to find diverse ways to engage these men, in hopes of helping them make better choices in this regard. (See chapter 11.)

There are at least three different theories regarding why men do not seek assistance when they need it. The first is that men do not know how to detect problems, as they are unaware of their bodies and their own experiences (Addis & Mahalik, 2003). The second is that men are aware of their bodies and experiences, but that discussing them presents additional pain for them. This is known as **double jeopardy**. Men can feel extremely uncomfortable when they are vulnerable and therefore it feels like a losing scenario for them either way. Discussing problems is viewed as a weakness, as is having the problem in the first place (Addis & Mahalik, 2003; Mahalik et al., 2006). Finally, researchers are exploring men's conformity to male role norms as related to help seeking, with results suggesting that men are less likely to ask for help if they think doing so would be deviating from traditional masculinity (Addis & Mahalik, 2003). Interventions that put them in contact with other men with similar concerns can help alleviate these problems (Addis & Mahalik, 2003).

To illustrate this overall effect of masculinity and health consider this scenario, the leading cause of death for White men is cancer and heart disease. Sex differences in the rates of developing these illnesses on average are very slight (about 101 women to 100 men) (Kilmartin, 2001). However, men ages 25 to 44 are almost three times as likely to die from heart-related illnesses (Kilmartin, 2001). Men at this age are likely working in stressful environments, making choices to deal with stress that make it worse, and then not asking for or getting assistance when they need it.

Summary

This chapter has briefly reviewed three areas in which men are displaying significant problems. Men are less likely to apply and be admitted to college than women, and once admitted are less likely to complete their degree. Men have alarming problems with violence that harms others and themselves at increasing rates. Their overall health is suffering in a variety of ways. And finally, they are not likely to ask for the help that they probably need. This is only a brief review of a few problems men are experiencing at staggering rates, which constitute a crisis for men.

But why, you may ask, are men in crisis? Why do we see such alarming concerns for men? The answers to these questions are viewed by many in this field as a crisis in masculinity, a concept explored in the next three chapters of this text. In other words, the problems that many male-identified people experience is not due to the mere fact of "being men" but rather the struggle and negotiaton of what masculinity means for them and others in today's world. As you will soon see, the definition, cause, and cure for this crisis in masculinity varies depending on the perspective.

Review and Questions to Ponder

1. What is meant by the "crisis for men"?
2. How is this crisis affecting men's enrollment to college?
3. How is this crisis affecting men's aspirations for college?
4. How is this crisis affecting men's completion of college?
5. How does being a person of color affect questions 2–4 above?
6. What does it mean to say that some men view college as feminine?
7. How are women different than men in their approach to college? Have you noticed this difference? Where? How?
8. What is persistency? How is this related to men and women differently?
9. Why do Katz (and others) call youth violence male violence?
10. Why do people seem reluctant to discuss male violence?
11. Why is it hard to define violence?
12. What is the difference between a community and clinical sample?
13. What is domestic violence and how does it impact women?
14. What is the difference between intimate terrorism and common couple violence? Why is that differentiation important when studying violence?
15. What is intimate partner violence and how does it affect women?
16. How can violence be other than physical?
17. What is the difference between rape, sexual assault, sexual abuse, and sexual harassment?

18. How are women impacted by the above?
19. What is blaming the victim?
20. What do researchers mean by a rape culture?
21. What does it mean to say men are the largest group targeted by violence?
22. What is bullying? What are different ways it manifests itself?
23. What is hypermasculinity?
24. What is a hate crime?
25. Why might men be more successful at suicide than women? What does that have to do with masculinity?
26. What other issues might contribute to the troublesome increase in Native American suicides?
27. Why is it hard to study rape and sexual abuse of men?
28. What does it mean to say that most men who rape other boys and men are heterosexual?
29. What makes it particularly difficult to study intimate partner violence with gay male couples?
30. How is longevity different between men and women?
31. How is risk taking different between men and women and what does that have to do with health? With masculinity?
32. What health problems are associated with masculinity?
33. Why might we be misdiagnosing major depression in men?
34. What are three reasons men may not be seeking help when they need it?
35. In what ways are boys of color discriminated against in the educational system?
36. Why are Native Americans committing suicide at 2.5 times the rate of other groups in the United States?

9

The Crisis in Masculinity

Essentialist Perspective

The previous chapter addressed the crisis in men. The chapter argued that men are experiencing psychosocial problems in greater proportion than one would predict. We focused upon specific areas of men's lives to illustrate these problems: education; violence; and health and health-seeking. In all these areas, men seem to be struggling in a unique and critical way that is disproportionate to the problems of other genders.

This chapter (and the two that follow) will argue that the problem in men is a problem with masculinity. In other words, scholars are arguing that one primary reason why men are experiencing problems as a group is due to various problems with what masculinity means to them and the cultures in which they live. But exactly what that problem *is* and how to solve it differs depending on whether one adopts an essentialist, sociocultural, or social constructionist perspective. While many people have perspectives that overlap with these three major views, these views are presented separately, as they represent three major schools of thought in the field. This chapter focuses on the essentialist perspective on the crisis in men and masculinity.

The Essentialist Explanation for the Masculinity Crisis

The first approach to explaining this crisis of masculinity is referred to here as the **essentialist explanation** (Hearn, 1993; White, 1996). There are various offshoots of this perspective, but what they all have in common is an essentialized description of masculinity: specifically, that there is a right and natural way to be masculine. The essentialist perspective assumes that there is a determined and expected role for each gender that is rooted in biology and expressed through a variety of behaviors (Haslam & Levy, 2006; Yoder, Fischer, Kahn, & Groden, 2007). The basic argument is that, over the last 30 years, changes in the family and society have prohibited biological males from naturally developing into men, which has resulted in problematic behaviors.

The bulk of these theories draw insight from psychoanalytic and Jungian models about masculinity and are based on several assumptions. Colman (2001) outlines three major psychoanalytic assumptions that lay the groundwork for this essentialist explanation. The first is that boys and girls are biologically different from one another. The second is that this biological difference fuels psychological experiences as boys and girls try to come to terms with these differences. The final assumption is that boys and girls must recognize that anatomy has a certain symbolic value in the culture (Colman, 2001). For the developing boy, the psychological task becomes understanding the symbolism of the penis.

> The **phallus** is felt to be an instrument whose tremendous power has both creative and destructive potential . . . on the one hand, the universal male preoccupation with violence and warfare invokes sexual symbolism through the association of swords, knives, and spears with the penetrative phallus; while on the other, men frequently symbolize their sexual activity in terms of tools, weapons, and screwing, etc. (Colman, 2001, p. 126).

To the psychoanalysts, it is in the identification with the penis as a symbol of power and male virility that boys become men (Colman, 2001).

While Jungians have less of a focus on the symbolic nature of the penis, they place equal emphasis on the biologically based differences of men and women. These differences are connected to cultural archetypes and images that are associated with men and women and are argued to differentiate them (Jung, 1989; Moore & Gillette, 1990). These archetypes are presumably similar in cultures throughout the world and represent potential energies stored in our collective unconscious upon which we draw to enact our determined gender (Jung, 1989; Moore & Gillette, 1990).

As discussed previously (see chapter 6), specific requirements are necessary to instill masculinity in the developing boy as he struggles to understand his differences (Axlerod, 2001). To analytic thinkers, a boy's gender identity is viewed as dependent upon resolving the Oedipus complex through separating from his mother and identifying with his father (Axlerod, 2001). During this Oedipal process, the boy develops a healthy **ego ideal**, the aspect of the ego that deals with growth and accomplishment (Axlerod, 2001). The unconscious sexual basis of the separation and identification is not as emphasized by Jungians, but the emphasis of separation from mother and femininity is viewed as an important archetypal aspect of masculinity and the psychology of men (Colman, 2001; Moore & Gillette, 1990). For example, the **hero** is described by Moore and Gillette as the archetype that assists boys in becoming men (Moore & Gillette, 1990). "What the hero does is mobilize the boy's delicate ego structures to enable him to break with the mother at the end of boyhood and face the difficult tasks that life is beginning to assign him" (Moore & Gillette, 1990, p. 40).

In addition to the specific familial requirements, social requirements exist for boys to develop into men. In order for a boy to identify with his father, there must be **socially sanctioned** and supported opportunities to do so (Colman, 2001). Jungians often emphasize the importance of rituals to help establish this bond between boys and their fathers (Barton, 2000; Gilbert, 1992; Richard, 2000; Wehr, 1987). **Social rituals** are group activities that convey the meaning and values within a cultural group. These types of rituals are said to help boys adapt by providing both practice in their learning to be boys (and eventually) men and fuel for their psychological development (Axlerod, 2001, Nye, 2005; Vinner, 2007). Modern social rituals can range from large-scale events such as high school proms or bar mitzvahs to the daily activities in which boys and men find themselves engaged (Gilbert, 1992; Nye, 2005).

The Problem

As stated, proponents of this perspective believe that significant changes in the culture (particularly in the last 30 years) have prevented boys from making this transition to manhood in a healthy way, resulting in a variety of problematic behaviors. While there has been much written on this topic, we will cover three major areas of change that essentialists believe contribute to men's problems in actualizing manhood: economics, public space, and the family.

Economic change public & family

In the last 200 years, there have been major shifts in the economic base of industrialized nations. These countries went first from a primarily agricultural economy to an industrial one (Crafts, 2004; Gilbert, 1992). With the **industrial revolution** beginning in the late eighteenth century, men left the home to work in factories, mills, and other businesses in order to provide economically for their families (Crafts, 2004; Gilbert, 1992). Prior to this time, work and home were not separate entities (Gilbert, 1992). The home was a place of work where families were committed to specific tasks that helped them survive. The division of labor was often segregated, but families worked together to tend to animals, crafts (such as ironworking, and leatherworking) and other activities that contributed to their survival (Crafts, 2004; Gilbert, 1992).

This shift to an industrial economy created an atmosphere in which men competed more directly with other men (Gilbert, 1992). This competitive world made it difficult for men to have positive connections with one another, which lead to the devaluing of men by men (Gilbert, 1992). In particular, the devaluing of elder men in the occupational sphere left younger men without mentors to learn from and to develop more mature masculinities (Gilbert, 1992). In the past, many young men were mentored by their fathers in their fathers' area of expertise. Boys learned the crafts of their fathers in order to take over the family farm or family business. With shifts in the economy, the rituals associated with connecting boys to their fathers' work have been declining (Gilbert, 1992).

In the last 20 years, this change has increased as a result of the economy shifting in another direction. Economists describe our current state of affairs as an age of information and technology (also known as the **information age**) that seems to be in constant flux (Annand, 2007; Moller-Leimkuhler, 2003). While we still produce material objects, we are increasingly selling information and ideas as opposed to tangible things. This ability to focus on the "non-material" has become even more extreme as a result of modern technology. For example, computer games such as Lineage, Ultima, and World of Warcraft have inspired people to make a living selling *virtual* objects for *actual* money. The virtual items that characters need to advance in the game are acquired by these paid gamers and then the items are sold on websites like e-bay for *actual* money (Lee, 2005). In some countries, this has resulted in a new form of **sweatshop**, where people are paid very low wages to play video games while their bosses make profits through selling their acquisitions in the video games (Lee, 2005).

This is, of course, just one example of a changing marketplace. It is cited here as a stark contrast to the kinds of occupations held in the past, which seemed to be grounded in specific skills and tangible products (Forrest & Sullivan, 2002). This constantly changing information age atmosphere increases the strain between fathers and sons, as the kinds of career skills required for today's youth are often not possessed by their fathers, or are so abstract and ever-changing that it would be difficult to understand how they would be passed down through ritual (Forrest & Sullivan, 2002; Gilbert, 1992; Moyer, 2004).

Public space

In addition to economic change, the **public space** that men have interacted in has changed much over the last 30 years. Women have increasingly entered the public sphere in areas previously inaccessible to them (Abramson, 2006; Jefferson, 2002; Kahane, 1998; MacInnes, 2001). Over time, occupations that were primarily (if not entirely) staffed by men are becoming more gender balanced. Of course not all occupations are doing so at the same rate and women find themselves underrepresented in positions of authority (Abramson, 2006; Begley, 2005; Matlin, 2004). However, the workplace is a much different space than it was 50 years ago. More competition in the workforce has led to an increase in dual-career couples and single women professionals. Such workplace shifts have led to psychological struggles for men in that they have had to contend with being less able to be the primary provider for their families, a role previously assigned to them (Levant, 1997; MacInnes, 2001).

Simultaneously, women have begun to incorporate aspects of femininity into traditionally masculine spaces (MacInnes, 2001; Poddar & Krishan, 2004). Not only have the proportions of women increased in a variety of social institutions, but the way the institutions operate has slowly been changing as well (MacInnes, 2001; Poddar & Krishan, 2004; Simpson, 2006). Women have questioned many of the "givens" of the work culture and have been offering different ways to explore the world of work. Women's leadership style, for instance, is beginning to be seen as an advantage in a variety of settings (Poddar, & Krishan, 2004; Simpson, 2006; Whitehead, 2001). And while it may be advantageous, men are not always welcoming of these "feminized" work

spaces. These changes seem to have affected traditional men of previous generations dramatically (Carey, 1996; MacInnes, 2001).

In addition to social changes in the workforce, there have also been
social changes in the family. The divorce rate has generally increased
since the 1970s (although it has declined slightly in the last few years
(Hurley, 2005; Levant, 1997; Varcoe & Irwin, 2004). With what Weitzman
(1985) called the **divorce revolution**, the advent of **no-fault divorce** led
to an extraordinary increase in divorces. Today the divorce rate is
over 50 percent (Shackelford, Weekes-Shackelford, & Schmitt, 2005;
Varcoe & Irwin, 2004).

Proponents of this essentialist perspective argue that, since the
majority of mothers are awarded custody for their children (Varcoe &
Irwin, 2004), fathers end up spending much less time with their sons.
It is estimated that 30 percent of all children in the United States do not
live with their biological father and 50 percent will live in a single-
parent family that is headed by a woman (Shackelford et al., 2005).

From a family culture perspective, the media has been harmful to
boys and men as well (Levant, 1997; MacInnes, 2001). With an emphasis
on men's violence, "deadbeat dads," and a variety of other problems,
boys are said to associate masculinity with negativity. Traditional male
characteristics have been linked to social problems rather than being
viewed as positive characteristics of manhood (Gilbert, 1992; Levant,
1997).

What were once claimed to be manly virtues (heroism, independence,
courage, strength, rationality, will, backbone, virility) have become masculine vices (abuse, destructive aggression, coldness, emotional inarticu-
lacy, detachment, isolation, an inability to be flexible, to communicate, to
empathize, to be soft, supportive, or life supporting). (MacInnes, 2001,
pp. 313–314)

These social changes have created an atmosphere that makes it difficult for boys to identify with their fathers. As men find the world
changing and becoming "feminized," they have fewer and fewer
spaces to "be men." Men are increasingly spending less time with their
sons, who do not know how to internalize a healthy gender identity of
maleness (Gilbert, 1992). As a result, many boys develop a problematic
gender identity (Flouri & Buchanan, 2002; Rekers, Mead, Rosen, &
Bringham, 1982; Rekers & Swihart, 1989). "The father is the parent

whose role behavior may be most likely to generate sex-appropriate behaviors in children . . . The sex-role learning process is adversely affected when fathers are either physically or psychologically absent from the home." (Rekers et al., 1982, pp. 31–32). When boys are disconnected from, and long for, their fathers, they develop into men with a **father wound** (Pease, 2000).

The father wound is suggested to result in men who embody the extremes of masculinity. Clinical terms used to describe those who differ from the norms of gender and masculinity include **gender-disturbed** (Rekers & Morey, 1990a, 1990b), **gender deviant** (Harry, 1983), **gender/boyhood non-conformists** (Beard & Bakeman, 2000), **low masculine boys** (Klein & Bates, 1980; Rekers & Swihart, 1989, Rekers & Morey, 1990a, 1990b) and **unmasculine boys** (Savin-Williams, 2001).

Rekers, Bentler, Rosen, & Lovaas (1977) argued that there are two classifications of "gender atypical" people. The two classifications include people with a **gender *identity* disturbance** or a **gender *behavior* disturbance**. Gender identity disturbance (now called **gender identity disorder**) refers to a biological boy or girl who psychologically identifies and/or desires to be the other sex, while gender behavior disturbance refers to a boy or girl who participates in a wide range of gender atypical behaviors (Rekers et al., 1977; Rekers & Morey, 1990a, 1990b). This differentiation is used to explain the significant difference in extremes within a general group of men that do not know how to "be men." While those with gender identity disturbance are argued to need psychological treatment (Harry, 1983; Rekers et al., 1977, Rekers & Morey, 1990a, 1990b), those with gender behavior disturbance suffer much pain as a function of their non-conformity to masculine behavioral norms and are argued to also be in need of assistance (Rekers et al., 1977).

The two extremes of deviance result in men who are essentially too masculine and those who are not masculine enough. The first extreme are the men who are often described in the literature as possessing a super-masculinity (Rekers et al., 1977) or **hypermasculinity** (Scharrer, 2001a, 2001b; Ward, 2005). From the essentialist perspective, the hyper-aggressive male results from a wounded sense of what masculinity really is (Colman, 2001; Gilbert, 1992, Kipnis, 1995). The argument purports that when a boy or man is unable to be the man he is meant to be, he may "act- out" in aggressive ways, hurting those around him (White, 1996). Physical and sexual abuse, drug and alcohol addiction, and other forms of harm to others are viewed as a result of an unbalanced male psyche (Moore & Gillette, 1990; Kipnis, 1995).

On the other end of the spectrum, the "too feminine" males have had *several* common terms used to describe their experience, including soft-man, sissy, faggot, new man, soft, mama's boys, effeminate, sensitive, pansy, woman, sissy/sissy-boy, girl, homo, pussy, pussy-whipped, fruit, gay, gaylord, fairy, priss, she-male, women-driven, bitch, and queer (Connell, 1989; Friedan, 1989; Harry, 1983; Hunter, 1993; Kimmel, 1995; Kupers, 1995; Miedzian, 1991; Silverstein & Rashbaum, 1994; Simpson, 1995; Weed, 1995; White, 1996). These terms unsurprisingly carry misogynistic and heterosexist overtones of dominant masculinity in the implication that men who do not know how to be "men" must be women or gay, two things that a "normal" man would presumably not want. Academic terms for the "too-feminine" include feminine males (Lobel, 1994), cross-sexed (Rotter & O'Connell, 1982), counter-stereotypic males (Kolbe & Langenfeld, 1993), gender atypical males (Richardson, 1999) and unmasculine (Savin-Williams, 2001). "The sensitive man of the 1970's and 1980's is better able to express vulnerability, compassion, and closeness. However, this increased sensitivity is often associated with a diminished sense of vitality, decisiveness, radiance and sexuality" (Gilbert, 1992, p. 42).

From the essentialist perspective, because boys are being denied the opportunity to incorporate masculinity, they develop a range of problems to cope with their father wounds (Barton, 2000; Gilbert, 1992). As stated, these problems are often described in a dichotomous fashion of being either "too masculine" or "not masculine enough". The problem is not within men or about manhood, but about the lack of integrating masculinity into the psyche of men. "If men behave badly it is because something has happened to their masculinity that has obscured its essential goodness." (Kipnis, 1995, p. 281).

Solutions

From an essentialist perspective, interventions must take place to assist men struggling with manhood to learn how to be men and to work on changing society to value masculinity (Barton, 2000). The interventions have come in two major areas: clinical interventions and social interventions.

Who's Who in Masculinities Research: Edward Read Barton, J.D., Ph.D.

Edward Barton teaches and does research at Michigan State University. He has edited several anthologies, including *Mythopoetic Perspectives of Men's Healing Work: An Anthology for Therapists and Others*, a thematic issue on *Myth, Legend, and Lore: Powerful Tools for the Transformation of Individuals, Families, Groups, and Organizations*, and has written numerous academic articles and performed many presentations on men's work and the contemporary men's movement. He is the Volunteer Curator of the Changing Men Collections (CMC), Special Collections, Michigan State University Libraries.

Email: bartoned@msu.edu

Clinical intervention

From the clinical perspective, several treatment modalities have been offered to assist men in their learning to be "real men." These programs have ranged from those that attempt to cure homosexuality and transgendered experiences, to those that help men regain their inner strength (Duberman, 2001; Furnham & Taylor, 1990; Gilbert, 1992; Harry, 1983, Neff, 2004; Rekers et al., 1977, 1982; Rekers & Morey, 1990a, 1990b). This is an important range to consider because, while differences in sexual preference have been viewed by some essentialist-influenced men's groups as oppositional to masculinity, others have viewed them as a uniqueness to be integrated into a deep masculinity.

Psychoanalytic and social learning models have been argued to be helpful, as they offer specific connections to behaviors that can assist in resolving prior unresolved Oedipal complexes and/or learning the specific skill sets required for masculine behavior (Rekers et al., 1977). Clinical groups and support groups have also been offered to help men support one another as they claim their true masculinity (Barton, 2000).

Social interventions

This reclaiming of manhood has also taken social form. One such form is known as the **men's rights movement** (also known as the

patriarchy movement), which began around 1973, but did not become well known until the mid-1980s (Clatterbaugh, 1997; Fox, 2004; Lingard & Douglas, 1999). Men's rights groups, often associated with religious doctrine (particularly Christian), view men as a group of people who have been oppressed by the various social changes that have occurred in the last 50 years (Clatterbaugh, 1997; Fox, 2004; Mann, 2008; Rickabaugh, 1994). They refer to themselves as **masculinist, liberationists, post-feminist**, and **anti-feminist**, and some of their major concerns are child support and alimony issues and domestic violence against men (Fox, 2004; Lingard & Douglas, 1999; Mann, 2008). They claim that it is men, not women, who are victims of society and that men must "take back" the culture from women and establish a true patriarchy (see Rickabaugh, 1994, Mann, 2008). Because men are suffering from a variety of problems (as discussed in chapter 8), the argument is that men are the oppressed ones, not women. The assumption is that restoring the world to its "proper place" will diminish the problems associated with men (Lingard & Douglas, 1999, Mann, 2008). For example, one concern of some essentialists has been the sharing of family roles, which, they argue, obscures men's natural place.

> Except for a handful of Christian families around the country who refuse to be assimilated into the modern culture, most people, including most Christians, have accepted the feminist hypothesis that men and women should be treated the same. For more than 6,000 years of earth history, Christians and Jews have held to a worldview in which God established a hierarchy for the family. This hierarchy presupposed that man would be the protector and defender of womankind. (Leggewie, 1999)

Well-known modern organizations that advocate for a patriarchal perspective are: the Promise Keepers, the Men's Rights Association, the National Coalition of Free Men, the Men's Defense Association, the National Organization for Men, the National Congress for Men and the National Center for Men (Bliss, 1995; Fox, 2004; Lingard & Douglas, 1999; MacInnes, 2001, Messner, 2001; Rickabaugh, 1994). Websites such as patriarchy.com and mensactivism.org also promote these ideals. In the last ten years, these movements have been steadily increasing, although often under a variety of names (Fox, 2004).

Making Connection: The Million Man March

One cannot discuss men's movements without mentioning the **Million Man March**, the largest march designed by and for Black men in the twentieth century (West, 1999). The march (which was more like a rally, in that people did not march) took place on the Mall in Washington, DC, October 16, 1995 and has been repeated every year since then. The first Million Man March drew between 400,000 and 1.5 million people, depending on the source of estimation (Watkins, 2001; West, 1999).

The march has been described as a form of American **Black nationalism** (West, 1999). In fact, the mission of the march was written by Maulana Ron Karenga, the "fountainhead of modern black nationalism" (West, 1999, p. 1). Black nationalism, emphasizing the need for Americans of African descent to reject integration with White culture, has been an important movement within Black communities to increase solidarity and address unique cultural and shared historical experiences of Black people. The perspective has also assisted in creating a vision for the complete emancipation of American descendants from Africa (West, 1999).

Black men from all over America (and the world) joined together on this day to discuss a variety of concerns for Black men. Speeches were made by prominent Black leaders including the Reverend Jesse Jackson, Rosa Parks, and Maya Angelou, who stressed the need for Black people to work together for the benefit of all (Poling & Kirkley, 2000). Topics that men discussed with one another included racial profiling, stereotypes of Black men, imprisonment, families, anti-violence, and brotherhood (Poling & Kirkley, 2000; Watkins, 2001). The issues were confronted under a Christian umbrella of atonement and reconciliation, emphasizing connection to other men (West, 1999). "It was love, peace, joy, tears, warmth, sacred, strength, power, spirit-filled, fun and laughter" (Winbush in Poling & Kirkley, 2000, p. 18).

Black women were asked by leaders not to attend, which had mixed reactions from Black women (West, 1999). Polls suggested many women supported Black men for efforts of uniting with one another (West, 1999). Others felt that the march was a large scale representation of problems within the Black community, men connecting with other

Continued

men at the exclusion of women and the needs of others (Watkins, 2001; West, 1999). The march has also been criticized by some for being an essentialized heterosexist attempt to argue for one kind of masculinity (Poling & Kirkley, 2000).

The march was organized primarily by the Nation of Islam minister Louis Farrakhan and the former National Association for the Advancement of Colored People (NAACP) director Reverend Benjamin Chavis, Jr. to unify Black men and to confront issues in the Black community (Poling & Kirkley, 2000; Watkins, 2001; West, 1999). The march itself has largely been associated with Farrakhan, resulting in other leaders often being absent from mention in the media and in the literature (West, 1999). While Farrakhan was a prominent leader in the march, the media focus may have been a way to emphasize his controversial politics (he has made **xenophobic** and **anti-Semitic** and anti-Catholic comments) and controversial aspects of the march rather than its unifying aspects (Watkins, 2001; West, 1999).

While it had an enormous turn-out and facilitated much discussion, some claimed the march lacked vision (West, 1999). Perhaps because it was inclusive and drew from men from a variety of places and belief systems, it was hard to have an overriding ideology that would assist men in moving forward. Since the first march took place in 1995 several other events have occurred. Women's marches and the formation of a Black radical congress resulted from the march (West, 1999). In 2005, a gender-integrated march took place in which some leaders chastised President Bush for neglecting Black victims of Hurricane Katrina (Frank, 2005).

The Million Man March was a pivotal event of the twentieth century. Never before in America's history have so many men come together to discuss issues related to masculinity. In particular, the march was by and for Black men, which also sets it apart from many protest movements in the United States, which have been historically White dominated (West, 1999). While the march was controversial, it has resulted in several other experiences that assist in keeping discussions open and on-going about the difficulties that men (and particularly Black men) face in the United States (Frank, 2005).

In contrast, some men's groups have focused on men's psychological experiences and men's healing, as opposed to men's "rights." Perhaps the most well-known self-help men's movement is the **mythopoetic men's movement** (Barton, 2000; Carey, 1996; Fox, 2004; Lingard

& Douglas, 1999, Magnuson, 2007). This movement can be traced to early work in the 1970s stressing men's liberation through self-healing and therapeutic connections to other men (Barton, 2000; Carey, 1996). Based in Jungian archetypal work, spirituality, and mythology, mythopoetic men hope to determine the true nature of what masculinity is and help other men discover that truth through confronting unconscious archetypal shadow energy (Barton, 2000; Fee, 1992). A major focus has been on forgiveness and reconciliation with fathers, men and masculinity (Pease, 2000). The movement has sought to bring together men who have experienced significant pain around areas of masculinity with a goal to learn how to reclaim a mature version of it (which is often called **deep masculinity**) (Barton, 2000; Bliss, 1995; Fee, 1992; Gilbert, 1992; Magnuson, 2007).

The term "mythopoetic" comes from the concept of mythopoesis, which means remythologizing or creating new mythologies (Bliss, 1995). It has appealed to a wide variety of people with diverse interests (Gilbert, 1992). Perhaps its most well-known contributor has been the poet Robert Bly, but several others have contributed to this approach, including writers Robert Moore, Douglas Gillette, Sam Keen, John Rowan, Mark Gerzon, and Shepard Bliss (Barton, 2000; Kipnis, 1995, Rickabaugh, 1994).

Mythopoetic work has been made famous by wilderness retreats in which men come together to support one another to reclaim manhood (Gilbert, 1992; Barton, 2000; Richard, 2000). The retreats are often based in ritualistic behaviors of various cultures (especially Native American) in order to take back what society has been denying men: positive connections with other men engaging in **positive masculinity** (Barton, 2000; Richard, 2000). Examples of these retreats include wild men weekends, vision quests, warrior trainings, inner king trainings, woodland passages, and a variety of other retreats and workshops (Barton, 2000; Gilbert, 1992; Magnuson, 2007). The retreats might include poetry readings, mythic storytelling, singing, dancing, drumming circles, sharing circles, shadow work, and various activities that address issues of masculinity and men's healing (Barton, 2000; Gilbert, 1992; Kipnis, 1995; Richard, 2000).

The Mankind Project (MKP) is a fairly recent offshoot of the mythopoetic movement that stresses the assisting of men in reclaiming the **sacred masculine** (Mankowski, Maton, Burke, Hoover, & Anderson, 2000; Maton, 2000; Pentz, 2000). Originally founded as the New Warrior Network by Bill Kauth, Rich Tosi, and Ron Hering, and publicizing a membership of over 30,000 men from many nations, the Mankind Project appears to be revitalizing the mythopoetic vision as a new social movement (Mankowski et al., 2000; Pentz, 2000). The Mankind Project encourages diverse men to attend their New Warrior Training Adventures to address the project's core values: accountability and integrity, feelings, leadership, fatherhood, and respect for elders (Mankowski et al., 2000). Much like other mythopoetic groups, MKP stresses that much of men's pain comes from being disconnected from their fathers and the wounding that results from that disconnection (Mankowski et al., 2000). The goal is to heal that pain through acknowledging the shadow and creating positive interactions with other men to reclaim sacred masculinity (Mankowski et al., 2000; Pentz, 2000).

While mythopoetic groups and the Mankind Project are often categorized together with groups like the National Coalition of Free Men, due to their stressing of essentialism (Clatterbaugh, 1995; Levant, 1997; Messner, 2001; Rickabaugh, 1994; White, 1996), they are not identical. As Dr. Edward Barton, a scholar at Michigan State University, has stressed, the mythopoetic and mankind perspective stress the balance and integration of masculinity within men (Barton, 2000; Maton, 2000; Pentz, 2000). They address the problems associated with men withholding experiences and pain from others (Barton, 2000). In describing the power of mythopoetic work, Barton says, "It is a masculine voice speaking from the masculine experience of consciousness, pain, vulnerability, and healing" (p. 12). In other words, this balance includes characteristics often thought of as being feminine, but instead described as human by proponents of this perspective (Barton, 2000; Gilbert, 1992). Mythopoetic men don't advocate for the "macho man" of the 1950s, nor the so-called "soft man" of the 1970s, but for a new balanced man (Barton, 2000; Gilbert, 1992). "It appears from the research that the overall mission of MKP is to lead men to lives of service. That is not a dominant patriarchy." (Pentz, 2000, p. 222).

Other men's groups (such as the Promise Keepers) seem to argue for a male more reminiscent of the idealized American 1950s male, one who is separate, dominant and in control, rather than for a balanced masculinity (Barton, 2000; Moore & Gillette, 1990; Maton, 2000). Much like any social group, there will be diverse voices within the group. Mythopoetic men do share an assumption in essentialism and have several proponents who have been patriarchal in their views (Fox, 2004; Kimmel & Kaufman, 1995). They also have advocates that see the connections between their work and others:

The change in consciousness resulting from the second great wave of feminism along with various types of spiritualism, seems to mean almost as if there were a permission given to seek and find this new voice for men who want to do things other than dominate in the ways that seem to be ascribed by the dominant culture. (Barton, 2000, p. 12)

Summary

This chapter has briefly outlined the essentialist perspective on the crisis of masculinity. This perspective assumes that there is a natural way for men to be men. This natural way to be a man is rooted in men's biology and ultimately affects them psychologically in a way that makes them unique from women. If men as a social group are experiencing problems (whether through aggression or through despondency) it is because the culture is not supporting boys and men to act in the ways that they are naturally intended to. The essentialist view argues that the crisis in masculinity exists because changes in the culture have prevented boys from developing into men and establishing a positive male masculinity.

The solution to this dilemma for men is to work on integrating true masculinity into their psyches. This can come about through individual work, where men learn how their past and present experiences have kept them at a distance from positive masculinity. It can also come about through group work in organizations that emphasize men's spending more time with one another and reclaiming masculinity to achieve balance.

Rather than presenting concerns with this perspective here, we will discuss this in the next chapter, which takes a psychosocial perspective on the crisis of masculinity. As you will soon learn, not all researchers in this field view this problem in the same way that essentialists do, nor do they see an essentialist solution as viable or likely to lead to positive change for men.

Review and Questions to Ponder

1. What is the basic essentialist explanation for the masculinity crisis?

2. What are the basic psychoanalytic assumptions essentialists rely on for their arguments?
3. What are the Jungian assumptions essentialists often rely on for their arguments?
4. What are the social changes essentialists claim are responsible for the crisis in masculinity? Be sure to discuss social rituals, changes since the industrial revolution to the information age, public space, and changing roles of men.
5. What is the divorce revolution? How does it relate to the crisis of masculinities?
6. What is no-fault divorce? How does it relate to the crisis of masculinities?
7. What is a father wound? Can you give examples of it?
8. What are terms for men not viewed as masculine?
9. Why do you think there are so many terms for "non-masculine men"?
10. How do essentialists hope to solve this crisis?
11. What is the men's rights movement?
12. What does it mean to be masculinist, liberationist, post-feminist, or anti-feminist?
13. What is the mythopoetic movement?
14. What is the Mankind Project (MKP)?
15. What is the purpose of MKP?
16. What is meant by positive masculinity?
17. What is the Million Man March?
18. What are different views on the accomplishments of the march?
19. What are different names used to refer to men that are seen as atypical?
20. Do you have any hypotheses why so many names exist for men that are "more like women" than for men who are "too manly"?

10

The Crisis in Masculinity

Psychosocial Perspective

The previous chapter summarized the essentialist perspective on the crisis in masculinity. As you will recall, this perspective views men and women's gender expression as a natural and determined outgrowth of their sex. This view advocates that men are experiencing problems in the world because the environment has changed in such a way to be welcoming for women and not for men. Because of these changes men have difficulties knowing what it means to be a man and, as a result, develop all kinds of problems.

The Psychosocial Explanation

While the essentialist explanation is adopted by some people in the field, it is not the only understanding of the crisis in masculinity. The **psychosocial explanation** integrates theory and research from several perspectives, including psychological (in areas such as psychoanalytic, social learning, cognitive-behavioral, and social psychology), sociological and anthropological work (Nye, 2005, Peoples, 2001; Pollack, 1995).

First and foremost, this view purports that men are experiencing problems at alarming rates that need to be addressed (Levant, 1997; Pollack, 1995, 1998). Issues discussed previously in this text such as violence towards others, self, drug and alcohol use, and mental health problems are said to plague boys and men (Addis & Mahalik, 2003; Galvani, 2004; Levant, 1997; Locke & Mahalik, 2005; Pollack, 1990, Styver, 2007). Men, for a variety of reasons, are also not likely to ask for and get the help they need to resolve their concerns (Addis & Mahalik, 2003).

The psychosocial view agrees with many of the premises set forth by the essentialist perspective. The economic and historical changes suggested to have occurred are not debated by this view. The United States' economy has shifted. Women have entered the workplace at increased rates, which is beginning to change the nature of work (Kimmel & Kaufman, 1995; MacInnes, 2001). It is also not debated that the rising divorce rate has been a problem for children and their families, particularly for women and children, who are over-represented in poverty statistics and not likely to receive child support (Cook, Davis, & Davies, 2008; Huang, Mincy & Garfinkel, 2005; Levant, 1997; Pollack, 1998; Shackleford, Weekes-Shackleford, & Schmitt, 2005). Of those who do receive child-support, barely 50 percent receive the full payment as determined by the court (Shackleford et al., 2005). It is not debated that men have increasingly spent less time with their children and that that is a problem for families in general (Levant, 1997; Pease, 2000; Pollack, 1998; Thomas, Krampe, & Newton, 2008).

In fact, proponents of the psychosocial view have added additional data to support the contention that historical changes have contributed to problems for men. Feminist and Pulitzer Prize winner Susan Faludi discussed these social changes in her text *Stiffed: The Betrayal of the American Man* (1999). Her argument is that as a society we are moving toward glorifying the ornamental aspects of culture rather than the functional. We worship consumerism, glamour, and entertainment rather than actual craft and skill, which is having a detrimental impact on men. While there is some attention given to a few public roles often associated with masculinity, our culture seems obsessed with glitz over substance. The kinds of occupations that *actual* men have, that were regarded as solid and important in the past, today are looked down upon and cannot garner a sense of male identity in the way they once did (Faludi, 1999).

So what is different between the essentialist and psychosocial view? There are four major distinctions between them. The first is the assumption of essentialism. The psychosocial view rejects the idea of essentialism (Levant, 1997; Pollack, 1995). This view assumes that men are diverse in the way that they experience masculinity, and that there is no correct way to be a man (Levant, 1997; Pollack, 1995; Stoltenberg, 1993, 2000). So the first difference in views concerns the legitimacy of viewing masculinity in an essentialized way.

Following that logic, the second difference advocated by the psychosocial view acknowledges that cultures have different norms with different expectations about masculinity (Abreau, Goodyear, Campos, & Newcomb, 2000; Levant, 1997; Schwartz & Waldo, 2003). This means that, in order to understand the experience of masculinity (or a crisis of masculinity), one must understand the interaction between the experience of masculinity and the differing psychosocial norms (Levant, 1997; O'Neil, 1981; O'Neil, Helms, Gable, David & Wrightsman, 1986; Pleck, 1995). Masculinity does not exist within a person, but within an interaction between a person's experience and the norms of their culture (Levant, 1997; O'Neil, 1981; Pleck, 1995).

The third difference in views relates to the valuing of these changing gender norms. Over the last 50 years, gender role expectations have been changing. Women, in expanding their roles in the world, have been making gains in order to have equal opportunities (Crary, 2008; Faludi, 1999; Levant, 1997, MacInnes, 2001; Okeowo, 2007; Vance, 2007). As stated in chapter 9, the essentialist perspective is concerned that those changes have resulted in a "feminized" environment, one that is unfriendly to men. As a general rule, proponents of the psychosocial view, like liberal feminists, believe that men and women should have equal access to cultural resources and any changes that increase access are positive ones (Addis & Mahalik, 2003; Brooks & Levant, 1999; Levant, 1997). Men, however, have not adjusted to these changes well (Addis & Mahalik, 2003; Faludi, 1999; Levant, 1997). The reason they haven't dealt well with these changes is not because there is a "right" way to be masculine, but because men are not prepared to effectively adapt to change due to the rigidity of the male gender role (Addis & Mahalik; 2003; Brooks & Levant, 1999; Deachan, 1998; Levant, 1997; Pollack, 1995).

The final difference is the focus on research and data as a primary source of knowledge gathering. While the essentialist perspective does include research and data at times, it also includes clinical and individual examples not always based in thorough research. The cornerstone for the psychosocial approach is a focus on research and data to understand the questions raised by the crisis in masculinity (Brooks & Levant, 1999). In fact, proponents of this view have historically been active in creating the very tools used to measure the phenomenon of masculinity and how it relates to a host of other factors (Brooks & Levant, 1999).

The Problem

From the psychosocial perspective, in order to understand the difficulties boys and men are having, one must investigate the relationship between internal experiences of masculinity and psychosocial norms. Joseph Pleck's revolutionary **male role strain** paradigm can assist us in our exploration of the general ways in which gender roles contribute stress to men's lives (Garnets & Pleck, 1979; Levant, 1997; Mahalik, Cournoyer, DeFranc, Cherry, & Napolitano, 1998). Ronald Levant, Dean and Professor of Psychology at Buchtel College of Arts and Sciences at the University of Akron, and James O'Neil, a researcher and Professor of Family Studies and Educational Psychology at the University of Connecticut, have also been prominent investigators of this overall issue. Their analyses are extremely useful and representative of this section of the chapter. We will focus on three aspects of this strain paradigm: gender role discrepancy; gender role trauma; and gender role conflict (Blazina, Pisecco, & O'Neil, 1986; Levant, 1997; Mahalik et al., 1998; O'Neil, 1981; O'Neil et al., 1986; Pleck, 1995).

Who's Who in Masculinities Research: Ronald Levant, Ed.D., ABPP

Ronald F. Levant is Dean and Professor of Psychology, Buchtel College of Arts and Sciences, University of Akron. Dr. Levant has authored, coauthored, edited, or coedited fourteen books and more than 175 peer-reviewed journal articles and book chapters. One of Levant's contributions is in helping to pioneer the new psychology of men. He was also the co-founder and first President of APA Division 51 (the Society for the Psychological Study of Men and Masculinity). His books include *Between Father and Child, Masculinity Reconstructed, A New Psychology of Men, Men and Sex: New Psychological Perspectives* and *New Psychotherapies for Men.*

Website: www.DrRonaldLevant.com

Who's Who in Masculinities Research: James O'Neil, Ph.D.

James M. O'Neil is Professor of Family Studies and Educational Psychology in the Neag School of Education at the University of Connecticut in the School Counseling and Counseling Psychology Programs. He is one of the founding members of the Society for the Psychological Study of Men and Masculinity (SPSMM), Division 51 of the American Psychological Association. His last book (with Michele Harway) was *What Causes Men's Violence against Women?* He has dedicated 25 years to studying gender role conflict in men.

Website: http//web.uconn.edu/joneil/

Gender role discrepancy (body image)

Gender role discrepancy is a discrepancy (or difference) between your **ideal self**, what is idealized (desired), and your **real self**, or what is actually attained (Chu, Porche, & Tolman, 2005; Pleck, 1995; Levant, 1997). This can be connected to the idea of prescriptive norms and descriptive norms. In other words, there is potentially a difference in the way that men *actually* are in a culture and that particular culture's expectations of the way they *should* be (Monk & Ricciardelli, 2003; Pleck, 1995).

Large numbers of men experience gender role discrepancy because they cannot attain the requirements of their particular culture (Chu et al., 2005; Monk & Ricciardelli, 2003; Pleck, 1995; Levant, 1997). Unfortunately, many internalize this failure and view it as their own fault, rather than a defect in the societal expectations themselves (Monk & Ricciardelli, 2003; Pleck, 1995). This can lead to feelings of worthlessness or lowered self-esteem (Monk & Ricciardelli, 2003; Pleck, 1995). Levant (1997) connects gender role discrepancy to the "good provider role." Men are increasingly not being viewed as the sole provider in their households, which is contributing to a discrepancy strain for men (Levant, 1997). Unfortunately, they are having difficulty negotiating this strain.

Men are caught in a trap both because they do not have incentives (to change their view of the social expectations) and because they are ill-equipped to address the loss of the good provider role in a collaborative and equitable fashion with the women in their lives and as a result act with anger and defensiveness. (Levant, 1997, p. 222)

Discrepancy strain is described as a process, not as a fixed experience (Pleck, 1995). In other words, when strain occurs, men try to make sense of the strain through a variety of factors. Men are rarely either in a state of discrepancy or not in one, but fluctuate in and out of strain as they try to make sense of what that strain means to their identity and to their relationships (Bergman, 1996; Pleck, 1995; Pleck, Sonestein, & Ku, 1993).

Finally, discrepancy strain can also have advantages. Viewed as a process, the strain involves a cognitive component which can lead to awareness of oneself and questioning of gender role expectations (Pleck, 1995). Nonconformity to gender role expectations can have positive results, particularly when negative norms are not internalized (Mahalik, Good, & Englar-Carlson, 2003; Pleck, 1995).

One of the gender role norms that I can relate to personally is in relation to asking for assistance. I have internalized the male role of being self-sufficient, sometimes to my own dismay. There are times where I am distraught, but it does not even occur to me to pick up the phone and call a friend. And when I do think of that option, I often start to create reasons why I shouldn't call (they are probably busy, or I don't want to bring them down, etc.). And the truth is that I am fortunate enough to have people in my life who would love for me to call them when I need support. Awareness of the strain between a social role expectation of being independent and "handling my own problems" and my own internal feelings of vulnerability has helped me to make better choices in reaching out to others to get assistance. And I feel much better when I do. This kind of awareness and nonconformity to the expectation has been very helpful as I try to improve this area of my life.

Gender role trauma

While proponents of this view believe that father absence has had negative effects on children, they have focused on another familial problem: the detachment process of boys from mothers in early childhood. As discussed in chapter 3, some authors believe that boys have been pushed away from their mothers at a crucial time in their psychological development, resulting in a problematic sense of self called a **gender role trauma** (Pollack, 1995). Dr. William Pollack, an Assistant Clinical Professor of Psychiatry at Harvard Medical School, has been a major contributor in understanding the gender trauma of boys (Pollack, 1995, 1998).

> **Who's Who in Masculinities Research: William S. Pollack, Ph.D.**
>
> Dr. Pollack is a clinical psychologist, Assistant Clinical Professor of Psychiatry at Harvard Medical School, the director of the Center for Men at McLean Hospital, and a founding member and fellow of the American Psychological Association's Society for the Psychological Study of Men and Masculinity. He is best known for his "Real Boys" series of books examining problematic masculinity in boys.
>
> Website: http://www.williampollack.com/contact.html.

This trauma has also been referred to as the **mother wound** (Kimmel, 1995; Kimmel & Kaufman, 1995; Silverstein & Rashbaum, 1994). The mother wound, stated simply, is a wound that young men carry because they have not developed a full sense of self, due to being forced to detach from their mothers before being ready to slowly become more interdependent (Pollack, 1995, 1998; Schwartz & Waldo, 2003). Researchers interested in attachment have argued that a solid sense of oneself is established in childhood in relationships with primary caregivers and if those relationships are severed, deleterious results for the child can result (Defranc & Mahalik, 2002; Schwartz & Waldo, 2004; Mahalik, Aldarondo, Gilbert-Gokhale, & Shore, 2005).

Many cultures' gender role socialization, stressing independence and autonomy for men, literally forces boys to detach psychologically from their parents before they are ready to do so (DeFranc & Mahalik, 2002; Good et al., 1995, Mahalik et al., 1998, 2005; Pollack, 1995). The socialization process essentially strips boys from experiencing the full range of their human qualities and forces them to adopt characteristics associated with men while they are still boys (Pollack, 1995, 1998). Parents, teachers, and many other well-meaning people in boys' lives collude to socialize boys in this way (Blazina et al.,1986; Jefferson, 2002; Pollack, 1995, 1998). The result is a man who has a rigid version of the self, denying himself the experiential aspects of the world associated with femininity (O'Neil, 1981; O'Neil et al., 1986; Mahalik et al., 1998).

The communication of this rigid masculinity is sometimes referred to as **code masculinity** or the **boy code**, which entails the various complex ways in which people communicate to men the ways in which they believe they need to act, think, and feel in order to meet the criteria of this rigid gender role (Deachan, 1998; Nye, 2005; Pollack, 1998; Risner, 2007). This boy code can be communicated through what are called **masculinity scripts**. Masculinity scripts can be thought of as dominant masculine norm-based behavioral expectations for men (Mahalik et al., 2003). These scripts are culturally and historically specific in that they differ across cultures and across time (Abreau et al., 2000; Fracher & Kimmel, 1989; Kimmel & Levine, 1989; Risner, 2007; Stoltenberg, 1989). The best way to think of it is like a script in a play. It is as if in life, men's lines have already been written for them and that there are very few choices to make and still remain "in character" or to be "a man."

Men continue to adhere to these unattainable scripts largely because they struggle with knowing, understanding, and being able to express other ways of communicating masculinity (Pollack, 1998; Redman, 2005; Wetherell & Edley, 1999). "The boy code puts boys and men into a gender straitjacket that constrains not only them but everyone else, reducing us all as human beings, and eventually making us strangers to ourselves and to one another" (Pollack, 1998, p. 6).

This underdeveloped sense of self leads to what some researchers call a **fragile masculine self** (Blazina, 2001; Blazina & Watkins, 2000). The fragile masculine self involves a rigid and constricted set of internal rules for what it means to be male, resulting in an insecure and detached person (Blazina, 2001; Blazina & Watkins, 2000; Deachan, 1998). Because the young boy was denied attachments and experiences associated with femininity, he begins to internalize guilt and fear whenever he experiences the world in a way perceived as feminine by the culture. As Blazina (2001) explains,

The fragile masculine self encompasses the woundedness that many boys and then men carry as a result of their restrictive gender role experiences from the period of disidentification onward. These psychic wounds arise in part from the empathic failure of caregivers (both male and female) regarding masculine self issues . . . The child is not able to account for the rejection and failings of his parental objects other than to blame himself. (p. 54)

Another way of conceptualizing this problem is being referred to by researchers as **normative male alexithymia,** which is described as an inability to describe or even be aware of one's emotions (Berger, Levant, McMillan, Kelleher, & Sellers, 2005; Levant, 1998). It is unfortunately described as "normal" because it seems to be a phenomenon that many boys and men experience (Berger et al., 2005; Levant, 1998; Pollack, 1995; Stoltenberg, 1993). Researchers have found this restricted emotionality to be related to overall anxiety, psychosomatic illness, substance abuse, and other mental health concerns (Berger et al., 2005; Levant et al., 2006; Wong, Pituch, & Rochlen, 2006). (literally can't describe emotions)

To better understand this description perhaps you can imagine the following scenario. Many women have had the experience of asking men what they think or feel in response to certain situations and then received a "blank look" in return. That look is sometimes interpreted as resistance or a lack of wanting to communicate, when in actuality for many men it may be an inability to even know what they are experiencing (Berger et al., 2005; Levant, 1998). This inability also gets internalized and fault is seen as within oneself, which further complicates the problem (Berger et al., 2005; Levant, 1998).

Others have preferred to frame the problem as being between people as opposed to within the person. From a relational perspective, the dissociation results in what is called relational dread. **Male relational dread** has been described as a discomfort in connecting to others, rather than an uncomfortable identity. It entails the uncomfortable, anxiety-ridden psychological experience that many men have when they are in a situation that requires them to be empathic, to communicate, and to connect to others (Stoltenberg, 1993). Researchers have argued that male relational dread should be described as an interactional problem and not an internal pathology (Bergman, 1995; Chu et al., 2005). "It is a disconnecting from the very process of growth in relationship, a learning about turning away from the whole relational mode. The turning away means that the boy never learns how to do it, how to be in process with another and grow" (Bergman, 1995, p. 74).

So what boys do is deny their "**psychic femininity**" (human characteristics men possess that are associated with women) (DeFranc &

Mahalik, 2002). The detachment the child is forced to endure becomes a psychological metaphor for the way that men live their lives; they essentially detach from characteristics associated with femininity that they actually need in order to adapt and connect with others (DeFranc & Mahalik, 2002; Stoltenberg, 1993). This disconnection itself is referred to in chapter three as masculine dread (of femininity) (Horney, 1968) and is also referred to as the flight from or fear of women/femininity (Grinnell College, 2003; Kimmel, 1995; O'Neil, 1986; Stoltenberg, 1993).

Gender role conflict

The basic premise and understanding of gender role strain has led researchers to develop a widely researched topic referred to today as gender role conflict (Blazina et al., 1986; O'Neil, 1981; O'Neil et al., 1986). In fact, an extensive research program exists to study and investigate this phenomenon with hundreds of studies to its credit (see http://web.uconn/joneil).

   Gender role conflict assumes that the male gender role as an ideal in most western cultures is inherently problematic and has expectations for men that lead them to develop all kinds of problems (Blazina et al., 1986; Blazina & Watkins, 2000; Fragoso & Kashubeck, 2000; Monk & Ricciardelli, 2003; Morardi, Tokar, Schaub, Jome & Serna, 2000; O'Neil, 1981; O'Neil et al., 1986; Pleck, 1995; Poddar & Krishan, 2004; Rando, Rogers, & Britain-Powell, 1998). In particular, the rigidity in denying characteristics associated with femininity has contributed to men not developing a whole human self and suffering emotional and physical strain as a result (Blazina & Watkins, 2000; Miedzian, 1991; O'Neil et al., 1986). While gender trauma refers to a familial disconnection from femininity, gender role conflict could be seen as referring to a conflict that is connected to an overall psychosocial disconnection from femininity (O'Neil et al., 1986).

   O'Neil and colleagues (1986) identified six areas of a man's life related to this disconnection from femininity as aspects of gender role conflict. The areas are: restrictive emotionality (as mentioned above), homophobia, **socialized control**, power and competition, restricted sexual and **affective behavior**; obsession with achievement and success, and health-care problems (Mahalik et al., 1998). Many of these themes overlap descriptions of dominant masculinity and concerns presented in chapter three (David & Brannon, 1976; Mahalik et al., 2003; Pleck, 1995; Silverstein & Rashbaum, 1994; Stoltenberg, 1993).

Making Connections: The Trap of Fatherhood and Masculinity

As stated, gender role conflict results when the gender role requirements of a culture contribute to problems in one's life. One example of
this conflict lies within the relationship between fathers and their children. Many people today grow up in single-parent households, typically headed by women. Others who grow up in two-parent households
may have nearly as little contact with their fathers as those in single-
parent households. Fathers' lack of involvement with their own children in many ways can be viewed as following the male gender role.

O'Neil and colleagues (1986) cited the obsession with achievement
and success and restrictive emotionality as two aspects of potential
gender role conflict. These two characteristics seem to be common in
many men who focus on work and work relationships over those at
home. These men work overtime. They make sacrifices for their jobs so
they can move up and earn more income. They do not know their
children intimately: who they are, what their dreams are, who they
hope to be. They see them infrequently and view this as part of being
a man.

Men suffering from gender-role conflict often judge their self-worth
by their title, how much money they have in the bank, how big their
house is, and what kind of car they drive. They often rationalize that
these decisions are made for the benefit of the family and yet, if they
bothered to ask their family members whether they wanted this lifestyle, they might find that they do not.

While some children were fortunate to have had financial stability
contributed by their fathers, they often lack the emotional and loving
connection with them. This strips these men of moments in life they can
never regain. It disconnects them from aspects of their humanness. It
also strips the children (and the man's partner) from having a relationship with them. This can impact the way children view themselves and
the role of a father in others' lives. These fathers can, without realizing
it, spend their lives trying to meet the cultures definition of masculinity,
while ignoring the most important relationships in their lives.

The degree to which conflict occurs for individual men has been said
to be related to many variables, including a man's expectations about

what the roles are, what they believe they should be and what a person's ideal is for themselves (Chu et al., 2005; Garnets & Pleck, 1979; Mahalik et al., 2003). The process of struggling with these norms also affects men differently on the basis of social issues such as racial and ethnic identity, as well as having different behavioral, cognitive, and emotional consequences for men (Abreau et al., 2000; Chu et al., 2005; Fragoso & Kashubeck, 2000; Mahalik et al., 1998; Schwartz & Waldo, 2003).

For example, researchers Liu & Iwamoto (2006) found that, in a sample of Asian American men, the men who conformed to traditional Asian cultural values (such as collectivism, emotional restraint, and deference to authority) were more likely to experience gender role conflict in relation to issues of success, power, and competition. The interpretation of this conflict also becomes important considering the cultural background of the participants. "For many Asian American men, emotional self-control may be associated with saving-face (for self and other) or upholding their family name" (p. 160).

Research has demonstrated a connection between the problematic behaviors and experiences of men discussed earlier in this chapter and overall gender role strain. Research has also shown a connection between violence, relationship problems and the internalization of dominant male norms (Blazina & Watkins, 2000; Chu et al., 2005; Defranc & Mahalik, 2002; Jakupcak, Lisak, & Roemer, 2002; Liu & Iwamoto, 2006; Mahalik et al., 2005; Schwartz & Waldo, 2003). Divorce and parental separation have been shown to be more problematic for boys who have internalized dominant masculine gender norms and perceive their fathers as experiencing role strain (Defranc & Mahalik, 2002; Levant, 1997). The excessive use of alcohol and other drugs has also been linked to anti-feminine attitudes and the adoption of dominant male norms (Monk & Ricciardelli, 2003; Styver, 2007). Finally, mental and physical health problems have been linked to the adoption of dominant masculine norms (Fragoso & Kashubeck, 2000; Levant et al., 2006).

What we can summarize in this section on gender role strain and of the psychosocial model that the crisis in masculinity for men is the rigidity of masculinity. This should not be construed as suggesting that all men have a problem, but that the rigid social role for men that seems exalted in many cultures, and unfortunately supported by child-rearing practices, is having dire consequences for men. The problems that boys and men face are not viewed here a function of not being *masculine* enough, but as not being *feminine* enough. Rejecting femininity is at the heart of the crisis of masculinity. The bottom line from this perspective is not to find lost masculinity, as suggested by essentialists, but to reject dominant masculinity and discover characteristics associated with femininity.

Solutions

Solutions from a psychosocial perspective begin with a general criticism of the essentialist solutions. Because essentialists view the crisis of masculinity as being one that involves reclaiming maleness, their activities speak to reconnecting with men. While proponents of the psychosocial approach believe that men connecting with other men can be beneficial, as a solution it is viewed as misguided (Bergman, 1996; Pease, 2000; Pleck, 1995; Kimmel & Kaufman, 1995). "Men are now getting together with men. This is of value and I applaud the sharing of grief and loss and the healing of male-male wounds that can take place. Yet there are disturbing concerns . . . Sending men off into the woods à la Bly, will not, by itself, lead to something new, we must also bring men back into relationships with women" (Bergman, 1996, pp. 86 & 88). The solution entails bringing men in connection with characteristics associated with femininity and with others.

In fact, this perspective has historically aligned itself with women and with feminism. Referring to members of Division 51 of the American Psychological Association (The Society for the Psychological Study of Men and Masculinity (SPSMM)), Brooks & Levant state, "Most members of the SPSMM believe that men often face disadvantages in American culture, whether from the draft, the courts, or the demands of the workplace . . . But unlike antifeminists, they do not see women or feminism as the cause of problems. Instead, the men and women of SPSMM (women make up 20–25 percent of the membership) have joined collegially with women to discuss ways to end gender oppression" (p. 214).

Organizing

In order to begin this process of collegiality, one important step is to get people who have an interest in this topic together to give support, share research, and further the understanding of men and masculinity. This is not an easy task to undertake. People who have had interest in this area have been involved with multiple activities ranging from clinical work, community support organizing, research at universities, and activism against male violence (Brooks & Levant, 1999; Doyle & Femiano, 2008). While these areas have clear overlap in interest, they are often pursued in a variety of ways and by diverse people with unique professional backgrounds and goals (Brooks & Levant, 1999; Doyle & Femiano, 2008). Regardless, much progress has been made due to work by organizations such as SPSMM and the American Men's Studies Association.

SPSMM, as mentioned, is one of the several professional divisions of the American Psychological Association (Brooks & Levant, 1999). These specialty divisions within the field allow people with specific interests to meet other psychologists, learn about their work and research, form collaborations for future projects to better understand men and masculinity, and devise ways of improving men's lives. In order to assist in the meeting of these goals, SPSMM holds an annual conference, has an active LISTSERV, and publishes the journal *Psychology of Men and Masculinity* (Brooks & Levant, 1999).

Becoming a division was a lot of work for the progenitors (people like Joseph Pleck, Robert Brannon and Murray Scher), many of whom worked closely alongside the Association for Women in Psychology (AWP), the organization responsible for the creation of Division 35, the Society for the Psychology of Women (Brooks & Levant, 1999). SPSMM began as a result of (a) conversations about gender at early AWP meetings, (b) pioneering works such as Pleck's *The Myth of Masculinity*, and (c) connections with members of other organizations with similar interests like the National Organization for Changing Men (Brooks & Levant, 1999). Divisionary status was granted in 1997, and today the division is a very active area within the APA, promoting research, scholarship, and programming to assist in improving men's lives (Brooks & Levant, 1999).

While SPSMM is an area specific to psychologists, other professionals are of course interested in this topic and also needed a community space to meet similar goals. One such organization, the National Organization for Men, was formed by university students in 1975. After taking a women's studies class, University of Tennessee students decided that they could model a men's movement that could build on what feminist women had already established (Clatterbaugh, 1997; Fox, 2004, Lingard & Douglas, 1999).

NOM began with the formation of small task groups with the goal of learning about men and helping them as a social group (Doyle &

Femiano, 2008). Eventually, the organization became known as the National Organization for Changing Men and then the National Organization for Men Against Sexism (NOMAS, discussed in more detail in the next chapter) (Doyle & Femiano, 2008).

Within this organization, a specific task-group originally called the Men's Studies Task Group (MSTG) was created. This group was formed to address teaching and research as it relates to men's studies (Doyle & Femiano, 2008). As the organization progressed, interest in the work of the task force grew and it was eventually named the Men's Studies Association. Over time, it became difficult to balance the needs of NOMAS, who wanted an exclusively feminist perspective and the growing association that represented more diverse ideas (Doyle & Femiano, 2008; Newton, 2005). In 1989, the organization moved away from NOMAS and the MSA and is now known as the American Men's Studies Association (AMSA). AMSA, much like SPSMM, is an active organization that also holds academic and scholarly conferences every year, publishes a journal called *The Journal of Men's Studies* and as an organization appeals to a variety of professionals who are concerned about men's lives (Doyle & Femiano, 2008; Kilmartin, 2000).

SPSMM and AMSA are two organizations who share in common a history of bringing people together, focusing on research and knowledge, and an interest in exploring psychosocial issues impacting men and masculinity. AMSA is open to professionals in a variety of disciplines, while SPSMM focuses on work within the field of psychology. These are not the only organizations that exist in this arena and certainly not every member of each organization adheres strictly to a psychosocial view. However, members of these organizations have had a major impact on interventions that fall within a psychosocial perspective. The psychosocial perspective advocates a reconnection with femininity through both clinical interventions and educational activism.

Clinical interventions

Clinical interventions are those that utilize professionals in the field of mental health in order to help men make changes in their lives. Proceeding clinically in this manner is not easy. Because this view recognizes the pain men experience, the pain that men cause others, and a focus on the incorporation of femininity as a solution, men may be resistant to addressing these issues (Levant, 1997). Their resistance makes sense given the assumptions of gender-role-related strain. "Reared to compete and see things in terms of winning and losing, criticism for men is inherently shaming; in the context of an intimate relationship, it might even connote the end of the relationship" (Levant, 1997, p. 226).

The first step, then, involves approaching men empathically and with an understanding of the pain they experience (Addis & Mahalik, 2003; Levant, 1997; Pollack, 1995). As with any client, it becomes a matter of trust building and a demonstration of empathy for the client's subjective experiences (Levant, 1997). It is also important throughout this process to help them identify positive aspects of masculinity that have contributed to their adaptation and their own and others' well being (Levant, 1997; Addis & Mahalik, 2003). Because the goal is for men to recognize the problems with the rigid aspects of masculinity, it is important for them to recognize that being male in and of itself is not bad and that aspects of masculinity can be important aspects of the self (Levant, 1997).

Once trust and positive masculinity has been established, clinicians can begin to move forward. Psychologists who advocate for this view emphasize that individual clinical work with men needs to both recognize how men's problems relate to gender role strain and help men to identify how masculinity scripts have impeded them from living authentic and genuine lives (Levant, 1997; Mahalik et al., 2003, 2005; Pollack, 1995). This means that men's general psychosocial functioning, in terms of the diagnosis, assessment, and treatment of their problems, should come under the scrutiny of a gendered lens as radical feminists have proposed (Kaschak, 1992; Mahalik et al., 2003, 2005; O'Neil, 1996). By helping them identify their problem areas and the connection of those areas to masculine scripts, men can both see the unrealistic standards imposed upon them and their own role in maintaining them at a cost to their and others' development (Mahalik et al., 2003, 2005; O'Neil, 1996). This view advocates a need to assist men in learning what professionals know about the connections between dominant masculinity and problematic behavior (Addis & Mahalik, 2003; Levant, 1997; Mahalik et al., 2003; Pollack, 1995).

> These findings highlight the need for clinicians to better understand masculine socialization, to make efforts to explore the linkages between masculine scripts and men's presenting problems in their work with men, and to anticipate men's possible ambivalence to seeking help by finding ways to make the therapeutic experience more comfortable and effective. Our suggestion to the field is that we begin training

psychologists to understand the psychosocial context of men in the same way in which we have already recognized how the psychosocial context shapes the experiences of persons of color and women. (Mahalik et al., 2003)

Clinical groups have been run with homogenous groups of men in hopes of creating an atmosphere in which men can be honest about their problems with masculinity (O'Neil, 1996; Schwartz & Waldo, 2003). Clinical groups based on research and theory in **group process** can be tied to issues of gender role conflict to help men develop a consciousness about the constrictive nature of masculinity (Levin-Rozalis, Bar-on, & Hartaf, 2003; O'Neil, 1996; Schwartz & Waldo, 2003). Psychologists trained in group process pay particular attention to what people say in groups and more importantly, how they act and relate to other people in the group. This process often reveals much about their current concerns and their connections to masculinity and to others in the group and in their world (O'Neil, 1996).

In addition, by helping men see how they interact in social groups **in the moment** men can begin to get a sense of how others view them and the social roles they play (Schechtman, 1994; Schwartz & Waldo, 2003). Groups can help men develop communication skills that can assist them in relationships and in getting help when they need it (Bartholomew, Hiller, Knight, Nucatola, & Simpson., 2000; Schechtman, 1994). They can also help men challenge the way their cognitions are related to gender role attitudes (Brooks-Harris, Heesacker, & Mejia-Millan, 1996). Professionals can help men learn about the often restrictive ways that men express themselves (Bartholomew et al., 2000; Brooks-Harris et al., 1996; Schwartz & Waldo, 2003). A very powerful feature of groups in this regard is that they can help men view their problems as something that they can change, rather than merely a pathology within them (Brooks-Harris et al., 1996; Levin-Rozalis et al., 2003; Schechtman, 1994).

Other suggestions are workshops, groups, and trainings that bring men and women together to work on relational issues (Bergman, 1996). Including women in this process is not to reinforce men's reliance on women for the learning of emotion and characteristics associated with femininity (Bergman, 1996). Rather, it is to help men view how women experience them in a safe space and to help women see the pain that men struggle with in dealing with masculine dread (Bergman, 1996). This can be done in a group or family therapy format that helps family members see the role that sexism and rigid gender roles play in their daily lives (Dienhart & Myers Avis, 1991; Goodrich, Rampage, Ellman, & Halstead, 1992; Kaschak, 1992).

Educational activism

Because the psychosocial view believes the cause of the crisis to be rigid gender roles for men, activism includes methods that will connect men to women, and to each other. It also includes teaching men how to create spaces that support more fluid roles for them. There are several institutions in the community that could develop programs for expanding gender roles for men. In recognizing that many men will not seek assistance in traditional clinical settings, community centers can be an important place to engage men in confronting gender role conflict and stress (Lee, 2004).

One method employed by community centers is focus groups that utilize aspects of gender role conflict for points of discussion and process (Lee, 2004). Issues such as family roles and domestic violence can be discussed in a context that both recognizes the damaging effects of rigid masculine gender roles and traces their development throughout men's lives (Lee, 2004; Newton, 2005). The group format can provide a space that allows for **normalizing** the pain through support from others in the group. These groups work with boys as well as men with the hope of breaking early socialization of male dominance. Close to Home, a community domestic violence prevention program in Dorchester, Massachusetts, is an example of such a center. In addition to many programs, Close to Home runs groups with teen boys in the neighborhood to teach them about the links between sexism, racism, homophobia, and domestic violence. (www.c2home.org). Having these groups in the community emphasizes that confronting masculinity is something that should be done within our normal lives, as opposed to only within the context of clinical treatment (Lee, 2004).

Successful educational programs have also been implemented to assist men in challenging dominant gender scripts (O'Neil, 1996; Stoltz, 2005). O'Neil's **gender role journey workshop** is an example of such a program (O'Neil, 1996). The workshop takes place in an informal setting and combines traditional aspects of an educational environment, such as lecture and readings, with therapeutic interventions (O'Neil, 1996). The intent of these workshops is to help people (regardless of gender) understand how gender role conflicts have constrained people's lives. The workshops, incorporating both cognitive and emotional work, hope to make people more aware of their beliefs and emotions as they relate to gender roles (O'Neil, 1996). "Sexism is assumed to be a form of psychopathology that is dangerous and delusional. Healing alliances between men and women can be created if safe group environments are developed for both intellectual and emotional dialogues" (O'Neil, 1996, p. 195). Educational workshops akin to community groups also stress that this kind of work should be incorporated into our regular lives (O'Neil, 1996; Stoltz, 2005).

Research supports the contention that men and others can help men overcome the restrictions of a rigid gender role (Kearney, Rochlen, & King, 2004; McKelley & Rochlen, 2007). While these changes could occur in a clinical or community center, they don't have to take place in a formal setting. For example, Spencer (2006) found that in male youth mentoring relationships, men who are able to challenge dominant norms of masculinity (particularly in embracing emotional connectedness) assisted boys in feeling safe and more able to find a way to integrate expressiveness with their own sense of masculinity. These mentoring relationships, often centered around activities, can challenge dominant masculinity on the basketball court, at a movie, or while making dinner together.

Overall, the psychosocial approach argues that we need structural support to engage men and to praise them when they take risks to incorporate and express themselves in ways that are associated with femininity (Pollack, 1998; Stoltz, 2005). This has been a controversial request, as some would see it as ridiculous to praise men for doing things they should be doing (spending time with their children, communicating with others, seeking help, etc.). However, if men have difficulty doing this and do not receive any reinforcement for doing so, they essentially have no incentive for changing their rigid roles (Pollack, 1995, 1998). The psychosocial perspective argues that we must work toward integrating programs in all aspects of culture that will challenge men to endorse characteristics associated with femininity while simultaneously supporting them and recognizing their efforts towards change (Pollack, 1998).

Summary

This chapter reviews the psychosocial view for understanding the crisis of masculinity. Those that adhere to this perspective see a problem that begins with the rigid and unrealistic social and interpersonal expectations of men. Due to our ways of viewing boys and men, we strip them of all the qualities they need to be adaptable, form relationships and cope with life's changes. We essentially defeminize men. From the psychosocial view, in contrast to the essentialist view, it is the *lack* of incorporating characteristics associated with femininity that is the root of their problems.

The solution is largely aimed at assisting men in seeing this problem and learning how to reincorporate those qualities we view as feminine into their lives. This view also suggests that we revisit current child rearing practices. As suggested in the chapter, many people involved in boys' lives collude to deny them characteristics associated with femininity, which results in men who lack aspects of their human potential. The psychosocial view suggests that we need to keep pushing for social changes that promote equity in the culture in addition to those changes that will promote femininity in men.

The next chapter of this text will review the social constructionist perspective on the crisis of masculinity. It shares some assumptions with the psychosocial view but also emphasizes other issues that are seen to be the root of the masculinity crisis. These different assumptions about the cause will also suggest different interventions to resolve this crisis.

Review and Questions to Ponder

1. What does the psychosocial perspective have in common with the essentialist perspective?
2. How does the psychosocial perspective differ from the essentialist perspective?
3. What is the male role strain paradigm?
4. What is the difference between the real and ideal self?
5. How does that difference (above) connect to our study of masculinities?
6. What is the basic argument from the psychosocial perspective as to the reason for the masculinity crisis?
7. What is gender role discrepancy? Can you give examples of it?
8. What is gender role trauma? Can you give examples of it?
9. How does the socialization process contribute to gender role trauma?

10. What is the boy code? Masculinity scripts? Can you give examples of them?
11. What is the fragile masculine self?
12. What is normative male alexithymia?
13. What is male relational dread?
14. What is gender role conflict?
15. Why is traditional fatherhood seen as a potential conflict with dominant masculinity?
16. What areas do O'Neil and colleagues cite as potential sources for conflict?
17. What might be difficult in working with men to confront problems with masculinity?
18. Why do you think trust is such an important issue when working with men on issues of masculinity?
19. What is SPSMM? What are its goals?
20. What is AMSA? What are its goals?
21. Why are groups seen as potential places to help men with masculinity?
22. What advantages does a community center have in reaching men?
23. What is the gender role journey workshop? How does it help men (and women)?

The Crisis in Masculinity

Social Constructionist Perspective

The previous chapter summarized the psychosocial perspective on the crisis in masculinity. As you will recall, this perspective views the crisis of masculinity as occurring due to the conflict between what the culture expects from men and the actual lived lives of men. This view purports that men are experiencing problems in the world because various representatives of culture essentially strip boys and men of aspects of themselves that are seen as feminine, making them less able to respond adaptively in ever-changing cultures. These cultures then expect men to conform to unrealistic expectations about what it means to be a man (which often means neglecting characteristics associated with being feminine). Because of these harmful expectations and behaviors toward men, they have a variety of problems that they are ill-equipped to handle.

The Social Constructionist Explanation

This chapter reviews the social constructionist perspective on the crisis of masculinity. It shares some assumptions with the sociocultural view, but also emphasizes other issues that are seen to be at the root of the masculinity crisis. These different assumptions about the root causes will also suggest different interventions to resolve the masculinity crisis.

The social constructionist approach has much in common with the sociocultural approach for explaining the current crisis in masculinity. The social constructionist approach recognizes (a) social and historical changes and their effects on men's lives, (b) rigid gender roles and the

Power approach (handwritten in left margin)

adherence to gender role norms as a problem for men, and (c) the mother wound and denial of femininity by men as a source of problems (Kimmel & Kaufman, 1995). In addition, the rejection of essentialism is a cornerstone of the social constructionist approach (Connell, 2005; Kimmel & Kaufman, 1995). What makes this approach different from the sociocultural approach is its emphasis of addressing power and how power relates to essentialism, gender roles, and domination, all of which makes this type of analysis akin to radical feminism (Connell, 2005; Kimmel & Kaufman, 1995).

> My approach to social change is based on the relational perspective on masculinity. Relations of hegemony reflect and produce a social dynamic: struggles for resources and power, processes of exclusion and incorporation, splitting and reconstitution of gender forms. To understand this dynamic is to explore the crisis tendencies of the gender order as a whole (Connell, 2005, p. 736).

To understand the gender order and current cause of this crisis from the social constructionist approach, we must first explore the relevant history of masculinity. Much of the analysis in this section comes from renowned scholar Michael Kimmel, a Sociologist at the State University of New York at Stony Brook and official spokesperson of the National Organization for Men Against Sexism (Fox, 2004).

Who's Who in Masculinities Research: Michael Kimmel, Ph.D

Michael Kimmel is a sociologist, author, and researcher at the State University of New York at Stony Brook and official spokesperson of the National Organization for Men Against Sexism. Kimmel's work on masculinity has been described as groundbreaking and transformative. He has written several influential texts, including *Manhood in America: A Cultural History*.

Website: http://www.sunysb.edu/sociology/faculty/Kimmel/contactinfo.htm.

History with Masculinity

The term "crisis" has been described as a cliché by advocates of this view (Kimmel & Kaufman, 1995). This is partially due to the popular media capitalizing on this term to churn out self-help books and advice columns which purportedly deal with the crisis (Kimmel & Kaufman, 1995). But it is also because most people seem to be uninformed about past "crises" in various cultures throughout time and the current economic and historical changes that have affected masculinity (Kimmel & Kaufman, 1995). This ignorance has resulted in the avocation of essentialism and the blaming of women for faulty social systems designed and implemented by men (Connell, 2005; Kimmel & Kaufman, 1995).

As stated, masculinity can be viewed as having been in crisis in various cultures throughout the world in different stages of their history and development (Guest, 2007; Hastings, 2008). The masculinity crisis of the past 30 years typically refers to masculinity as it exists in industrialized nations, without necessarily making that information explicit. There is also an assumption that masculinity has been on some kind of trajectory of normalcy prior to this current crisis. This is in fact argued to be in error (Kimmel & Kaufman, 1995). As an illustration of understanding the social constructionist approach to this crisis, we turn to a brief historical overview of modern masculinity as it has taken place in the United States.

At the turn of the twentieth century, within 50 years of the Civil War, the majority of men went from predominantly owning and controlling their means of work to working outside the home for someone else (Kimmel & Kaufman, 1995). In addition, freed slaves, new immigrants from Europe, and women were moving into institutions in unprecedented ways (Kimmel & Kaufman, 1995; White, 2006). With the **abolitionist movement** and **suffrage movement** in the earlier part of the century, the world of men was beginning to shift (Kimmel & Kaufman, 1995; Rickabaugh, 1994). This change was not welcomed by many Americans (Kimmel & Kaufman, 1995). Many resisted women's and people of color's attempts to have equal access and representation in the culture (Kimmel & Kaufman, 1995). Power was threatened

The country reacted by arguing for essential differences between men and women that often had religious overtones (Kimmel, 1995; Kimmel & Kaufman, 1995). In fact, the **Muscular Christianity Movement** started campaigns during this era to change the image of Jesus from a soft, gentle man to a strong, virile, and muscular man (Kimmel & Kaufman, 1995). A variety of programs and interventions also resulted to separate boys from girls (and men from women) in order to protect men from being "feminized." Educational systems began to develop brochures and child rearing manuals to ensure that boys were treated like "boys" (Kimmel, 1995). This form of propaganda continued into the 1950s and beyond, taking advantage of newer technologies with advertisements on television and preceding feature films to remind its audience what being masculine meant. These themes, of course, continued in the actual themes of the entertainment programs and within the institutions themselves (Kimmel, 1995; Kimmel & Kaufman, 1995).

The revitalization of organizations for boys such as the Young Men's Christian Association (YMCA) and the creation of the Boy's Brigades, Knights of King Arthur and the Boy Scouts all served to reinforce dominant masculinity (Kimmel, 1995; Kimmel & Kaufman, 1995). Men's organizations also flourished with the rise of the lodge and male fraternity designed to organize against the "feminization" of men (Kimmel, 1995; Kimmel & Kaufman, 1995; Lyman, 2004). According to Ernest Thompson Seton (1910), founder of the Boy Scouts, women were turning "robust, manly, self-reliant boyhood into a lot of flat chested cigarette smokers with shaky nerves and doubtful vitality." (quoted by Kimmel & Kaufman, 1995, p. 34). Tensions between men and women were prevalent at the turn of the century, as men often complained about having relationships with women who they described as too controlling and dominant, particularly in their adherence to moral values (Dubbert, 1974). Ironically, these women were raised with their own fathers' **Victorian values**, which conflicted with the desires of many men of their own "modern" generation (Dubbert, 1974).

Since that time, as discussed previously, the economy in the US continued to shift. The US moved from an economic atmosphere in which individuals with specific crafts and skills produced products to trade with others to one in which people (mostly men) competed with one another over largely intangible services. This has decreased men's autonomy and control over their work. "This century has witnessed a steady erosion of economic autonomy; from 90 percent of United States men who owned their shop or farm at the time of the Civil War to less than 1 out of 10 today" (Kimmel & Kaufman, 1995, p. 17). By the 1950s, the cultural landscape emphasized masculinity as almost purely related to production, whereas in the past part of being masculine was connected to one's faith and connection to others (Dubbert, 1974).

In the last 50 years, this trend has been coupled with increasing corporate behavior that neglects the human needs of its employees, seeking to maximize profit at the cost of people's needs. Today, many companies constantly downsize, change policies, move plants to maximize profits and maintain their often bimodal distributions of wealth. Corporate greed, while certainly nothing new, seems to be the order of the day in the twenty-first century (Dobbs, 2004; Jett, 2002; Porter, 2004).

The concerns and reactions to changes in the culture in the early part of the twentieth century seem quite parallel to those of the latter part. The focus on essentialism and the creation of modern "male only" activities also seem to be parallel solutions to the crisis of masculinity. Interestingly, the most vociferous advocates of essentialism and men's separation to reclaim masculinity have been White, heterosexual, upper-middle-class men (Connell, 1992, 2005; Kimmel & Kaufman, 1995; Levant, 1997). Why would these men in particular be so angry about these social changes and so invested in holding onto dominant masculinity?

The Problem

According to the social constructionist approach, based in a radical feminist concern, the problem that men are experiencing is the slow deterioration of patriarchy and patriarchal privilege (Connell, 1992, 2005; Kimmel & Kaufman, 1995; Nye, 2005). They are experiencing less access to something that they believed was within their natural right to define, dominate, and control (Connell, 1992; 2005; Kimmel & Kaufman, 1995; Levant, 1997; Pease, 2000; White, 2001a). The experience of powerlessness, confusion, and alienation men experience around masculinity is not merely the result of a rigid gender role, but also a result of a firm belief in male privilege, which most men are often unaware of and unwilling to relinquish (Connell, 2005; Johnson, 1997; Levant, 1997; Pease, 2000; White, 2001a).

One of the main problems for men in acknowledging their male privilege is confusing normal day-to-day feelings of powerlessness while belonging to a social group that is powerful (Johnson, 1997; Kimmel, 1995; Levant, 1997; White, 2001a). For example, some members of the men's movement often blame women for making men feel powerless (Farrell, 1994; Kipnis, 1995). As discussed by Kimmel (1995), the metaphor sometimes used by these men is "the chauffeur" derived by anti-feminist Warren Farrell (1994). The metaphor goes something like this: The different social positions of men and women can be understood by imagining a car driven by a chauffeur. Men are viewed as the chauffeur, with the outfit, access to keys, and job to drive a car. Because they are in the front seat driving, it appears that they are in control of the car. However, someone else sits in the back seat giving them directions. The person in the back seat is a woman. According to this perspective, men appear to be in control but are actually not; behind these men, women actually pull the strings (Farrell, 1994).

According to the social constructionist approach, this type of analysis misses is the larger social structure. Who has been given access to jobs, money, education, etc. to purchase cars? Did women prevent men from getting college educations, voting, buying property, marrying, accumulating wealth, etc.? In other words, if someone is in the position of buying a car and hiring a chauffeur, it is likely that person is also a man (Kimmel, 1995). And if the social structure is preventing men from equality, then it is men who are largely responsible for that problem. "Men's pain is caused by men's power. Would we say the unhappiness of White people was caused by Black people's power?" What else could it be? The pains and sexual problems of heterosexuals were caused by gays and lesbians?" (Kimmel, 1995, p. 366). It is very much the case that many individual men are not powerful and struggle with feelings of powerlessness. But that does not mean that the source of their powerlessness is women. In fact, it's patriarchy (Connell, 1992, 2001, 2005; Kimmel, 1995; Levant, 1997).

Essentialists often cite the crisis in men (data as presented in chapter eight of this text) of a matriarchal culture (Kipnis, 1995). In other words, if our culture is patriarchal, why are men hurt so much by it? Shouldn't men be benefiting by a system that they rule? As discussed in chapter one, from a social constructionist approach, the answer is that men receive both benefits and pain from patriarchy (Connell, 2005; Levant, 1997).

Hegemonic masculinity results in a minority of men who can aspire to the dominant sphere by excluding women and other marginalized and subjugated men from participating equally in the culture. These men struggle with the pressure of having to maintain that dominance (stress, overworking, physical problems, etc.). Other men suffer from trying to achieve dominance and being unable to because of structures built into the system. These men then internalize their "failures" as having to do with being "less than men." The system of patriarchy, while benefiting men by giving some men access to certain kinds of opportunities, ultimately destroys men (Connell, 2005; Johnson, 1997; Levant, 1997; MacInnes, 2001; Stoltenberg, 1989).

The term **masculine mystique**, borrowed from the famous term **feminine mystique** of the activist and author Betty Friedan (1963), has been used to explain this phenomenon. The masculine mystique is seen as a front that men put up by giving up their femininity (expression and emotion) in order to maintain positions of power (Good , Borst & Wallace, 1994; Miedzian, 1991; O'Neil, 1981, Robertson & Fitzgerald, 1992; Sattel, 1989). While similar to sociocultural perspectives on a rigid gender role, the social constructionist approach emphasizes that this rigidity serves to maintain power and patriarchy.

In summary, according to the social constructionist approach, male-identified people's current problems are a result of privilege over others. Privilege results in problems for those few who are able to maintain dominant masculinity due to the physical, emotional and psychological sacrifices necessary to maintain that power. It also hurts men who believe they should be able to maintain dominance and yet for a variety of reasons cannot, internalize those perceived failures, and have to deal with the ensuing pain (Kaura & Allen, 2004; MacInnes, 2001; Mahalik, Good, & Englar-Carlson, 2003; Silverstein & Rashbaum, 1994).

Solutions

Influenced by radical feminist theory, the social constructionist approach conceives that patriarchy is the overarching problem that contributes to men's experiences of pain around masculinity. In order to solve this problem, men must contribute to the dismantling of patriarchy by supporting efforts that achieve equality for women and marginalized and subjugated men. For this reason, proponents of this perspective are actively in opposition to groups that reinforce essentialism. Social constructionists and radical feminists have been particularly critical of aspects of the men's movement and mythopoetic perspectives that are anti-feminist and essentialist in their writings (see Carey, 1996; Jefferson, 2002; Whitehead, 2001). The social constructionist approach provides a number of alternatives to addressing patriarchy.

Deconstructing

The first step in addressing problems associated with masculinity is critically deconstructing masculinity and its "problems." In other words, it is important to see how the way we define and understand problems set us up for the ways in which we solve them (Whitehead, 2001). This deconstructing is discussed here in three primary ways: Definitions of masculinity, definitions of relationships, and research methods.

Masculinities   A major focus of the social constructionist approach in studying this area is on emphasizing masculinities rather than masculinity (Messner, 2004; Wetherell & Edley, 1999). This is both a form of research methodology and a form of activism. It is a form of research methodology because it allows researchers to view the various possibilities of manhood that exist and to understand them all as legitimate perspectives on what it is like to be a man. Allowing for multiple perspectives enables people to view gay men, straight men, transgendered men, Native men, Latino men, intersexed men, etc. as having unique aspects and also something that ties them together in their identities as men. The study of *masculinity* assumes that there is *a* way to be masculine and a way *not* to be masculine, which might cause scholars to miss various human experiences or pathologize those that don't meet authorities' and experts' current sociocultural criteria for manhood (Messner, 2004; Whitehead, 2001).

Advocating for masculinities is a form of activism because multiple masculinities counter an essentialist perspective and the patriarchal assumptions on which essentialism is based. By realizing that there is no one way to be a man and that the dominant masculinity that men aspire to is associated with all kinds of problems, we can move on to rethinking what masculinities can look like without dominance (Messner, 2004; Nye, 2005; White, 2001a, 2001b). At the heart of the masculinities perspectives is a questioning of the typically binary and homogenous way we think about gender. There have been three primary groupings of people doing this initial questioning of traditional ways of understanding masculinity: gay liberation, transgender communities, and queer communities.

One of the first organized groups of men to challenge the dominant view of masculinity was what has been come to be known as the gay liberation movement (Brooks & Levant, 1999). The first incarnation of this movement, the Mattachine society, was named after medieval-Renaissance French folk dance societies that often explored and critiqued binary gender identity through costume and dance (Newton, 2005).

The society was started by Harry Hay in the early 1950's (Newton, 2005). Hay identified himself as a communist and gay man and spent much of his life making connections between his own struggles with identity in a heterosexist climate and others' struggles with other types of political and social freedoms (Newton, 2005).

Hay's influence in the society emphasized two crucial elements consistent with a social constructionist approach. First, he questioned the very nature of masculinity and what it means to be a man (Newton, 2005). The Mattachine society often embraced qualities associated with femininity and emphasized that possessing these qualities makes you a *different* kind of man. Hay argued that there are many different kinds of men and, questioned the use of the term "men" as a useful catch-all in the first place (Newton, 2005).

In addition, Hay reasoned for making the connection between the stigmatization of gay men and the oppression of women. Hay envisioned a movement that would bring together women, straight men, and gay men to end male domination. "Male chauvinism," Hay wrote in 1970, during the early days of the women's movement, "was a perversion of the social order that gay men had experienced alongside women." (Newton, 2005, p. 86). Throughout the 1960s and 1970s and up to the present time, gay men (at times, alongside other genders) continued a movement that challenged dominant masculinity (Brooks & Levant, 1999; Newton, 2005).

Transgender writers and activists like Riki Wilchins, Alan Sinfield and Judith Lorber have also been at the forefront of an approach consistent with social constructionism and the questioning of definitions of dominance (Burdge, 2007; Drescher, 2002; Mills, 2006). The term "transgender" has been generally understood as an umbrella term that refers to the discrepancies between the socially expected behaviors presumably linked to a person's biological sex and one's unique understanding of one's gender identity (Broad, 2002; Burdge, 2007; Cochran, Stewart, Ginzler, & Cauce, 2002; Ellis & Eriksen, 2002; Gainor, 2000; Harley, Nowak, Gassaway, & Savage, 2002; Wilchins, 1997). In other words, people who identify as being transgendered do not adhere to significant characteristics/roles/behaviors associated with their biological sex (Ellis & Eriksen, 2002; Gainor, 2000; Harley et al., 2002; Wilchins, 1997).

Transgender writing and analysis raises the fundamental question regarding what gender actually *is* and whether categorizing human behavior by this construct is even possible (Broad, 2002; Burdge, 2007; Roen, 2002; Stryker, 2008; Wilchins, 1997). Discussions in this realm are quite consistent with a social constructionist approach, in that they question the very definitions of what is being studied.

Queer identity reflects a similar theme, but can also reflect experiences of individuals who view themselves as having multiple genders, no gender, a shifting gender identity or a unique queered identity (Mills, 2006; Sedgwick, 1993; Slagle, 1995). Being queer includes "the open mesh of possibilities, gaps, overlaps, dissonances and resonances, lapses and excesses of meaning [that occur] when the constituent elements of anyone's gender, of anyone's sexuality aren't made (or can't be made) to signify monolithically" (Sedgwick, 1993, p. 8). This radical understanding of what gender is (or isn't) has had a profound impact on those studying masculinities in that it has raised questions about all of the assumptions that go into this work (Burdge, 2007; Roughgarden, 2004; Slagle, 1995; Stryker, 2008; Thomas, 2000). It has even caused much discussion and debate within gay- and lesbian-focused organizations, since definitions and agendas for political change between these groups do not always coincide (Stryker, 2008).

The on-going and current political activism of transgender and queer organizations such as GenderPAC, the National Center for Transgender Equality, Queer Nation, the International Foundation for Gender Education, Queer is Here and FTM International, have also been a driving force in this exploration (Drescher, 2002; Stryker, 2008; Wenzel, 2007). By making people aware of the unique struggles of transgender communities, the legalized discriminatory practices that affect transgender and queer folks, and by questioning the very definitions of gender, gender identity, and gender expression, transgender and queer perspectives have offered much to the social constructionist approach (Burdge, 2007).

Relationships   In addition to deconstructing the concept of masculinity, it is important to deconstruct the relationships in which men are involved. For example, the introduction to this chapter discussed the role of people in families and the difficulties that families endure when members are disengaged from their children in various ways. The undertone of that discussion is heterosexist, as it assumes that couples are heterosexual and of two distinct genders and that there is some inherent connection between young boys and male role models. In fact, human history provides us examples of cultures throughout the world that have raised children in a variety of ways, many of which include children being raised by non-genetic family members, multiple adults, and other types of configurations (DeLoache & Gottlieb, 2000; Maital & Bornstein, 2003).

Making Connections: Constructing a Family

The Amish in America and the Kibbutzim in Israel offer us examples of communal childrearing practices in contrast to dominant practices in many Western countries (DeLoache & Gottlieb, 2000; Maital & Bornstein, 2003). It is important when having discussions about child-rearing to remember that these practices vary in different countries and have changed over time. It seems clear that children need consistent and loving adults in their lives to depend on and recognize their self-worth, but that can be accomplished in a variety of ways.

In the last ten years, with political changes such as the legalization of marriage for LGBT couples in the Netherlands, Belgium, Spain, Sweden, the UK, and parts of the US and changing social attitudes, gay men and women have been becoming parents in larger proportions (Hicks, 2005; Pawelski et al., 2006). It is important to note that, while LGBT-identified couples struggle with similar issues to heterosexual couples (communication issues, setting boundaries/limits, how/when to punish children), research does *not* support that children who have gay and lesbian parents have any more difficulty with negotiating gender than their peers who have heterosexual parents (Ciano-Boyce & Shelley-Sireci, 2002; Hicks, 2005; McCann & Delmonte, 2005; Pawelski et al., 2006). What families with gay-identified parent(s) *do* face uniquely include the different dynamics between gay men and gay women in relationships and the unfortunate continuing heterosexism and discrimination that results from not recognizing legal marriages between lesbian, gay, bisexual, and transgendered people (Hicks, 2005; McCann & Delmonte, 2005).

This is not to suggest that gay, lesbian, and transgendered parents won't have unique conflicts and human struggles (Ciano-Boyce & Shelley-Sireci, 2002; Clarke, 2002). It is only to reinforce the idea that,

Continued

242 *Chapter 11*

as we continue to deconstruct this crisis of masculinities, it is important to address the various kinds of relationships that people will be engaged in and understand how these relationships are affected by the social context in which they live.

Critical research

In addition to being critical of the definitions of what is studied, the social constructionist approach is also critical of research. While similar to the psychosocial approach in emphasizing data gathering in systematic ways, this approach takes a judicious view of the knowledge gathered.

What makes this perspective unique is its emphasis on the construction of knowledge and research that is critical of power and of those who represent knowledge. In other words, consistent with the social constructionist approach to understanding masculinity, a critical research approach applies the same concerns it has about the phenomena it studies to the people who do the research, the methods they use, and the conclusions they draw (Richmond, 2007).

Dr. Jeff Hearn, a Professor at the Swedish School of Economics, exemplifies this approach through his work in the Critical Research Network on Men in Europe (CROME). CROME is a research network that brings together transnational researchers of all genders who wish to study men and masculinity critically (see www.cromenet.org).

Who's Who in Masculinities Research: Jeff Hearn, Ph.D.

Dr. Jeff Hearn, Professor at the Swedish School of Economics, Helsinki, Finland, has been working with other European colleagues in creating and maintaining the Critical Research Network on men in Europe (CROME) over the last 10 years. CROME examines men as part of historical gender relations, through a wide variety of analytical and methodological tools and approaches. This work is documented in the text *European Perspectives on Men and Masculinities: National and Transnational Approaches* (co-edited with Keith Pringle).

Website: http://www.cromenet.org/[hearn@hanken.fi]

The first step a critical approach takes is to question the very nature of the construct one is studying (Hearn & Pringle, 2006; Richmond, 2007). Critical researchers assume that researchers will use different definitions of masculinity in their approaches and that issues of power, culture, and privilege will affect how they come to understand what masculinity is, who has access to it, and how it may lend itself to various human experiences (Hearn & Pringle, 2006).

CROME also emphasizes that work on men and masculinity must be done by a diverse group of scholars. "Research on men that draws only on the work of men is likely to neglect the very important research contribution that has been and is being made by women to research on men" (www.crome.net). This collaboration is argued to be necessary not only for the purposes of research but for the purposes of social activism and working toward the achievement of gender equity across the board (www.cromnet.org).

Finally, what sets a social constructionist approach apart, is the intent of utilizing research and knowledge for social action. CROME, for example, emphasizes addressing social policies, welfare practices, family structures, and work organizations that contribute to men's suffering and the gender inequality of women and others (Hearn & Pringle, 2006). It is through work in organizations such as CROME that people turn knowledge into action.

The social constructionist approach first sets itself apart by questioning the definitions of masculinities. In order to know how to address a crisis or whether a crisis exists, the first step is to be clear about what is actually being examined. A brief review of concerns of social constructionists on the definitions of masculinities, presumptions about relationships, and research reveals a perspective that is critical of every step in takes. This continues when considering how to respond to the crisis as well.

Individual work

In terms of taking action, it probably won't come as a surprise that there is less focus on individual work from the social constructionist approach, since the focus of the problem is dismantling patriarchy, which is a social system. However, there is an emphasis on working on patriarchal aspects of ourselves in our day to-day relationships with others (Holmes & Lundy, 1990; Pease, 2000).

Profeminist men suggest that individual therapy, men's groups, workshops, religious affiliations, and other kinds of activities can be useful in helping men get in touch with their own pain and using those experiences to help men develop empathy for others (Holmes & Lundy, 1990; Pease, 2000; Trute, 1998). The development of empathy should help men see how others have been affected by patriarchy and how they themselves have harmed others through benefiting from patriarchy (Holmes & Lundy, 1990; Pease, 2000; Poling, Grundy & Min, 2002). This process must also include teaching men what they have to gain by dismantling patriarchy (Holmes & Lundy, 1990; Kahn & Ferguson, in press; Whitehead, 2001).

Bob Pease, an Associate Professor of Social Work at RMIT University in Melbourne, Australia, has written about the need to deconstruct men's pains and frustrations in order to help men and empower them to help others. Men must first understand the consequences of their privilege toward women and others (Bartky, 1998; Pease, 2002). They must also develop empathy for marginalized others while simultaneously learning to differentiate between feelings of powerlessness that come from human struggles and those that come from entitled expectations (Bartky, 1998; Pease, 2000; 2002). In confronting this paradox, Pease (2002) suggests, "to encourage men to change their perception of what constitutes their self-interests is to be involved in the reconstitution of their social and personal identities" (p. 172). In addition, men must learn to truly express their pain to themselves and to others (Pease, 2000). This will help them transform themselves and ally with others (Pease, 2000). As Kevin Powell, poet and journalist, describes,

Who's Who in Masculinities Research: Bob Pease, MSW

Bob Pease is Chair of Social Work at Deakin University. He has published extensively in the fields of critical masculinity studies and critical social work practice. His current research focus is on men's violence against women and cross-cultural and global perspectives on men and masculinities. His most recent books are *International Encyclopedia of Men and Masculinities* (co-edited), *Critical Social Work Practice* (co-edited) and *Men and Gender Relations*. He is currently writing a book titled *Undoing Privilege* and co-editing a book titled *Migrant Masculinities*.

Email: bob.pease@deakin.edu.au.

I felt fragile, fragile as a bird with clipped wings, that day my ex-girlfriend stepped up her game and spoke back to me. Nothing in my self-definition prepared me for dealing with a woman as an equal . . . I am no hero. I am no saint. I remain a sexist male. But one who has been waging an internal war for several years . . . It is very lonely to swim against the stream of American male-centeredness, of black-man bravado and nut grabbing . . . I am ashamed of my ridiculously sexist life, of raising my hand to my girlfriend. But with that shame has come a consciousness, and as the activists said during the civil rights movement, this consciousness, is a river of no return. (Powell, 2000, p. 75–77).

Making Connections: The Position of Women

A male-identified colleague of mine sent me this example to illustrate how men can connect individual pain to other's suffering. My friend Bill was in the dining room of his family home with his father, mother, and his male friend, Tony. His father and Tony had engaged each other in some conversation about NASCAR auto-racing (or some subject that Bill was not particularly interested in or knowledgeable about). Bill began to get irritated as this carried on and on. He felt alienated and ignored.

In that moment, rather than focusing on his anger, he watched his mother. He saw how she tried to be involved in the conversation and, eventually, how she became resigned and went into the kitchen. He sat in that space wondering if at any point these two men, with their raised voices and factual explanations and demonstrations of overconfidence, would ever turn to him or to his mother to include them. They did not. He realized that the only way to enter this conversation was to adopt the same kinds of characteristics being displayed. In other words, he would have to act more confrontational, knowledgeable, factual, objective, etc. He would have to be a "man".

He also realized in this moment that he felt like a woman. For that moment, in that position, he could somewhat understand what it's like to be a woman from the position of patriarchy. His own feelings of displacement and alienation, anger, and confusion about how to be engaged may be similar to the feelings that women and marginalized others have multiple times throughout the day. While this experience is relatively innocuous, it is an example of recognizing how one's own pain caused by dominance can be linked to women and others.

In order to take on this challenge of transforming pain, John Stoltenberg, a well-known author and activist, has asked men to abandon masculinity and to literally "refuse to be a man" (Stoltenberg, 1989). Stoltenberg has been active in understanding men's violence against women, particularly as related to pornography and rape. His connecting of sexual identity with positions of power and politics have informed his views on interactions amongst people and provide some interesting and important insights on masculinity (Stoltenberg, 1989; Stoltenberg, 1993).

Who's Who in Masculinities Research: John Stoltenberg, M.F.A.

John Stoltenberg holds a Master of Divinity degree in Theology and Literature from Union Theological Seminary and an M.F.A. in Theater Arts from Columbia University School of the Arts. A long-time activist against sexual violence and philosopher of gender, John Stoltenberg is the author of *Refusing to Be a Man: Essays on Sex and Justice*, *The End of Manhood: Parables on Sex and Selfhood*, and *What Makes Pornography "Sexy"?*, as well as numerous articles and essays in anthologies. John conceived and creative-directs a media campaign based on the theme line "My strength is not for hurting." Widely recognized as the nation's best-designed and most effective public service advertising sexual-assault-prevention outreach to young men, media materials was creative-directed by www.mencanstoprape.org.

In his landmark text, *Refusing to Be a Man*, he answers the question "Why do men rape?" by drawing an analogy to acting (Stoltenberg, 1989). Stoltenberg claims that one theory of acting suggests that, in order to seem realistic, actors have to pretend (no matter the dialogue) that they are in fact the character (Stoltenberg, 1989). Rather than *playing* a part they need to *become* the part by believing that their perspective is simply truthful (whether playing a hero, villain, etc.). This becomes analogous to the male psyche.

The impersonation of male sexual identity in life bears several striking resemblances to the techniques by which an actor portrays a character . . . when men are held accountable for what they do in their lives to women, which happens very rarely, their tunnel vision, their obliviousness to consequences, their egotism, their willfulness, all tend to excuse, rather than compound, their most horrific interpersonal offenses. (Stoltenberg, 1989, p. 15–16)

To Stoltenberg, the only way to be truly human is to renounce masculinity, because by definition its existence depends on the subjugation of others.

Kahn and Ferguson (in press) suggest that any new insights men gain about patriarchy through individual work should be discussed and understood in a manner that minimizes paralysis of **agency**. Unfortunately, insights about patriarchy's insidious grip on one's life can lead to a painful paralysis of agency for men, which can result in men disengaging from activities and support of women or others. Similarly, insights about patriarchy can go to men's heads, as it were, manifesting as a mentality of superiority in relation to other men who are perceived as being *less* socially adept. Neither paralysis nor a "power-over" mentality are productive, according to a social constructionist approach, as they do not lead to social action and often reinforce dominance.

In addition to confronting and recognizing how privilege has served us, ultimately we must also be responsible enough to take social action, be willing to make some mistakes, be responsible for those mistakes, learn from them, make changes, and continue to work toward connecting with one another while working toward social justice (Kahn and Ferguson, in press, p. 8).

In fact, researchers are beginning to notice some differences in men who resist dominance and patriarchy. "Non-traditional men" are more likely to want children and less likely to divorce (Kaufman, 2000). They are more likely to communicate their emotions and to experience fewer relationship problems (Blazina & Watkins, 2000; Stake & Hoffman, 2000). And not surprisingly, the less traditionally masculine a man views himself, the more positive his views are toward feminism (Toller, Suter & Trautman, 2004). In fact, research has demonstrated that a profeminist identity differentiates profeminists from other leftist men, who claim to be progressive about issues that involve women, but who are typically actually no different than the norm (Kahn, 1981).

Political activism

The most powerful form of change, according to the social constructionist approach, comes from political activism, particularly the kind
of activism that supports women and all marginalized and subordinated men. It is argued that men must identify all spheres of their social
lives (educational, vocational, political, religious, families, etc.) and
work to promote equal access and choice in each sphere by all members
of humanity (Connell, 2005). Men must do so by allying themselves
with women and listening and learning from what women have
experienced in patriarchy. Men must go beyond their workshops and
individual therapy into the streets and advocate for equality (Connell,
2005; Johnson, 1997; Nye, 2005; Whitehead, 2001).

Allying

There are multiple ways in which men can be engaged in social actions
to work toward ending patriarchy. This chapter includes activism that
can be in the form of working toward egalitarian social policy and in
activities that challenge the status quo by allying with women.

Pushing for social policies that make the oppression of women illegal
is one form of activism that can contribute to this concern. For example,
The Violence Against Women Act (VAWA), written for women who
have been victims of violence, provides specific treatment and advocacy guidelines and support for resources such as shelter services,
housing, and legal services (Seelau, Seelau & Poorman, 2003). It also
provides funding for training for a variety of professionals involved
with the welfare of women and children (Seelau et al., 2003). Men's
groups such as Men's Resources International actively sought to get
men to sign the act in order to pledge themselves to end violence
against women (Men's Resources International, 2005). Because patriarchy is viewed as the problem, any behavior that can address men's
power over women can assist in changing patriarchy. While this act
does not change the system in which these behaviors develop, by
involving men and recognizing men's power over women, it can be
viewed as a type of **ally activism**.

There are many forms of ally activism. An ally can be defined as "a
member of the 'dominant group' or 'majority group' who works to end
oppression in his or her personal and professional life through support
of and as an advocate with and for the oppressed population" (Fabiano,
Wesley, Berkowitz, & Linkenbach 2003, p. 106). Much ally work focuses

on issues of violence against women due to the severe problem that violence against women presents internationally.

While there are many organizations dedicated to this issue, the White Ribbon Campaign is perhaps the most well known ally campaign. It began in Montreal, Canada after the **Montreal massacre**, in which fourteen women were brutally killed and nine women and four men were injured by Marc Lépine in 1991 (Flood, 2001; Hearn, 2001; Odendaal, 2001; Rosenberg, 2003). After the rampage, he ended his own life. In his suicide note, he claimed his suicide would be for political reasons. "Because I have decided to send the feminists who ruined my life, to their maker" (Rosenberg, 2003, p. 4).

This shocking act and claim precipitated an "activist-memorial response" (Rosenberg, 2003, p. 7). The White Ribbon Campaign is an international movement described as "the first large scale male protest against violence in the world." (Flood, 2001, p. 43). The campaign includes participants in Canada, the USA, Africa, Europe, Australia and Asia. Men are encouraged to wear white ribbons and dedicate themselves to ending violence against women, raising money for women's shelters, and educating and working with others to end violence (Flood, 2001; Hearn, 2001).

Other examples of ally programs include the Mentors in Violence Prevention Program (Katz, 1995), Men Overcoming Violence (Flood, 2001; Lingard & Douglas, 1999), Men Against Violence, Men Against Sexual Violence (Lingard & Douglas, 1999), Men Against Sexual Assault (Lingard & Douglas, 1999), Men Stopping Violence, Men's Rape Prevention Project, Men Can Stop Rape, and the Men's Resource Center for Change (formerly the Men's Resource Center) (Flood, 2001) (see table 11.1). These programs attempt to ally with women and marginalized men to address men's power and patriarchy and ultimately to empower one another to end these forms of dominance through profeminist activism and education (Adams, 1988; Choate, 2003; Fabiano et al., 2003; Flood, 2001; Hearn, 2001).

As introduced in the last chapter, one of the best-known ally activist organizations in the United States that advocates for this view is the National Organization for Men Against Sexism (NOMAS). In addition to a national membership, NOMAS has local chapters in areas like California, Colorado, Georgia, Illinois, Ohio, Massachusetts, New Jersey and New York (NOMAS, 2005). While branches exist in several states, overall membership has been declining over the years (Fox, 2004). The reasons for declining membership may be due to the

Table 11.1: Feminist Men and Ally Organizations

Title	URL/Contact
A Call to Men: National Association of Men and Women Committed to Ending Violence Against Women	http://www.acalltomen.com/
All Men Are Sons	http://allmenaresons.com/
American Men's Studies Association	http://www.mensstudies.org/
Centro Bartolome de las Casas	http://www.centrolascasas.org
Coaching boys into Men	http://endabuse.org/programs/ display.php3?DocID=9916
Dads and Daughters	http://www.dadsanddaughters.org
Emerge	http://www.emergedv.com/
European Men Profeminist Network	http://www.europrofem.org
Founding Fathers	http://www.founding-fathers.org/
Gay Men's Domestic Violence Project	http://www.gmdvp.org
Gloucester Men Against Domestic Abuse	http://www.strongmendontbully.com/
International Society for Men's Health and Gender	http://www.ismh.org
Karelian Centre for Gender Studies	http://www.owl.ru/eng/women/ aiwo/karelia.htm
Mad Dads	http://www.maddads.com/
Mainely Men Against Violence & Sexism	http://www.mmavs.org/home
Male Survivor	http://www.malesurvivor.org/
Men Against Sexual Assault	http://www.borderlands.org.au/masa/
Men Against Sexual Violence	http://www.menagainstsexualviolence. org
Men Can Stop Rape	http://www.mencanstoprape.org
Men Ending Violence	http://www.vahealth.org/civp/ sexualviolence/menendingviolence/ index.html

Table 11.1: *Continued*

Title	URL/Contact
Men for Change	http://www.chebucto.ns.ca/ CommunitySupport/Men4Change/ index.htm
Men for HAWC	http://www.danverspolice.com/ domviol9.htm
Men Stopping Rape	http://danenet.wicip.org/msr/
Men Stopping Violence	http://www.menstoppingviolence.org/ index.php
Meninist	http://www.feminist.com/resources/ links/men.htm
Men's Health Network	http://www.menshealthnetwork.org/
Men's Initiative for Jane Doe Inc.	http://www.mijd.org
Men's Network Against Domestic Violence	http://www.mcnagainstdv.org/
Men's Resource Center	http://www.mrcforchange.org
Men's Resources International	http://www. mensresourcesinternational.org
Mentors in Violence Prevention	http://www.sportinsociety.org/mvp/
Montreal Men Against Sexism	c/o Martin Dufresne 913 de Bienville Montreal, QC H2J 1V2
MVP Strategies	http://www.jacksonkatz.com/mvp. html
National Organization for Men Against Sexism	http://www.nomas.org
New Hampshire Tree (Trans Pride)	http://www.transpride.org/
NOMAS-Boston Chapter	http://www.nomasboston.org
NOMORE	http://www.nomorerape.org/
OneinFour	http://www.student.virginia.edu/ ~1in4/
RAVEN (Rape And Violence End Now)	7314 Manchester 2nd Floor St. Louis, MO 63143
The Campaign to End Homophobia	http://www.endhomophobia.org
Tulane Men Against Rape	http://www.tulane.edu/~tmar/
Twin Cities Men's Center	http://www.tcmc.org/index.html
White Ribbon Campaign	http://www.whiteribbon.com

isolation of feminist voices in academia and infighting within the organization (Clatterbaugh, 2000). Participating in NOMAS is also a difficult sell to men, since men are asked to explore their own role in participating in sexism, while recognizing their own negative experiences that have come of it, which is no easy task (Clatterbaugh, 2000).

Who's Who in Masculinities Research: Kenneth Clatterbaugh, Ph.D.

Kenneth Clatterbaugh is a Professor and Chair of Philosophy of the department at the University of Washington. He teaches and publishes in the areas of modern philosophy, social philosophy, and gender studies. He has written numerous articles on men and masculinities and is particularly known for work documenting the historical struggle of profeminist men.

Email: clatter@u.washington.edu.

NOMAS principles include four major tenets (NOMAS, 2004). The first is **profeminism**. This means that NOMAS members view themselves either as feminists or as being in support of feminist causes such as being pro-choice, against violence against women, and advocates for equal pay and equal access to cultural institutions (NOMAS, 2004). "[Profeminism] is a call from and to men to develop feminist and profeminist personal and political actions." (Brod, 1998, p. 208). The second tenet is gay affirmation. NOMAS members represent a variety of gender and sexual orientations and advocate for the equality of **gender expression** and multiple ways of being masculine. Fighting homo/**transphobia** and heterosexism are an important part of NOMAS' goals (NOMAS, 2004). In fact, the official adoption of this tenet in the late 1980s resulted in some members leaving NOMAS, suggesting that there is still much work to be done in the recognition of multiple masculinities and addressing homophobia (Mirandé, 2001). The third tenet is anti-racism and is one that connects NOMAS members to broader movements concerned with social justice (NOMAS, 2004). The recognition exists that marginalization happens at all levels and that racism has been a dominant system of oppression that marginalizes men of color (NOMAS, 2004). The last tenet is enhancing men's lives. This tenet charges NOMAS members in their work to enhance the lives of men in general, as well as the lives of the people in the organization (NOMAS, 2004).

Activities in which NOMAS members might participate include those of activist, community, and social natures. Activist activities in the past have included attending the March for Women's Lives in Washington, DC, equal marriage rallies, supporting the White Ribbon Campaign and raising money and awareness for women's shelters and organizations (NOMAS-Boston, 2005). Community/social activities are geared to connect members of NOMAS and the community together to bring them in relationship with one another. These activities could include movies, basketball games, lectures, or profeminist process groups around issues of privilege (NOMAS-Boston, 2005). NOMAS members challenge one another within the organization and in their own individual lives to address patriarchy in multiple, creative, and repeated ways.

New programs addressing patriarchy and domination are also beginning to emerge. One example of such an organization is Centro Bartolomé de las Casa (CBC) in San Salvador, El Salvador. The CBC trains community leaders (such as police, justices, organizers) in intensive workshops and activities to learn about the impact of patriarchy and dominant masculinity on relationships and communities (Hochachka, 2007). As reflective of many of the organizations above, the primary goal is to reduce and eliminate gender-based violence. The center utilizes several methodologies to empower men to move beyond the harmful effects of conditioned dominance (Hochachka, 2007).

> CBC's work goes all the way down to deal with the psychological trauma in the deeper layers of the psyche that show up in various layers of the body. And it goes all the way up: creating conditions in which individuals can form a healthy ego, build capacity, confidence and collaboration for community work, and transcend their egos in service of a wider identity, embrace and care. (p. 30)

There are multiple programs throughout the world that focus on ending violence and domination toward women and marginalized others. Not all of them identify themselves as feminist organizations nor do all explicitly identify patriarchy as the systemic organization that must change. However, the work that they do is committed to both personal and social changes that work towards equity and violence-free communities. While historically done primarily by women, over the last 30 years, the work is also being done by men and others who recognize that having male privilege means that an obligation exists to be in the service of others.

Men's Involvement: Divergent Views

On the face of it, it might seem that men being involved with these causes would generally be welcomed (especially by women). However, finding ways of allying and doing it well can be a difficult endeavor. In fact, some do not think men should be doing it at all. Concerns come primarily from two camps.

The first group that provides resistance is men. The majority of men seem to reject feminism as an ideology, although many endorse feminist attitudes (particularly liberal ones such as equal pay, non-discrimination in the workplace, etc.) (Kimmel, 1987; Pease, 2002). The most vociferous male voices seem to come from those who represent and aspire to dominant masculinity, men Kimmel (1998) calls "angry white men in training" who staunchly oppose men's involvement in feminism. This would be true of those essentialists who are self-proclaimed anti-feminists, who view men's pain as a function of domi-nance by women and being exploited in the culture.

The second source of resistance comes from feminist women who are divided on the issue (Clatterbaugh, 1997; Digby, 1998, Kimmel, 1998; Morra & Smith, 1993). A strong voice of resistance has come from academics involved with feminism (Digby, 1998, Kimmel, 1998; Morra & Smith, 1993). Some academic feminists have tended to oppose the infusion of profeminist men in the feminist movement.

There are several concerns voiced by feminists in regard to men's involvement. While not all are reviewed here, several of the most common in the literature are summarized here. The first concern is rooted in an assumption of the differences between men and women. Since men as a social group have been socialized into identities that are not only different from women's, but hostile to women and women's interests, how is it possible that they could understand women's concerns (Digby, 1998)? Since men cannot understand what it is like to *be a woman*, to some feminist women it makes no sense that they could *be feminists*, since feminism is an extension of an existence that men can never relate to (see Douglas, 1994; Schacht & Ewing, 1997).

If understanding women's experiences (at least from an intellectual perspective) *could* be achieved by some men, the question then becomes what could possibly motivate the privileged to give up their power (Digby, 1998)? Some women understandably are skeptical of privileged men who identify with, and advocate for, losing their privilege (Digby, 1998). Underlying such skepticism is the fear that men who adopt feminism do so for their own gain. Feminist men have been described as helping women only when it meets their own agenda, which ultimately is **androcentric** (Duelli Klein, 1983). For example, advocating for choice in birth control and other matters in relation to sexual freedom (concerns often advocated by women feminists) have been argued to be the most supported male agenda items, reflecting men's desires rather than women's interests (Dworkin, 1987). Women who have been working alongside men have noted men's self-interest and questioned their general motivations (Austin-Smith, 1992; Douglas, 1994; Duelli Klein, 1983; Dworkin, 1987).

And if men somehow achieved some sense of understanding and interest in relinquishing privilege, that does not mean that they *should* be given the ability to voice their concerns (see Morra & Smith, 1993). Some feminist women have compared the encouragement of men to join as allies in feminism to welcoming wolves into the sheep ranch (Duelli Klein, 1983). The concern is that men will do exactly what they have done in all other areas of human life: dominate, control, and push women out of positions of authority and leadership (Duelli Klein, 1983). To some women, it is fine if men want to be on the sidelines, but having a voice in feminism should be reserved for women. "In my view, there is no room for men in women's studies, none whatsoever" (Duelli Klein, 1983, p. 413).

These concerns are included here because they are legitimate. The issues raised by these authors represent areas that have been problematic in some settings. I have witnessed some of the problems expressed here and have likely participated in them. It is important to acknowledge these concerns as very real and potential ways that members of dominant groups can disrupt progress rather than ally with those concerns.

Despite these very real concerns, many women have embraced men and all genders for identifying with feminism (hooks, 2004; White, 2002). Feminists of all genders have suggested that men can be powerful allies as long as they are continually examining the role of privilege and how that might affect the work they do with others (Pease, 2002; Powell, 2000; Stoltenberg, 1989; White, 2002).

The women's movement has a long history of working alongside men and including men as allies. The National Organization for Women

(NOW), one of the best-known organizations advocating for women, has had men as members (and in leadership positions) from its inception (Forman, 2003; The Founding of NOW, 2008). What has been difficult for feminist women in this regard is the media's portrayal of feminism and feminists as being anti-men (Barnett, 2005).

Academic feminists have also sought to illuminate the important work that men are doing. Aaronette White, an Associate Professor of Women's Studies at University of California, Santa Cruz, has been both a scholar and advocate for profeminist men – profeminist Black men, in particular. She has written several articles exploring the meaning of profeminism for black men and the ways in which racial and gender identity can connect within men and serve as a form of empowering others (White, 2001a, 2001b, 2002, 2006). Her work in this area celebrates the voice of a community that is not always known to others – black men advocating for women and femininity.

Who's Who in Masculinities Research: Aaronette White, Ph.D.

Aaronette M. White, is a Associate Professor of Psychology at the University of California-Santa Cruz. She has written numerous articles on profeminist black men and has a forthcoming book on the life stories of black men active in the feminist movement titled *Ain't I A Feminist? African American Men Speak Out on Fatherhood, Friendship, Forgiveness, and Freedom.*

Email: aaronette.white@gmail.com.

Profeminist black men

In recent work to support and understand profeminist men, White (2002) sheds some light on the uniqueness of black profeminist men (White, 2002). Through qualitative interviews she located themes within their ideologies: stretching, blending, and transforming (White, 2002).

Stretching, the first profeminist identity theme, implies going beyond normal or ordinary limits. By definition, feminist men are non-conventional. Stretching captures this identity with recognition of being an "other" or a purposeful outsider (White, 2002). It is not just a question of differing attitudes or beliefs, but a difference in behavior and engagement with the world. "They [profeminist black men] stretch themselves as they develop the skills and values necessary to listen to women and accept how women define their reality" (White, 2002; p. 8). Stretching requires moving beyond what one is expected on multiple dimensions of the human experience to challenge expectations of dominant masculinity (Lemons, 1997; White, 2002).

This engagement often takes the form of personal ethics, values, and spirituality (Bordo, 1998; Whitehead, 2001; Youmans, 2004). While there is still much resistance within many mainstream religions to addressing issues that feminist men concern themselves with, there are spiritual communities that are profeminist and LGBTQ friendly. For example, Unitarian Universalist congregations have a history of supporting social justice and civil rights (Barol & Miller, 1988; Green, 2003).

Blending, the second profeminist identity theme, implies a combining into an integrated whole. As members of a historically oppressed group, black men have an opportunity to connect with marginalization in a unique way. Their identity as profeminist men is not just a reaction to coping with dominant masculinity and racism. "What distinguishes profeminist men from other men who also experience various forms of powerlessness and oppression but do not develop profeminist outlooks, is their progressive interpretation of their experiences and their ability to see how various forms of oppression interact and reinforce each other." (White, 2002, p. 16). Profeminist black men are not trying to be other men and not succeeding, they have their own legitimate masculinity (White, 2002). It is a blending of these experiences of marginalization with cultural and personal experiences that result in an activist black profeminist identity, one that sits well with womanism (Lemons, 1997).

In struggling with their role and place in profeminism, men work toward developing an interdependent style. Due to being aware of their paradoxical role as an ally and as a privileged member of culture, they attempt to blend independence with connection to others. This act causes many men anxiety and difficulty in finding that balance, but the struggle is also viewed as an aspect of their feminism (White, 2002).

> Most profeminist black men have to prove themselves to feminists and nonfeminists alike. That is, many people in our society are not used to the radical notions of manhood that profeminist men are choosing to explore, nor are they used to the radical notion that men, particularly black men, can be feminists. (White, 2002, p. 5).

The final profeminist identity theme is transforming, implying a change in character or condition. This theme suggests that profeminist men must change themselves and others. The first step according to White (2002) is practice. One of the most difficult struggles for profeminist black men (and perhaps feminist men in general) is to put feminism into practice (Lemons, 1997; White, 2002). However, to truly transform, men must participate in daily activities that will assist them as they develop feminist identities. Feminist men often understand feminism intellectually, prior to being able to live it in the world (White, 2002). Profeminist men transform their personal consciousness and work towards transforming the institutions in which they interact and live (White, 2002).

Profeminism for these men then becomes a commitment to marginalized others (White, 2002). Profeminism, to many men, seems to be an ethical system or guide to living an authentic and genuine life. The ethics for many of these men seem to require an attention to social justice as a whole in connecting the many types of oppressions that exist within diverse cultures (Lemons, 1997; White, 2002).

White's research is, of course, just one example of the embracing of profeminist men's work by other genders. In my own experience doing this kind of work, I have met with very little resistance from others and much encouragement. The majority of people I have had interactions with have been incredibly supportive and encouraging, and have been wonderful influences on me and my own work. The stereotype of feminists (and especially of radical feminists) of being cold, distant, and "men hating" has not had any merit in my engagement in this work. In *all* social groups there are people who express themselves with anger and fury. Sometimes that fury is warranted because of injustice and sometimes that fury represents their own pain and difficulties. Feminists are no different in this regard. Overall I have been fortunate to have been welcomed in several feminist communities. I am very thankful to the feminist women who have had a profound influence on me (and the writing of this text).

Summary and Integration

This chapter reviewed the social constructionist view for the crisis in masculinity, which focuses on men's entitlement and privilege as the primary source of men's problematic behaviors. As the world has been moving in more gender equitable directions, men as a social group have had a hard time letting go of their entitlement. Problems men face are often the result of their anger and frustration as they attempt to maintain their power and privilege over women.

The solution to the masculinity crisis from social constructionist approach is to continue to work towards equity and justice. Men who have become aware of this problem have an obligation to work alongside other genders to end forms of systematic exclusion of women and femininity. Men also have an obligation to examine the ways in which this entitlement has affected their lives and relationships, take responsibility for it and change it. Though divergent views regarding men's involvement with feminism exist, dismantling patriarchy and addressing any "masculinity crisis" ultimately requires men to adopt a pro-feminist ideology and work towards social justice.

Review and Questions to Ponder

1. What are the major concerns of men being involved with feminism?
2. How is the social constructionist approach (social constructionist approach) similar to the sociocultural?
3. How is the social constructionist approach different?
4. What do social constructionists mean when they say that masculinity crises have existed in various cultures at various times?
5. How was the crisis of masculinity at the turn of the twentieth century similar to the one described in this chapter?
6. How was the crisis of masculinity at the turn of the twentieth different from today?
7. Why does the social constructionist approach think it is important to discuss this previous crisis?
8. How does the social constructionist approach criticize the essentialist perspective on this crisis?
9. What is the masculine mystique? Can you think of examples of this?
10. How does the social constructionist approach deconstruct the crisis? (Three primary ways.)
11. How does work in gay liberation, transgender and queer activism add to the work of a social constructionist approach?

12. How does recognizing diverse family configurations coincide with the social constructionist approach? Can you think of other examples not given in this chapter?
13. What is critical research?
14. What is CROME? What are its goals?
15. What kind of individual work does the social constructionist approach advocate for?
16. What were Pease's suggestions for men?
17. What did Stoltenberg mean when suggesting that men should refuse to be men? Do you think that is a good strategy? Why or why not?
18. What were Kahn's and Ferguson's suggestions for men?
19. What kind of political/community work does social constructionist approach advocate for?
20. What is ally activism?
21. What is VAWA?
22. What is the Montreal massacre and white ribbon campaign?
23. What are groups that would fit into ally activism? What is NOMAS? How does it address this crisis?
24. What is the CBC? Are you aware of other organizations like it in your area? What is unique to the identities of profeminist black men? How might this uniqueness extend itself to other communities (gay, queer, Latino, etc.)?
25. What are some men's concerns with the social constructionist approach and men involving themselves in feminism?
26. What are some women's concerns with the social constructionist approach and men involving themselves in feminism?
27. How have women supported men in embracing feminism? What are your thoughts about it?

12

Putting It All Together

Next Steps for Masculinities

In this text we've explored the field of masculinities. The discipline is dedicated to understanding the many ways that people who self-identify as men experience themselves and their world and how that world contributes to this process. While this text did not explore the multiple manifestations of masculinity (e.g., White masculinity, trans-gendered masculinity, etc.) nor the social worlds of men in detail (men at work, in the family, etc.) it set the tone for understanding and appreciating that type of investigation. Upon finishing this text, my hope is that you will be equipped with new understandings and motivated to learn more about the worlds of men and masculinities.

I wrote this book using a feminist perspective. I chose this perspective for several reasons, including: (a) feminist scholars were the first to address and emphasize gender as an important construct to study; (b) feminist theory and understanding of marginalization helps us understand the ways in which men can be marginalized, an appreciation of which can help us understand important aspects of masculinities; and (c) the diverse perspectives of feminist theory (introduced in chapter two) also allow us to investigate the unique worlds of men from various vantage points.

Feminist theory, in concert with a social constructionist lens, also helped us set the stage in our exploration of masculinities struggles. One of the fundamental social struggles for men in understanding themselves and evaluating masculinities is how to do that from the vantage point of identifying with a social group that holds social power and privilege (discussed in chapter three). As reviewed, not all men have the same access to power and privilege and some even try to resist and better understand how this privilege has affected their lives. Regardless, all men struggle within a context of male privilege to understand masculinities.

In addition to utilizing feminist theory to help set the stage for social context, feminist ideology was used throughout this text in several other ways. Perhaps one of the most pervasive was the critical eye utilized to evaluate each of the perspectives examined in the text. Within each chapter are various ideas about masculinities, all of which end with concerns and criticisms. These concerns often are motivated by feminist concerns of equity, recognizing uniqueness and difference, and asking whether the ways in which we view a phenomenon ultimately lead to more humane ways of living.

Chapters 3 and 4 of this text reminded us that the first difficulty in understanding masculiniti(es) is that scholars in this area do not agree on a definition of what masculinity is. Various arguments were presented in these chapters, including an exploration of masculinity as a gender role, form of power, trait-based identity, ideology, and as a social construction. Understanding these differences is important because the way in which we define something ultimately sets the stage for how we respond to a particular phenomenon.

Following multiple definitions, we explored origins of masculinities. Chapters five through seven covered several theories within the social sciences that describe the origins of masculinities. These theories included evolutionary psychology, behaviorism, social learning theory, psychoanalytic and psychodynamic approaches, cognitive/gender schema, conformity to masculine norms, masculinity as discourse and masculinity as relational self. These are not the only models available, but they represent both historical and modern views of masculinity.

In chapter eight we examined what is known as a modern crisis in men. Simply stated, this crisis suggests that in many realms of life men are suffering in greater proportions, with more severity and in a unique way that differentiates them from other genders. This chapter focused on problems with education, violence, health and help-seeking. Of course, these are not the only areas with which men find themselves struggling. The aim was to present issues that might interest readers in exploring other areas that men might be struggling with and perhaps learn and discover new insights about men's experiences. Perhaps it will lead to working with men to help alleviate these problems.

Chapters nine through eleven explained a source for the crisis of men referred to as a crisis in masculinity. Three views on this crisis included here were the essentialist, sociocultural and social constructionist. Masculinity scholars often agree that men are having problems in their lives and difficulty understanding and making sense of masculinities, and therefore having trouble in their interactions and relationships with others. What they do not agree on is what masculinity is, where it comes from, and what it is that men are having trouble with.

Presenting these views separately was largely for the purposes of education and learning, as these views are not absolutely distinct (i.e., most people's views on masculinities reflect a blending of perspectives). There are, however, people who represent each distinct perspective and seem to adhere to the basic premises therein.

Some perspectives, however, are simply hard to reconcile. Research indicates that the least likely overlap will occur with essentialist men (particularly those who are anti-feminist) and profeminist men, since they disagree upon many basic assumptions (Fox, 2004). While scant research exists on profeminist men, a recent study comparing profeminist and masculinist men suggests that profeminist men tended to have graduate degrees and be working in professional fields, while the majority of masculinist men did not have college degrees and tended to work in blue-collar occupations (Fox, 2004). This may make it difficult for these groups to bridge their concerns and find common ground since their experiences in the world are so different. It is particularly a concern for profeminist men who have been chastised for being against patriarchy and the domination of subjugated masculinities, while having difficulty connecting with members of those groups in terms of building membership in profeminist organizations (Douglas, 1994).

However, as life often is, the real story is much more complicated. While there are people who definitely fall exclusively into one of the perspectives, many people draw from various perspectives to inform their views about the crisis in masculinity (Fox, 2004; Hearn, 1993). For example, there are members from all three movements that advocate ending physical violence against women (Fox, 2004). There are mythopoetic men incorporating feminism and profeminist men incorporating spirituality into their work (Fox, 2004; Youmans, 2004). And we still know very little about the diverse men who wish to see changes made to masculinity.

One important advocate for an integrated perspective is Steven Botkin, who is the head of Men's Resources International. Men's Resources International works with men to assist them in developing a positive masculinity while advocating for women and femininity (see

Who's Who in Masculinities Research: Steven D. Botkin, Ed.D.

Steven Botkin founded the Men's Resource Center (MRC) of Western Massachusetts in 1982 and received his doctoral degree in Social Justice Education from the University of Massachusetts several years later. He guided the MRC from a grass-roots group of volunteers into a successful non-profit organization, whose programs have become a model for community-based men's groups around the world. In 2004, Steven left this position and founded Men's Resources International to "mobilize networks of men as allies with women for violence prevention and positive masculinity." Dr. Botkin lectures, leads workshops and trainings, and provides consultations for organizations throughout the United States and around the world, most recently in Zambia, Nigeria, Rwanda and Liberia.

Website: www.mensresourcesinternational.org.

http://www.mensresourcesinternational.org/template.php?page=aboutus). Botkin has argued that for too long men have split themselves along the line of whether personal healing or political activism is the method to assist men. In his view, men must do both. Men must acknowledge their own pain and engage in activism to ally with others.

> One essential foundation of our approach is a firm understanding that men are both privileged and damaged by gender roles and sexism. By creating opportunities for men to learn how to safely and compassionately attend to their own and others' emotional experience, we help men reclaim their full selves, teach an essential life skill, build a strong community of connection and support, and create a new culture of masculinity. It is also clear that we have an important part as men in challenging rigid gender roles and dominating forms of masculinity. (Botkin, 2002)

Some of the difficulty of bridging between these groups of men may be a difficulty in separating individual psychological experiences from sociological and political contexts. Some of the pain men experience is likely due to masculinity in terms of privileged expectations and restricted gender roles. Some of it is likely related to basic human issues with which all people struggle, including loss, misunderstanding, disconnection, and feeling unimportant and unable to make change in one's life.

The social power to exclude specific social groups defines the difference. In many countries, women, marginalized men, and others have been and continue to be prevented from participating as equals in various cultures. This does not mean that individual men do not have unfair consequences that result from this the patriarchal system, or that individual men do not suffer individualized injustices. From a sociological and historical perspective, a social system that is hierarchical and has historically excluded members from participating equally in that system will have social and psychological ramifications for both those at the top of the hierarchy and those who struggle to move up, those who are displaced, and for those who try to understand and/or resist this system (Goodman, 2001).

Next Steps for Masculinities

In order for this field to progress, we will need to continue to learn how to separate these feelings of individual frustration from those that come from privilege. As scholars and representatives of this field, we need to learn how to recognize historical and systemic processes that maintain inequity and how to differentiate those from individual instances of injustice and personal pain. This is extraordinarily difficult for people to do because when people are in pain, they often look to outside forces to explain that pain, rather than looking within, and when explaining *other's* problems often minimize those social forces. This will be a difficult step and struggle.

We also will need to continue to do work that examines intersections of masculinities. Not only is masculinity experienced differently by different people, but the struggle outlined above will be unique as a function of one's race, class, country of origin, age, etc. We will also need to remind ourselves that, while the struggle will be unique, the struggle will still exist.

Another necessary step for this field to progress will be to continue to increase collaboration across perspectives and across disciplines. While some perspectives may be insurmountable, several people in this field share a genuine concern and interest in improving the lives of men and others. Academics in particular can be guilty of spending more time quibbling about theoretical differences in analysis and research methodology when they could be working with one another on projects that would have an actual positive impact on others. We need to continue moving beyond our theoretical foundations and our academic disciplines to find shared concerns.

The inclusion of various perspectives in this text is in-part a goal to that end. Not only are there different perspectives, but each perspective also had advantages and disadvantages. Sociological and anthropological perspectives are wonderful in that they give a larger picture view of human interaction, but they are less useful in understanding the unique internalized experiences of individuals. Psychological perspectives can often give insight into the internal struggles people face, but are often neglectful of the sociohistorical forces that exist and how they contribute to those experiences. Feminist and social constructionist perspectives as used throughout this text can be wonderful in assisting us to see the unique and various ways in which we define, measure, and understand phenomenon, but at times can make it difficult to see the common threads.

This becomes another step for us in this field. How do we recognize the common themes that affect this work while honoring the unique experiences and needs of individuals? We need to continue to find the common areas that ground this field and find ways that speak to unique experiences without losing sight of the bigger picture.

In addition, we need to continue to be critical of this overall work, but ultimately generate knowledge that will result in action. And we need to take action. That action may come in various forms depending on one's own training, skills, background, interests, etc., but we cannot allow our sophisticated critical view to keep us from acting in ways that connect and emancipate us.

Now that you have completed this text, I hope you will be able to keep this struggle in mind as you continue to learn about a diverse array of people's experiences with masculinities. These people struggle with hegemonic masculinity and their place in it. They struggle with their own human interactions and psychological experiences of selfhood. They are real people with real lives and real relationships. Through their lives they attempt to make sense of what it means to be "masculine" and how to relate to others. Through their struggles and their triumphs we can learn about the various ways in which people experience masculinities.

In closing, I hope that you are now inspired to learn more about the diverse worlds of men and masculinities. In particular, I hope that you can begin to piece together how complex aspects of our identities (race, culture, gender expression, gender identity, etc.) contribute to the diverse ways in which people make sense of masculinities. Every chapter in this text has included an extensive reference section and a list of people who influenced the writing of this text. These are not all of the people who have contributed to this field, but represent many important contributors. Through exploring their work you will undoubtedly discover others who will also enlighten and inspire you to learn more. Please take the time to examine those references more carefully.

I have really enjoyed writing this book. I learned so much in my own investigation of masculinities. I am continually impressed by the brilliant people who debate about these complex issues in ways that attempt to empower marginalized peoples. Perhaps that is one of the most important things I have learned in putting together this text. In thinking about all of the debates in the field, in the end, it may be the *process* of engaging in these conversations that is one of the most important. In other words, as time evolves, we will likely have new terms and ideas as they relate to men, gender, masculinities and feminisms. If we can continue to learn from these views, we can engage each other in ways that empower us to be critical of ourselves, work towards social justice, make changes where they are necessary and ultimately be nurturing, and understanding as we continue to explore masculinities.

Review and Questions to Ponder

1. Were you surprised that a text about men utilized feminist theories to understand men?
2. Has your view changed at all about the use of feminist theory to study men? How?
3. Which of the definitions of masculinity best fits your view?
4. Do you think it is possible to have multiple definitions of masculinity? Why/why not?
5. Which of the views on the origins of masculinity best fits your view?
6. Do you think any of these views can be combined? If so which?

7. Do you think that there really is a crisis in men?
8. Do you think men have always been in crisis and that we are just now recognizing it?
9. Do you think the crisis in men is due to the crisis in masculinity? Which version(s)?
10. What other social factors might influence the crisis in men?

Masculinities Terms

Abolitionist movement   A movement of social reformers that advocated ending slavery.

Acculturation   The process of adjusting to the expectations of a culture.

Acquaintance rape   When one is raped by someone one knows.

Adaptation   The process of learning to ensure continued survival by complying with social and environmental demands.

Adaptive value   A behavior that is useful for survival.

Addicted lover   An aspect of Moore's and Gillette's **Archetypes for Masculine Energies model**, emphasizing a person who derives all of their self-worth through others.

Affect   The way in which a person expresses emotion.

Affective behavior   The expression of emotion.

African Latino/Asian Native American (ALANA)   A student group made up of people of diverse ethnic and racial backgrounds and identities who wish to educate others about diversity and form feelings of community and belonging.

Agency   The belief and ability to affect change, to have an impact on one's environment.

Aggregate   (*n*) A combination or general trend found in data; (*v*) identify this trend

Alexythymia   A syndrome which involves difficulties with the experience and expression of emotion.

Ally activism   The process of identifying and working towards justice with groups outside of one's own. The work methods and goals are largely determined by target group members, as opposed to those outside of the particular target community.

Anatomy/anatomical   Parts of the body. (See **physiology**.)

Androcentrism   From a male-centered perspective (often touted as "neutral").

Androgyne   A person who identifies as having no gender.

Androgynous   A person who identifies as male or female but combines characteristics from the other-sex group.

Anima   The emotional aspect of our psyche. It often serves a function of self-protection.

Animus/Persona   Our social self. What we are aware of in the world. Our knowable self based on our own insight into ourselves and interactions in the world.

Anti-feminist   A person who believes that feminist thinking is inaccurate and harmful. May also include actions to protest feminist activities.

Anti-Semitic   Hostile attitudes or behaviors directed towards people of Semitic origins, typically used in reference to those of Jewish ancestry.

Anti-sexist man   A man who identifies with feminist principles and works against privilege and patriarchy. (See **pro-feminist, profeminist, feminist man**.)

Anxiety   To Freud, an uncomfortable state of physiological tension which results when the id is confronted with the demands of the environment.

Archetype/archetypal energies   A potential energy that resides in the unconscious manifested in symbols and themes of ancient cultures (hero, mother, warrior, king, etc.).

Archetypes for Masculine Energies model   See **Archetypal model**.

Archetypal model   A model that utilizes the concepts of archetypes to explain something (the Archetypes for Masculine Energies Model proposed by Robert Moore and Douglas Gillette is an example of an archetypal model).

Assimilation   The process of gathering information from the environment.

Attention   The ability to focus on a particular stimulus to the exclusion of others (see noise).

Attentional processes   Processes used to pay attention to stimuli in order to set the stage for future modeling behavior.

Basic anxiety   To Karen Horney, anxiety that results from a person not getting their relational needs met in the environment.

Be a Big Wheel   A theme of David's and Brannon's **Blueprint for Manhood** model for masculinity that emphasizes the idea that being a man involves being in charge.

Behavioral   Observable actions.

Binary   Based on a concept in computer code in which everything is thought of as only being a "0" or "1." In language, the idea is that there are only two distinct groups as an aspect of some phenomenon. So for gender we sometimes think of male *or* female.

Biological   Pertaining to any physical aspects of our experiences including genetics and hormones.

Black nationalism   An ideology and movement that seeks to unite people of African descent in order to survive and prosper.

Blaming the victim   Making the victim of a crime feel that it is their fault for being harmed.

Blueprint for Manhood   Deborah David's and Robert Brannon's role model for masculinity. Includes four major themes: No Sissy Stuff, Be a Big Wheel, The Sturdy Oak, and Give 'em Hell.

Botanist   A type of biologist that specializes in plants.

Boy code/Code masculinity   The various complex ways in which people communicate to boys and men the ways in which they believe they need to act, think, and feel in order to meet the criteria of a rigid masculine gender role.

Bullying   Aggressive behavior that is consistent and unwarranted and perpetrated by someone that has more power than another.

Castration anxiety   An unconscious fear boys experience after demonstrating sexual desire for their mothers. Literally, boys' concern about being castrated due to feelings about their mothers.

Code masculinity/boy code   See **boy code**.

Characteristics   Descriptors of various aspects or abilities of a person. (See **traits**.)

Class privilege   Unearned social granting of a route to accessing **cultural resources** as a function of being of middle- or upper-class economic status.

Clinical samples   A sample that involves people who have come into professional settings seeking help. (See **community sample**.)

Cognitive   Referring to the process of gathering, storing and retrieving information. The school of psychology interested in understanding how thinking occurs.

Cognitive revolution   A movement in psychology that focuses on understanding how cognitions (thoughts) primarily organize our psychological experiences.

Cohesive norms   The norms of influential and powerful people whom others look up to and often wish to emulate.

Collective unconscious A sub-sphere of the unconscious that is a storehouse of archetypal energies.

Color vision deficiency (those who are "color blind") The difficulty recognizing certain colors, usually red or green.

Common couple violence Violence that is less severe, less frequent, and does not escalate over time but remains relatively stable and causes stress to couples. (See **intimate terrorism**.)

Community samples A sample that involves a more general group of people from the community. (See **clinical sample**.)

Comparative research Research done on non-human animals to draw analogies to humans.

Complicit masculinity When one acts in such a way to support or ignore behaviors of men in order to perpetuate dominant masculinity.

Condition To learn how to adapt through automatic responses to environmental demands.

Conditioned response A response that has been learned by being paired to a specific stimulus.

Conditioned stimulus A stimulus that has been learned to be connected to a response through interaction with the environment.

Conscious Sphere of the mind associated with information that one is currently processing.

Construct (*v*) To create one's own perception of the world.

Constructed truths Perceptions of reality based on one's own interaction with others, the world, and one's sense of oneself.

Contextual/contextual cues Related to situational factors. When we say something is contextual we mean that aspects of the situation help us understand that phenomenon (such as time of day, gender of participants, and location it took place).

Conversational analysis A method for analyzing language that does not presuppose any meaning to constructs prior to the analysis. The meaning of constructs is assumed to be socially constructed in every new situation in novel ways through language.

Copulate To insert the penis into the vagina (coitus or intercourse).

Correlate Associate or co-vary. If two variables are correlated it means they influence one another.

Countercultural revolution A period in history usually associated with the late 1960s and early 1970s in which people defied norms, particularly dealing with drug use, sexuality, and the US involvement in Vietnam.

Counteridentification   After a resolution of the Oedipus complex, an attempt by a son to be like his father and maintain competition with him.

Crisis for men   The assumption that men are experiencing problems at a disproportionate rate and with more severity than other genders.

Crisis of masculinity   The suggestion that boys and men do not know what it means to be male and are suffering as a result.

Cross-sexed schema   A person born of one sex who processes the world with a gender schema of the other sex.

Cultural feminism   A feminist model that claims there are significant differences between men and women that make them unique and distinct social groups. Cultural feminists believe that many characteristics associated with women have been undervalued, ignored, or harmed.

Cultural/historical context   Specific situational factors related to the culture or history of that culture. (See **contextual**.)

Cultural materials   Physical creations made by humans. Could range from forks to buildings to televisions.

Cultural norm   An expectation of how the majority of people will express some aspect of human experiences (what is considered "normal").

Cultural resource   A social tool to enhance one's ability to adapt and live within one's culture (a bank account, driver's license, etc.).

Cultural symbol   The meaning that is assigned to stimuli in the overall culture.

Date rape   When one is raped in the context of a dating relationship.

Deconstruct   The act of examining the factors that affect what we believe to be true, including the source(s) of truth(s).

Deep masculinity   A mature form of masculinity associated with being responsible, mature and concerned for others.

Defensive autonomy   An unconscious denial of experiences of pain and hurt in order to maintain a sense of independence.

Dehumanizing   A situation that makes someone feel less than human. Something one would not expect a human being should be exposed to.

Denying innocent one   An aspect of Moore's and Gillette's **Archetypes for Masculine Energies model**, describing a person who utilizes a quasi-independence to gain attention from others.

Descriptive norms The most common experience amongst people. The actual way in which a majority of people think, behave, or feel.

Determinism A belief that outcomes are controlled by something outside of one's ability (fate, destiny, etc).

Deviant Outside of the norm or what is expected

Deviate To be different from what is expected.

Diagnosis The specific medical term used to refer to a syndrome (a cluster of abnormal symptoms).

Diagnostic and Statistical Manual for Mental Disorders A manual for practicing mental health clinicians to assist in diagnosis of mental health concerns.

Direct modeling When a person directly observes a behavior and imitates it.

Discriminate To deny a person equal participation in culture as a function of belonging to a social group.

Discursive psychology A sub-branch of psychology interested in understanding how language is used to construct meaning and relationships amongst people.

Disequilibrium When information a person has assimilated does not predict a new situation.

Disidentification The boy's resolution of the Oedipus complex by distancing himself from his mother.

Dividend A benefit or advantage.

Divorce revolution The dramatic increase in divorces following the advent of no-fault divorce.

Doing gender The idea that gender is a socially active and constructed activity rather than an identity or role.

Domestic violence Violence that occurs within the home typically perpetrated by a person one is in a romantic relationship with.

Dominant culture Aspects of human culture that are given the most attention and are viewed as the most worth pursuing. It does not mean necessarily that the majority of people live this way.

Dominant masculinity Aspects of masculinity that are given the most attention and are viewed as the most worth pursuing. Typically includes a focus on competition, aggression, and control.

Double jeopardy In relation to men and health seeking, the concept that some men are uncomfortable with vulnerability and the expression of emotion. Asking for help is often associated with a weakness and vulnerability, but it is necessary to improve. In order to get better, men have to engage in something that makes them feel worse.

Dynamic   Changing, adaptive.

Effects of conformity/nonconformity   How conformity or nonconformity affects an individual's experience (cognitively, behaviorally, emotionally, etc.).

Egalitarian   Equal in a relationship.

Ego   The conscious part of the mind involved with memory and reasoning.

Ego ideal   The aspect of the ego that deals with growth and accomplishment.

Emotional   The way the world impacts us or our feelings about the world and ourselves.

Empathy   The experience of understanding and concerning oneself for the plight of another.

Empirical/empiricism   Based on observable, testable, and measurable information. Assumes that there is a correct/objective answer to be discovered.

Encoding   The process of the mind assigning a code to information that has been assimilated in order to store it in memory.

Engendered lives   The idea that all aspects of our lives are affected by the way we understand and act upon our beliefs in gender.

Entitlement   The belief that one should be guaranteed certain privileges and benefits due to one's belonging to some social group.

Equilibration   The process of the mind balancing what has been assimilated to what will be accommodated to better predict and understand the world.

Equilibrium   A state in which information the mind has assimilated is useful in predicting and understanding the world.

Eros   The life instinct.

Essentialist   A view of examining human nature that assumes that people have a true "essence" that typically is caused by their biological makeup.

Essentialist explanation   An explanation for the crisis of masculinity that assumes there is a "right" way to be masculine.

Essentialized   Pre-determined and presumably natural connection between a physiological characteristic and psychosocial set of behaviors (sex and gender for example).

Evolutionary Sociology   A sub-field of sociology interested in the links between biology, the study of societies, and adaptation.

Experience/psychological experience   The sum of one's behaviors, cognitions and emotions in a given social situation.

Exploitation   Taking advantage of others for personal gain.

Expressive   The quality in the way in which we carry ourselves. So while behavior refers to a specific act, expressiveness refers to the way in which that act comes across.

Expressiveness   A trait associated with femininity that emphasizes communication and concern for others.

Extent of conformity/nonconformity   The degree to which a person approximates a cultural norm.

External hegemony   When men marginalize women to try to achieve dominant masculinity.

Extreme conformer   A person who accepts the majority of the norms of their culture.

Extreme nonconformer   A person who rejects a majority of the norms of their culture.

Father wound   A psychological wound caused by a father not being available to a young boy. Results in incomplete development of the male psyche.

Feminine gender schema   A person who processes information primarily through endorsing characteristics associated with femininity.

Feminine mystique   The mask that women wear to help them cope with their relegated roles as only being capable of domestic duties. The mask keeps them protected from realizing their own feelings of disconnection and depression about being viewed as less important than men.

Femininity   What is expected of women per the gender role in any given culture.

Feminist (for men)   A man who adheres to the ideologies of one of many forms of feminisms and believes the use of the term is not a problem and rather a way to honor the ideas put forth by women.

Feminist models   While there are many feminisms, all feminists are interested in understanding and bettering the lives of women and others that are marginalized.

Feminist standpoint theory   A model for understanding masculinity that suggests that men's experiences are directly related to their position of social dominance.

Fertile   Capable of reproducing.

Forced-choice questions   Questions that have a limited choice for the correct answer. Multiple-choice tests are usually forced-choice.

Fragile masculine self Involves a rigid and constricted set of internal rules for what it means to be male that results in an insecure and detached person.

Freewill The belief that one's choices have an impact on the way they interact in the world.

Function Purpose or outcome of something.

Gay Referring to a sexual and/or romantic affiliation for someone of the same sex (typically used for men).

Gender General social and cultural beliefs about the ways in which individuals and societies think about people and what differentiates them based on assumptions about sex.

Gender as performance See **doing gender**.

Gender-aschematic processing/non-sex-typed processing A process by which a person does not utilize stereotypical views about sex or gender in order to interpret what is going on in the world and to discover how to react. (See **androgynous**.)

Gender behavior disturbance When a boy or girl behaves in a way more expected of the other gender.

Gender-bias (in language) When language favors one gender over the other through attributing positive attributes to one gender over others or through omission.

Gender/boyhood nonconformists A term used in the psychology literature for a boy who has in some way not demonstrated "appropriate" masculinity.

Gender deviant / Gender-disturbed Terms used in the psychology literature for a boy who has in some way not demonstrated 'appropriate' masculinity.

Gender expression The behaviors in which one engages to express oneself believed to connect to gender (use of hands, arms etc. to convey a point).

Gender gap A situation in which a gender group is underrepresented in an institution relative to their actual proportional existence – typically used to explain historical discrimination (the gender gap in women participating in government, religion, etc).

Gender identity How individuals make sense of their own way of being gendered.

Gender identity disturbance When a person is born of one biological sex but desires to be another.

Gender identity disorder A disorder in which a person experiences distress and discomfort when their biologically viewed sex does not match their internal experiences of gender. People who experience this disorder often identify as belonging to the "other sex" from which they are expected to experience.

Gender identity/role development A process of gender formation involving the incorporation of behaviors, thoughts, emotions and self-concept expected of one's gender.

Gender role conflict The conflict men experience as a function of trying to aspire to a rigid gender role.

Gender role discrepancy A discrepancy (or difference) between your ideal self, what is idealized (desired) and your real self in terms of gender.

Gender role journey workshop An educational workshop that takes place in an informal setting and combines traditional aspects of an educational environment such as lecture and readings with therapeutic interventions to help people see how rigid gender roles may contribute to limiting life options.

Gender role orientation The specific ways in which a particular culture has expectations about the ways in which people's behaviors, thoughts, and feelings should be based on presumably distinct genders.

Gender role stereotype A belief that all members of a particular gender act in consistent and predictable ways.

Gender role trauma The trauma boys suffer due to being separated from their mothers prematurely due to beliefs about the needs of boys to be independent.

Gender schema theory A cognitive model for explaining gender. Through interactions in the culture we form schemas about gender which extend to understandings of ourselves and the world. Assumes that the basic structure of schemas is similar across people. (See **self schema theory**.)

Gender-schematic processing/sex-typed processing A process by which a person utilizes stereotypical views about their own sex in order to interpret what is going on in the world and to discover how to react.

Gender-specific demands Specific tasks assumed to be inherently linked to a specific sex.

Gender trauma Coercing boys to reject aspects of themselves denoted as "feminine."

Genderqueer An umbrella term used for people who defy conventional notions of gender (such as that gender must exist, or be dichotomous or stable).

Give 'em Hell A theme of David's and Brannon's **Blueprint for Manhood** model for masculinity that emphasizes the idea that being a man involves persevering and getting things done at any cost.

Global approach (to studying gender role) Assumes that there is a general expected set of expectations of being masculine or feminine which is assumed to be carried with you as you interact with others in the environment.

Grandiosity An exaggerated sense of self-importance.

Group and individual factors in conformity The effect of belonging to social groups as contributions to the degree to which one conforms or does not conform to cultural norms.

Group process The way in which group members interact and bring issues from their individual lives to the ways in which they interact with the group.

Hate crime A crime that is committed under the auspices of prejudice and creates fear for members of historically oppressed minority groups.

Hegemonic masculinity A theory that states that people will act in ways that reinforce male privilege by reinforcing conformity to an idealized version of masculinity even when it may not be in their best interest, in order to maintain the system of patriarchy. (See **complicit, marginalized**, and **subjugated masculinities**.)

Hermeneutics A philosophical school of thought that strives to understand the ways in which language is delivered and interpreted.

Hero The archetype that assists boys in becoming men by taking risks and distancing themselves from mother.

Heterosexism The tendency to see heterosexual norms as correct or superior to the norms of other sexual identities.

Heterosexual privilege Unearned social granting of a route to accessing cultural resources as a function of being heterosexual.

Hierarchical relationship A type of relationship in which different people have different amounts of power over each other. In a hierarchical relationship, some people have more power than others.

Homeostasis A system that has achieved normalcy or is at average.

Homophobia Literally means "fear of sameness." Usually used to refer to discomfort about, and fear of, homosexuality.

Hormones/hormonal Chemicals produced in the endocrine glands that travel in the blood and have a specific effect on target organs.

Hypermasculinity   A heightened sense of dominant masculinity. A hypermasculine person is extremely aggressive and egocentric.

Hypothetical construct   A conceptual way of explaining something we cannot directly observe or measure (intangible) but we assume is made up of a cluster of human experiences which may include behaviors, thoughts, or emotions.

Hypothesis   A testable prediction about the relationship between two or more variables.

Id   The unconscious part of the mind where instincts operate.

Ideal self   The person you would like to be. (See **real self**.)

Idiographic   An approach to studying trait differences between groups that assumes that the uniqueness between any compared groups is due to a trait that belongs to one and not the other. (See **nomothetic**.)

In the moment   Referring to experiences that are currently happening and paid attention to.

Imaginal representation   An image in the mind that represents a potential behavior.

Impotent lover   An aspect of Moore's and Gillette's **Archetypes for Masculine Energies model**, emphasizing a person who lacks the ability to connect intimately with others.

Individual factors in conformity   One's unique experiences in social groups as a contributor to the degree to which one conforms or does not conform to cultural norms.

Industrial revolution   A period of history beginning in the late eighteenth century that emphasized the producing of material goods in large quantities, often in factories.

Information age   See **age of information and technology**.

Injunctive norms   Expectations of how one is supposed to behave or act that often come with negative consequences when violated.

Institutionalized   When the very institutions of a society (governments, religions, businesses, families, etc.) are responsible for the maintenance of the rules. To say that something is institutionalized means that the very fabric of that society supports and perpetuates it.

Instrumentality   A trait typically associated with masculinity that stresses goal-directed and action-oriented behavior.

Interactional level   The actual behaviors that people engage in that indicate they are doing gender.

Internal hegemony   When men marginalize other men to try to achieve dominant masculinity.

Internalization   The process by which people take ideas about gender role and incorporate them to their own identity.

Intersectional approach   An approach to knowledge that suggests that various social categories (race, class, gender, etc.) interact in unique ways and that we must understand that interaction to fully understand the phenomenon.

Intersexed   A general term for people who have less than common genetic sexual combinations or less than common sexual anatomical features.

Intimate partner violence   Violence committed in the context of a dating or social relationship.

Intimate terrorism   Violence that is frequent, severe, and presents a major health risk for the victim. (See **common couple violence**.)

Intra-psychic   Within one's mind.

Intrinsic work dimensions   Motivations for doing work that are based on internal rewards such as pride, achievement, or growth.

Introspection   The process of looking within oneself for truth.

Items   The specific stimuli used to measure aspects of a construct. On a scale the items are typically **forced-choice questions**.

Judeo-Christian   Cultures that come from Jewish or Christian heritages.

Jungian theorists   Theorists who are influenced by the work of psychotherapist Carl Jung.

Kinesthetic   Pertaining to touch and sensations related to touching.

King   Part of Gillette's and Moore's **Archetypes for Masculine Energies model**. The king is the part of the male psyche representing potential leadership.

Klinefelter's syndrome   A situation in which a person is born with the combination of XXY chromosomes.

Learning style   A way in which one gathers information about the world.

Lesbian   Referring to a romantic and/or relational affiliation for someone of the same sex (typically used for women).

Liberal feminism   A feminist model that believes that general social systems are worthwhile and that all people should have equal access to cultural resources within that system.

Liberal profeminism   An incorporation and celebration of qualities associated with women.

Liberationist   A man who identifies with the men's rights movement (also known as an **anti-feminist**).

Libido   The sexual instinct.

Location   A general term used to refer to the place where something (masculinity) resides/comes from.

Long-term memory   Stored information in the mind of events that took place in the past. Ranges from minutes to years in the past.

Looking glass self   A theory that suggests that the way in which we view ourselves is largely influenced by how the social world defines us.

Lover   Part of Gillette's and Moore's **Archetypes for Masculine Energies model**. The lover is the aspect of the male psyche that connects to and cares for others.

Low masculine boys   A term used in the psychology literature for a boy who has in some way not demonstrated "appropriate" masculinity.

Magician   Part of Gillette and Moore's **Archetypes for Masculine Energies model**. The magician is the aspect of the male psyche that involves spirituality, wisdom, and self-reflection.

Major depressive disorder   A clinical syndrome involving significant and overwhelming feelings of sadness and alienation that prevents a person from living their normal life. This must occur for at least one two-week period.

Male centered   A system that puts men's accomplishments in the forefront.

Male dominated   A system where men or men's values heavily outnumber others.

Male identified   A system where men's ways of being are considered normal and expected.

Male privilege   Unearned social granting of a route to accessing cultural resources as a function of being male.

Male relational dread   A discomfort in connecting to others.

Male role strain   Strain that results from men attempting to meet societal expectations of them as men.

Male Sex Role Identity Paradigm (MSRI)/Gender identity theory   An approach to masculinity based on an assumption that there is a normal/expected sex role for men and for women and one's identity is essentially being able to internalize that norm.

Manipulator   An aspect of the magician part of Moore's and Gillette's **Archetypes for Masculine Energies model**, emphasizing a person who uses personal skills to gain interest from others.

The Mankind Project   A fairly recent offshoot of the mythopoetic movement that stresses the assisting of men in reclaiming the "sacred masculine."

Marginalization   When experiences and the worth of one person are not seen as equal or as valid as other people's in the dominant culture in which one lives and when this is actively supported by the culture.

Marginalized masculinities   Masculinities that are largely ignored by the culture or are "in the margins"

Masculine dread (of femininity)   The loathing of anything associated with women experienced and expressed by men.

Masculine gender schema   A person who processes information primarily through endorsing characteristics associated with masculinity.

Masculine mystique   The mask that men wear psychologically which prevents them from experiencing aspects of themselves associated with femininity and helps them maintain distance and power over others.

Masculinist   A man that identifies with the men's rights movement (also known as **anti-feminist** and **liberationist**).

Masculinist epistemology   A way of viewing the world espoused by men and reflecting men's values and ideas, often described as neutral or objective.

Masculinities   There are multiple ways to think about masculinity and multiple ways in which people may experience this phenomenon.

Masculinity   The variety of ways that cultures make sense of the social, behavioral, emotional, expressive-laden experiences of men and characteristics associated with them.

Masculinity ideology   One's attitudes about what gender norms exist for men, which are appropriate, and which apply to the individual.

Masculinity scripts   Dominant masculine norm based behavioral expectations for men.

Masochist   An aspect of the warrior part of Moore's and Gillette's **Archetypes for Masculine Energies model**, emphasizing a person who makes choices to harm themselves, which results in immobilization

Mating behavior   Behaviors associated with attracting and pursuing a mate for reproduction.

Mature masculinity   A balanced masculinity that involves all aspects of the male psyche.

Men of color   The term "of color" is usually used to refer to people whose ancestors are from African, Asian, Latin and Native American ancestries.

Men's rights movement   A broad social movement that believes in **essentialism**, that men have less power than women, and that men's rights must be restored to their "proper place."

Mental disorder   According to the **Diagnostic and Statistical Manual for Mental Disorders** a syndrome that impairs functioning, is clinically significant (extreme) and contributes distress to self and/or others.

Methodology   Methods and techniques used to measure phenomenon or accomplish a task.

Million Man March   The largest scale men's march of the twentieth century, organized by and for Black men to address issues pertinent to Black men.

Mirroring   A process where parents and significant others infuse children with their own view of them which ultimately becomes children's views of themselves.

Misogynistic   Hating women and aspects of femininity.

Model   A way of organizing information in order to bring it closer to one's awareness and to make it make more sense.

Modeling   A process of observing, internalizing, and practicing behavior in a social environment.

Modern philosophy of science   A framework for discovering truth based on **empiricism**.

Monarchy   A social structure in which one primary person (or small group of people) makes decisions for an entire group of people.

Moderate conformers   People who conform to some but not all of the norms of their culture.

Moderate nonconformers   People who rebel against some but not all of the norms of their culture.

Montreal massacre   A tragic event in Montreal in which Marc Lépine brutally killed fourteen women and injured nine women and four men. This brutal killing is remembered every year to support an end to violence.

Mother wound   The trauma boys suffer due to being separated from their mothers prematurely because of beliefs about the needs of boys to be independent.

Muscular Christianity movement A movement that was dedicated to displaying images of Jesus as strong and virile in hopes of attracting men to attend religious services.

Mythopoetic men's movement A broad term for men who have found dissatisfaction with traditional ways of thinking about masculinity and have used the ideas of Jung and other Jungians (such as Moore and Gillette) to develop other ways of considering masculinities.

Narcissistic injury An unconscious wound to the psyche caused by a shaming of instinctual needs resulting in an over-focus on the self.

Narcissistic self-protection A focus on the self to the exclusion of others. An inability to view things from others' points of view or recognize others needs in order to protect oneself from pain.

National Organization for Men Against Sexism (NOMAS) A national organization that embraces four tenets: **profeminism**, gay affirmation, **anti-racism**, and enhancing men's lives.

Naturalized See **essentialized**.

Negative advantages of privilege When privileges are not granted equally across people tensions arise across social groups, and hierarchies form to keep the privileged privileged.

Negative feedback loop A self-correcting or self-stabilizing system in which parts of a system will contribute when necessary to keep a system at homeostasis.

Negotiate masculinity To figure out what it means to connect to masculinity, considering the ways in which society and people change. Understanding which thoughts, feelings, and behaviors one possesses are attributed to masculinity.

Negotiation See **negotiate masculinity**.

Negative punishment Something wanted is taken away in the environment, which results in a decrease in behavior.

Negative reinforcement Something not wanted is taken away in the environment, which results in an increase in behavior.

NeoFreudian/neoanalyst A person who incorporates the basics of Freud's model into their version of psychoanalytic theory.

Neurological Referring to brain functioning by way of the nerves or the nervous system in general

No-fault divorce The ability to get divorced without having to prove why divorce should be granted. Usually relies on "irreconcilable differences."

Nobility An elite social class that one must be born into or marry into.

Noise Unwanted stimuli that affect attention.

Nomothetic An approach to measuring traits that assumes that people have the same traits but in different amounts.

Non-sex typed processing/gender aschematic processing A process by which a person does not utilize stereotypical views about sex or gender in order to interpret what is going on in the world and to discover how to react. (See **androgynous**.)

Non-traditional masculinity ideology Attitudes about male norms that reflect less common attitudes.

Norm communication An understanding of how norms get internalized.

Normal See **descriptive/sociocultural/prescriptive/cohesive/injunctive norms**.

Normalizing A social process by which something (a behavior, belief, etc.) becomes known as "normal" or expected.

Normative male alexithymia An inability to describe or even be aware of one's emotions.

Norms Expected rules that govern the behavior, thoughts, and feelings of members of a social group. Violation of norms often results in feedback intended to persuade the violator to conform.

No Sissy Stuff A theme of David's and Brannon's **Blueprint for Manhood** model for masculinity that emphasizes the idea that being a man involves figuring out whatever women do and not doing whatever that is.

Object A thing or a possession to be used by others for some purpose. A passive member of culture.

Objectify/objectification To engage another human being as if they are an object or a thing for you to enjoy or use, rather than a person with unique experiences, rights, and feelings.

Objective truth Something that is absolutely true and indisputable fact.

Oedipus complex A Freudian stage of development in which a boy has an unconscious sexual crush on his mother.

Oppressive A situation in which social groups are dominated by others and it is extremely difficult to get basic human needs met.

Other report The reliance on the observation of an "expert" to describe the experience of a participant in a study. (See **self report**.)

Others   Those who are marginalized or hold less power in the culture.

Pairing   The co-occurring of two stimuli.

Pan-Africanism   A movement to assist people of African nations to become more self-sufficient (and in some cases totally separate from non-Africans) and united to African people of other nations.

Paradigm   A way of looking at something that makes certain assumptions about what it is and how to understand it.

Parental investment   Behaviors related to ensuring the survival of one's children.

Pathological   Outside of the norm in a way that displays a mental disorder.

Patriarchal cultures   Those cultures that are male dominated, male identified and male centered.

Patriarchy   A social system that is male dominated, identified and centered.

Patriarchy movement   A movement of men's rights, often associated with religious doctrine (particularly Christian) that views men as a group of people that has been oppressed by the various social changes that have occurred in the last fifty years and believes men need to be restored to their "proper place" of dominance.

People of color   A term used primarily in North America to refer to people who do not identify themselves as White.

Persistence   A term used by educators to refer to a collection of behaviors related to whether a person completes college.

Persona/Animus   Our social self. What we are aware of in the world. (Similar to the conscious mind.)

Phallic stage   One of the psychosexual stages of development in which the Oedipus complex and castration anxiety occur.

Phallus   The male organ (penis) as a representation of power.

Philosophy of science   A phrase referring to the overall assumptions and methods used within a scientific discipline.

Physiology/physiological   The relationship between the parts of the body (one's **anatomy**). How the parts of the body interact and affect one another.

Physiological psychology   A sub-branch of psychology concerned with the connections between human **anatomy** and **physiology** such as hormones, genetics, and brain structure and their relationship to psychological phenomenon.

Polygamous sexuality   Having multiple sexual partners in the same time period.

Positive advantages of privilege   When privileges are granted equally they can help communities sustain themselves by ensuring that all members have access to resources they need to survive.

Positive masculinity   Positive characteristics associated with men.

Positive punishment   Something not wanted that is added to the environment and decreases a behavior.

Positive reinforcement   Something wanted that is added to the environment and increases a behavior.

Positivist   A way of trying to find truth by relying on accepted scientific methods such as the measurement of observable characteristics and then drawing theory or explanation from the summary of what has been observed.

Post-feminist   A person (who often identifies with the men's rights movement) who believes feminism is no longer necessary.

Post-modern feminism   Feminist models that emphasize the ways we use to discover what we think is true is socially constructed. Truth is seen as always relative to cultural and historical context.

Post-modern philosophy of science   A philosophy that stresses that an understanding and investigation of scientists and scientific methods must be included in a science. Truths are believed to be constructed rather than discovered.

Power (over)   To a social constructionist, the ability to have your construction of events be the truth rather than just one alternative.

Pre-conscious   The sphere of the mind associated with information in our mind we have access to but just not currently in our consciousness. Accessible memories would be in the preconscious.

Pre-modern philosophy of science   A philosophy that stresses rationalism and introspection for discovering truths.

Prescriptive norms   The expected ways in which a society assumes people *should* experience the world. Expected ways of thinking, feeling or behaving in a given society. Also called **sociocultural norms**.

Privilege   An unearned social granting of a route to accessing cultural resources.

Procreative   The sexual process of making children.

Pro-feminist   Men who subscribe to many of the tenets that women feminists do but see feminism as something that women identify with and women do. (See **anti-sexist, profeminist, feminist man**).

Profeminist   Men who do feminism who wish to indicate a respect for an ideology that is grounded in women's experiences as well as recognize the connection men must have with feminism. (See **anti-sexist, pro-feminist, feminist man**). Profeminists support feminist principles and advocate for women and for traits associated with femininity.

Psyche A synonym for mind.

Psychic femininity Human characteristics men possess that are associated with women.

Psychic trauma A trauma in which a person's normal instincts are forced to be unmet and simultaneously the person is shamed for expressing the need.

Psychoanalytic theory A model proposed by Freud to explain personality development as well as to provide treatment for mental health problems. It assumes unconscious material is at the root of many of our behaviors.

Psychodynamic model A form of psychoanalytic theory that emphasizes early relationships as the causal factor in determining personality and gender.

Psychological experiences A summary term for a complex combination of affect, behavior, and cognition within a given context.

Psychologist A social scientist who primarily focuses on individual and/or group experiences (often categorized as thoughts, emotions, and feelings) and the factors that influence them.

Psychosexual stages A series of unconscious stages that infants go through in order to develop an ego and superego (as well as gender).

Psychosocial Involving both psychological and social factors. This means there is a continual interactive relationship between our internal processes (cognitions, emotions, unconscious drives) and external ones (such as the way others use language, behave, and respond to us).

Psychosocial explanation An approach to viewing the crisis in masculinity as a function of rigid gender roles.

Public space Parts of the social world that are theoretically accessible to all. In contrast to people's private homes, etc.

Punishment Anything that decreases a response in the environment.

Qualitative research An approach to research that involves examining the perceptions and voices of those whom you wish to understand.

Queer See **genderqueer**.

Racial privilege   Unearned social granting of a route to accessing cultural resources as a function of being White (or any privileged racial group in a diverse culture).

Radical behaviorist   A behaviorist who believes all behavior is determined by conditioned responses that come from the environment.

Radical feminism   A feminist model that purports that a masculinist epistemology has dominated the way in which we live our lives. Radical feminists believe that the basic ways in which we understand the world and ultimately the way we live with one another must be called into question in order to make life more equal for all.

Radical profeminism   A type of profeminism that stresses the dismantling of patriarchy as its intended goal.

Rape   A specific type of sexual assault which includes the unwanted penetration into any orifice.

Rape culture   Cultures that devalue women and emphasize male violence and aggression, resulting in rape being accepted as normal behavior.

Rationalism   A philosophy that stresses the importance of using pure reason and logic to arrive at the truth.

Real self   One's actual traits and characteristics. (See **ideal self**.)

Reinforcement   Anything that increases a behavior.

Relational   Recognition of how relationships affect our sense of self and others.

Relational self   The idea that the self or one's sense of self shifts as one moves in and out of relations with others.

Relational-self construal   The process of having a self-image which is impacted by the quality of our past relationships with other people.

Reliable   Consistent and time-tested. A test that is reliable shows consistency in a variety of situations.

Reproductive processes   An individual's ability to follow through on what they have learned.

Reservation   An area of land that is viewed as under Native jurisdiction. While still members of the country in which the land exists, laws specific to that tribe may exist within the reservation.

Response   A reaction in the environment (follows a stimulus).

Retentional processes   The ability of a person to retain and remember past information they have learned.

Retrieval   The cognitive accessing of information previously stored.

Risky identity   A new identity that appears to require changes and conflicts with the way one views oneself.

Role definitions Defining a person by the role they are in (father, brother, friend, etc.).

Sacred masculine The "true," balanced, and mature masculine, as defined by the **Mankind Project**.

Sadist An aspect of the warrior part of Moore's and Gillette's **Archetypes for Masculine Energies model,** emphasizing a person who makes choices to harm others.

Scale A **forced-choice** questionnaire said to measure a construct or series of constructs.

Schemas A network of organizations that organizes and guides an individual's perceptions of the world.

Second-order conditioning When two conditioned stimuli are paired to produce the same response the original stimuli did.

Self The ability to interpret the world, reflect on and recognize one's consciousness, and plan for and contemplate the future.

Self report The reliance on the observation of a participant to describe their experience rather than an "expert" testimony. (See **other report**.)

Self-report scale Questionnaires with questions pertaining to specific constructs (intelligence, self-esteem, etc.) that rely on participants to answer **forced-choice questions** and then compare their answers to established norms.

Self-schema A network of mental categories that organizes and guides an individual's perceptions of themself.

Self-schema theory A schema model that suggests that the content, type, and organization of schemas are unique to the individual. (See **gender schema theory**.)

Sensory information Information that is gathered through your sense organs (eyes, ears, tongue, skin, and nose).

Sensory memory Extremely brief memory (less than 1 second) based on the senses.

Sex A biological difference that results in separating humans into distinct groups on the basis of that difference. The most common biological difference is a genetic one separating people by their **sex chromosomesinto** males (XY) and females (XX).

Sex chromosomes Chromosomes that contain genetic information about sex related physiological differences. These specific chromosomes separate humans into two major separate categories male (XY) and female (XX) resulting in physiological differences between the two groups.

Sex role See **gender role**.

Sex-role differentiation　An expectation that due to one's sex one will have specific roles or tasks in life.

Sex typing　See **gender identity/role development**.

Sexism　The belief that one sex is inherently superior to another. In patriarchal cultures this term usually is used to refer to men's beliefs and actions towards others.

Sexual abuse　Any unwanted sexual contact involving physical contact and behaviors not specifically involving touching such as verbal intimidation, coercion, or unwanted sexual attention.

Sexual assault　A legal term for any unwanted physical sexual contact.

Sexual harassment　When unwanted sexual contact or an uncomfortable atmosphere exists (due to sexually inappropriate behavior, language, etc.) in public work spaces.

Sexual selection　The process of choosing a sexual mate.

Shadow　The unknown part of you that resides in your unconscious.

Short-term memory　Also called working memory, the ability to hold a small amount of information in one's mind for a limited time (typically 20–30 seconds).

Social characteristics　Information about people that is related to social groups they belong to that relate to identity (gender, race, religion, etc.)

Social comparison　The process of comparing others to oneself in order to determine the appropriateness of one's experiences.

Social constructionism　A theory that claims that knowledge is historically, temporally, and situationally based and created by people, rather than discovered. Often there is an interest in understanding who has the most say in how things get constructed.

Social constructionist approach (SCA)　An approach to studying phenomenon that emphasizes an understanding of how the phenomenon is defined, who defines it and how context shapes its meaning.

Social disintegration　When the changing nature of societies make it difficult to meet the needs of their community members.

Social group　A group with shared norms in which one belongs that informs your identity.

Social learning theory/model　An approach that sees humans as learning behavior through interacting in the social world. The learning is affected by individual, behavioral, and environmental components that result in imitations of learned behaviors.

Social position The position of power you occupy in a society. (See **subject, object, other.**)

Social roles Positions that have certain expectations associated with them which tell a person how to interact with others.

Socialized control The general need to control others.

Socialization process The complex psychosocial process that involves assisting members of a culture to adapt.

Social institutions Specific sub-groupings of people within a society who hold specific positions and have specific rules about their relationships to one another and their relationships to other organizations.

Social rituals An activity that takes place between two or more people and involves some behavior that represents a larger meaning to those involved and the culture from which they come.

Social role theory A theory that examines how belonging to different roles can impact our sense of self and behavior.

Social scientist A scientist who studies social phenomenon. Sociologists, anthropologists, and psychologists are often thought of as social scientists.

Social structure The specific ways that the different parts of a society relate to one another and function.

Socialist feminism Socialist feminists question the validity of our modern capitalist economic system as a system that even has the potential to include women equally. Socialist feminists believe that our economic systems can help explain gendered concerns.

Socializing/socialization The process by which social structures (family, schools, media, religion) shape the ways people learn about various roles.

Socially constructed To say that something is socially constructed means that what that thing "is" will depend on social and cultural characteristics. What something means is contingent on social context.

Socially desirable Characteristics that are seen as positive or good in any given culture.

Socially integrated A feeling that one belongs in an environment.

Socially sanctioned Approved by the norms of society.

Sociocultural Sociocultural refers to the fact that a phenomenon has both social (local) and cultural (broader) influences.

Sociocultural influences Social and cultural influences on the self.

Sociocultural norms The expected ways in which a society assumes people *should* experience the world. Expected ways of thinking, feeling or behaving in a given society. Also called **prescriptive norms**.

Sociologist   A social scientist who focuses interest on the functioning of societies and how that affects the individuals within them.

Soft men   Men who are gentle and more soft-spoken than what is expected from the dominant norm. A term used to describe men, but not adopted by most men who are described in such a fashion.

Spiritual   Referring to a belief system which involves some higher meaning which may or may not involve religious affiliation. In general, there is an interest in understanding one's place in the world and relationship to others, given a belief in a higher power, meaning, or god/goddess, etc.

State of detachment   A period in a boy's life when they are encouraged not to have a relationship with their mothers.

Stimulus   Anything that can cause an effect in the environment.

Storage   The cognitive transference of information to memory.

Structural context   The larger social structure of an event (who is in charge, what the rules are, who makes the rules, etc.).

Sturdy Oak   A theme of David's and Brannon's **Blueprint for Manhood** model for masculinity that emphasizes the idea that men must be strong and keep their feelings inside.

Subject   An active member of culture with power and intent.

Subjugated   The process of putting a person's needs and rights below others.

Subliminal   Referring to stimuli presented in such a way that it is not apparent to the conscious mind.

Subordinated masculinities   Masculinities that are viewed as inferior or "not masculine."

Subscale   A smaller set of items grouped together on a scale believed to represent a construct related to the overall construct being measured.

Suffrage movement   A movement to ensure that all people have equal access to voting (largely started by and maintained by women).

Superego   The part of the mind that includes beliefs, morals, ethics and a general concern for others.

Sweatshop   A place where people are paid very low wages to perform a menial task and a small number of people profit greatly from others' hard work.

Symbolic modeling   A behavior that is viewed or represented in some medium but not directly observed.

Syndrome   A cluster of co-occurring abnormal characteristics.

System   A collection of individual parts in which all parts affect each other. The system accomplishes something greater than any individual part could.

Thanatos   The death or aggressive instinct.

Traditional masculinity ideology   Attitudes about male norms that reflect common attitudes.

Traits (gender traits)   Stable predispositions or characteristics of a socio-affective nature linked to one's sex. Often thought of as genetic in nature.

Transformative   A change that really reflects a meaningful difference.

Transgendered   An umbrella term for a disconnection between the socially expected gender to which one is assigned and the lived sense of one's own gender identity.

Transphobia   Fear or discomfort with people who choose to live their lives in ways believed to be inconsistent with their biological sex (particularly in gender identity and expression).

Triadic reciprocal causation   Human behavior is caused by individual, behavioral, and environmental factors.

Trial and error learning   The process of trying different behaviors until one finds a behavior that is more adaptive in the environment.

Two-factor model of gender   A view that sees gender as comprised of two heterogeneous traits (typically masculinity or femininity).

Tyrant   An aspect of the king part of Moore's and Gillette's **Archetypes for Masculine Energies model**, emphasizing a person who harshly punishes others.

Unconditioned   "not learned" or automatic.

Unconditioned response   A response that is automatically/naturally paired to a specific stimulus.

Unconditioned stimulus   A stimulus that is automatically/naturally connected to a response.

Unconscious   The sphere of the mind associated with material we are not conscious of but then affects us. Some people believe dreams are derived from material in the unconscious.

Undifferentiated gender schema processing   Someone who does not appear to have sex-typed gender schemas, but who still incorporates some gendered information in their interpretation of the world

Unifactorial model of gender   A view that sees gender as comprised of one trait that places masculinity on one end of a pole and femininity on the other end.

Universal   Applying to all people in various parts of the world. Not specific to any one group.

Unmasculine boys   A term used in the psychology literature for a boy who has in some way not demonstrated "appropriate" masculinity.

Vagina/womb envy   An unconscious envy that boys and men have of women due to their ability to give birth.

Valid   A scale is known as valid if it actually measures what it says it does.

Variation   An emphasis on the differences across a subset. To suggest that there is variation means that individual instances of that phenomenon differ from one another in some relevant way.

Verbal representation   The actual words used to describe and communicate behaviors to others, which reinforce those same behaviors.

Vertebrate   Animal with a backbone. A common biological way of grouping similar animals.

Viable   Healthy, able to survive.

Victorian values   A traditional view of the family in which women are seen as being in control of the domestic sphere and men of the work sphere of life. Women are also seen as responsible for the "values" of the family, which include a very conservative view of women, sex, and expression of oneself.

Warrior   Part of Gillette's and Moore's **Archetypes for Masculine Energies model**. The warrior is the part of the masculine psyche representing drive and energy.

Weakling prince   An aspect of the king part of Moore's and Gillette's **model of masculine archetypal energy**, emphasizing a person who does not take responsibility for leading.

Women-of-color feminism/womanism   A model of feminism that is interested in understanding the role of race and racism and their impact on identity formation and marginalization, particularly for people of color.

Working class   People who engage in occupations that primarily involve manual (hands-on) skilled/semi-skilled activities that often result in low wages.

Xenophobic   Fear or discomfort with strangers or "others" (often used for people from other nations than one's own).

References

Preface

Hammond, W. P. & Mattis, J. S. (2005). Being a man about it: Manhood meaning among African American men. *Psychology of Men and Masculinity, 6,* 114–126.

Moore, T. M. & Stuart, G. L. (2005). A review of the literature on masculinity and partner violence. *Psychology of Men and Masculinity, 6,* 46–61.

Chapter 1

Addis, Michael E. & Cohane, Geoffrey H. (2005). Social scientific paradigms of masculinity and their implications for research and practice in men's mental health. *Journal of Clinical Psychology, 61,* 633–647.

Amaya, H. (2007). Amores perros and racialised masculinities in contemporary Mexico. *New Cinemas: Journal of Contemporary Film, 5,* 201–216.

Amer, M. L. (2007). CRS Report for congress: membership of the 109th congress: a profile. (http://www.senate.gov/reference/resources/pdf/RL30261.pdf). Retrieved December 19, 2007.

Bambert, M. (2005). Young masculinities: understanding boys in contemporary society/adolescent boys: Exploring diverse cultures of boyhood. *Journal of Adolescent Research, 5,* 604–608.

Banks-Wallace, J. (2000). Womanist ways of knowing: Theoretical considerations for research with African American women. *Advanced Nursing Science, 22,* 33–45.

Barret, F. J. (2001). Hegemonic masculinity: The US Navy. In S. M. Whitehead & F. J. Barrett (Eds.), *The masculinities reader* (pp. 77–99). Malden, MA: Blackwell.

Barrett, M. & McIntosh, M. (2005). Ethnocentrism and socialist-feminist theory. *Feminist Review, 80,* 64–86.

Bergdahl, E., Allard, P., Alex, L., Lundman, B., & Gustafson, Y. (2007). Gender differences in depression among the very old. *International Psychogeriatrics; 19,* 1125–1140.

Broad, K. L. (2002). GLB+T?: Gender/sexuality movements and transgender collective identity (de) constructions. *International Journal of Sexuality and Gender Studies, 7,* 241–264.

Bushweller, K. (2004). Instructional materials are biased, report says. *Education Week, 23,* 14.

Campbell, A. (2007). Weaving women into the science curriculum. *Science Scope, 31,* 54–58.

Carlton-LaNey, I. (1997). Elizabeth Ross Haynes: An African American reformer of womanist consciousness, 1908–1940. *Social Work, 42,* 573–583.

Connell, B. (1989). Masculinity, violence and war. In M. S. Kimmel & M. A. Messner (Eds.), *Men's lives* (2nd ed., pp. 176–182). New York: Macmillan.

Connell, R. W. (1995). *Masculinities.* Berkeley, CA: University of California Press.

Cranford, C. J. (2007). It's time to leave machismo behind! Challenging gender inequality in an immigrant union. *Gender and Society, 21,* 409–438.

Edwards, D. (1997). *Discourse and cognition.* Thousand Oaks, CA: Sage.

Efetie, E. R. & Salami, H. A. (2007). Domestic violence on pregnant women in Abuja, Nigeria. *Journal of Obstetrics and Gynaecology, 27,* 379–382.

Enns, C. Z. & Sinacore, A. L. (2005). Second-wave feminisms and their relationship to pedagogy. In C. Z. Enns & A. L. Sinacore (Eds.), *Teaching and social justice: Integrating multicultural and feminist theories in the classroom* (pp. 25–39). Washington, DC: APA.

England, P. (1999). The impact of feminist thought on sociology. *Contemporary Sociology, 28,* 263–268.

Erlanger, S. (2006, November 7). Violence against Palestinian women is increasing, study says. *New York Times,* pA8.

Foley, K. M. (1993). A feminist response to Heesacker and Prichard's "In a different voice, revisited: Men, women, and emotion". *Journal of Mental Health Counseling, 15,* 438–445.

Furnham, A., Petrides, V. K., & Martin, G. N. (2004). Estimates of emotional and psychometric intelligence: Evidence for gender-based stereotypes. *Journal of Social Psychology, 144,* 149–162.

González-López, G. (2004). Beyond machos and machismo: Mexican immigrant men, sexuality, and intimacy. Conference Papers. American Sociological Association, 2004 Annual Meeting, San Francisco, CA, 1–13.

Harrison, K. (2005). Emotional bond in relational masculinity: A phenomeno-logical study. Dissertation Abstracts International: Section B: The Sciences and Engineering, Vol. 65(10-B), pp. 54–59.

Harvey, K. (2005). The history of masculinity, circa 1650–1800. *Journal of British Studies, 44,* 296–311.

Hercus, C. (1999). Identity, emotion, and feminist collective action. *Gender and Society, 13,* 34–55.

Hearn, J. (2004). From hegemonic masculinity to the hegemony of men. *Feminist Theory, 5,* 49–72.

Hrdy, S. B. (1997). Raising Darwin's consciousness: Female sexuality and the prehominid origins of patriarchy. *Human Nature, 8,* 1–49.

Huang, C. C. & Pouncy, H. (2005). Why doesn't she have a child support order?: Personal choice or objective constraint. *Family Relations: Interdisciplinary Journal of Applied Family Studies, 54,* 547–557.

Husky, M, Mazure, C., Paliwal, P., & McKee, S. (2008). Gender differences in the comorbidity of smoking behavior and major depression. *Drug and Alcohol Dependence, 93,* 176–179.

Iseke-Barnes, J. (2005). Misrepresentations of indigenous history and science: Public broadcasting, the Internet, and education. *Discourse: Studies in the Cultural Politics of Education, 26,* 149–165.

Jackson, T. L. & Petretic-Jackson, P. A. (1996). The definition, incidence, and scope of acquaintance rape and sexual assault. In T. L. Jackson (Ed.), *Acquaintance rape: Assessment, treatment, and prevention* (pp. 1–15). Sarasota, FL: Professional Resource Press.

Jefferson, T. (2002). Subordinating hegemonic masculinity. *Theoretical Criminology, 6,* 63–75.

Jimenez, M. & Vogel, L. (2005). Marxist-feminist thought today. *Science and Society, 69,* 5–10.

Johnston, R. & McIvor, A. (2004). Dangerous work, hard men and broken bodies: Masculinity in the Clydeside heavy industries. *Labour History Review, 69,* 135–151.

Kaschak, E. (1992). *Engendered Lives: A new psychology of women's experience.* New York: BasicBooks.

Kimmel, M. (1998). Who's afraid of men doing feminism? In T. Digby & S. Bartky (Eds.), *Men doing feminism* (pp. 57–69). New York: Routledge.

Kimmel, M. & Messner, M. A. (2001). Introduction. In M. S. Kimmel & M. A. Messner (Eds.), *Men's lives* (5th ed., pp. ix–xvii). Boston, MA: Pearson.

King, S. R. (2002). *Blue coat or powdered wig: Free people of color in pre-revolutionary Saint Domingue.* Athens, GA: University of Georgia Press, 2001.

Kronsell, A. (2005). Gendered practices in institutions of hegemonic masculinity: Reflections from feminist standpoint theory. *International Feminist Journal of Politics, 7*, 280–298.

Kurdek, L. A. (2004). Are gay and lesbian cohabiting couples really different from heterosexual married couples? *Journal of Marriage and Family, 66*, 880–900.

Levant, R. F. (1996). The new psychology of men. *Professional Psychology: Research and Practice, 27*, 259–265.

Lipton, R., Ghannam, J. H., & Beinin, J. (2003). Definitions of terrorism. *JAMA: Journal of the American Medical Association, 290*, 22–54.

Luepnitz, D. A. (1988). The family interpreted: Psychoanalysis, feminism, and family therapy. New York: BasicBooks.

Luo, L. & Hing-Luan, W. (1998). Gender-role traits and depression: Self-esteem and control as mediators. *Counseling Psychology Quarterly, 11*, 95–108.

MacLeod, C. (2000). Silk stockings not fine and dandy with all elite British men. *Christian Science Monitor, 92*, P7.

Mahalik, J. R., Locke, B. D., Theodore, H., Cournoyer, R. J., & Lloyd, B. F. (2001). A cross-national and cross-sectional comparison of men's gender role conflict and its relationship to social intimacy and self-esteem. *Sex Roles: A Journal of Research, 45*, 1–15.

Macys.com (2007). www.Macys.com. http://www1.macys.com/catalog/product/index.ognc?ID=254169&CategoryID=31504&LinkType=SiteAd&LinkLoc=269&AdID=39128. Retrieved December 19, 2007.

Mirehya, N. (2005, March 24). Learning to walk in size 17 pumps. *New York Times*, B1–B4.

Mirgain, S. A. & Cordova, J. V. (2007). Emotion skills and marital health: The association between observed and self-reported emotion skills, intimacy, and marital satisfaction. *Journal of Social and Clinical Psychology, 26*, 983–1009.

Morardi, B. (2005). Advancing womanist identity development: Where we are and where we need to go. *The Counseling Psychologist, 33*, 225–253.

Newman, R. J. (2005). The rise of a new power. *U.S. News and World Report, 138*, 40–51.

Nonn, T. (2004). Hitting bottom: Homelessness, poverty, and masculinity. In M. S. Kimmel & M. A. Messner (Eds.), *Men's lives* (6th ed., 258–267). New York: Pearson.

Nuzzo, A. (2004). Reasons for conflict: Political implications of a definition of terrorism. *Metaphilosophy, 35*, 330–344.

Ossana, S. M., Helms, J. E., & Leonard, M. M. (1992). Do "womanist" identity attitudes influence college women's self-esteem and perceptions of environmental bias? *Journal of Counseling and Development, 70*, 402–408.

Pateman, B. (2000). Feminist research or humanistic research? Experiences of studying prostatectomy. *Journal of Clinical Nursing, 9*, 310–316.

Paulsen, M. (1999). Deconstructing hegemonic masculinity: An approach for high school students. *Youth Studies Australia, 18*, 12–20.

Pendergast, S. & Pendergast, T. (2004). Eighteenth-century headwear: Fashion, costume, and culture: Clothing, headwear, body decorations, and footwear through the ages. In Pendergast & Pendergast (Eds.), *European culture from the Renaissance to the modern era* (575–576). Detroit, MI: UXL.

Pleck, J. H. (1976). The male sex role: Definitions, problems, and sources of change. *Journal of Social Issues, 32*, 155–164.

Pleck, J. H. (1989). Men's power with women, other men, and society: A men's movement analysis. In M. S. Kimmel & M. A. Messner (Eds.), *Men's lives* (2nd ed., 19–27). New York: Macmillan.

Prilleltensky, I. (1994). *The morals and politics of psychology: Psychological discourse and the status quo*. Albany, New York: SUNY Press.

Raskin, J. D. (2002). Constructivism in psychology: Personal construct psychology, radical constructivism, and social constructionism. In J. D. Raskin & S. K. Bridges, *Studies in meaning: Exploring constructivist psychology* (pp. 1–25). New York: Pace University Press.

Rosser, S. V. (2005). Through the lenses of feminist theory: Focus on women and informational technology. *Frontiers, 26*, 1–23.

Rothblum, E. (2004). Diversity and size acceptance: Lessons from the lesbian experience. *Health at Every Size, 18*, 41–43.

Russell, S., Crockett, L., Shen, Y.-L., & Lee, S.-A. (2008). Cross-ethnic invariance of self-esteem and depression measures for Chinese, Filipino, and European American adolescents. *Journal of Youth and Adolescence, 37*, 50–61.

Schreurs, K. (1994). Intimacy, autonomy, and relationship satisfaction in Dutch lesbian couples and heterosexual couples. *Journal of Psychology and Human Sexuality, March 1996, 7*, 41–57.

Sen, S. (2005). Diversity and North American planning curricula: The need for reform. *Canadian Journal of Urban Research, 14*, 121–144.

Serra, A. (2005). The "New Woman" in Cuban revolutionary discourse: Manuel Cofiño's the Last Woman and the Next Combat (1971). *Journal of Gender Studies, 14*, 33–43.

Shackelford, T. K., Weeks-Shackelford, V. A., & Schmitt, D. P. (2005). An evolutionary perspective on why some men refuse or reduce their child support payments. *Basic and Applied Social Psychology, 27*, 297–306.

Silverstein, O. & Rashbaum, B. (1994). *The courage to raise good men.* New York: Viking.

Simon, R. W. & Nath, L. (2004). Gender and emotion in the United States: Do men and women differ in self-reports of feelings and expressive behavior? *American Journal of Sociology, 109,* 1137–1176.

Sinacore, A. L. & Enns, C. Z. (2005). Diversity feminisms: Postmodern, women-of-color, antiracist, lesbian, third-wave, and global perspectives. In C. Z. Enns & A. L. Sinacore (Eds.), *Teaching and social justice: Integrating multicultural and feminist theories in the classroom* (pp. 41–67). Washington, DC: APA.

Soban, C. (2006). What about the boys?: Addressing issues of masculinity within male anorexia nervosa in a feminist therapeutic environment. *International Journal of Men's Health,5,* 251–267.

Stobbe, L. (2005). Doing machismo: Legitimating speech acts as a selection discourse. *Gender, Work and Organization, 12,* 1–20.

Tappan, M. B. (2000). Power, privilege, and critique in the study of moral development. *Human Development, 43,* 165–169.

Tietz, W. (2007). Women and men in accounting textbooks: Exploring the hidden curriculum. *Issues in Accounting Education, 22,* 459–480.

Tuwor, T. (2007). Equal education for girls in Ghana: Analysis of representation of women in social studies textbooks and curriculum. Dissertation Abstracts International: Section A: Humanities and Social Sciences, *Vol. 68 (4-A),* pp. 13–14.

Uhlmann, A. J. & Uhlmann, J. R. (2005). Embodiment below discourse: The internalized domination of the masculine perspective. *Women's Studies International Forum, 28,* 93–103.

Wetherell, M. & Edley, N. (1999). Negotiating hegemonic masculinity: Imaginary positions and psycho-discursive practices. *Feminism and Psychology, 9,* 335–356.

Whitehead, S. M. & Barrett, F. J. (2001). The sociology of masculinity. In S. M. Whitehead & F. J. Barrett (Eds.), *The masculinities reader* (pp. 1–26). Malden, MA: Blackwell.

Chapter 2

Academy of Motion Picture Arts & Sciences (2005). 77th Academy Awards. Retrieved October 1, 2005 from: http://www.oscars.org/77academyawards/nomswins.html.

Ackerman, L. & Klein, L. (1995). *Women and Power in Native North America.* Norman, OK: University of Oklahoma Press, 1995.

Albury, R. M. (2005). Unpacking queer politics: A – lesbian feminist perspective. *Culture, Health and Sexuality, 7*, 414–416.

Anderson, S., Balme, J., & Beck, W. (1995). Archaeology as legitimizing feminist historiography: A case for a deconstruction of the Australian historical archaeological record. *Gendered archaeology: The second Australian Women in Archaeology Conference*, 80–83.

Austin-Smith, B. (1992). A man's place. *Canadian Dimension, 26*, 35–36.

Barrett, F. J. (2001). Hegemonic masculinity: The US Navy. In S. M. Whitehead & F. J. Barrett (Eds.), *The masculinities reader* (pp. 77–99). Malden, MA: Blackwell.

Bell, D. A. (2006). The idea of a patriot queen? The monarchy, the constitution, and the iconographic order of greater Britain, 1860–1900. *Journal of Imperial and Commonwealth History, 34*, 3–21.

Bolger, D. (1966). Figurines, fertility, and the emergence of complex society in prehistoric Cyprus. *Current Anthropology, 37*, 365–372.

Branscombe, N. R. (1998). Thinking about one's gender group's privileges or disadvantages: Consequences for well-being in women and men. *British Journal of Social Psychology, 37*, 167–184.

Brod, H. (1998). To be a man or not to be a man, that is the feminist question. In T. Digby (Ed.), *Men doing feminism* (pp. 197–212). New York: Routledge.

Brown, T. M. & Fee, E. (2003). William Edward Burghardt DuBois: Historian, social critic, activist. *American Journal of Public Health, 93*, 274–275.

Buddington, S. A. (2001). Barbie.com and Racial Identity. Paper presented at the Annual National Conference of the National Association of African American Studies and the National Association of Hispanic and Latino Studies (Houston, TX, February 21–26, 2000).

Cheng, C. (1999). Marginalized masculinities and hegemonic masculinities and hegemonic masculinity: An introduction. *The Journal of Men's Studies, 7*, 295–315.

Clatterbaugh, K. (1997). *Contemporary perspectives on masculinity*. Oxford, UK: Westview Press.

Connell, B. (1989). Masculinity, violence and war. In M. S. Kimmel & M. A. Messner (Eds.), *Men's lives* (2nd ed., pp. 176–182). New York: Macmillan.

Connell, R. W. (1995). *Masculinities*. Berkeley, CA: University of California Press.

Connell, R. W. (2001). The social organization of masculinity. In S. M. Whitehead & F. J. Barrett (Eds.), *The masculinities reader* (pp. 27–47). Malden, MA: Blackwell.

Constantine, S. (2006). Monarchy and constructing identity in "British" Gibraltar, *c.* 1800 to the present. *Journal of Imperial and Commonwealth History, 34,* 23–44.

Davies-Netzley, S. A. (2002). Women above the glass ceiling: Perceptions on corporate mobility and strategies for success. In A. E. Hunter & C. Forden (Eds.), *Readings in the psychology of gender* (pp. 300–314). Boston, MA: Allyn & Bacon.

Deegan, M. J. (2001, Winter). W. E. B. Dubois and the women of Hull House, 1895–1899. *The American Sociologist, 19,* 301–311.

Dekeseredy, W. S., Schwartz, M. D., & Alvi, S. (2000). The role of profeminist men in dealing with woman abuse on the Canadian college campus. *Violence against Women, 6,* 918–935.

Demetriou, D. (2001). Connell's concept of hegemonic masculinity: A critique. *Theory and Society, 30,* 337–361.

Digby, T. (1998). Introduction. In T. Digby & S. Bartky (Eds.), *Men doing feminism* (pp. 1–17). New York: Routledge.

Disney, R. H. (1999). *The lion king.* New York, Random House.

Donnelley, D., Cook, K. J., Van Ausdale, D., & Foley, L. (2005). White privilege, color blindness, and services to battered women. *Violence against Women, 11,* 6–37.

Douglas, P. (1994). "New Men" and the tensions of profeminism. *Social Alternatives, 12,* 32–36.

Duelli Klein, R. (1983). The "men problem" in women's studies: The expert, the ignoramus, and the poor dear. *Women's Studies International Forum, 6,* 413–421.

Dunbar, M. (1999). Dennis Rodman – "Barbie doll gone horribly wrong": Marginalized masculinity, cross-dressing, and the limitations of commodity culture. *Journal of Men's Studies, 99,* 317–336.

Dworkin, A. (1987). Look dick, look. See Jane blow it. In A. Dworkin (Ed.), *Letters from a warzone* (pp. 126–132). London: Secker & Warburg.

Erickson, J. (2007). Women make progress under title IX, but barriers persist. *National NOW Times, 39,* 6–7.

Farough, S. D. (2003). Structural aporia and white masculinities: White men respond to the white male privilege critique. *Race, Gender and Class, 10,* 38–53.

50 Cent. "Make Money by any Means" from *The power of the dollar.* http://display.lyrics.astraweb.com:2000/display.cgi?50_cent%2E%2Ethe_power_of_the_dollar%2E%2Emake_money_by_any_means. http://www.50cent.com/ (Retrieved September 20, 2005).

Finley, N. J. (1996). Relinquishing dominant privilege: A study of feminist men. *Sociological Spectrum, 16,* 159–172.

Fisher, C., Hauck, Y., & Fenwick, J. (2006). How social context impacts on women's fears of childbirth: A Western Australian example. *Social Science and Medicine, 63,* 64–75.

Gero, J. M. (2001). Field knots and ceramic beaus: Interpreting gender in the Peruvian early intermediate period. In C. F. Klein & J. Quilter (Eds.), *Gender in Pre-Hispanic America* (pp. 15–55). Washington, DC: Harvard University Press.

Gilligan, C. (1982). *In a different voice: Psychological theory and women's development.* Cambridge, MA: Harvard University Press.

Gleitzman, M. (2003). When minority group members stereotype: Comparing lesbians' and gay men's stereotypes of each other. *Australian Journal of Psychology, 55,* 44.

Goldenberg, I. & Goldenberg, H. (1991). *Family therapy: An overview.* Belmont, CA: Brooks/Cole.

Gutterman, D. S. (2001). Postmodernism and the interrogation of masculinity. In S. M. Whitehead & F. J. Barrett (Eds.), *The masculinities reader* (pp. 56–72). Malden, MA: Blackwell.

Hall, R. E. (2004). Entitlement disorder. *Journal of Black Studies, 34,* 562–579.

Harvey, K. (2005). The history of masculinity, circa 1650–1800. *Journal of British Studies, 44,* 296–311.

Hearn, J. (2004). From hegemonic masculinity to the hegemony of men. *Feminist Theory, 5,* 49–72.

Hooks, B. (2003). Class and race: The new black elite. In M. Kimmel & A. Ferber (Eds.), *Privilege: A reader* (pp. 243–252). Boulder, CO: Westview Press.

Hopkins, P. D. (1998). How feminism made a man out of me: The proper subject of feminism and the problem of men. In T. Digby & S. Bartky (Eds.), *Men doing feminism* (pp. 33–56). New York: Routledge.

Huffman, M. L. & Cohen, P. (2004). Occupational segregation and the gender gap in workplace authority: National versus local labor markets. *Sociological Forum, 19,* 121–147.

Hurwich, J. J. (2003). Bastards in the German nobility in the fifteenth and early sixteenth centuries: Evidence of the Zimmerische Chronik. *The Sixteenth Century Journal, 34,* 701–728.

Jaffee, S. & Hyde, J. S. (2000). Gender differences in moral orientation: A meta-analysis. *Psychological Bulletin, 126,* 703–726.

Jefferson, T. (2002). Subordinating hegemonic masculinity. *Theoretical Criminology, 6,* 63–75.

Johannson, T. & Hammarén, N. (2007). Hegemonic masculinity and pornography: Young people's attitudes toward and relations to pornography. *The Journal of Men's Studies, 15*, 57–70.

Johnson, A. G. (1997). *The gender knot: Unraveling our patriarchal legacy.* Philadelphia, PA: Temple University Press.

Johnson, M. P. (2001). Patriarchal terrorism and common couple violence: Two forms of violence against women. In T. F. Cohen (Ed.), *Men and masculinity: A text reader* (pp. 248–260). Stamford, CT: Wadsworth.

Johnson, P. (2001). Under wraps. *American Legacy: Celebrating African-American History, 7*, 14–17.

Johnston, D. C. (2002, May 12). As salary grows, so does a gender gap. *New York Times, 151*, 8.

Kahane, D. (1998). Male feminism as oxymoron. In T. Digby & S. Bartky (Eds.), *Men doing feminism* (pp. 213–236). New York: Routledge.

Kantrowitz, B. & Juarez, V. (2005). When women lead. *Newsweek, 146*, 46–47.

Kaschak, E. (1992). *Engendered Lives: A new psychology of women's experience.* New York: BasicBooks.

Kimmel, M. (1998). Who's afraid of men doing feminism? In T. Digby & S. Bartky (Eds.), *Men doing feminism* (pp. 57–69). New York: Routledge.

Kimmel, M. S. (2003). Masculinity as homophobia: Fear, shame, and silence in the construction of gender identity In M. Kimmel & A. Ferber (Eds.), *Privilege: A reader* (pp. 51–74). Boulder, CO: Westview Press.

Kimmel, M. S. & Messner, M. A. (2001). *Men's lives* (5th ed.). Needham Heights, MA: Allyn & Bacon.

Kronsell, A. (2005). Gendered practices in institutions of hegemonic masculinity: Reflections from feminist standpoint theory. *International Feminist Journal of Politics, 7*, 280–298.

Levant, R. F. (1996). The new psychology of men. *Professional Psychology: Research and Practice, 27*, 259–265.

Levine, G. C. (2003). *The princess tales: volume one.* New York: HarperCollins.

Lingard, B. & Douglas, P. (1999). *Men engaging feminisms.* Philadelphia, PA: Open University Press.

MacInnes, J. (2001). The crisis of masculinity and the politics of identity. In S. M. Whitehead & F. J. Barrett (Eds.), *The masculinities reader* (pp. 311–329). Malden, MA: Blackwell.

McIntosh, P. (1990). White privilege: Unpacking the invisible knapsack. *Independent School, Winter*, 32–37.

McIntosh, P. (1993). Examining unearned privilege. *Liberal Education, 79*, 61–63.

McIntosh, P. (2000). White privilege and male privilege: A personal account of coming to see correspondences through work in women's studies. In T. E. Ore (Ed.), *The social construction of difference and Inequality* (pp. 475–485). Mountain View, CA: Mayfield.

Mantsios, G. (2003). Class in America: Myths and realities. In M. Kimmel & A. Ferber (Eds.), *Privilege: A reader* (pp. 33–50). Boulder, CO: Westview Press.

Mead, M. (1963). Sex and temperament in three primitive societies. New York: Morrow.

Messner, M. A. (2004). Barbie girls versus sea monsters: Children constructing gender. In M. Kimmel & M. A. Messner (Eds.), *Men's lives* (6th ed., pp. 87–102). New York: Pearson.

Murray, C. & Greenberg, M. T. (2006). Examining the importance of social relationships and social contexts in the lives of children with high-incidence disabilities. *Journal of Special Education, 39,* 220–233.

Nevo, J. (1998, July). Religion and National Identity in Saudi Arabia. *Middle Eastern Studies, 34.*

Okoampa-ahoofe, K. (1997). Dubois was a talented "profeminist". *New York Amsterdam News, 88,* 26–28.

Oppliger, P. A. (2004). Wrestling and hypermasculinity. London: McFarland Press.

Ossana, S. M., Helms, J. E., & Leonard, M. M. (1992). Do "womanist" identity attitudes influence college women's self-esteem and perceptions of environmental bias? *Journal of Counseling and Development, 70,* 402–408.

Page, S. & Tyrer, J. (1995). Gender and prediction of Gilligan's Justice and Care orientation. *Journal of College Student Psychotherapy, 10,* 43–56.

Paulsen, M. (1999). Deconstructing hegemonic masculinity: An approach for high school students. *Youth Studies Australia, 18,* 12–20.

Penterits, E. J. (2004). The White Privilege Attitudes Scale: Construction and initial validation. Dissertation Abstracts International: Section B: The Sciences and Engineering, Vol. 65, p. 448.

Peralta, R. (2007). College alcohol use and the embodiment of hegemonic masculinity among European American men, *Sex Roles, 56,* 741–756.

Petrzelka, P. (2005). They make how much? Investigating faculty salaries to examine gender inequalities. *Teaching Sociology, 33,* 380–388.

Pewewardy, N. & Severson, M. (2003). A threat to liberty: White privilege and disproportionate minority incarceration. *Journal of Progressive Human Services, 14,* 52–74.

Phillips, D. A. (2005). Reproducing normative and marginalized masculinities: Adolescent male popularity and the outcast. *Nursing Inquiry, 12,* 219–230.

Price, D. (2007). Closing the gender gap in retirement income: What difference will recent UK pension reforms make? *Journal of Social Policy, 36,* 561–583.

Python, M. (1976). *Monty Python and the Holy Grail.* http://en. thinkexist.com/ quotation/watery_women_laying_in_ponds_giving_out_swords_is/ 346883.html. Retrieved June 28, 2006.

Roy, D. (2006). Cooperation and conflict in the factory: Some observations and questions regarding conceptualization of intergroup relations within bureaucratic social structures. *Qualitative Sociology, 29,* 59–85.

Rucker, W. (2002). "A negro nation within the nation": W. E. B. DuBois and the creation of a revolutionary Pan-Africanist tradition, 1903–1947. *The Black Scholar, 32,* 37–47.

Sargent, P. (2005). The gendering of men in early childhood education. *Sex Roles, 52,* 251–259.

Schacht, S. P. (2003). Teaching about being an oppressor: Some personal and political considerations. In M. Kimmel & A. Ferber (Eds.), *Privilege: A reader* (pp. 161–171). Boulder, CO: Westview Press.

Schacht, S. P. & Ewing, D. (1997). The many paths of feminism: Can men travel any of them? *Journal of Gender Studies, 6,* 159–176.

Schwarz, S. (2004). The privilege gap. *Tikkun, 19,* 66–69.

Sivaraksa, S. (2002). Take pride, and the rest will follow: Democratic movements, reformed monarchy good for Thailand. *Times Higher Education Supplement, 1540,* 22.

Smith, P. (1987). Men in feminism: Men and feminist theory. In A. Jardine & P. Smith (Eds.), *Men in feminism* (pp. 33–40). London: Methuen.

Smith, J. (2007). "Ye've got to 'ave balls to play this game sir!" Boys, peers and fears: the negative influence of school-based "cultural accomplices" in constructing hegemonic masculinities. *Gender and Education, 19,* 179–198.

Smith, R. A. (2002). Race, gender, and authority in the workplace: Theory and research. *Annual Review of Sociology, 28,* 509–542.

Sobel, T. (2005). Personal communication. Girls, Women, and Media Project. (www.mediaandwomen.org).

Speer, S. A. (2001). Reconsidering the concept of hegemonic masculinity: Discursive psychology, conversation analysis and participant's observation. *Feminism and Psychology, 11,* 107–135.

Stearns, P. (2006). Part III: Reintroducing and refining social structure in social history. *Journal of Social History, 39,* 779–781.

Stoltenberg, J. (1993). *The end of manhood.* New York: Penguin Books.

Szarycz, I. (2001). Morsels on the tongue: Evidence of a Pre-Christian matriarchy in Russian fairy tales. *Stadia Slavica Academiae Scientarum Hungaricae, 46,* 63–73.

Tulloch, J. (2004). Art and archaeology as an historical resource for the study of women in early Christianity: An approach for analyzing visual data. *Feminist Theology: The Journal of the Britain and Ireland School of Feminist Theology, 12,* 277–304.

Turner, J. (2006). Tyranny, freedom and social structure: Escaping our theoretical prisons. *British Journal of Social Psychology, 45,* 41–46.

Vicario, B. A. (2004). A qualitative study of profeminist men. (Doctoral Dissertation, 2004). Auburn University, Auburn Alabama. Vol. 64(11-A), 2004.

Vogel, K. (2003). Female shamanism, goddess cultures, and psychedelics. *Revision, 25,* 18–28.

Voon, C. P. (2007). Contesting and maintaining hegemonic masculinities: Gay Asian American men in mate selection. *Sex Roles, 57,* 909–918.

Waite, C. L. (2001). DuBois and the invisible talented tenth. In K. Weiler (Ed.), *Feminist engagements: Reading, resisting, and revisioning male theorists in education and cultural studies* (pp. 33–45). New York: Routledge.

Watanabe, H. (2007). Media women in Japan have achieved slow but steady progress. *Media Report to Women, 35, Issue 4,* 5.

Weeks, W. B. & Wallace, A. E. (2007). Gender differences in ophthalmologists' annual incomes. *Ophthalmology, 114,* 1696–1701.

Wetherell, M. & Edley, N. (1999). Negotiating hegemonic masculinity: Imaginary positions and psycho-discursive practices. *Feminism and Psychology, 9,* 335–356.

Whitehead, S. M. & Barrett, F. J. (2001). The sociology of masculinity. In S. M. Whitehead & F. J. Barrett (Eds.), *The masculinities reader* (pp. 1–26). Malden, MA: Blackwell.

Wilson, M. C. (2004). Closing the leadership gap. *Ms., 14,* 14–15.

Windelspect, E. (2004). *Human body systems.* Westport, CT: Greenwood Press.

Winton, C. A. (1995). *Frameworks for studying families.* New Jersey: Dushkin.

Woods, C. (1996). Gender differences in moral development and acquisition: A review of Kohlberg's and Gilligan's models of justice and care. *Social Behavior and Personality, 24,* 375–384.

Chapter 3

Abdullah, K. (2005). Mirrors of masculinity: Defining the state of the black male has never been easy, but a few selections can offer clues as to what's on the minds of many who make an effort to do so. *Black Issues, 7,* 50–51.

Bandura, A. & Bussey, K. (2004). On broadening the cognitive, motivational, and sociostructural scope of theorizing about gender development and functioning: Comment on Martin, Ruble, and Szkrybalo (2002). *Psychological Bulletin, 30*, 691–701.

Barton, E. R. (2000). Parallels between mythopoetic men's work/men's peer mutual support groups and selected feminist theories. In E. Read (Ed.), *Mythopoetic perspectives of men's healing work, an anthology for therapists and others* (pp. 3–20). Westport, CT: Bergin & Harvey.

Bengtsson, H. & Johnson, L. (1992). Perspective taking, empathy, and prosocial behavior in late childhood. *Child Study Journal, 22*, 11–22.

Berger, J. M., Levant, R., McMillan, K. K., Kelleher, W., & Sellers, A. (2005). Impact of gender-role conflict, traditional masculinity ideology, alexithymia, and age on men's attitudes toward psychological help seeking. *Psychology of Men and Masculinities, 1*, 73–78.

Bergman, S. J. & Surrey, J. (1993). Changing nature of relationships on campus: Impasses and possibilities. *Educational Record, 74*, 13–20.

Bernard, J. (1989). The good provider role: It's rise and fall. In M. Kimmel & M. A. Messner (Eds.), *Men's lives* (2nd ed., pp. 203–220). New York: Macmillan.

Bowker, A., Gabdois, S., & Cornock, B. (2003). Sports participation and self-esteem: variations as a function of gender and gender role orientation. *Sex Roles, 49*, 47–58.

Burger, J. M. (2004). *Personality.* Belmont, CA: Wadsworth/Thomson Learning.

Cazenave, N. A. (1984). Race, socioeconomic status, and age: The social context of American Masculinity. *Sex Roles, 11*, 639–657.

Changfoot, N. (2004). Feminist standpoint theory, Hegel and the dialectical self. *Philosophy and Social Criticism, 30*, 477–502.

Collins, P. H. (1989). The social construction of black feminist thought. *Signs, Journal of Women in Culture and Society, 14*, 745–773.

Collins, P. H. (1997). How much difference is too much? Black feminist thought and the politics of postmodern social theory. *Current Perspectives in Social Theory, 17*, 3–37.

Connell, R. W. (1995). *Masculinities.* Berkeley, CA: University of California Press.

Connell, R. W. (2001). The social organization of masculinity. In S. M. Whitehead & F. J. Barrett (Eds.), *The masculinities reader* (pp. 27–47). Malden, MA: Blackwell.

Daniels, E. & Leaper, C. (2006). A longitudinal investigation of sport participation, peer acceptance, and self-esteem among adolescent girls and boys. *Sex Roles, 55*, 11–12, 875–880.

David, D. S. & Brannon, R. (Eds.). (1976). *The forty-nine percent majority*. Reading, MA: Addison-Wesley.

Demetriou, D. Z. (2001). Connell's concept of hegemonic masculinity: A critique. *Theory and Society, 30*, 337–361.

Edwards, D. (1997). *Discourse and cognition*. Thousand Oaks, CA: Sage.

Eisenberg, N. & Fabes, R. A. (1998). Prosocial development. In W. Damon & N. Eisenberg (Eds.), *Handbook of child psychology, Vol. 3: Social, emotional, and personality development* (pp. 701–778). New York: Wiley.

Fausto-Sterling, A. (1999). Is gender essential? In M. Rottnek (Ed.), *Sissies and tomboys* (pp. 52–57). New York: New York University Press.

Frable, D. E. (1989). Sex typing and gender ideology: Two facets of the individual's gender psychology that go together. *Journal of Personality and Social Psychology, 56*, 95–108.

Franklin, C. W. II (1988). *Men and society*. Chicago, IL: Nelson-Hall.

Freedberg, S. (2007). Re-examining empathy: A relational-feminist point of view. *Social Work, 52*, 251–259.

Freud, S. (1963). *General psychological theory*. New York: Macmillan & Co.

Furby, L. (1983). Consistency and contradiction in the development of gender role characteristics. *New Ideas in Psychology, 1*, 285–297.

Gallagher, E. V. (2006). Autobiography of Malcolm X imparts important lessons about teaching and learning. *Diverse: Issues in Higher Education, 23*, 47.

Gergen, K. J. (1999). *An invitation to social construction*. London: Sage.

Geschwind, D. H. & Dykens, E. (2004). Neurobehavioral and psychosocial issues in Klinefelter syndrome. *Learning Disabilities Research and Practice, 19*, 166–173.

Gilbert, R. K. (1992). Revisiting the psychology of men: Robert Bly and the mythopoetic movement. *Journal of Humanistic Psychology, 32*, 41–67.

Good, G. E., Borst, T. S., & Wallace, D. L. (1994). Masculinity research: A review and critique. *Applied and Preventative Psychology, 3*, 3–14.

Gray, J. (2004). *Men are from Mars women are from Venus: The classic guide to understanding the opposite sex*. New York: HarperCollins.

Green, R. (2000). Family co-ocurrence of "gender dysphoria" ten sibling or parent-child pairs. *Archives of Sexual Behavior, 29*, 499–507.

Grinnel College (2001). *Gay Masculinities*. http://web. grinnel. edu/courses/ lih/s01 /lih397_01,/rostructuring maoculinities/documents/gaymasc.pdf. Retrieved February 12, 2003.

Harré, R. (1988). *The singular self: An introduction to the psychology of personhood*. London: Sage.

Harrington, L. & Liu, J. H. (2002). Self-enhancement and attitudes toward high achievers: A bicultural view of the independent and interdependent self. *Journal of Cross-Cultural Psychology, 33,* 37–55.

Harvey, K. (2005). The history of masculinity, circa 1650–1800. *Journal of British Studies, 44,* 296–311.

Hayslett-McCall, K. L. & Bernard, T. J. (2002). Attachment, masculinity, and self-control: A theory of male crime rates. *Theoretical Criminology, 6,* 5–33.

Hekman, S. (1997). Truth and method: Feminist standpoint theory revisited. *Signs: Journal of Women in Culture and Society, 22,* 341–365.

Hoffman, R. M. (2001). The measurement of masculinity and femininity: Historical perspective and implications for counseling. *Journal of Counseling and Development, 79,* 472–485.

Hofstede, G. (1998). *Masculinity and femininity: The taboo dimension of national cultures.* Thousand Oaks, CA: Sage.

Hopcke, R. H. (1999). *A guided tour of the collected works of C. G. Jung.* Boston, MA: Shambhala Productions.

Hyde, J. S., Kranjik, M., & Skuldt, K. (1991). Androgyny across the lifespan: A replication and follow-up. *Developmental Psychology, 27,* 516–519.

Johnson, A. G. (1997). *The gender knot.* Philadelphia, PA: Temple University Press.

Jung, C. J. (1971). *Aspects of the masculine, aspects of the feminine.* New York: MJF Books.

Kagitcibasi, C. (2005). Autonomy and relatedness in cultural context: Implications for self and family. *Journal of Cross-Cultural Psychology, 36,* 403–422.

Kaschak, E. (1992). *Engendered lives: A new psychology of women's experience.* New York: BasicBooks.

Kelly, G. (1963). *A theory of personality: The psychology of personal constructs.* Toronto: W. W. Norton & Co.

Kimmel, M. S. (2003). Toward a pedagogy of the oppressor. In M. S. Kimmel & A. L. Ferber (Eds.), *Privilege: A reader* (pp. 1–10). Boulder, CO: Westview.

Kimmel, M. S. & Kaufman, M. (1995). Weekend warriors: The new men's movement. In M. S. Kimmel (Ed.), *The politics of manhood: Profeminist men respond to the mythopoetic movement (and the mythopoetic leaders answer* (pp. 15–43). Philadelphia, PA: Temple University Press.

Kimmel, M. S. & Messner, M. A. (2001). Introduction. In M. S. Kimmel & M. A. Messner (Eds.), *Men's lives* (5th ed., pp. ix–xvii). Boston, MA: Allyn & Bacon.

Kirshner, H. (2002). *Behavioral neurology: Practical science of mind and brain.* Boston, MA: Butterworth-Heinemann.

Kitayama, S., Markus, H. R., & Kurokawa, M. (2000). Culture, emotion, and well-being: Good feelings in Japan and the United States. *Cognition and Emotion, 14,* 93–124.

Krishna, S. (2007). Quest for harmony and postmodern Gandhi and other essays: Gandhi in the world and at home. *Perspectives on Politics, 5,* 814–816.

Kronsell, A. (2005). Gendered practices in institutions of hegemonic masculinity: Reflections from feminist standpoint theory. *International Feminist Journal of Politics, 7,* 280–298.

León, L. (2007). Cesar Chavez in American religious politics: Mapping the new global spiritual line. *American Quarterly, 59,* 857–881.

Levant, R. F. (1998). Desperately seeking language: Understanding, assessing, and treating normative male alexithymia. In W. S. Pollack & R. F. Levant (Eds.), *A new psychology of men* (pp. 424–442). New York: John Wiley & Sons.

Levant, R. F., Cuthbert, A., & Richmond, K. (2003). Masculinity ideology among Russian and U.S. young men and women and its relationship to unhealthy lifestyle habits among young Russian men. *Psychology of Men and Masculinity, 4,* 26–36.

Liew, J., Eisenberg, N., Losoya, S. H., Fabes, R, A., Guthrie, I. K., & Murphy, B. C. (2003). Children's physiological indices of empathy and their socioemotional adjustment: Does caregivers expressivity matter? *Journal of Family Psychology, 17,* 584–597.

Mahalik, J. R., Cournoyer, R. J., DeFranc, W., Cherry, M., & Napolitano, J. M. (1998). Men's gender role conflict and use of psychological defenses. *Journal of Counseling Psychology, 45,* 247–255.

Mahalik, J. R., Good, G. E., & Englar-Carlson, M. (2003). Masculinity scripts, presenting concerns, and help seeking: Implications for practice and training. *Professional Psychology Research and Practice, 34,* 123–131.

May, R. (1986). Concerning a psychoanalytic view of maleness. *The Psychoanalytic Review, 4,* 579–587.

Mead, M. (1963). *Sex and temperament in three primitive societies.* New York: William Morrow and Company.

Messner, M. A. (1995). "Changing men" and feminist politics. In M. S. Kimmel (Ed.), *The politics of manhood: Profeminist men respond to the mythopoetic men's movement* (pp. 97–114). Philadelphia, PA: Temple University Press.

Moore, R. & Gillette, D. (1990). *King, warrior, magician, lover: Rediscovering the archetypes of the mature masculine.* New York: HarperCollins.

O'Leary, C. M. (1997). Counteridentification or counterhegemony? Transforming feminist standpoint theory. *Women and Politics, 18,* 45–72.

O'Neil, J. M. (1981). Male sex role conflicts, sexism, and masculinity: Psychological implications for men, women, and the counseling psychologist. *The Counseling Psychologist, 9,* 61–81.

Paulsen, M. (1999). Deconstructing hegemonic masculinity: An approach for high school students. *Youth Studies Australia, 18,* 12–20.

Peyser, M. (2005). Round six for "Rocky". *Newsweek, 146,* 69.

Pleck, J. H. (1976). The male sex role: Definitions, problems, and sources of change. *Journal of Social Issues, 32,* 155–164.

Pleck, J. H. (1989). Men's power with women, other men, and society: A men's movement analysis. In M. S. Kimmel & M. A. Messner (Eds.), *Men's lives* (2nd ed., pp. 19–27). New York: Macmillan.

Pleck, J. H. (1995). The gender role strain paradigm: An update. In R. F. Levant & W. S. Pollack (Eds.), *A new psychology of men* (pp. 11–32). New York: BasicBooks.

Pleck, J. H., Sonnestein, F. L., & Ku, L. C. (1993). Masculinity ideology: Its impact on adolescent males' heterosexual relationships. *Journal of Social Issues, 49,* 11–29.

Pogun, S. (2001). Sex differences in brain and behavior: emphasis on nicotine, nitric oxide and place learning. *International Journal of Psychophysiology, 42,* 195–208.

Polani, P. E. (1969). Abnormal sex chromosomes and mental disorder. *Nature, 223,* 680–686.

Pollack, W. S. (1995). No man is an island: toward a new psychoanalytic psychology of men. In R. F. Levant & W. S. Pollack (Eds.), *A new psychology of men* (pp. 33–67). New York: BasicBooks.

Pollack, W. S. (1998). *Real boys: Rescuing our sons from the myths of boyhood.* New York: Henry Holy & Co.

Potter, J. & Wetherell, M. (1987). *Discourse and social psychology: Beyond attitudes and behavior.* London: Sage.

Prilleltensky, I. (1994). *The morals and politics of psychology: Psychological discourse and the status quo.* Albany, New York: SUNY Press.

Pronger, B. (1998). On your knees: Carnal knowledge, masculine dissolution, doing feminism. In T. Digby (Ed.), *Men doing feminism* (pp. 69–80). New York: Routledge.

Reitman, M. (2007). The geography of Malcolm X: Black radicalism and the making of American space, by James Tyner. *Journal of Regional Science, 47,* 1024–1026.

Roberts, W. & Strayer, J. (1996). Empathy, emotional expressiveness, and prosocial behavior. *Child Development, 67*, 449–470.

Rowland, S. (2002). *Jung: A feminist revision*. Malden, MA: Blackwell.

Satinover, J. (1986). The myth of the death of the hero: A Jungian view of masculine psychology. *The Psychoanalytic Review, 73*, 149–161.

Sattel, J. W. (1989). The inexpressive male: Tragedy or sexual politics? In M. S. Kimmel & M. A. Messner (Eds.), *Men's lives* (2nd ed., pp. 350–357). New York: Macmillan.

Shimoda, H. & Keskinen, S. (2004). Ideal gender identity related to parental images and locus of control: Jungian and social learning perspectives. *Psychological Reports, 94*, 1187–1201.

Silverstein, O. & Rashbaum, B. (1994). *The courage to raise good men*. New York: Viking.

Spence, J. T. & Buckner, C. (1995). Masculinity and femininity: Defining the undefinable. In P. J. Kalbfleisch & M. J. Cody (Eds.), *Gender, power, and communication in human relationships* (pp. 105–138). Washington, DC: American Psychological Association.

Steinberg, W. (1993). *Masculinity: Identity, conflict, and transformation*. Boston, MA: Shambhala.

Stoltenberg, J. (1989). *Refusing to be a man: Essays on sex and justice*. New York: Penguin.

Strate, L. (2004). Beer commercials: A manual on masculinity. In M. Kimmel & M. A. Messner (Eds.) *Men's lives* (6th ed., pp. 533–542). Boston, MA: Pearson.

Swain, A. & Jones, G. (1991). Gender role endorsement and competitive anxiety. *International Journal of Sports Psychology, 22*, 50–65.

Thompson, E. H. & Pleck, J. H. (1986). The structure of male role norms. *American Behavioral Scientist, 29*, 531–543.

Thompson, E. H., Pleck, J. H., & Ferrera, D. L. (1992). Men and masculinities: Scales for masculinity ideology and masculinity-related constructs. *Sex Roles, 27*, 573–607.

Uhlmann, A. J. & Uhlmann, J. R. (2005). Embodiment below discourse: The internalized domination of the masculine perspective. *Women's Studies International Forum, 28*, 93–103.

Weiner, A. (2006, November 21). Yo, Rocky, or Rambo, gonna fly now at 60. *New York Times, 156*, e1–e8.

Wehr, D. S. (1987). *Jung and feminism: Liberating archetypes*. Boston, MA: Beacon Press.

Weiten, W. (2004). *Psychology: Themes and variations*. Belmont, CA: Thomson/ Wadsworth.

Wetherell, M. & Edley, N. (1999). Negotiating hegemonic masculinity: Imaginary positions and psycho-discursive practices. *Feminism and Psychology, 9*, 335–356.

Whitehead, S. M. & Barrett, F. J. (2001). The sociology of masculinity. In S. M. Whitehead & F. J. Barrett (Eds.), *The masculinities reader* (pp. 1–26). Malden, MA: Blackwell.

Wise, D. & Stake, J. E. (2002). The moderating roles of personal and social resources on the relationship between dual expectations (for instrumentality and expressiveness) and well-being. *The Journal of Social Psychology, 14*, 109–119.

Woods, S. (2007, November). Live free or die hard. *Rolling Stone, 1040*, 92.

Youmans, S. (2004). *Always moving: Using memoir and theoretical constructions of masculinity to generate a unique perspective on mature male transformation.* Thesis, Goddard College.

Chapter 4

Abreau, J. M., Goodyear, R. K., Campos, A., & Newcomb, M. D. (2000). Ethnic belonging and traditional masculinity ideology among African Americans, European Americans, and Latinos. *Psychology of Men and Masculinity, 1*, 75–86.

Addis, M. E. & Mahalik, J. R. (2003). Men, masculinity, and contexts of help seeking. *American Psychologist, 58*, 5–14.

Aune, B. (1970). *Rationalism, empiricism, pragmatism: An introduction.* New York: Random house.

Auster, C. J. & Ohm, S. C. (2000). Masculinity and femininity in contemporary American society: A reevaluation using the Bem Sex-role inventory. *Sex Roles: A Journal of Research, 43*, 499–528.

Bem, S. L. (1974). The measurement of psychological androgyny. *Journal of Consulting and Clinical Psychology, 42*, 155–172.

Bem, S. L. (1981a). The BSRI and gender schema theory: A reply to Spence and Helmreich. *Psychological Review, 88*, 369–371.

Bem, S. L. (1981b). Gender schema theory: A cognitive account of sex typing. *Psychological Review, 4*, 354–364.

Bem, S. L. (1984). Androgyny and gender schema theory: A conceptual and empirical investigation. In T. B. Sonderegger (Ed.), Psychology and Gender (pp. 179–226). Omaha, NE: University of Nebraska Press.

Benjamin, L. T. Jr. (1997). *A history of psychology: Original sources and contemporary research* (2nd ed.). New York: McGraw-Hill.

Berger, J. M., Levant, R., McMillan, K. K., Kelleher, W., & Sellers, A. (2005). Impact of gender-role conflict, traditional masculinity ideology, alexithymia, and age on men's attitudes toward psychological help seeking. *Psychology of Men and Masculinities, 1*, 73–78.

Brickell, C. (2005). Masculinities, perfomativity, and subversion: A sociological reappraisal. *Men and masculinities, 8*, 24–43.

Bund, S. & Do, E. Y. (2005). SPOT! Fetch Light: Interactive navigable 3D visualization of direct sunlight. *Automation in Construction, 14*, 181–188.

Chan, J. W. (2000). Bruce Lee's fictional model of masculinity. *Men and Masculinities, 4*, 371–387.

Cheng, C. (1999). Marginalized masculinities and hegemonic masculinity: An introduction. *The Journal of Men's Studies, 7*, 295–315.

Choi, N. (2004). A psychometric examination of the Personal Attributes Questionnaire. *Journal of Social Psychology, 144*, 348–352.

Chu, J., Porche, M. V., & Tolman, D. (2005). The adolescent masculinity ideology in relationships scale: Development and validation of a new measure for boys. *Men and Masculinities, 8*, 93–115.

Connell, R. W. (1995). *Masculinities*. Berkeley, CA: University of California Press.

Constantinople, A. (1973). Masculinity-femininity: An exception to the famous dictum? *Psychological Bulletin, 80*, 389–407.

Cornwall, A. (1997). Men, masculinity, and gender in development. *Gender in Development, 5*, 8–13.

David, D. S. & Brannon, R. (Eds.). (1976). *The forty-nine percent* majority. Reading, MA: Addison-Wesley.

Edwards, D. (1997). *Discourse and cognition*. Thousand Oaks, CA: Sage.

Epstein, R. & Liverant, S. (1963). Verbal conditioning and sex-role identification in children. *Child Development, 34*, 99–106.

Fetterman, M. (2006, December 12). Boy gets in touch with his feminine side. *USA Today*, 01b.

Fitzpatrick, M. K., Salgado, D. M., Suvak, M. K., King, L. A., & King, D. W. (2004). *Psychology of Men and Masculinity, 2*, 93–102.

Foucault, M. (1965). *Madness and civilization: A history of insanity in the age of reason*. New York: Pantheon Books

Foucault, M. (1995). *Discipline and punish: The birth of the prison*. New York: Vintage Books, 1995.

Franklin, C. W. II (1988). *Men and society*. Chicago, IL: Nelson-Hall.

Galambos, R., Juhász, G., Lorincz, M., & Szilágyi, N. (2005). The human retinal functional unit. *International Journal of Psychophysiology, 57*, 187–194.

Gergen, K. J. (1999). *An invitation to social construction.* London: Sage.

Gerull, F. C. & Rapee, R. M. (2002). Mother knows best: Effects of maternal modeling on the acquisition of fears and avoidance behavior in toddlers. *Behavior Research and Therapy, 40*, 279–287.

Harper, K. (2000). From a feminist nation to a Barbie nation. *Oral History Review, 27*, 143–148.

Hathaway, S. R. & McKinley, J. C. (1943). *The Minnesota Multiphasic Personality Inventory.* New York: Psychological Corporation.

Herman, K. S. & Betz, N. E. (2004). Path models of the relationships of instrumentality and expressiveness to social self-efficacy, shyness, and depressive symptoms. *Sex Roles, 51*, 55–66.

Hibbins, R. (2006). Sexuality and constructions of gender identity among Chinese male migrants in Australia. *Asian Studies Review, 30*, 289–303.

Hoffman, R. M. (2001). The measurement of masculinity and femininity: Historical perspective and implications for counseling. *Journal of Counseling and Development, 79*, 472–485.

Jamieson, D. (2007). Marketing androgyny: The evolution of the Backstreet Boys. *Popular Music, 26*, 245–258.

Johnson, M. E., Jones, G., & Brems, C. (1996). Concurrent validity of the MMPI-2 feminine gender role (GF) and masculine gender role (GM) scales. *Journal of Personality Assessment, 66*, 153–168.

Kimmel, M. & Messner, M. A. (1989). Introduction. In M. Kimmel & M. A. Messner (Eds.), *Men's Lives* (2nd ed., pp. 1–11). New York: Macmillan.

Konrad, A. M. & Harris, C. (2002). Desirability for the Bem sex-role inventory items for women and men: A comparison between African-Americans and European Americans. *Sex roles: A Journal of Research, 47*, 259–272.

Lenney, E. (1991). Sex roles: The measurement of masculinity, femininity, and androgyny. In J. P. Robinson & P. R. Shaver (Eds.), *Measures of Personality and Social Psychological Attitudes* (pp. 573–660). San Diego, CA: Academic Press.

Levant, R. F., Cuthbert, A., Richmond, K., Sellers, A., Matveev, A., Mitina, O., Sokolovsky, M., & Heesacker, M. (2003a). Masculinity ideology among Russian and U.S. young men and women and its relationship to unhealthy lifestyle habits among young Russian men. *Psychology of Men and Masculinity, 4*, 26–36.

Levant, R. F., Richmond, K., Majors, R. G., Inclan, J. E., Rossello, J. M., Heesacker, M., Rowan, G. T., & Sellers, A. (2003b). A multicultural investigation of masculine ideology and alexithymia. *Psychology of Men and Masculinity, 4,* 91–99.

Lucke, J. C. (2003). Gender roles and sexual behavior among young women. *Sex Roles: A Journal of Research, 39,* 273–298.

Lustig, T. (2001). Ink dryback: Effect and cause. *Graphic Arts Monthly, 73,* 94–97.

May, R. (1986). Concerning a psychoanalytic view of maleness. *The Psychoanalytic Review, 4,* 579–587.

Meier, S. T. (1994). *The chronic crisis in psychological measurement and assessment: A historical survey.* San Diego, CA: Academic Press.

Meissner, W. W. (2005). Gender identity and the self: Gender formation in general and in masculinity. *The Psychoanalytic Review, 92,* 1–27.

Messner, M. A. (2004). Barbie girls versus sea monsters: Children constructing gender. In M. Kimmel & M. A. Messner (Eds.), *Men's lives* (6th ed., pp. 87–102). Boston, MA: Pearson.

Minter, S. (1999). Diagnosis and treatment of gender identity disorder in children. In M. Rottnek (Ed.), *Sissies and tomboys* (pp. 9–33). New York: New York University Press.

Muris, P., Mesters, C., & Knoops, M. (2005). The relation between gender role-orientation and fear and anxiety in non-clinic-referred children. *Journal of Clinical Child and Adolescent Psychology, 34,* 326–332.

Murphy, K. R. & Davidshofer, C. O. (2004). *Psychological testing: Principles and applications.* (6th ed.). Upper Saddle River, NJ: Prentice Hall.

Nola, R. (2004). Pendula, models, constructivism and reality. *Science and Education, 13,* 349–377.

Nye, R. A. (2005). Locating masculinity: Some recent work on men. *Signs: Journal of Women in Culture and Society, 30,* 1937–1962.

Pardo, P. J., Perez., A. L., & Suero, M. I. (2004). The validity of TFT-LCD displays for *colour vision deficiency* research and diagnosis. *Displays, 25,* 159–163.

Peng, T. (2006). Construct validation of the Bem Sex Role Inventory in Taiwan. *Sex Roles, 55,* 843–851.

Pleck, J. H. (1995). The gender role strain paradigm: An update. In R. F. Levant & W. S. Pollack (Eds.), *A new psychology of men* (pp. 11–32). New York: BasicBooks.

Pleck, J. H., Sonnestein, F. L., & Ku, L. C. (1993). Masculinity ideology: Its impact on adolescent males' heterosexual relationships. *Journal of Social Issues, 49,* 11–29.

Raskin, J. D. & Bridges, S. K. (2002). *Studies in meaning: Exploring constructivist psychology.* New York: Pace University Press.

Reid-Walsh, J. & Mitchell, C. (2000). "Just a doll"?: "Liberating" accounts of Barbie-play. *Review of Education, Pedagogy and Cultural Studies; 22,* 175–191.

Sampson, E. E. (1993). *Celebrating the other: A dialogic account of human nature.* Boulder, CO: Westview Press.

Sinnacore, A. L. & Enns, C. Z. (1995). Diversity feminisms: Postmodern, women-of-color, antiracist, lesbian, third-wave, and global perspectives. In C. Z. Enns & A. L. Sinnacore (Eds.), *Teaching and social justice: Integrating multicultural and feminist theories in the classroom* (pp. 41–67). Washington, DC: American Psychological Association.

Spence, J. T. & Buckner, C. (1995). Masculinity and femininity: Defining the undefinable. In P. J. Kalbfleisch & M. J. Cody (Eds.), *Gender, power, and communication in human relationships* (pp. 105–138). Washington, DC: American Psychological Association.

Spence, J. T., Helmreich, R. L., & Stapp, J. (1974). The Personal Attributes Questionnaire: A measure of sex-role stereotypes and masculinity and femininity. *JSAS: Catalog of Selected Documents in Psychology, 4,* 43–44.

Stake, J. E. (1997). Integrating expressiveness and instrumentality in real-life settings: A new perspective on the benefits of androgyny. *Sex Roles, 37,* 541–564.

Stake, J. E. (2000). When situations call for instrumentality and expressiveness: Resource appraisal, coping, strategy choice, and adjustment. *Sex Roles, 42,* 865–885.

Strong, T. (2004). Psychological *constructivism* and the social world. *Journal of Constructivist Psychology, 17,* 258–263.

Thompson, E. H. & Pleck, J. H. (1986). The structure of male role norms. *American Behavioral Scientist, 29,* 531–543.

Thompson, E. H., Jr., Pleck, J. H., & Ferrera, D. L. (1992). Men and masculinities: scales for masculinity ideology and masculinity-related constructs. *Sex Roles, 27,* 573–607.

Tierney, J. (1995). 5 things you should never say to people of the opposite sex. *Forbes, 156,* 135.

Uhlmann, A. J. & Uhlmann, J. R. (2005). Embodiment below discourse: The internalized domination of the masculine perspective. *Women's Studies International Forum, 28,* 93–103.

Ward, C. A. (2000). Models and measurement for psychological androgyny: A cross-cultural extension of theory and research. *Sex Roles: A Journal for Research, 43,* 529–552.

Ward, L., Thorn, B. E., Clements, Kristi L., Dixon, K. E., & Sanford, S. D. (2006). Measurement of agency, communion, and emotional vulnerability with the Personal Attributes Questionnaire. *Journal of Personality Assessment, 86,* 206–216.

Weiten, W. (2004). *Psychology: Themes and variations.* Belmont, CA: Thomson/Wadsworth.

Wise, D. & Stake, J. E. (2002). The moderating roles of personal and social resources on the relationship between dual expectations (for instrumentality and expressiveness) and well-being. *The Journal of Social Psychology, 14,* 109–119.

Chapter 5

Adreon, D. & Durocher, J. S. (2007). Evaluating the college transition needs of individuals with high-functioning autism spectrum disorders. *Intervention in School and Clinic, 42,* 271–279.

Alegre, C. & Murray, E. J. (1973). Locus of control, behavioral intention, and verbal conditioning. *Journal of Personality, 42,* 668–681.

Bandura, A. (1977). *Social Learning Theory.* Englewood Cliffs, NJ: Prentice-Hall.

Bandura, A. & Bussey, K. (2004). On broadening the cognitive, motivational, and sociostructural scope of theorizing about gender development and functioning: Comment on Martin, Ruble, and Szkrybalo (2002). *Psychological Bulletin, 30,* 691–701.

Beasley, B. & Standley, T. C. (2002). Shirts vs. skins: Clothing as an indicator of gender role stereotyping in video games. *Mass Communication and Society, 5,* 279–293.

Bem, S. L. (1984). Androgyny and gender schema theory: A conceptual and empirical investigation. In T. B. Sonderegger (Ed.), Psychology and Gender (pp. 179–226). Omaha, NE: University of Nebraska Press.

Bercovitch, F. B. (2002). Sex-biased parental investment in primates. *International Journal of Primatology, 23,* 905–921.

Burger, J. M. (2004). *Personality.* Belmont, CA: Wadsworth/Thomson Learning.

Buss, D. M. (1994). *The evolution of desire.* New York: Basic Books.

Bussey, K. & Bandura, A. (2004). Social cognitive theory of gender development and functioning. In F. Hendrickson, A. F. Beall, & R. J. Sternberg (Eds.), *The Psychology of gender* (pp. 92–119). New York: Guilford Press.

Connell, B. (1989). Masculinity, violence, and war. In M. Kimmel & M. A. Messner (Eds.), *Men's lives* (2nd ed., pp. 176–183). New York: Macmillan.

Connell, R. W. (1995). *Masculinities.* Berkeley, CA: University of California Press.

Connell, R. W. (2001). The social organization of masculinity. In S. M. Whitehead & F. J. Barrett (Eds.), *The masculinities reader* (pp. 27–47). Malden, MA: Blackwell.

de Heer, J., Bloem, S. J. G., & Paijmans, S. E. W. M. (2004). Diversity in advertising: The influence of contextual conditioning effects on attitudes: Advertising and consumer psychology. In J. D. Williams, W. N. Lee, & C. P. Haugtvedt (Eds.), *Diversity in advertising: Broadening the scope of research directions* (pp. 237–244). Mahwah, NJ: Lawrence Erlbaum Associates.

Dietz, T. L. (1998). An examination of violence and gender role portrayals in video games: Implications for gender socialization and aggressive behavior. *Sex Roles, 38,* 425–442.

Dowd, E. T. (2004). Cognition and the cognitive revolution in psychotherapy: Promises and advances. *Journal of Clinical Psychology, 60,* 415–428.

Ellis, K. M. & Eriksen, K. (2002). Transsexual and transgenderist experiences and treatment options. *The Family Journal: Counseling and Therapy for Couples and Families, 10,* 289–299.

Epstein, R. & Liverant, S. (1963). Verbal conditioning and sex-role identification in children. *Child Development, 34,* 99–106.

Fischer, A. H. & Rodriguez Mosquera, P. M. (2001). What concerns men? Women or other men? A critical appraisal of the evolutionary theory of sex differences in aggression. *Psychology, Evolution, and Gender, 3, 1,* 5–25.

Fitzpatrick, S. (2006, December). TV wrestling has nation in headlock. *The Australian,* 13.

Franklin, C. W. II (1988). *Men and society.* Chicago, IL: Nelson-Hall.

Gamber, J. S. (2006). The relationship of self efficacy and job culture to job satisfaction among certified athletic trainers. Dissertation Abstracts International: Section A: Humanities and Social Sciences, Vol. 66(12-A).

Gannon, L. (2002). A critique of evolutionary psychology. *Psychology, Evolution, & Gender, 4. 2,* 173–218.

Glassner, B. (1989). Men and muscles. In M. Kimmel & M. A. Messner (Eds.), *Men's lives* (2nd ed., pp. 287–297). New York: Macmillan.

Guterman, L. (2005). Chimpanzee genome mapped by scientists. *Chronicle of Higher Education, 52,* 16–21.

Hamilton, C. J. (1995). Beyond sex differences in visio-spatial processing: The impact of gender trait possession. *British Journal of Psychology, 86,* 1–20.

Hantover, J. P. (1989). The boy scouts and the validation of masculinity. In M. Kimmel & M. A. Messner (Eds.), *Men's lives* (2nd ed., pp. 123–130). New York: Macmillan.

Hasher, L. & Griffin, M. (1978). Reconstructive and reproductive processes in memory. *Journal of Experimental Psychology, 4,* 318–330.

Hekman, S. (1997). Truth and method: Feminist standpoint theory revisited. *Signs: Journal of Women in Culture and Society, 22,* 341–365.

Henry, G. K. (1987). Symbolic modeling and parental behavioral training: Effects of non compliance of hyperactive children. *Journal of Behavioral Therapy and Experimental Psychiatry, 18,* 105–113.

Herzog, H. A. (2005). Dealing with the animal research controversy. In C. K. Akins, S. Panicker, & C. L. Cunningham (Eds.), *Laboratory animals in research and teaching: Ethics, care, and methods* (pp. 9–29). Washington, DC: American Psychological Association.

Hoffman, H., Janssen, E., & Turner, S. L. (2004). Classical conditioning of sexual arousal in women and men: Effects of varying awareness and biological relevance of the conditioned stimulus. *Archives of Sexual Behavior, 33,* 43–53.

Hrdy, S. B. (1997). Raising Darwin's consciousness: Female sexuality and the prehominid origins of patriarchy. *Human Nature, 8,* 1–49.

Hunt, L. L. (2001). Religion, gender and the Hispanic experience in the United States: Catholic/Protestant Differences in religious involvement, social status, and gender-role attitudes. *Review of Religious Research, 43,* 139–160.

Hurtz, W. & Durkin, K. (2004). The effects of gender-stereotyped radio commercials. *Journal of Applied Social Psychology, 34,* 1974–1992.

Ickes, W. (1993). Traditional gender roles: Do they make and then break our relationships? *Journal of Social Issues, 49,* 71–85.

Imwalle, D. B. & Schillo, K. K. (2004). Masculinity and femininity: The taboo dimensions of national cultures (book review). *Archives of Sexual Behavior, 33,* 174–177.

Johnson, A. G. (1997). *The gender knot.* Philadelphia, PA: Temple University Press.

Kelly, G. (1963). *A theory of personality: The psychology of personal constructs.* Toronto, Canada: W. W. Norton & Co.

Kimmel, M. & Messner, M. A. (1989). Introduction. In M. Kimmel & M. A. Messner (Eds.), *Men's lives* (2nd ed., pp. 1 11). New York: Macmillan.

Kronsell, A. (2005). Gendered practices in institutions of hegemonic masculinity: Reflections from feminist standpoint theory. *International Feminist Journal of Politics, 7,* 280–298.

Leadbeater, B., Banister, E., Ellis, W., & Yeung, R. (2008). Victimization and relational aggression in adolescent romantic relationships: The influence of parental and peer behaviors, and individual adjustment. *Journal of Youth and Adolescence, 37*, 359–372.

Lott, B. & Maluso, D. (1993). The social learning of gender. In A. Beall & R. J. Sternberg (Eds.), *The psychology of gender* (pp. 99–123). New York: Guilford Press.

Mahalik, J. R., Locke, B. D., Theodore, H., Cournoyer, R. J., & Lloyd, B. F. (2001). A cross-national and cross-sectional comparison of men's gender role conflict and its relationship to social intimacy and self-esteem. *Sex Roles: A Journal of Research, 45*, 1–15.

Maibach, E. & Flora, J. A. (1993). Symbolic modeling and cognitive rehearsal: Using video to promote AIDS prevention self-efficacy. *Communication Research, 20*, 517–545.

Messner, M. (1989). Boyhood, organized sports, and the construction of masculinity. In M. Kimmel & M. A. Messner (Eds.), *Men's lives* (2nd ed., pp. 161–175). New York: Macmillan.

Miller, L. C., Putcha-Bhagavatul, A., & Pederson, W. C. (2002). Men's and women's mating preferences: Distinct evolutionary mechanisms? *Current Directions in Psychological Science, 11*, 88–93.

Morgan, M. (1987). The impact of religion on gender-role attitudes. *Psychology of Women Quarterly, 11*, 301–310.

Murai, T. (2006). Mating behaviors of the proboscis monkey (Nasalis larvatus). *American Journal of Primatology, 68*, 832–837.

Newcomb, M. D., Huba, G. J., & Bentler, P. M. (1983). Mother's influence on the drug use of their children: Confirmatory tests of direct modeling and mediational theories. *Developmental Psychology, 19*, 714–726.

Paulsen, M. (1999). Deconstructing hegemonic masculinity: An approach for high school students. *Youth Studies Australia, 18*, 12–20.

Pavlov, I. V. (1927). *Conditioned reflexes.* London: Oxford University Press.

Pike, J. J. & Jennings, N. A. (2005). The effects of commercials on children's perceptions of gender appropriate toy use. *Sex Roles, 52*, 83–91.

Pleck, J. H., Sonnestein, F. L., & Ku, L. C. (1993). Masculinity ideology: Its impact on adolescent males' heterosexual relationships. *Journal of Social Issues, 49*, 11–29.

Pogun, S. (2001). Sex differences in brain and behavior: emphasis on nicotine, nitric oxide and place learning. *International Journal of Psychophysiology, 42*, 195–208.

Pollack, W. S. (1995). No man is an island: toward a new psychoanalytic psychology of men. In R. Levant & W. S. Pollack (Eds.), *A new psychology of men* (pp. 33–67). New York: Basic Books.

Pollack, W. (1998). *Real boys: Rescuing our sons from the myths of boyhood*. New York: Henry Holy & Co.

Pryke, S. (2001). The boy scouts and the "girl question." *Sexualities, 4,* 191–210.

Roopnarine, J. L. & Mounts, N. S. (1987). Current theoretical issues in sex roles and sex typing. In D. B. Carter (Ed.), *Current theoretical issues in sex roles and sex typing.* (pp. 7–31). New York: Praeger.

Roughgarden, J. (2004). *Evolution's rainbow: Diversity, gender, and sexuality in nature and people.* Berkeley, CA: University of California Press.

Schad, M., Szwedo, D., Antonishak, J., Hare, A., & Allen, J. (2008). The broader context of relational aggression in adolescent romantic relationships: Predictions from peer pressure and links to psychosocial functioning. *Journal of Youth and Adolescence, 37,* 346–358.

Schwartz, B. & Lacey, H. (1982). *Behaviorism, science, and human nature.* Toronto, Canada: W. W. Norton & Co.

Skinner, B. F. (1953). *Science and human behavior.* New York: The Free Press.

Skinner, B. F. (1971). *Beyond freedom and dignity.* New York: Bantam Books.

Smuts, B. (1995). The evolutionary origins of patriarchy. *Human Nature, 6,* 1–32.

Stevenson, L. & Haberman, D. L. (1998). *Ten theories of human nature.* New York: Oxford University Press.

Tapper, K. & Boulton, M. J. (2005). Victim and peer group responses to different forms of aggression among primary school children. *Aggressive Behavior, 31,* 238–253.

Thorndike, E. L. (1911). *Animal intelligence: Experimental studies.* New York: Macmillan.

Tirodkar, M. & Jain, A. (2003). Food messages on African American television shows. *American Journal of Public Health, 93,* 439–441.

Urani, M. A., Miller, S. A., Johnson, J. E., & Petzel, T. P. (2003). Homesickness in socially anxious first year college students. *College Student Journal, 37,* 392–400.

Van Leeuwen, M. S. (2001). Of hoggamus and hogwash: Evolutionary psychology and gender relations. *Journal of Psychology and Theology, 2,* 101–111.

Vervaecke, H., Vries, H. D., & Elsacker, L. V. (1999). An experimental evaluation of the consistency of competitive ability and agnostic dominance in different social contexts in captive bonobos. *Behaviour, 136,* 423–443.

Watson, J. (1913). Psychology as the behaviorist views it. *Psychological Review, 20,* 158–177.

Watson, J. (1919). *Psychology from the standpoint of a behaviorist.* Philadelphia, PA: Lippincott.

Weiten, W. (2004). *Psychology: Themes and variations*. Belmont, CA: Thomson/ Wadsworth.

Wencelblat, P. (2004). Boys will be boys? An analysis of male-on-male hetero-sexual sexual violence. *Columbia Journal of Law and Social Problems, 38,* 37–66.

Wilks, D. (2000). Toward a comprehensive theory of counseling: A historical review of counseling theory development in relation to definitions of freewill and determinism. *TCA Journal, 28,* 66–77.

Chapter 6

American Psychiatric Association. (1994). *Diagnostic and statistical manual of mental disorders* (4th ed.). Washington, DC: American Psychiatric Association.

Bandura, A. & Bussey, K. (2004). On broadening the cognitive, motivational, and sociostructural scope of theorizing about gender development and functioning: Comment on Martin, Ruble, and Szkrybalo (2002). *Psychological Bulletin, 30,* 691–701.

Barbera, E. (2003). Gender schemas: Configuration and activation processes. *Canadian Journal of Behavioral Sciences, 35,* 176–184.

Bem, S. L. (1981a). Gender schema theory: A cognitive account of sex typing. *Psychological Review, 4,* 354–364.

Bem, S. L. (1981b). The BSRI and gender schema theory: A reply to Spence and Helmreich. *Psychological Review, 88,* 369–371.

Bem, S. L. (1984). Androgyny and gender schema theory: A conceptual and empirical investigation. In T. B. Sonderegger (Ed.), Psychology and Gender (pp. 179–226). Omaha, NE: University of Nebraska Press.

Blazina, C. & Watkins, C. E. (2000). Separation/individuation, parental attach-ment, and male gender role conflict: Attitudes toward the feminine and the fragile masculine self. *Psychology of Men and Masculinity, 1,* 126–132.

Bryant, K. (2006). Making gender identity disorder of childhood: Historical lessons for contemporary debates, *Sexuality Research and Social Policy, 3,* 23–39.

Burger, J. M. (2004). *Personality*. Belmont, CA: Wadsworth/Thomson Learning.

Chodorow, N. (1978). Mothering, object-relations, and the female oedipal configuration. *Feminist Studies, 4,* 137–158.

Chodorow, N. J. (1990). Gender, relation, and difference in psychoanalytic perspective. Essential papers in psychoanalysis. In C. Zanardi (Ed), *Essential papers on the psychology of women* (pp. 420–436). New York: New York University Press.

Christiansen, A. (1996). Masculinity and its vicissitudes: Reflections on some gaps in the psychoanalytic theory of male identity formation. *Psychoanalytic Review, 83*, 97–124.

Colman, W. (2001). Celebrating the phallus. In C. Harding (Ed.), *Sexuality: Psychoanalytic perspectives* (pp. 121–136). New York: Brunner-Routledge.

Connell, R. W. (1995). *Masculinities*. Berkeley, CA: University of California Press.

Crane, M. & Markus, H. (1982). Gender identity: The benefits of a self-schema approach. *Journal of Personality and Social Psychology, 43*, 1195–1197.

Deachan, D. F. (1998). Masculine self-ascribed attachment style, its relationship to gendered self concept, impressions of the mother, and attitudes toward women. Dissertation Abstracts International, Vol. 58(8-B), p. 4521.

Derry, S. J. (1996). Cognitive schema theory in the constructivist debate. *Educational Psychologist, 31*, 163–174.

Diamond, M. J. (2004). The shaping of masculinity: Revisioning boys turning away from their mothers to construct male gender identity. *International Journal of Psychoanalysis, 85*, 359–380.

Dowd, E. T. (2004). Cognition and the cognitive revolution in psychotherapy: Promises and advances. *Journal of Clinical Psychology, 60*, 415–428.

Frable, D. E. (1989). Sex typing and gender ideology: Two facets of the individual's gender psychology that go together. *Journal of Personality and Social Psychology, 56*, 95–108.

Freud, S. (1961). *Civilization and its discontents*. New York: W. W. Norton & Co.

Freud, S. (1963). *General psychological theory*. New York: Macmillan & Co.

Gelman, S. A. & Taylor, M. G. (2000). Gender essentialism in cognitive development. In P. H. Miller & S. E. Kofsky (Eds.), *Toward a feminist developmental psychology* (pp. 169–190). Florence, KY: Taylor & Francis/Routledge.

Goldberg, H. (1993). Masculine process/masculine pathology: A new psychodynamic approach. *Journal of Mental Health Counseling, 15*, 298–309.

Gruber, O. & Goschke, T. (2004). Executive control emerging from dynamic interactions between brain systems mediating language, working memory and attentional processes. *Acta Psychologica, 115*, 105 121.

Hayslett-McCall, K. L. & Bernard, T. J. (2002). Attachment, masculinity, and self-control: A theory of male crime rates. *Theoretical Criminology, 6*, 5–33.

Hofstede, G. (1998). *Masculinity and femininity: The taboo dimension of national cultures*. Thousand Oaks, CA: Sage.

Horney, K. (1966). *Our inner conflicts*. New York: W. W. Norton & Co.

Horney, K. (1968). The dread of woman. *The International Journal of Psychoanalysis, 13*, 348–360.

Huang, C. C. & Pouncy, H. (2005). Why doesn't she have a child support order?: Personal choice or objective constraint. *Family Relations: Interdisciplinary Journal of Applied Family Studies, 54*, 547–557.

Hudak, M. A. (1993). Gender schema theory revisited: Men's stereotypes of American Women. *Sex Roles, 28*, 279–293.

Hurvich, M. (1997). Classics revisited: The ego in anxiety (Max Schur, 1953) and an addendum to Freud's theory of anxiety (Charles Brenner, 1953). *The Psychoanalytic Review, 4*, 483–504.

Jakupcak, M., Tull, M. T., & Roemer, L. (2005). Masculinity, shame and fear of emotions as predictors of men's expressions of anger and hostility. *Psychology of men and masculinity, 4*, 275–284.

Johnson, A. G. (1997). *The gender knot*. Philadelphia, PA: Temple University Press.

Kantrowitz, R. E. & Ballou, M. (1992). A feminist critique of cognitive-behavioral therapy. In L. S. Brown & M. Ballou (Eds.), *Personality and psychopathology: Feminist reappraisals* (pp. 70–87). New York: Guilford Press.

Kaschak, E. (1992). *Engendered lives: A new psychology of women's experience*. New York: BasicBooks.

Katz, P. A., Silvern, L. S., & Coultier, D. K. (1990). Gender processing and person perception. *Social Cognition, 8*, 186–202.

Kelly, G. (1963). *A theory of personality: The psychology of personal constructs*. Toronto, Canada: W. W. Norton & Co.

Kimmel, M. & Messner, M. A. (2004). Introduction. In M. S. Kimmel & M. A. Messner (Eds.), *Men's lives* (6th ed., pp. ix–xvii). Boston, MA: Pearson.

Kissen, M. (1992). Gender and superego development. In M. Kissen (Ed.), *Gender and psychoanalytic treatment*. Philadelphia, PA: Brunner/Mazel.

Lemons, M. & Parzinger, M. (2007). Gender schemas: A cognitive explanation of discrimination of women in technology. *Journal of Business and Psychology; 22*, 91–98.

Lenney, E. (1991). Sex roles: The measurement of masculinity, femininity, and androgyny. In J. P. Robinson & P. R. Shaver (Eds.), *Measures of personality and social psychological attitudes* (pp. 573–660). San Diego, CA: Academic Press.

Levant, R. F. (1997). The masculinity crisis. *The Journal of Men's Studies, 5*, 221–232.

Lobel, T. E., Rothman, G., Abramovitz, E., & Maayan, Z. (1999). Self perception and deceptive behavior: The uniqueness of feminine males. *Sex Roles, 41,* 577–587.

Luepnitz, D. A. (1998). *The family interpreted: Psychoanalysis, feminism, and family therapy.* New York: BasicBooks.

Maguire, M. & Dewing, Hilary (2007). New psychoanalytic theories of female and male femininity: The Oedipus complex, language and gender embodiment. *British Journal of Psychotherapy, 23,* 531–545.

Mahler, M. S. & McDevitt, J. B. (1982). Thoughts on the emergence of the sense of self, with particular emphasis on the body self. *Journal of the American Psychoanalytic Association, 30,* 827–848.

May, R. (1986). Concerning a psychoanalytic view of maleness. *The Psychoanalytic Review, 4,* 579–587.

Mayo, C. (2006). Pushing the limits of liberalism: Queerness, children, and the future. *Educational Theory, 56,* 469–487.

Meissner, W. W. (2005). Gender identity and the self: Gender formation in general and in masculinity. *The Psychoanalytic Review, 92,* 1–27.

Miller, C. T. (1984). Self-schemas, gender, and social comparison: A clarification of the related attributes hypothesis. *Journal of Personality and Social Psychology, 46,* 1222–1229.

Miller, G. A. (2003). The cognitive revolution: A historical perspective. *Trends in Cognitive Sciences, 7,* 141–144.

Minter, S. (1999). Diagnosis and treatment of gender identity disorder in children. In M. Rottnek (Ed.), *Sissies and tomboys* (pp. 9–33). New York: New York University Press.

Newman, L. K. (2002). Sex, gender and culture: Issues in the definition, assessment and treatment of Gender Identity Disorder. *Clinical Child Psychology and Psychiatry, 7,* 352–359.

Paris, B. J. (2000). Feminine psychology and the relations between the sexes. In B. J. Paris (Ed.), *Karen Horney: The unknown Karen Horney.* New Haven, CT: Yale University Press.

Pearson, D. G., Logie, R. H., & Gilhooly, K. J. (1999). Verbal representations and spatial manipulation during mental synthesis. *European Journal of Cognitive Psychology, 11,* Special issue: Imagery in working *memory* and in mental discovery.

Pease, B. (2000). Beyond the father wound: Memory-work and the deconstruction of the father son relationship. *A. N. J. Z. Family Therapy, 21,* 9–15.

Piaget, J. (1954). *The construction of reality in the child.* New York: Ballantine Books.

Pollack, W. S. (1995). No man is an island: Toward a new psychoanalytic psychology of men. In R. Levant & W. S. Pollack (Eds.), *A new psychology of men* (pp. 33–67). New York: BasicBooks.

Pollack, W. (1998). *Real boys: Rescuing our sons from the myths of boyhood*. New York: Henry Holy & Co.

Prilleltensky, I. (1994). *The morals and politics of psychology: Psychological discourse and the status quo*. Albany, NY: SUNY Press.

Proctor, R. & Vu, Kim-Phuong L. (2006). The cognitive revolution at age 50: Has the promise of the human information-processing approach been fulfilled? *International Journal of Human-Computer Interaction, 21*, 253–284.

Richardson, J. (1999). Response: Finding the disorder in gender identity disorder. *Harvard Review of Psychiatry, 7*, 43–50.

Roopnarine, J. L. & Mounts, N. S. (1987). Current theoretical issues in sex roles and sex typing. In D. B. Carter (Ed.), *Current theoretical issues in sex roles and sex typing* (pp. 7–31). New York: Praeger.

Satinover, J. (1986). The myth of the death of the hero: A Jungian view of masculine psychology. *The Psychoanalytic Review, 73*, 149–161.

Scherer, R. & Petrick, J. A. (2001). The effects of gender role orientation on team schema: A multivariate analysis of indicators in a U.S. Federal Health Care Organization. *The Journal of Social Psychology, 14*, 7–22.

Schwartz, J. P., Waldo, M., & Higgins, A. J. (2004). Attachment styles: Relationship to masculine gender role conflict in college men. *Psychology of Men and Masculinities, 5*, 143–146.

Shackelford, T. K., Weeks-Shackelford, V. A., & Schmitt, D. P. (2005). An evolutionary perspective on why some men refuse or reduce their child support payments. *Basic and Applied Social Psychology, 27*, 297–306.

Signorella, M. L. (1999). Multidimensionality of gender schemas: Implications for the development of gender-related characteristics. In W. B. Swann & J. Langlois (Eds.), *Sexism and stereotypes in modern society: The gender science of Janet Taylor Spence* (pp. 107–126). Washington, DC: American Psychological Association.

Silverstein, O. & Rashbaum, B. (1994). *The courage to raise good men*. New York: Viking.

Smith, J. H. (1997). The ego and anxiety in Freud and Lacan. *Clinical Studies International Journal of Psychoanalysis, 3*, 11–24.

Spence, J. T. & Buckner, C. (1995). Masculinity and femininity: Defining the undefinable. In P. J. Kalbfleisch & M. J. Cody (Eds.), *Gender, power, and communication in human relationships* (pp. 105–138). Washington, DC: American Psychological Association.

Tennenbaum, H. R. & Leaper, C. (2002). Are parents gender schemas related to their children's gender related cognitions? A meta-analysis. *Developmental Psychology, 38,* 615–630.

Thorpe, H. (1994, September 22). It's Pat. *Rolling Stone, 691,* 9–15.

Tyson, P. (1982). A developmental line of gender identity, gender identity, gender role, and choice of love object. *Journal of the American Psychoanalytic Association, 30,* 61–86.

Ullian, D. Z. (1977). The development of conceptions of masculinity and femininity. Dissertation Abstracts International, Vol. 37(7-B).

Weiten, W. (2004). *Psychology: Themes and variations.* Belmont, CA: Thomson/ Wadsworth.

Wikepedia. (2006). *Androgyne.* Retrieved August 3, 2006 from http://en. wikipedia.org/wiki/Androgyne.

Chapter 7

Ackerman, A. (Executive Producer). (1994a, May 6). *Seinfeld.* [Television series]. The keys. New York: NBC.

Ackerman, A. (Executive Producer). (1994b, May 19). *Seinfeld.* [Television series]. The opposite. New York: NBC.

Ackerman, A. (Executive Producer). (1994c, October 6). *Seinfeld.* [Television series]. The sledge drive. New York: NBC.

Addis, M. E. & Mahalik, J. R. (2003). Men, masculinity, and contexts of help seeking. *American Psychologist, 58,* 5–14.

Andersen, S. M. & Chen, S. (2002). The relational self: An interpersonal social-cognitive theory. *Psychological Review, 4,* 619–645.

Aoki, E. (2005). Coming out as "we 3": Using personal ethnography and the case study to assess relational identity and parental support of gay male, three-partner relationships. *Journal of GLBT Family Studies, 1,* 29–48.

Avsec, A. (2003). Masculinity and femininity personality traits and self-construal. *Studia Psychological, 45,* 151–159.

Bouhnik, A. D. (2006). Unsafe sex with casual partners and quality of life among HIV-infected gay men: Evidence from a large representative sample of outpatients attending French hospitals. *Journal of Acquired Immune Deficiency Syndromes (JAIDS), 42,* 597–603.

Bower, B. (2005). Reflections of primate minds. *Science News, 1,* 168.

Boyles, D. R. (1994). Considering hermeneutics and education: *Hermes,* teachers, and intellectualism. Viewpoints, ERIC Document: ED379260 (19 pp.).

Brannon, R. (1976). The male sex-role and what it's done for us lately. In R. Brannon & D. David (Eds.), *The forty-nine percent majority* (pp. 1–40). Reading, MA: Addison-Wesley.

Burn, S. M. & Ward, Z. A. (2005). Men's conformity to traditional masculinity and relationship satisfaction. *Psychology of Men and Masculinity, 6,* 254–263.

Chen, S., Boucher, H. C., & Tapias, M. P. (2006). The relational self revealed: Integrative conceptualization and implications for interpersonal life. *Psychological Bulletin, 132,* 151–179.

Cialdini, R. B, Kallgren, C. A., & Reno, R. R. (1991). A focus theory of normative conduct: A theoretical refinement and reevaluation of the role of norms in human conduct. In M. P. Zanna (Ed.), *The development of prosocial behavior* (pp. 339, 341). New York: Academic Press.

Cooley, C. H. (1902). *Human nature and social order.* New York: Scribner.

Coulter, J. (2004). What is discursive psychology? *Human studies, 27,* 335–340.

Cross, S. E. & Morris, M. L. (2003). Getting to know you: The relational self-construal, relational cognition and well being. *Personality and Social Psychology Bulletin, 29,* 512–523.

Edwards, D. (1997). *Discourse and cognition.* Thousand Oaks, CA: Sage.

Ellis, A. (1989). The history of cognition in psychotherapy. In A. Freeman, K. M. Simon, L. E. Beutler, & H. Arkowitz (Eds.), *Comprehensive handbook of cognitive therapy* (pp. 5–19). New York: Plenum Press.

Evans, C. S. (2005). The relational self: psychological and theological perspectives. In W. R. Miller & H. D. Delaney (Eds.), *Judeo-Christian perspectives on psychology: Human nature, motivation, and change* (pp. 73–93). Washington, DC: American Psychological Association.

Foley, T. & Safran, S. (1004). Gender-biased language in learning disability textbooks. *Journal of Learning Disabilities, 27,* 309–315.

Fosshage, J. L. (2002). A relational self psychological perspective. *Journal of analytical psychology, 47,* 67–82.

Frolund, L. (1997). Early shame and mirroring. *Scandinavian Psychoanalytic Review, 20,* 35–57.

Gabriel, S., Renaud, J. M., & Tippin, B. (2007). When I think of you, I feel more confident about me: The relational self and self-confidence. *Journal of Experimental Social Psychology, 43,* 772–779.

Gill, R. (1995). Relativism, reflexivity and politics: Interrogating discourse analysis from a feminist perspective. In S. Wilkinson & C. Kitzinger (Eds.), *Feminism and discourse: Psychological perspectives* (pp. 165–186). Thousand Oaks, CA: Sage.

Gore, J. S., Cross, S. E., & Morris, M. L. (2006). Let's be friends: Relational self-construal and the development of intimacy. *Personal Relationships, 13*, 83–102.

Harrison, L. A. (2005). Social role theory and the perceived gender role orientation of athletes. *Sex Roles: A Journal of Research, 52*, 227–236.

Hepburn, A. & Wiggins, S. (2005). Developments in discursive psychology. *Discourse and Society, 16*, 595–601.

Heyes, C. M. (1994). Reflections on self-recognition in primates. *Animal Behaviour, 47*, 909–920.

Ickes, W. (1993). Traditional gender roles: Do they make and then break our relationships? *Journal of Social Issues, 49*, 71–85.

Jensen, R. (2004). Homecoming: The relevance of radical feminism for gay men. *Journal of Homosexuality, 47*, 75–81.

Ludlow, L. H. & Mahalik, J. R. (2001). Congruence between a theoretical continuum of masculinity and the Rasch model: Examining the conformity to masculine norms inventory. *Journal of Applied Measurement, 2*, 205–226.

Maguire, N. A. (1995). The relational self: A theory of human development in a postmodern world. Masters Thesis, Widener University (83 pp.).

Mahalik, J. R., Burns, S. M., & Syzdek, M. (2007). Masculinity and perceived normative health behaviors as predictors of men's health behaviors. *Social Science and Medicine, 64*, 2201–2209.

Mahalik, J. R., Cournoyer, R. J., DeFranc, W., Cherry, M., & Napolitano, J. M. (1998). Men's gender role conflict and use of psychological defenses. *Journal of Counseling Psychology, 45*, 247–255.

Mahalik, J. R., Good, G. E., & Englar-Carlson, M. (2003b). Masculinity scripts, presenting concerns, and help seeking: Implications for practice and training. *Professional Psychology Research and Practice, 34*, 123–131.

Mahalik, J. R., Locke, B. D., Ludlow, L. H., Diemer, M. A., Scott, R. P. J., Gottfried, M., et al. (2003a). Development of the conformity to masculine norms inventory. *Psychology of Men and Masculinity, 4*, 3–25.

Mahalik, J. R., Locke, B. D., Theodore, H., Cournoyer, R. J., & Lloyd, B. F. (2001). A cross-national and cross-sectional comparison of men's gender role conflict and its relationship to social intimacy and self-esteem. *Sex Roles: A Journal of Research, 45*, 1–15.

Mahalik, J. & Rochlen, A. (2006). Men's likely responses to clinical depression: What are they and do masculinity norms predict them? *Sex Roles, 55*, 659–667.

Mahalik, J. R., Talmadge, W. T., Lockhe, B. D., & Scott, R. P. J. (2005). Using the conformity to masculine norms inventory to work with men in a clinical setting. *Journal of Clinical Psychology, 61*, 661–674.

Markus, H. R. & Cross, S. (1990). The interpersonal self. In L. A. Pervin (Ed.), *Handbook of personality* (pp. 576–608). New York: Guilford Press.

McBirney, K. (2004). Nested selves, networked communities: A case study of Diablo II: Lord of destruction as an agent of cultural change. *Journal of American Culture, 27,* 415–421.

McCormack, D. (2006). Masculinities without men? Female masculinity in twentieth-century fictions. *Journal of the History of Sexuality, 15,* 333–338.

Nichols, S. (2002). Parents' constructions of their children as gendered, literate subjects: A critical discourse analysis. *Journal of Early Childhood Literacy, 2,* 123–144.

Potter, J. & Wetherell, M. (1987). *Discourse and social psychology: Beyond attitudes and behavior.* London: Sage.

Raskin, J. D. (2002). Constructivism in psychology: Personal construct psychology, radical constructivism, and social constructionism. In J. D. Raskin & S. K. Bridges (Eds.), *Studies in meaning: Exploring constructivist psychology* (pp. 1–25). New York: Pace University Press.

Rifkin, L. (2002). The suit suits whom? Lesbian gender, female masculinity, and women-in-suits. *Journal of Lesbian Studies, 6,* 157–174.

Riley, S. C. E. (2003). The management of the traditional male role: A discourse analysis of the constructions and functions of provision. *Journal of Gender Studies, 12,* 99–113.

Speer, S. A. (2001). Reconsidering the concept of hegemonic masculinity: Discursive psychology, conversation analysis and participant's observation. *Feminism and Psychology, 11,* 107–135.

Speer, S. A. (2002). What can conversation analysis contribute to feminist methodology? Putting reflexivity into practice. *Discourse and Society, 6,* 801–821.

Stokoe, E. H. & Smithson, J. (2001). Making gender relevant: Conversational analysis and gender categories in interaction. *Discourse and Society, 12,* 217–228.

Sunderland, J. & Litosseliti, L. (2002). Gender identity and discourse analysis. In L. Litosseliti & J. Sunderland (Eds.), *Gender identity and discourse analysis: Theoretical and empirical considerations* (pp. 1–39). Philadelphia, PA: John Benjamin's.

Tan, S. C. & Tan, A. L. (2006). Conversational analysis as an analytical tool for face-to-face and online conversations. *Educational Media International, 43,* 347–361.

Wetherell, M. & Edley, N. (1999). Negotiating hegemonic masculinity: Imaginary positions and psycho-discursive practices. *Feminism and Psychology, 9,* 335–356.

Winter, J. & Pauwels, A. (2006). "Trajectories of agency" and discursive identities in education: A critical site in feminist language planning. *Current Issues in Language Planning, 7,* 171–198.

Chapter 8

Aberle, C. C. & Littlefield, R. P. (2001). Family functioning and sexual aggression in a sample of college men. *Journal of Interpersonal Violence, 16,* 565–579.

Addis, M. E. & Cohane, G. H. (2005). Social scientific paradigms of masculinity and their implications for research and practice in men's mental health. *Journal of Clinical Psychology, 61,* 633–647.

Addis, M. E. & Mahalik, J. R. (2003). Men, masculinity, and contexts of help seeking. *American Psychologist, 58,* 5–14.

Allebeck, P. & Allgulander, C. (1990). Suicide among young men: Psychiatric illness, deviant behavior, and substance abuse. *Acta Psychiatrica Scandinaviva,* 565–570.

American Psychiatric Association. (1994). *Diagnostic and statistical manual for mental disorders* (4th ed.). Washington, DC: American Psychiatric Association.

Anderson, T. (2005). Workable sisterhood and the political journey of stigmatized women with HIV/AIDS. *Theoretical Criminology, 9,* 515–518.

Archer, L. & Hutchings, M. (2000). "Bettering yourself?" Discourses of risk, cost and benefit in ethnically diverse, young working class non-participants' constructions of higher education. *British Journal of Sociology of Education, 21,* 555–574.

Archer, L., Pratt, S. P., & Phillips, D. (2001). Working-class men's constructions of masculinity and negotiations of (non) participation in higher education. *Gender and Education, 13,* 431–449.

Arenson, K. W. (2004. May 27). Study faults colleges on graduation rates. *New York Times,* a23.

Banerji, S. (2004). Report: Higher education fiscal crisis hardest on Hispanic, low-income students. *Black Issues in Higher Education, 21,* 10.

Bannerman, E. D. (1996). Female police officers: The relationship between social support, interactional style and occupational stress and strain. *Dissertation Abstracts International,* Vol. 58 (4-B), pp. 2162–2163.

Barlas, S. (2005). Concerns raised about high suicide rates in Native Americans. *Psychiatric Times, 22,* 83.

Baum, S. & Goodstein, E. (2005). Gender imbalance in college applications: Does it lead to a preference for men in the admission process? *Economics of Education Review, 24,* 665–675.

Beattle, I. R. (2002). Are all adolescent econometricians created equal? Racial, class, and gender differences in college enrollment. *Sociology of Education, 75,* 19–43.

Belcher, L., Sternberg, M. R., Wolitski, R. J., Halkitis, P., Hoff, C., and the Seropositive Urban Men's Study Team (2005). *AIDS Education and Prevention, 17,* 79–89.

Beneke, T. (2004). Men on rape. In M. S. Kimmel & M. A. Messner (Eds.), *Men's lives* (6th ed., pp. 406–411). Boston, MA: Pearson.

Bergen, R. K. (1996). *Wife rape: Understanding the response of survivors and service providers.* Thousand Oaks, CA: Sage.

Bevan, E. & Higgins, D. J. (2002). Is domestic violence learned? The contributions of five forms of child maltreatment to men's violence and adjustment. *Journal of Family Violence, 17,* 223–245.

Boswell, A. A. & Spade, J. Z. (2004). Fraternities and college rape culture: Why are some college fraternities more dangerous places for women? In M. S. Kimmel & M. A. Messner (Eds.), *Men's lives* (6th ed., pp. 155–178). Boston, MA: Pearson.

Bould, S. (2005). A population health perspective on disability and depression in elderly women and men. *Journal of Aging and Social Policy, 17,* 7–24.

Brannon, L. (2005). *Gender: Psychological perspectives.* Boston, MA: Pearson.

Burd, S. (2006). Working-class students increasingly end up at community colleges, giving up on a 4-year degree. *Chronicle of Higher Education, 52,* a23.

Burke, S. & McKeon, P. (2007). Suicide and the reluctance of young men to use mental health services. *Irish Journal of Psychological Medicine, 24,* 67–70.

Busch, A. L. & Rosenberg, M. S. (2004). Comparing women and men arrested for domestic violence: A preliminary report. *Journal of Family Violence, 19,* 49–57.

Canetto, S. S. (1995). Men who survive a suicidal act: Successful coping or failed masculinity? Research on men and masculinities series. In D. R. Sabo & D. F. Gordon (Eds.), *Men's health and illness: Gender, power, and the body* (pp. 292–304). Thousand Oaks, CA: Sage.

Carlson, S. (2008). Small colleges worry about cost of sustainability. *Chronicle of Higher Education, 54,* A14.

Castle, K., Duberstein, P. R., Meldrum, S., Conner, K. R., & Conwell, Y. (2004). Risk factors for suicide in Blacks and Whites: An analysis of data from the

1993 National Mortality Followback Survey. *American Journal of Psychiatry, 161*, 452–458.

Center for Disease Control and Prevention (2005). *AIDS amongst people ≥ 50.* Retrieved December 22, 2005 from: http://www.thebody.com/cdc/mmwr472.html#table1.

Chapple, C. & Johnson, K. (2005). Predicting gender differences in risk taking: Conference papers. *American Society of Criminology*, 2005 Annual Meeting, Toronto, pN. PAG.

Charles, C. Z., Roscigno, V. J., & Torres, K. C. (2007). Racial inequality and college attendance: The mediating role of parental investments. *Social Science Research, 36*, 329–352.

Choate, L. H. (2003). Sexual assault prevention programs for college men: An exploratory evaluation of the men against violence model. *Journal of College Counseling, 6*, 166–176.

Chronicle of Higher Education (1995, February 17). Fact file: projections of college enrollment, degrees, and high school graduates, 1994 to 2005. *Chronicle of Higher Education, 41*, A38, n23.

Connell, R. W. (1995). *Masculinities.* Berkeley, CA: University of California Press.

Connor, H., Dewson, S., Tyers, C., Eccles, J., Regan, J., & Aston, J. (2001). *Social class and higher education: Issues affecting decisions on participation by lower social class groups.* DfEE Research report 267. Nottingham: DfEE Publications.

Copenhaver, M. M. & Eisler, R. M. (1996). Masculine gender role stress: A perspective on men's health. In P. M. Kato & M. Traci (Eds.), *Handbook of diversity issues in health psychology.* New York: Plenum Press.

Courtenay, W. H. (1999). Youth violence? Let's call it what it is? *Journal of American College Health, 48*, 141–142.

Courtenay, W. H. (2004). Best practices for improving college men's health. *New Directions for Student Services, 107*, 59–74.

Cox, Matthews, and Associates. (2002). States to study rising costs of higher education. *Black Issues in Higher Education, 19*, 17.

Craft, S. M. & Serovich, J. M. (2005). Family-of-origin factors and partner violence in the intimate relationships of gay men who are HIV positive. *Journal of Interpersonal Violence, 20*, 777–791.

Cross, T. & Slater, R. B. (2000). The troublesome decline in African-American college student graduation rates. *The Journal of Blacks in Higher Education, 33*, 102–109.

D12 (2005). Revelation lyrics. http://www.lyricsmp3.net/D6000/kk5835.htm. Retrieved December 10, 2005.

References

Dickey, A. K., Asher, E. J. Jr., & Tweddale, R. B. (1989). Projecting headcount and credit hour enrollment by age group, gender, and degree level. *Research in Higher Education, 30*, 1–19.

DiMaria, F. (2006). Working-class students: Lost in a college's middle-class culture. *Education Digest, 72*, 60–65.

Dobashi, R. E., Dobashi, R., Cavanagh, K., & Lewis, R. (2004). Not an ordinary killer – just an ordinary guy: When men murder an intimate woman partner. *Violence Against Women, 10*, 577–605.

Eigenberg, H. M. (2000). Correctional officers' definitions of rape in male prisons. *Journal of Criminal Justice, 28*, 435–449.

Evelyn, J. (2002). Community colleges start to ask: Where are the men? *Chronicle of Higher Education, 48*, a32–a34.

Ewing, W. (1989). The civic advocacy of violence. In M. S. Kimmel & M. A. Messner (Eds.), *Men's lives* (2nd ed., pp. 358–363). New York: Macmillan.

Fasko, D., Grugg, D. J., & Osborne, J. S. (1995, November). An analysis of disciplinary suspensions. Paper presented at the annual meeting of the *Mid-South Educational Research Association*, Biloxi, MS. ERIC document: ED 393 169.

Felder, R. M. (1994). Gender differences in student performance and attitudes. A longitudinal study of engineering student performance and retention. Report no. NCSU-94A. North Carolina State University. ERIC document: ED 368 553.

Feminist Majority Foundation (2002). US: Discrimination against women police officers rampant. *Women's International Network News, 28*, 64–67.

Ferry, J. (2000). No easy answer to high native suicide rates. *Lancet, 355*, 906.

Finney Rutten, L. J., Meissner, H. I., Breen, N., Vernon, S. W., & Rimer, B. K. (2005). Factors associated with men's use of prostate-specific antigen screening: evidence from Health Information National Trends Survey. *Preventative Medicine, 40*, 461–468.

Fischer, A. H. & Rodriguez Mosquera, P. M. (2001). What concerns men? Women or other men? A critical appraisal of the evolutionary theory of sex differences in aggression. *Psychology, Evolution, and Gender, 3*, 5–25.

Flouri, E. & Buchanan, A. (2002). Life satisfaction in teenage boys: The moderating role of father involvement and bullying. *Aggressive Behavior, 28*, 126–133.

Frieze, I. H. (2005). *Hurting the one you love: Violence in relationships*. Belmont, CA: Wadsworth/Thomson Learning.

Frye, V., Manganello, J., Campbell, J. C., Walton-Moss, B., & Wilt, S. (2006). The distribution of and factors associated with intimate terrorism and situational couple violence among a population-based sample of urban women in the United States. *Journal of Interpersonal Violence, 21*, 1286–1313.

Gades, N. M., Nehra, A., Jacobson, D. J., McGree, M. E., Girman, C. J., Rhodes, T., et al. (2005). Association between smoking and erectile dysfunction: A population-based study. *American Journal of Epidemiology, 161,* 346–351.

Galdas, P. M., Cheater, F., & Marshall, P. (2004). Men and help-seeking behavior: Literature review. *Journal of Advanced Nursing, 49,* 616–623.

Garcia-Moreno, C., Jansen, H., Ellsberg, M., Heise, L., & Watts, C. H. L. (2006). Prevalence of intimate partner violence: findings from the WHO multi-country study on women's health and domestic violence. *Lancet, 368,* 1260–1269.

Garden, K. (2006, January). Real men read – fact not fiction. *Times Educational Supplement, 4668,* Special Section, 4.

Gary, F. (2005). Perspectives on suicide prevention among American Indian and Alaska Native children and adolescents: A call for help. *Online Journal for Nursing, 10,* 170–211.

Goldman, B. A., Blackwell, K. M., & Beach, S. S. (2003). Academically suspended university students: What percent return? What percent graduate? *Journal of the First-Year Experience and Students in Transition, 15,* 105–113.

Gowdy, E. A. & Robertson, S. A. (1994). Postsecondary learning assistance: Characteristics of the clientele. *Community College Journal of Research and Practice, 18,* 43–55.

Green, R. & Hill, J. H. (2003). Sex and higher education: Do men and women attend college for different reasons? *College Student Journal, 37,* 557–563.

Guilamo-Ramos, V., Jaccard, J., & Turrisi, R. (2005). Parental and school correlates of binge drinking among middle school students. *American Journal of Public Health, 95,* 894–899.

Gunnell, D., Middleton, N., Whitley, E., Dorling, D., & Frankel, S. (2003). Why are suicide rates rising in young men but falling in the elderly? A time-series analysis of trends in England and Wales 1950–1988. *Social Science and Medicine, 57,* 595–611.

Hamberger, L. K. & Guse, C. E. (2002). Men's and women's use of intimate partner violence in clinical samples. *Violence against Women, 8,* 1301–1331.

Harris, I. (1989). Media myths and the reality of men's work. In M. S. Kimmel & M. A. Messner (Eds.), *Men's lives* (2nd ed., pp. 225–231). New York. Macmillan.

Harlos, K. P. & Axelrod, L. J. (2005). Investigating hospital administrators' experience of workplace mistreatment. *Canadian Journal of Behavioural Science, 3,* 262–272.

Hearn, J. (2001). Men stopping men's violence against women. *The Society for International Development, 44,* 85–89.

Heise, L. L., Pitanguy, J., & Germain, A. (1994). Violence against women: The hidden health burden. *World Bank Discussion Papers, 255.* Washington, DC: The World Bank.

Henning, K. & Feder, L. (2004). A comparison of men and women arrested for domestic violence: Who presents the greater threat? *Journal of Family Violence, 19,* 69–80.

Herman, J. L. (1992). *Trauma and recovery.* New York: HarperCollins.

Hudson, J. B. (1988). The University of Louisville tutoring program: 1986–1987 operations and outcomes. *University of Louisville.* ERIC document: ED334915.

Isernhagen, J. & Harris, S. (2003). A comparison of 9th and 10th grade boys' and girls' bullying behaviors in two states. *Journal of School Violence, 2,* 67–80.

Isonio, S. (1995). Profile of students on probation/disqualification at Golden West college. *Golden West College.* ERIC document: ED 381 214.

Jackson, T. L. & Petretic-Jackson, P. A. (1996). The definition, incidence, and scope of acquaintance rape and sexual assault. In T. L. Jackson (Ed.), *Acquaintance Rape: Assessment, Treatment, and Prevention* (pp. 1–15). Sarasota, FL: Professional Resource Press.

Jefferson, T. (2002). Subordinating hegemonic masculinity. *Theoretical Criminology, 6,* 63–88.

Johnson, A, (1997). *The gender knot.* Philadelphia, PA: Temple University Press.

Johnson, M. P. (2004). Patriarchal terrorism and common couple violence: Two forms of violence against women. In H. T. Reis & C. E. Rusbult (Eds.), *Close relationships: Key readings* (pp. 471–482). New York: Psychology Press.

Kaslow, N. J., Sherry, A., Bethea, K., Wyckoff, S., Compton, M. T., Bender Grall, M., et al. (2005). Social risk and protective factors for suicide attempts in low income African American men and women. *Suicide and Life-threatening Behavior, 35,* 400–412.

Katz, J. (1995). Reconstructing masculinity in the locker room: The mentors in violence prevention project. *Harvard Educational review, 65,* 163–174.

Katz, J. (2003). Advertising and the construction of violent white masculinity: From Eminem to Clinique for men. In G. Dines & J. Humez (Eds.), *Gender, race and class in media: A text reader* (pp. 349–358). Thousand Oaks, CA: Sage.

Katz, J. (Producer & Director), Ericsson, S. & Talreja, S. (Producers) (2000). *Tough guise: Violence, media, and the crisis in masculinity.* [VHS/DVD]. (Available from Media Education Foundation. 60 Masonic Street, Northampton, Massachusetts 01060.)

Katz, J. & Jhally, S. (2000, June 25) Put the blame where it belongs: On men. *The Los Angeles Times*, M5.

Kaura, S. A. & Allen, C. M. (2004). Dissatisfaction with relationship power and dating violence perpetration by men and women. *Journal of Interpersonal Violence, 19*, 576–588.

Kilmartin, C. (2001). Surviving and thriving: Men and physical health. In T. F. Cohen (Ed.), *Men and masculinity: A text reader* (pp. 352–360). Stamford, CT: Wadsworth.

Kimmel, M. S. (2002). "Gender symmetry" in domestic violence: A substantive and methodological research review. *Violence against women, 8*, 1332–1363.

Kinloch, G. C., Frost, G. A., & MacKay, C. (1993). Academic dismissal, readmission conditions, and retention: A study of social science majors. *NACADA Journal, 13*, 18–22.

Korth, R. (2008, January). Today's college costs are unmanageable for most. *USA Today*, p. 100.

Koss, M. P., Gidycz, C. A., & Wisniewski, N. (1987). The scope of rape: Incidence and prevalence of sexual aggression and victimization in a national sample of higher education students. *Journal of Consulting and Clinical Psychology, 55*, 162–170.

Kus-Patena, S. T. (2004). The effects of learning strategy instruction on college students who are placed at risk of failure. Dissertation Abstracts International, 64 (10-A), 3610.

Lasane, T. P., Howard, W. L., Czopp, A. M., & Sweigard, P. N. (1999). Hyper-masculinity and academic goal-setting: An exploratory study. *Psychological Reports, 85*, 487–496.

Leander, K. (2002). Preventing men's violence against women. *Acta Psychiatrica Scandinavaca, 106*, 15–19.

Leppel, K. (2002). Similarities and differences in the college persistence of men and women. *The Review of Higher Education, 4*, 433–450.

Locke, B. D. & Mahalik, J. R. (2005). Examining masculinity norms, problem drinking, and athletic involvement as predictors of sexual aggression in college men. *Journal of Counseling Psychology, 52*, 279–283.

Lyon, M. R. (2004). No means no? Withdrawal of consent during intercourse and the continuing evolution of the definition of rape. *Journal of Criminal Law and Criminology, 95*, 277–314.

MacInnes, J. (2001). The crisis of masculinity and the politics of identity. In S. M. Whitehead & F. J. Barrett (Eds.), *The masculinities reader* (pp. 311–329). Malden, MA: Blackwell.

Mahalik, J. R., Lagan, H. D., & Morrison, J. A. (2006). Health behaviors and masculinity in Kenyan and U.S. male college students. *Psychology of Men and Masculinity, 7*, 191–202.

Mahalik, J. R., Levi-Minzi, M., & Walker, G. (2007). Masculinity and health behaviors in Australian men. *Psychology of Men and Masculinity, 8*, 240–249.

Marcus, J. (2000). Colleges urged to give men a break. *The Times Higher Education Supplement, 1461*, 11.

Mau, W. C. & Lynn, R. (2001). Gender differences on the scholastic aptitude test, the American college test and college grades. *Educational Psychology, 21*, 133–136.

Mayo, M. W. & Christenfeld, N. (1999). Gender, race, and performance expectations of college students. *Journal of Multicultural Counseling and Development, 27*, 93–104.

McNaught, A. & Spicer, J. (2000). Theoretical perspectives on suicide in gay men with AIDS. *Social Science & Medicine, 51*, 65–72.

Mickelson, R. A. (2003). Gender, Bordieu, and the anomaly of women's achievement redux. *Sociology of Education, 76*, 373–375.

Miedzian, M. (1991). *Boys will be boys.* New York: Doubleday.

Moller-Leimkuhler, A. M. (2003). The gender gap in suicide and premature death or: why are men so vulnerable? *European Archives of Psychiatric Clinical Neuroscience, 253*, 1–8.

Monk, D. & Ricciardelli, L. A. (2003). Three dimensions of male gender role as correlates of alcohol and cannabis involvement in young Australian men. *Psychology of Men and Masculinity, 4*, 57–69.

Murphy, G. E. (1998). Why women are less likely than men to commit suicide. *Comprehensive Psychiatry, 39*, 165–175.

Mustanski, B. (2008). Moderating effects of age on the alcohol and sexual risk taking association: An online daily diary study of men who have sex with men. *AIDS and Behavior, 12*, 118–126.

Nathan, R. (2005). *My freshman year: What a professor learned by becoming a student.* Ithaca, NY: Cornell University Press.

O'Donohue, W., McKay, S., & Schewe, P. A. (1996). Rape: The roles of outcome expectancies and hypermasculinity. *Sexual Abuse: A Journal of Research and Treatment, 8*, 133–141.

Ogunjuyigbe, P. O., Akinlo, A., & Ebigbola, J. A. (2005). Violence against women: An examination of men's attitudes and perceptions about wife beating and contraceptive use. *Journal of Asian and African Studies, 40*, 219–229.

Oklahoma State Regents (2000). Academic probation and suspension: Impact study of retention policy. Oklahoma State Regents for Higher Education. ERIC document: HE 033 774.

Oliver, M. I., Pearson, N., & Coe, N. (2005). Help-seeking behaviour in men and women with common mental health problems: Cross-sectional study. *British Journal of Psychiatry, Vol. 186*, pp. 297–301.

Ovadia, S. (2001). Race, class, and gender differences in high school seniors' values: Applying intersection theory in empirical analysis. *Social Science Quarterly, 82*, 340–356.

Özden, Y. (1996). Have efforts to improve higher education opportunities for low-income youth succeeded? *The Journal of Student Financial Aid, 26*, 19–39.

Parker, R. (2005). A review of gay, lesbian, bisexual and transgender adolescent research: Depression and suicide. Conference Papers – American Sociological Association; 2005 Annual Meeting, Philadelphia, 1–19.

Parrot, D. J. & Zeichner, A. (2003). Effects of hypermasculinity on physical aggression against women. *Psychology of Men and Masculinity, 4*, 70–78.

Peate, I. (2005). The effects of smoking on the reproductive health of men. *British Journal of Nursing, 14*, 362–366.

Peterson, Z. D. & Muehlenhard, C. L. (2004). "Was it rape?" The function of women's rape myth acceptance and definitions of sex in labeling their own experiences. *Sex Roles: A Journal of Research, 129*, 129–145.

Phoenix, A., Frosh, S., & Pattman, R. (2003). Producing contradictory masculine subject positions: Narratives of threat, homophobia, and bullying in 11–14 year old boys. *Journal of Social Issues, 59*, 179–195.

Pollack, W. S. (1995). No man is an island: toward a new psychoanalytic psychology of men. In R. Levant & W. S. Pollack (Eds.), *A new psychology of men* (pp. 33–67). New York: BasicBooks.

Pollack, W. (1998). *Real boys: Rescuing our sons from the myths of boyhood.* New York: Henry Holy & Co.

Polsky, J. Y., Aronson, K. J., Heaton, J. P. W., & Adams, M. A. (2005). Smoking and other lifestyle factors in relation to erectile dysfunction. *BJU International, 96*, 1355–1359.

Portner, J. (1994). Murder rate for young men soars, C. D. C. says. *Education Week, Issue 14*, 3.

Preuss, U. W., Schukit, M. A., Smith, T. L., Danko, G. P., Bucholz, K. K., Hesslebrock, M. N. et al. (2003). Predictors and correlates of suicide attempts over five years in 1,237 alcohol-dependent men and women. *American Journal of Psychiatry, 160*, 56–63.

Real, T. (2001). Men's hidden depression. In T. F. Cohen (Ed.), *Men and masculinity: A text reader* (pp. 361–367). Stamford, CT: Wadsworth.

Reese, V. & Dunn, R. (2007). Learning-style preferences of a diverse freshmen population in a large, private, metropolitan university by gender and GPA. *Journal of College Student Retention: Research, Theory and Practice, 9,* 95–112.

Rehman, S. U., Hutchison, F. N., Hendrix, K., Okonofua, E. C., & Egan, B. M. (2005). Ethnic differences in blood pressure control among men at veterans affairs clinics and other health care sites. *Archives of Internal Medicine, 165,* 1041–1047.

Reilly, J., Muldoon, O. T., & Byrne, C. (2004). Young men as victims and perpetrators of violence in Northern Ireland: A qualitative analysis. *Journal of Social Issues, 60,* 469–484.

Robertson, J. M. & Fitzgerald, L. F. (1992). Overcoming the masculine mystique: Preferences for alternative forms of assistance among men who avoid counseling. *Journal of Counseling Psychology, 39,* 240–246.

Rogers, R. (1990). A proposal for combating sexual discrimination in the military: Amendment of title VII. *California Law Review, 78,* 165–169.

Rosen, L. N., Knudson, K. H., & Fancher, P. (2003). Cohesion and the culture of hypermasculinity in U.S. army units. *Armed Forces and Society, 29,* 325–351.

Rudmin, F. W., Ferrada-Noli, M., & Skolbekken, J. (2003). Questions of culture, age and gender in the epidemiology of suicide. *Scandinavian Journal of Psychology, 44,* 373–381.

Russell, B. L. & Oswald, D. L. (2002). Sexual coercion and victimization of college men: The role of love styles. *Journal of Interpersonal Violence, 17,* 273–285.

Sabo, D. (2004). Masculinities and men's health: Moving toward post-superman era prevention. In M. S. Kimmel & M. A. Messner (Eds.), *Men's lives* (6th ed., pp. 321–334). Boston, MA: Pearson.

Scharrer, E. (2001a). Tough guys: The portrayal of hypermasculinity and aggression in televised police dramas. *Journal of Broadcasting and Electronic Media, 45,* 613–634.

Scharrer, E. (2001b). Men, muscles, and machismo: The relationship between television violence exposure and aggression and hostility in the presence of masculinity. *Media Psychology, 3,* 159–188.

Scher, M., Canon, H. J., & Stevens, M. A. (1988). New perspectives on masculinity in the college environment. In R. J. May & M. Scher (Eds.), *Changing Roles for Men on Campus* (pp. 19–35). San Francisco, CA: Jossey-Bass.

Sharpe, S. & Arnold, S. (1998). Men, lifestyle and health a study of health beliefs and practices. Unpublished Research Report. No. R000221950. Swindon, UK.

Shaughnessy, L., Doshi, S. R., & Jones, S. E. (2004). Attempted suicide and associated health risks among Native American high school students. *Journal of School Health, 74,* 177–182.

Sibulkin, A. E. & Butler, J. S. (2005). Differences in graduation rates between young black and white college students: Effect of entry into parenthood and historically black universities. *Research in Higher Education, 46,* 327–348.

Stillion, J. M. & McDowell, E. E. (2002). The early demise of the "stronger sex": Gender-related causes of sex differences in longevity. *Omega, 44,* 301–318.

Stoltenberg, J. (2000). Of microbes and manhood. *MS. August/September,* 60–63.

Su, L. (2006). What are Jane's secret weapons? Decomposing the gender gap in U.S. college attendance. Conference Papers – American Sociological Association, 2006 Annual Meeting, Montreal, *1,* 33.

Taylor Gibbs, J. (1989). Young black males in America: Endangered, embittered, and embattled. In M. S. Kimmel & M. A. Messner (Eds.), *Men's lives* (2nd ed., pp. 50–66). New York: Macmillan.

Thio, A. (1998). *Deviant behavior.* New York: Addison-Wesley.

Tileston, D. W. (2005). *10 best teaching practices: How brain research, learning styles, and standards define teaching competencies* (2nd ed.). Thousand Oaks, CA: Corwin Press.

Tilley, D. & Brackley, M. (2005). Men who batter intimate partners: A grounded theory study of the development of male violence in intimate partner relationships. *Issues in Mental Health Nursing, 26,* 281–291.

Toch, H. (1998). Hypermasculinity and prison violence. In L. H. Bowker (Ed.), *Masculinities and violence* (pp. 168–178). Thousand Oaks, CA: Sage.

Tracy, C. E., Fromson, T. L., & Else, J. (2001). A call to change the UCR definition of rape. *Sexual Assault Report, 5,* 1–16.

Tyre, P., Murr, A., Juarez, V., Underwood, K. S., & Wingert, P. (2006, January). The boy crisis: At every level they are falling behind. What to do? *Newsweek, 5,* 42–52.

Weiher, G. R., Hughes, C., Kaplan, N., & Howard, J. Y. (2006, September). Hispanic college attendance and the State of Texas GEAR UP Program. *Review of Policy Research, 23,* 1035–1051.

West, P. (1999). Boys' underachievement in school: Some persistent problems and some current research. *Issues in Educational Research, 9,* 33–54.

Wexler, D. (2006). *Is he depressed or what? What to do when the man you love is irritable, moody, and withdrawn.* Oakland, CA: New Harbinger.

Williams, S. L. & Frieze, I. H. (2005). Courtship behaviors, relationship violence, and breakup persistence in college men and women. *Psychology of Women Quarterly, 29*, 248–257.

Winters, M. F. (2003, July 25). What drives black men to suicide? *USA Today*, 15a.

Wood, K., Maforah, F., & Jewkes, R. (1998). "He forced me to love him": Putting violence on adolescent sexual health agendas. *Social Science and Medicine, 47*, 233–242.

Zamani, E. M. (2000). Aspiring to the baccalaureate: Attitudes of community college students toward affirmative action in college admissions. Doctoral Dissertation. University of Illinois at Urbana-Champaign.

Chapter 9

Abramson, G. (2006). Has the gender gap closed? Yes. *Learning and Leading with Technology, 33*, 6–7.

Annand, D. (2007). Re-organizing universities for the information age. *International Review of Research in Open and Distance Learning, 8*, 1–9.

Axlerod, S. D. (2001). The vital relationship between work and masculinity: A psychoanalytic perspective. *Psychology of Men and Masculinity, 2*, 117–123.

Barton, E. R. (2000). Parallels between mythopoetic men's work/men's peer mutual support groups and selected feminist theories. In E. R. Barton (Ed.), *Mythopoetic perspectives of men's healing work: An anthology for therapists and others* (pp. 3–20). Westport, CT: Bergin and Garvey.

Beard, A. J., Bakeman, R. (2000). Boyhood gender nonconformity: Reported parental behavior and the development of narcissistic issues. *Journal of Gay and Lesbian Psychotherapy, 4*, 81–97.

Begley, M. M. (2005, April 18). Corporate America's glass ceiling. *Business West, 21*, 18–20.

Bliss, S. (1995). Mythopoetic men's movements. In M. S. Kimmel (Ed.), *The politics of manhood: Profeminist men respond to the mythopoetic men's movement* (pp. 292–307). Philadelphia, PA: Temple University Press.

Carey, M. (1996). Perspective's on the men's movement. In C. McLean, M. Carey & C. White (Eds.), *Men's ways of being* (pp. 153–161). Boulder, CO: Westview Press.

Clatterbaugh, K. (1995). Mythopoetic foundations and new age patriarchy. In M. S. Kimmel (Ed.), *The politics of manhood: Profeminist men respond to the mythopoetic men's movement* (pp. 44–63). Philadelphia, PA: Temple University Press.

Clatterbaugh, K. (1997). *Contemporary perspectives on masculinity*. Oxford, UK: Westview Press.

Colman, W. (2001). Celebrating the phallus. In C. Harding (Ed.), *Sexuality: Psychoanalytic perspectives* (pp. 121–136). New York: Brunner-Routledge.

Connell, B. (1989). Masculinity, violence and war. In M. S. Kimmel & M. A. Messner (Eds), *Men's lives* (2nd ed., pp. 176–182). New York: Macmillan.

Crafts, N. (2004). Productivity growth in the industrial revolution: A new growth accounting perspective. *Journal of Economic History, 64*, 521–535.

Duberman, M. D. (2001). Excerpts from cures: A gay man's odyssey. *Journal of Gay and Lesbian Psychotherapy, 5*, 37–43.

Fee, D. (1992). Masculinities identity and the politics of essentialism. *Feminism and Psychology, 2*, 171–176.

Flouri, E. & Buchanan, A. (2002). Life satisfaction in teenage boys: The moderating role of father involvement and bullying. *Aggressive Behavior, 28*, 126–133.

Forrest, M. L. & Sullivan, S. E. (2002). A balanced scorecard approach to networking: A guide to successfully navigating career challenges. *Organizational Dynamics, 31*, 245–258.

Fox, J. (2004). How men's movement participants view each other. *Journal of Men's Studies, 12*, 103–118.

Frank, T. (2005, October 17). Farrakhan denounces Katrina response at anniversary of Million Man March. *USA Today*, 04a.

Friedan, B. (1989). Their turn: How men are changing. In M. S. Kimmel & M. A. Messner (Eds.), *Men's lives* (2nd ed., pp. 572–580). New York: Macmillan.

Furnham, A. & Taylor, L. (1990). Lay theories of homosexuality: Aetiology, behaviors and cures. *The British Journal of Social Psychology, 29*, 135–147.

Gilbert, R. K. (1992). Revisiting the psychology of men: Robert Bly and the mythopoetic movement. *Journal of Humanistic Psychology, 32*, 41–67.

Haslam, N. & Levy, S. R. (2006). Essentialist beliefs about homosexuality: Structure and implications for prejudice. *Personality and Social Psychology Bulletin, 32*, 471–485.

Harry, J. (1983). Parasuicide, gender, and gender deviance. *Journal of Health and Social Behavior, 24*, 350–361.

Hearn, J. (1993). The politics of essentialism and the analysis of the men's movement(s). *Feminism and Psychology, 3*, 405–409.

Hunter, A. (1993). Same door, different closet: A heterosexual sissy's coming out party. *Feminism and Psychology, 2*, 367–385.

Hurley, D. (2005, April 19). Divorce rate: It's not as high as you think. *The New York Times*, f7.

Jefferson, T. (2002). Subordinating hegemonic masculinity. *Theoretical Criminology, 6*, 63–88.

Jung, C. J. (1989). *Aspects of the masculine, aspects of the feminine*. New York: MJF Books.

Kahane, D. J. (1998). Male feminism as oxymoron. In T. Digby (Ed.), *Men doing feminism* (pp. 213–236). New York: Routledge.

Kimmel, M. S. (1995). *The politics of manhood: Profeminist men respond to the mythopoetic movement*. Philadelphia, PA: Temple University Press.

Kimmel, M. S. & Kaufman, M. (1995). Weekend warriors: The new men's movement. In M. S. Kimmel (Ed.), *The politics of manhood: Profeminist men respond to the mythopoetic movement (and the mythopoetic leaders answer)* (pp. 15–43). Philadelphia, PA: Temple University Press.

Kipnis, A. (1995). The postfeminist men's movement. (1995). In M. S. Kimmel (Ed.), *The politics of manhood : Profeminist men respond to the mythopoetic men's movement* (pp. 275–286). Philadelphia, PA: Temple University Press.

Klein, A. R. & Bates, J. E. (1980). Gender typing of game choices and qualities of boys' play behavior. *Journal of Abnormal Child Psychology, 8*, 201–212.

Kolbe, R. H. & Langefield, (1993). Appraising gender role portrayals in TV commercials. *Sex Roles, 28*, 393–417.

Kupers, T. A. (1995). Soft males and mama's boys: A critique of males. (pp. 222–230). In M. S. Kimmel (Ed.), *The Politics of manhood: Profeminist men respond to the mythopoetic men's movement*. Philadelphia, PA: Temple University Press.

Lee, J. (2005). From sweatshops to stateside corporations, some people are profiting off of MMO gold. http://www.1up.com/do/feat ure?cId=3141815. Retrieved December 2, 2005.

Leggewie, M. (1999). Interview with Douglas Phillips from the Vision Forum. http://www.homeschoolchristian.com/ChristianEd/Phillips.html. Retrieved December 1, 2005.

Levant, R. F. (1997). The masculinity crisis. *The Journal of Men's Studies, 5*, 221–232.

Lingard, B. & Douglas, P. (1999). *Men engaging feminisms*. Philadelphia, PA: Open University Press.

Lobel, T. E. (1994). Sex typing and the social perception of gender stereotypic and nonstereotypic behavior: The uniqueness of feminine males. *Journal of Personality and Social Psychology, 66*, 379–385.

MacInnes, J. (2001). The crisis of masculinity and the politics of identity. In S. M. Whitehead & F. J. Barrett (Eds.), *The masculinities reader* (pp. 311–329). Malden, MA: Blackwell.

Magnuson, E. (2007). Creating culture in the mythopoetic men's movement: An ethnographic study of micro-level leadership and socialization. *The Journal of Men's Studies, Vol 15 (1)*, 31–56.

Mankowski, E. S., Maton, K. I., Burke, C. K., Hoover, S. A., & Anderson, C. W. (2000). Collaborative research with a men's organization: Psychological impact, group functioning, and organizational growth. In E. E. Barton (Ed.), *Mythopoetic perspectives of men's healing work: An anthology for therapists and others* (pp. 183–203). Westport, CT: Bergin and Garvey.

Mann, R. M. (2008). Men's rights and feminist advocacy in Canadian domestic violence policy arenas: Contexts, dynamics, and outcomes of antifeminist backlash *Feminist Criminology, 3*, 44–75.

Matlin, M. W. (2004). *The psychology of women*. Belmont, CA: Wadsworth.

Maton, K. I. (2000). Making a difference: The social ecology of social transformation. *American Journal of Community Psychology, 28*, 25–57.

Messner, M. (2001). Essentialist retreats: The mythopoetic men's movement and the Christian promise keepers. In T. F. Cohen (Ed.), *Men and masculinity: A text reader* (pp. 397–408). Belmont, CA: Wadsworth.

Miedzian, M. (1991). *Boys will be boys*. New York: Doubleday.

Moller-Leimkuhler, A. M. (2003). The gender gap in suicide and premature death or: why are men so vulnerable? *European Archives of Psychiatric Clinical Neuroscience, 253*, 1–8.

Moore, R. & Gillette, D. (1990). *King, warrior, magician, lover: Rediscovering the archetypes of the mature masculine*. New York: HarperCollins.

Moyer, R. J. (2004). The function of ritual in the mythopoetic men's movement: A self-in-relation approach. Dissertation Abstracts International: Section B: The Sciences and Engineering, Vol. 64(12-B), 6336.

National Center for Health Statistics. (2004). Vital Statistics. World Almanac.

Neff, D. (2004). The cure of gay souls. *Christianity Today, 48*, 8.

Nye, R. A. (2005). Locating masculinity: Some recent work on men. *Signs, 30*, 1937–1962.

Pease, B. (2000). Beyond the father wound: Memory-work and the deconstruction of the father–son relationship. *A. N. J. Z. Family Therapy, 21*, 9–15.

Pentz, M. (2000). Heuristic and ethnographic study of the ManKind project: Initiating men into a "new masculinity" or a repackaging of dominant controlling patriarchy. In E. E. Barton (Ed.), *Mythopoetic perspectives of men's healing work: An anthology for therapists and others* (pp. 204–225). Westport, CT: Bergin and Garvey

Poddar, E. & Krishan, V. R. (2004). Impact of gender-roles on transformational leadership. *Abhigyan: The Journal of Foundation of Organizational Research, 22*, 2–13.

Poling, J. N. & Kirkley, E. A. (2000). Phallic spirituality: Masculinities in promise keepers, the Million Man March and sex panic. *Theology and Sexuality, 12,* 9–25.

Rekers, G. A., Bentler., P. M., Rosen, A. C., & Lovaas, O. I. (1977). Child gender disturbances: A clinical rationale for intervention. *Psychotherapy: Theory, Research and Practice, 14,* 2–11.

Rekers, G. A., Mead, S. L., Rosen, A. C., & Brigham, S. L. (1982). Family correlates of male childhood gender disturbance. *The Journal of Genetic Psychology, 142,* 31–42.

Rekers, G. A. & Morey, S. M. (1990a). Sex-typed body movements as a function of severity of gender disturbance in boys. *Journal of Psychology and Human Sexuality, 2,* 183–196.

Rekers, G. A. & Morey, S. M. (1990b). The relationship between measures of sex-typed play with clinician ratings on degree of gender disturbance. *Journal of Clinical Psychology, 46,* 28–34.

Rekers, G. A. & Swihart, J. J. (1989). The association of GID with parental separation. *Psychological Reports, 65,* 1272–1274.

Richard, D. J. (2000). The therapeutic status of the mythopoetic approach: A psychological perspective. In E. E. Barton (Ed.), *Mythopoetic perspectives of men's healing work: An anthology for therapists and others* (pp. 183–203). Westport, CT: Bergin and Garvey.

Richardson, J. (1999). Response: Finding the disorder in gender identity disorder. *Harvard Review of Psychiatry, 7,* 43–50.

Rickabaugh, C. A. (1994). Just who is this guy: Stereotypes of the men's movement. *Sex Roles: A Journal of Research, 30,* 459–471.

Rotter, N. G. & O'Connelll, A. N. (1982). The relationships among sex-role orientation, cognitive complexity, and tolerance for ambiguity. *Sex Roles, 8,* 1209–1220.

Savin-Williams, R. C. (2001). Memories of same-sex attractions. In M. S. Kimmel & M. A. Messner (Eds.), *Men's lives* (5th ed., pp. 73–87). Boston, MA: Allyn & Bacon.

Scharrer, E. (2001a). Tough guys: The portrayal of hypermasculinity and aggression in televised police dramas. *Journal of Broadcasting and Electronic Media, 45,* 613–634.

Scharrer, E. (2001b). Men, muscles, and machismo: The relationship between television violence exposure and aggression and hostility in the presence of masculinity. *Media Psychology, 3,* 159–188.

Shackelford, T. K., Weekes-Shackelford, V. A., & Schmitt, D. P. (2005). An evolutionary perspective on why some men refuse their child support payments. *Basic and Applied Social Psychology, 27,* 297–306.

Silverstein, O. & Rashbaum, B. (1994). *The courage to raise good men*. New York: Viking.

Simpson, M. (1995). Iron clint: Queer weddings in Robert Bly's *Iron John* and Clint Eastwood's *Unforgiven*. In M. S. Kimmel (Ed.), *The politics of manhood: Profeminist men respond to the mythopoetic men's movement* (pp. 257–270). Philadelphia, PA: Temple University Press.

Simpson, R. (2006). Masculinity and management education: Feminizing the MBA. *Academy of management learning and education*, 5, 182–193.

Stoltenberg, J. (2000 August/September). Of microbes and manhood. *MS*, 60–63.

Varcoe, C. & Irwin, L. G. (2004). "If I killed you, I'd get the kids." Women's survival and protection work with child custody and access in the context of woman abuse. *Qualitative Sociology*, 27, 77–99.

Vinner, S. (2007). Mathematics education: Procedures, rituals and man's search for meaning. *Journal of Mathematical Behavior*, 26, 1–10.

Ward, E. G. (2005). Homophobia, hypermasculinity and the US black church. *Culture, Health, and Sexuality*, 7, 493–504.

Watkins, S. C. (2001). Framing protest: News media frames of the Million Man march. *Critical Studies in Media Communication*, 18, 83–101.

Weed, D. M. (1995). Cultural daddy-ism and male hysteria. In M. S. Kimmel (Ed.), *The politics of manhood: Profeminist men respond to the mythopoetic men's movement* (pp. 243–256). Philadelphia, PA: Temple University Press.

Wehr, D. S. (1987). *Jung and feminism: Liberating archetypes*. Boston, MA: Beacon Press.

Weitzman, L. (1985). *The divorce revolution: The unexpected social and economic consequences for women and children in America*. New York: The Free Press.

West, M. O. (1999). Like a river: The Million Man March and the black nationalist tradition in the United States. *Journal of Historical Sociology*, 12, 81–100.

White, M. (1996). Men's culture: the men's movement, and the constitution of men's lives. In C. McLean, M. Carey, & C. White (Eds.), *Men's ways of being* (pp. 153–161). Boulder, CO: Westview Press.

Whitehead, S. M. (2001). Man: The invisible gendered subject. In S. M. Whitehead & F. J. Barrett, *The masculinities reader* (pp. 351–368). Cambridge, UK: Blackwell.

Yoder, J. D., Fischer, A. R., Kahn, A. S. & Groden, J. (2007). Changes in students' explanations for gender differences after taking a psychology of women class: More constructionist and less essentialist. *Psychology of Women Quarterly*, 31, 415–425.

Chapter 10

Abreau, J. M., Goodyear, R. K., Campos, A., & Newcomb, M. D. (2000). Ethnic belonging and traditional masculinity ideology among African Americans, European Americans, and Latinos. *Psychology of Men and Masculinity*, *1*, 75–86.

Addis, M. E. & Mahalik, J. R. (2003). Men, masculinity, and contexts of help seeking. *American Psychologist*, *58*, 5–14.

Bartholomew, N. G., Hiller, M. L., Knight, K., Nucatola, D. C., & Simpson, D. (2000). Effectiveness of communication and relationship skills training for men in substance abuse treatment. *Journal of Substance Abuse Treatment*, *18*, 217–225.

Berger, J. M., Levant, R., McMillan, K. K., Kelleher, W., & Sellers, A. (2005). Impact of gender-role conflict, traditional masculinity ideology, alexithymia, and age on men's attitudes toward psychological help seeking. *Psychology of Men and Masculinities*, *1*, 73–78.

Bergman, S. (1996). Male relational dread. *Psychiatric Annals*, *26:1*, 24–28.

Bergman, S. J. (1995). Men's psychological development: A relational perspective. In R. F. Levant & W. S. Pollack (Eds.), *A new psychology of men* (pp. 68–91). New York: BasicBooks.

Blazina, C. (2001). Analytic psychology and gender role conflict: The development of the fragile masculine self. *Psychotherapy*, *38*, 50–59.

Blazina, C., Pisecco, S., & O'Neil, J. M. (1986). An adaptation of the gender role conflict scale for adolescents: Psychometric issues and correlates with psychological distress. *Psychology of Men and Masculinity*, *6*, 39–45.

Blazina, C. & Watkins, C. E. (2000). Separation/individuation, parental attachment, and male gender role conflict: Attitudes toward the feminine and the fragile masculine self. *Psychology of Men and Masculinity*, *1*, 126–132.

Brooks-Harris, J. E., Heesacker, M., & Mejia-Millan, C. (1996). Changing men's male gender-role attitudes by applying the elaboration likelihood model of attitude change. *Sex Roles*, *35*, 563–580.

Brooks, G. R. & Levant, R. F. (1999). A history of Division 51 (The society for the psychological study of men and masculinity). *Unification through Division: Histories of the Divisions of the American Psychological Association*, *3*, 197–220.

Chu, J., Porche, M. V., & Tolman, D. (2005). The adolescent masculinity ideology in relationships scale: Development and validation of a new measure for boys. *Men and Masculinities*, *8*, 93–115.

Clatterbaugh, K. (1997). *Contemporary perspectives on masculinity*. Oxford, UK: Westview Press.

Clatterbaugh, K. (2000). Literature of the U.S. men's movements. *Signs: Journal of Women in Culture and Society, 25,* 883–895.

Close To Home (2008). Close to home in action. http://www.c2home.org/c2home_in_action.html. Retrieved August 25, 2008.

Cook, K., Davis, E., & Davies, B. (2008). Discrepancy between expected and actual child support payments: predicting the health and health-related quality of life of children living in low-income, single-parent families. *Child: Care, Health and Development, 34,* 267–275.

Crary, D. (2008). Black women make political, social gains but hardships persist, report finds. *Christian Science Monitor, 100,* 2.

David, D. S. & Brannon, R. (Eds.) (1976). *The forty-nine percent majority.* Reading, MA: Addison-Wesley.

Deachan, D. F. (1998). Masculine self-ascribed attachment style, its relationship to gendered self concept, impressions of the mother, and attitudes toward women. Dissertation Abstracts International, 58(8-B), 4521.

DeFranc, W. & Mahalik, J. (2002). Masculine gender role conflict and stress in relation to parental attachment and separation. *Psychology of Men and Masculinity, 3,* 51–60.

Dienhart, A. & Myers Avis, J. (1991). Men in therapy: Exploring feminist-informed alternatives. *Journal of Marital and Family Therapy, 20,* 397–417.

Doyle, J. & Femiano, S. (2008). Reflections on the early history of the American Men's Studies Association and reflections on the evolution of the field. http://www.mensstudies.org/history.html. Retrieved March 17, 2008.

Faludi, S. (1999). *Stiffed: The betrayal of the American man.* London: Chatto & Windus.

Fox, J. (2004). How men's movement participants view each other. *Journal of Men's Studies, 12,* 103–118.

Fracher, J. & Kimmel, M. S. (1989). Hard issues and soft spots. In M. S. Kimmel (Ed.), *Men's lives* (2nd ed., pp. 438–449). New York: Macmillan.

Fragoso, J. M. & Kashubeck, S. (2000). Machismo, gender role conflict, and mental health in Mexican American men. *Psychology of Men and Masculinity, 2,* 87–97.

Galvani, S. (2004). Responsible disinhibition: Alcohol, men and violence to women. *Addiction Research and Theory, 12,* 357–371.

Garnets, L. & Pleck, J. H. (1979). Sex role identity, androgyny, and sex role transcendence: A sex-role strain analysis. *Psychology of Women Quarterly, 3,* 270–283.

Good, G. E., Robertson, J. M., O'Neil, J. M., Fitzgerald, L. M., Stevens, M., DeBord, K. A., et al. (1995). Summarizing 25 years of research on men's gender role conflict using the gender role conflict scale. *Journal of Counseling Psychology, 42,* 3–10.

Goodrich, T. J., Rampage, C., Ellman, B., & Halstead, K. (1992). *Feminist family therapy.* New York: W. W. Norton & Company.

Grinnel College (2003). *Gay Masculinities.* http://www.grinnell.edu/courses/lib/s01/lib397-01/restructuring-masculinities/documents/gaymasc.pdf. Retrieved August 21, 2006.

Horney, K. (1968). The dread of woman. *The International Journal of Psychoanalysis, 13,* 348–360.

Huang, C. C., Mincy, R. B., & Garfinkel, I. (2005). Child support obligations and low-income fathers. *Journal of Marriage and Family, 67,* 1213–1225.

Jakupcak, M., Lisak, D., & Roemer, L. (2002). The role of masculinity ideology and masculine gender role stress in men's perpetration of relationship violence. *Psychology of Men and Masculinity, 3,* 97–106.

Jefferson, T. (2002). Subordinating hegemonic masculinity. *Theoretical Criminology, 6,* 63–88.

Kaschak, E. (1992). *Engendered lives: A new psychology of women's experience.* New York: BasicBooks.

Kearney, L. K., Rochlen, A. B., & King, E. B. (2004). Male gender conflict, sexual harassment tolerance, and the efficacy of a psychoeducative training program. *Psychology of Men and Masculinity, 5,* 72–82.

Kilmartin, C. T. (2000). *The masculine self.* Boston, MA: McGraw Hill.

Kimmel, M. S. (Ed.) (1995). *The politics of manhood: Profeminist men respond to the mythopoetic movement (and the mythopoetic leaders answer).* Philadelphia, PA: Temple University Press.

Kimmel, M. S. & Kaufman, M. (1995). Weekend warriors: The new men's movement. In M. S. Kimmel (Ed.), *The politics of manhood: Profeminist men respond to the mythopoetic movement (and the mythopoetic leaders answer)* (pp. 15–43). Philadelphia, PA: Temple University Press.

Kimmel, M. S. & Levine, M. P. (1989). Men and AIDS. In M. S. Kimmel (Ed.), *Men's lives* (2nd ed., pp. 318–330). New York: Macmillan.

Lee, R. B. (2004). Filipino men's familial roles and domestic violence: implications and strategies for community-based intervention. *Health and Social Care in the Community, 12,* 422–429.

Levant, R. F. (1997). The masculinity crisis. *The Journal of Men's Studies, 5,* 221–232.

Levant, R. F. (1998). Desperately seeking language: Understanding, assessing, and treating normative male alexithymia. In W. S. Pollack & R. F. Levant (Eds.), *A New Psychology of Men* (pp. 424–442). New York: John Wiley & Sons.

Levant, R. F., Cuthbert, A., Richmond, K., Sellers, A., Matveev, A., Mitina, O., et al. (2003). Masculinity ideology among Russian and U.S. young men and women and its relationship to unhealthy lifestyle habits among young Russian men. *Psychology of Men and Masculinity, 4*, 26–36.

Levant, R. F., Good, G. E., Cook, Stephen W., O'Neil, J. M., Smalley, K. B., Owen, K., & Richmond, K. (2006). The normative alexithymia scale: Measurement of a gender-linked syndrome. *Psychology of Men and Masculinity, 7*, 212–226.

Levin-Rozalis, M., Bar-On, N., & Hartaf, H. (2003). The structuring process of the social representation of violence in abusive men. *Culture and Psychology, 9*, 361–382.

Lingard, B. & Douglas, P. (1999). *Men engaging feminisms: Pro-feminism, backlashes and schooling*. Philadelphia, PA: Open University Press.

Liu, W. M. & Iwamoto, D. K. (2006). Asian American men's gender role conflict: The role of Asian values, self-esteem, and psychological distress. *Psychology of Men and Masculinity, 3*, 153–164.

Locke, B. D. & Mahalik, J. R. (2005). Examining masculinity norms, problem drinking, and athletic involvement as predictors of sexual aggression in college men. *Journal of Counseling Psychology, 52*, 279–283.

MacInnes, J. (2001). The crisis of masculinity and the politics of identity. In S. M. Whitehead & F. J. Barrett (Eds.), *The masculinities reader* (pp. 311–329). Malden, MA: Blackwell.

Mahalik, J. R., Aldarondo, E., Gilbert-Gokhale, S., & Shore, E. (2005). The role of insecure attachment and gender role stress in predicting controlling behaviors in men who batter. *Journal of Interpersonal Violence, 20*, 617–631.

Mahalik, J. R., Cournoyer, R. J., DeFranc, W., Cherry, M., & Napolitano, J. M. (1998). Men's gender role conflict and use of psychological defenses. *Journal of Counseling Psychology, 45*, 247–255.

Mahalik, J. R., Good, G. E., & Englar-Carlson, M. (2003). Masculinity scripts, presenting concerns, and help seeking: Implications for practice and training. *Professional Psychology Research and Practice, 34*, 123–131.

McKelley, R. A. & Rochlen, A. B. (2007). The practice of coaching: Exploring alternatives to therapy for counseling resistant men. *Psychology of Men and Masculinity, 8*, 53–65.

Miedzian, M. (1991). *Boys will be boys*. New York: Doubleday

Monk, D. & Ricciardelli, L. A. (2003). Three dimensions of male gender role as correlates of alcohol and cannabis involvement in young Australian men. *Psychology of Men and Masculinity, 4*, 57–69.

Morardi, B., Tokar, D. M., Schaub, M., Jome, L. M., & Serna, G. S. (2000). Revisiting the structural validity of the gender role conflict scale. *Psychology of Men and Masculinity, 1,* 62–69.

Newton, J. (2005). *From panthers to promise keepers: rethinking the men's movement.* Lanham, MD: Rowman & Littlefield.

Nye, R. A. (2005). Locating masculinity: Some recent work on men. *Signs, 30,* 1937–1962.

Okeowo, A. (2007, June). Women lawyers force big rights gains in Uganda. *Christian Science Monitor, 99,* 1–12.

O'Neil, J. M. (1981). Male sex role conflicts, sexism, and masculinity: Psychological implications for men, women, and the counseling psychologist. *The Counseling Psychologist, 9,* 61–81.

O'Neil, J. M. (1996). The gender role journey workshop: Exploring sexism and gender role conflict in a coeducational setting. In M. P. Andronico (Ed.), *Men in groups: Insights, interventions, and psychoeducational work* (pp. 193–213). Washington, DC: American Psychological Association.

O'Neil, J. M., Helms, B. J., Gable, R. K., David, L., & Wrightsman, L. S. (1986). Gender-role conflict scale: College men's fear of femininity. *Sex Roles, 14,* 335–350.

Pease, B. (2000). Beyond the father wound: Memory-work and the deconstructiuon of the father–son relationship. *A. N. J. Z. Family Therapy, 21,* 9–15.

Peoples, J. G. (2001). The cultural construction of gender and manhood. In T. F. Cohen (Ed.), *Men and masculinity: A text reader* (pp. 9–18). Stamford, CT: Wadsworth.

Pleck, J. H. (1995). The gender role strain paradigm: An update. In R. F. Levant & W. S. Pollack (Eds.), *A new psychology of men* (pp. 11–32). New York: BasicBooks.

Pleck, J. H., Sonestein, F. L., & Ku, L. C. (1993). Masculinity ideology: Its impact on adolescent males' heterosexual relationships. *Journal of Social Issues, 49,* 11–29.

Poddar, E. & Krishan, V. R. (2004). Impact of gender-roles on transformational leadership. *Abhigyan: The Journal of Foundation of Organizational Research, 22,* 2–13.

Pollack, W. S. (1995). No man is an island: toward a new psychoanalytic psychology of men. In R. Levant & W. S. Pollack (Eds.), *A new psychology of men* (pp. 33–67). New York: BasicBooks.

Pollack, W. (1998). *Real boys: Rescuing our sons from the myths of boyhood.* New York: Henry Holy & Co.

Rando, R. A., Rogers, J. R., & Brittan-Powell, C. S. (1998). Gender role-conflict and men's sexually aggressive attitudes and behavior. *Journal of Mental Health Counseling, 4,* 359–369.

Redman, P. (2005). Who cares about the psycho-social? Masculinities, schooling, and the unconscious. *Gender and Education, 17,* 531–538.

Risner, D. (2007). Rehearsing masculinity: challenging the "boy code" in dance education. *Research in Dance Education, 8,* 139–153.

Schechtman, Z. (1994). The effect of group psychotherapy on close same-gender friendships among boys and girls. *Sex Roles, 30,* 829–834.

Schwartz, J. P. & Waldo, M. (2003). Reducing gender role conflict among men attending partner abuse prevention groups. *Journal for Specialists in Group Work, 20,* 355–369.

Shackelford, T. K., Weekes-Shackelford, V. A., & Schmitt, D. P. (2005). An evolutionary perspective on why some men refuse their child support payments. *Basic and Applied Social Psychology, 27,* 297–306.

Silverstein, O. & Rashbaum, B. (1994). *The courage to raise good men.* New York: Viking.

Spencer, R. (2007). "I just feel safe with him": Emotional closeness in male youth mentoring relationships. *Psychology of Men and Masculinity, 8,* 185–198.

Stoltenberg, J. (1989). *Refusing to be a man: Essays on social justice.* New York: Penguin.

Stoltenberg, J. (1993). *The end of manhood.* New York: Penguin Books.

Stoltenberg, J. (2000 August/September). Of microbes and manhood. *MS,* 60–63.

Stoltz, J. (2005). Masculinity and school violence: Addressing the role of male gender socialization. *Canadian Journal of Counseling, 39,* 52–63.

Styver, H. (2007). Man, intoxication, addiction: Construction and crisis of masculinity. *Suchttherapie, 8,* 89–94.

Thomas, P. A., Krampe, E. M., & Newton, R. R. (2008). Father presence, family structure, and feelings of closeness to the father among adult African American children. *Journal of Black Studies, 38,* 529–546.

Vance, E. (2007, March). Women make gains in science studies. *Chronicle of Higher Education, 53,* A25–A25.

Wetherell, M. & Edley, N. (1999). Negotiating hegemonic masculinity: Imaginary positions and psycho-discursive practices. *Feminism and Psychology, 9,* 335–356.

Wong, Y. J., Pituch, K. A., & Rochlen, A. B. (2006). Men's restrictive emotionality: An investigation of associations with other emotion-related constructs, anxiety, and underlying dimensions. *Psychology of Men and Masculinity, 7,* 113–126.

Chapter 11

Adams, D. (1988). Treatment models of men who batter: A profeminist analysis. In M. K. Yllö (Ed.), *Feminist perspectives on wife abuse.* Thousand Oaks, CA: Sage.

Austin-Smith, B. (1992). A man's place. *Canadian Dimension, 26,* 35–36.

Axlerod, S. D. (2001). The vital relationship between work and masculinity: A psychoanalytic perspective. *Psychology of Men and Masculinity, 2,* 117–123.

Barnett, B. (2005). Feminists shaping news: A framing analysis of news releases from the National Organization for Women. *Journal of Public Relations Research, 17,* 341–362.

Barol, B. & Miller, M. (1988, March 7). The work goes on. *Newsweek, 111,* 31.

Bartky, S. (1998). Foreword. In T. Digby & S. Bartky (Eds.), *Men doing feminism* (pp. xi–1). New York: Routledge.

Blazina, C. & Watkins, C. E. (2000). Separation/individuation, parental attachment, and male gender role conflict: Attitudes toward the feminine and the fragile masculine self. *Psychology of Men and Masculinity, 1,* 126–132.

Bordo, S. (1998). My father the feminist. In T. Digby and S. Bartky (Eds.), *Men doing feminism* (pp. 17–32). New York: Routledge.

Broad, K. L. (2002). GLB+T?: Gender/sexuality movements and transgender collective identity (de)constructions. *International Journal of Sexuality and Gender Studies, 7,* 241–264.

Brod, H. (1998). To be a man or not to be a man, that is the feminist question. In T. Digby (Ed.), *Men doing feminism* (pp. 197–212). New York: Routledge.

Brooks, G. R. & Levant, R. F. (1999). A history of Division 51 (The society for the psychological study of men and masculinity). *Unification through division: Histories of the divisions of the American Psychological Association, 3,* 197–220.

Burdge, B. J. (2007). Bending gender, ending gender: Theoretical foundations for social work practice with the transgender community. *Social Work, 52,* 243–250.

Carey, M. (1996). Perspective's on the men's movement. In C. McLean, M. Carey & C. White (Eds.), *Men's ways of being* (pp. 153–161). Boulder, CO: Westview Press.

Choate, L. H. (2003). Sexual assault prevention programs for college men: An exploratory evaluation of the men against violence model. *Journal of College Counseling, 6*, 166–176.

Ciano-Boyce, C. & Shelley-Sireci, L. (2002). Who is mommy tonight? Lesbian parenting issues. *Journal of Homosexuality, 43*, 1–13.

Clarke, V. (2002). Sameness and difference in research on lesbian parenting. *Journal of Community and Applied Social Psychology, 12*, 210–222.

Clatterbaugh, K. (1997). *Contemporary perspectives on masculinity*. Oxford, UK: Westview Press.

Clatterbaugh, K. (2000). Literature of the U.S. men's movements. *Signs: Journal of Women in Culture and Society, 25*, 883–895.

Cochran, B. N., Stewart, A. J., Ginzler, J. A., & Cauce, A. M. (2002). Challenges faced by homeless sexual minorities: Comparison of gay, lesbian, bisexual, and transgender homeless adolescents with their heterosexual counterparts. *American Journal of Public Health, 92*, 773–777.

Connell, R. W. (1992). A very straight gay: Masculinity, homosexual experience, and the dynamics of gender. *American Sociological Review, 57*, 735–751.

Connell, R. W. (2001). The social organization of masculinity. In S. M. Whitehead & F. J. Barrett (Eds.), *The masculinities reader* (pp. 27–47). Malden, MA: Blackwell.

Connell, R. W. (2005). *Masculinities*. Berkeley, CA: University of California Press.

DeLoache, J. S. & Gottlieb, A. (2000). *A world of babies: Imagined childcare guides for seven societies*. Cambridge, UK: Cambridge University Press.

Digby, T. (1998). Introduction. In T. Digby & S. Bartky (Eds.), *Men doing feminism* (pp. 1–17). New York: Routledge.

Dobbs, L. (2004). *Exporting America: Why corporate greed in shipping American jobs overseas*. New York: Warner Business Books.

Douglas, P. (1994). "New Men" and the tensions of profeminism. *Social Alternatives, 12*, 32–36.

Drescher, J. (2002). An interview with GenderPAC's Riki Wilchins. *Journal of Gay and Lesbian Psychotherapy, 62*, 67–85.

Dubbert, J. L. (1974). Progressivism and the masculinity crisis. *The Psychoanalytic Review, 61*, 443–455.

Duelli Klein, R. (1983). The "men problem" in women's studies: The expert, the Ignoramus, and the poor dear. *Women's Studies International Forum, 6*, 413–421.

Dworkin, A. (1987). Look dick, look. See Jane blow it. In A. Dworkin (Ed.), *Letters from a warzone* (pp. 126–132). London: Secker & Warburg.

Ellis, K. M. & Eriksen, K. (2002). Transsexual and transgenderist experiences and treatment options. *The Family Journal: Counseling and Therapy for Couples and Families, 10,* 289–299.

Fabiano, P. M., Wesley, P. H., Berkowitz, A., & Linkenbach, J. (2003). Engaging men as social justice allies in ending violence against women: Evidence for a social norms approach. *Journal of American College Health, 52,* 105–112.

Farrel, W. (1994). *The myth of male power.* New York: Simon & Schuster.

Flood, M. (2001). Men's collective anti-violence activism and the struggle for gender justice. *The Society for International Development, 44,* 42–47.

Forman, G. (2003). USA: NOW – the National Organization for Women – an overview. *Women's International Network News, 29,* 74.

Fox, J. (2004). How men's movement participants view each other. *Journal of Men's Studies, 12,* 103–118.

Friedan, B. (1963). *The feminine mystique.* New York: W. W. Norton and Company.

Gainor, K. A. (2000). Including transgender issues in lesbian, gay, and bisexual psychology. In G. Beverly & G. L. Croom (Eds.), *Education, research, and practice in lesbian, gay, bisexual, and transgendered psychology: A resource manual (Vol. 5)* (pp. 131–160). Thousand Oaks, CA: Sage.

Good, G. E., Borst, T. S., & Wallace, D. L. (1994). Masculinity research: A review and critique. *Applied and Preventative Psychology, 3,* 3–14.

Green, J. C. (2003). A liberal dynamo: The political activism of the Unitarian-Universalist clergy. *Journal for the Scientific Study of Religion, 42,* 577–590.

Guest, K. (2007). The subject of money: Late-Victorian melodrama's crisis of masculinity. *Victorian Studies, 49,* 635–657.

Harley, D. A., Nowak, T. M., Gassaway, L. J., & Savage, T. A. (2002). Lesbian, gay, bisexual, and transgender college students with disabilities: A look at multiple cultural minorities. *Psychology in the Schools, 39,* 525–538.

Hastings, D. K. (2008). Fears of a feminized church: Catholicism, clerical celibacy, and the crisis of masculinity in Wilhelmine Germany. *European History Quarterly, 38,* 34–65.

Hearn, J. (1993). The politics of essentialism and the analysis of the men's movement(s). *Feminism and Psychology, 3,* 405–409.

Hearn, J. (2001). Men stopping men's violence against women. *The Society for International Development, 44,* 85–89.

Hearn, J. & Pringle, K. (2006). Studying men in Europe. In J. Hearn & K. Pringle (Eds.), *European perspectives on men and masculinities* (pp. 1–20). Basingstoke, UK: Palgrave Macmillan.

Hicks, S. (2005). Is gay parenting bad for kids? Responding to the "very idea of difference" in research on lesbian and gay parents. *Sexualities, 8*, 153–168.

Hochachka, G. (2007). Integral community development in post-war El Salvador. *Centro Bartolomé de las casas*. Canada's International Research Centre. University of Victoria, Vancouver, B.C.

Holmes, M. & Lundy, C. (1990, December). Group work for abusive men: A profeminist response. *Canada's Mental Health*, 12–17.

hooks, b. (2004). Men: Comrades in struggle. In M. S. Kimmel & M. A. Messner (Eds.), *Men's lives* (6th ed., pp. 555–563). New York: Macmillan.

Jefferson, T. (2002). Subordinating hegemonic masculinity. *Theoretical Criminology, 6*, 63–88.

Jett, D. (2002). Save colleges from the pitfalls of corporate greed. *Christian Science Monitor, 95*, 9.

Johnson, A. (1997). *The gender knot*. Philadelphia, PA: Temple University Press.

Kahn, A. (1981). Reactions of a profeminist and antifeminist men to an expert woman. *Sex Roles, 7*, 857–867.

Kahn, J. S. & Ferguson, K. (in press). Men as allies in feminist pedagogy in the undergraduate psychology curriculum. *Women and Therapy*.

Katz, J. (1995). Reconstructing masculinity in the locker room: The mentors in violence prevention project. *Harvard Educational Review, 65*, 163–174.

Kaufman, G. (2000). Do gender role attitudes matter? Family formation and dissolution among traditional and egalitarian men and women. *Journal of Family Issues, 21*, 128–144.

Kaura, S. A. & Allen, C. M. (2004). Dissatisfaction with relationship power and dating violence perpetration by men and women. *Journal of Interpersonal Violence, 19*, 576–588.

Kimmel, M. (1987). Men's responses to feminism at the turn of the century. *Gender and Society, 1*, 261–283.

Kimmel, M. S. (1995). *The politics of manhood: Profeminist men respond to the mythopoetic movement (and the mythopoetic leaders answer)*. Philadelphia, PA: Temple University Press.

Kimmel, M. S. (1998). Who's afraid of men doing feminism? In T. Digby & S. Bartky (Eds.), *Men doing feminism* (pp. 57–68). New York: Routledge.

Kimmel, M. S. & Kaufman, M. (1995). Weekend warriors: The new men's movement. In M. S. Kimmel (Ed.), *The politics of manhood: Profeminist men respond to the mythopoetic movement (and the mythopoetic leaders answer)* (pp. 15–43). Philadelphia, PA: Temple University Press.

Kimmel, M. & Messner, M. A. (2001). Introduction. In M. S. Kimmel & M. A. Messner (Eds.) *Men's lives* (5th ed., pp. ix–xvii). Boston, MA: Allyn & Bacon.

Kipnis, A. (1995). The postfeminist men's movement. (1995). In M. S. Kimmel (Ed.), *The politics of manhood: Profeminist men respond to the mythopoetic men's movement* (pp. 275–286). Philadelphia, PA: Temple University Press.

Lemons, G. L. (1997). To be black, male, and "feminist" – Making womanist space for black men. *International Journal of Sociology and Social Policy, 17,* 35–61.

Levant, R. F. (1997). The masculinity crisis. *The Journal of Men's Studies, 5,* 221–232.

Lingard, B. & Douglas, P. (1999). *Men engaging feminisms: Pro-feminism, backlashes and schooling.* Philadelphia, PA: Open University Press.

Lyman, P. (2004). The fraternal bond as a joking relationship: A case study of the role of sexist jokes in male group bonding. In M. S. Kimmel & M. A. Messner (Eds.), *Men's lives* (6th ed., pp. 169–189). Boston, MA: Pearson.

MacInnes, J. (2001). The crisis of masculinity and the politics of identity. In S. M. Whitehead & F. J. Barrett (Eds.), *The masculinities reader* (pp. 311–329). Malden, MA: Blackwell.

Mahalik, J. R., Good, G. E., & Englar-Carlson, M. (2003). Masculinity scripts, presenting concerns, and help seeking: Implications for practice and training. *Professional Psychology Research and Practice, 34,* 123–131.

Maital, S. L. & Bornstein, M. H. (2003). The ecology of collaborative child rearing: A systems approach to child care on the kibbutz. *Ethos, 31,* 274–306.

McCann, D. & Delmonte, H. (2005). Lesbian and gay parenting: Babes in arms or babes in the woods? *Sexual and Relationship Therapy, 20,* 333–347.

Men's Resources International (2005). About us. Retrieved December 22, 2005 from: http://www.mensresourcesinternational.org/about.php.

Messner, M. (2004). Becoming 100 percent straight. In M. S. Kimmel & M. A. Messner (Eds.), *Men's lives* (6th ed., pp. 421–427). New York: Macmillan.

Miedzian, M. (1991). *Boys will be boys.* New York: Doubleday.

Mills, R. (2006). History at large: Queer is here? Lesbian, gay, bisexual and transgender histories and public culture. *History Workshop Journal, 62,* 253–263.

Mirandé, A. (2001). "And aren't I a man?": Toward a Chicano/Latino men's studies. In S. M. Whitehead & F. J. Barrett (Eds.), *The masculinities reader* (pp. 341–350). Malden, MA: Blackwell.

Morra, N. & Smith, M. D. (1993). Men in feminism: Theorizing sexual violence. *The Journal of Men's Studies, 2,* 15–28.

Newton, J. (2005). *From panthers to promise keepers: rethinking the men's movement.* Lanham, MD: Rowman & Littlefield.

NOMAS (2004). Statement of principles. In M. S. Kimmel & M. A. Messner (Eds.), *Men's lives* (6th ed., p. 564). New York: Macmillan.

NOMAS (2005). *NOMAS Chapters.* Retrieved December 21, 2005 from: http://www.nomas.org/chapters.html.

NOMAS-Boston (2005). (www.nomasboston.org). Retrieved on January 2, 2007.

Nye, R. A. (2005). Locating masculinity: Some recent work on men. *Signs, 30,* 1937–1962.

Odendaal, W. (2001). The men against violence against women movement in Namibia. *The Society for International Development, 44,* 90–98.

O'Neil, J. M. (1981). Male sex role conflicts, sexism, and masculinity: Psychological implications for men, women, and the counseling psychologist. *The Counseling Psychologist, 9,* 61–81.

Pawelski, J. G., Perrin, E. C., Foy, J. M., Allen, C. F., Del Monte, M., Kaufman, M., et al. (2006). The effects of marriage, civil union, and domestic partnership laws on the health and well-being of children. *Pediatrics, 118,* 349–364.

Pease, B. (2000). Beyond the father wound: Memory-work and the deconstruction of the father–son relationship. *A. N. J. Z. Family Therapy, 21,* 9–15.

Pease, B. (2002). (Re)Constructing men's interests. *Men and Masculinities, 5,* 165–177.

Poling, J. N., Grundy, C., & Min, H. (2002). Men helping men to become profeminist. *Journal of Religion and Abuse, 4,* 107–122.

Porter, E. (2004, July 4). Corporate greed? The other guy started it. *The New York Times,* 3–4.

Powell, K. (2000, April/May). Confessions of a recovering misogynist. *MS Magazine,* 72–77.

Richmond, O. P. (2007). Critical research agendas for peace: The missing link in the study of international relations. *Alternatives, 32,* 247–274.

Rickabaugh, C. A. (1994). Just who is this guy: Stereotypes of the men's movement. *Sex Roles: A Journal of Research, 30,* 459–471.

Robertson, J. M. & Fitzgerald, L. F. (1992). Overcoming the masculine mystique: Preferences for alternative forms of assistance among men who avoid counseling. *Journal of Counseling Psychology, 39,* 240–246.

Roen, K. (2002). "Either/or" and "both/neither": discursive tensions in transgender politics. *Signs, 27,* 501–524.

Rosenberg, S. (2003). Neither forgotten nor fully remembered: Tracing an ambivalent public memory on the 10th anniversary of the Montréal massacre. *Feminist Theory, 4,* 5–27.

Roughgarden, J. (2004). *Evolution's rainbow: Diversity, gender, and sexuality in nature and people*. Berkeley, CA: University of California Press.

Sattel, J. W. (1989). The inexpressive male: Tragedy or sexual politics? In M. S. Kimmel & M. A. Messner (Eds.), *Men's lives* (2nd ed., pp. 350–357). New York: Macmillan.

Schacht, S. P. & Ewing, D. (1997). The many paths of feminism: Can men travel any of them? *Journal of Gender Studies, 6*, 159–176.

Sedgwick, E. K. (1993). *Tendencies*. Durham, NC: Duke University Press.

Seelau, E. P., Seelau, S. M., & Poorman, P. B. (2003). Gender and role-based perceptions of domestic abuse: Does sexual orientation matter? *Behavioral Sciences and the Law, 21*, 199–214.

Silverstein, O. & Rashbaum, B. (1994). *The courage to raise good men*. New York: Viking.

Slagle, R. A. (1995). In defense of queer nation: From identity politics to a politics of difference. *Western Journal of Communication, 59*, 85–102.

Stake, J. E. & Hoffman, F. L. (2000). Putting feminist pedagogy to the test. *Psychology of Women Quarterly, 24*, 30–38.

Stoltenberg, J. (1989). *Refusing to be a man: Essays on social justice*. New York: Penguin.

Stoltenberg, J. (1993). *The end of manhood*. New York: Penguin.

Stryker, S. (2008). Transgender history, homonormativity and disciplinarity. *Radical History Review, 100*, 145–157.

The Founding of Now (2008). http://www.now.org/history/the_founding.html. Retrieved April 1, 2008.

Thomas, C. (2000). *Straight with a twist: Queer theory and the subject of heterosexuality*. Chicago, IL: University of Illinois Press.

Toller, P. W., Suter, E. A., & Trautman, T. C. (2004). Gender role attitudes and attitudes toward feminism. *Sex Roles, 51*, 85–90.

Trute, B. (1998). Going beyond gender-specific treatments in wife battering: Profeminist couple and family therapy. *Aggression and Violent Behavior, 3*, 1–15.

Wenzel, R. (2007). A transgender history. *Advocate, 999*, 40–46.

Wetherell, M. & Edley, N. (1999). Negotiating hegemonic masculinity: Imaginary positions and psycho-discursive practices. *Feminism and Psychology, 9*, 335–356.

White, A. M. (2001a). Ain't I a feminist? Black men as advocates of feminism. *Womanist Theory and Research, 3(2)*, 28–34.

White, A. M. (2001b). I am because we are: Combined race and gender political consciousness among African American women and men anti-rape activists. *Women's Studies International Forum, 24*, 1–24.

White, A. M. (2002). John Coltrane's style of jazz and the improvisational lives of profeminist black men. *Journal of African American Men, 6,* 3–28.

White, A. M. (2006). African American feminist fathers' narratives on parenting. *Journal of Black Psychology, 32,* 43–71.

Whitehead, S. M. (2001). Man: The invisible gendered subject. In S. M. Whitehead & F. J. Barrett, *The masculinities reader* (pp. 351–368). Cambridge, UK: Blackwell.

Wilchins, R. A. (1997). *Read my lips: Sexual subversion and the end of gender.* Ithaca, NY: Firebrand Books.

Youmans, S. (2004). *Always moving: Using memoir and theoretical constructions of masculinity to generate a unique perspective on mature male transformation.* Thesis, Goddard College.

Chapter 12

Botkin, S. (2002, Fall). Twenty years of men showing up. *Voice Male Magazine.*

Douglas, P. (1994). "New Men" and the tensions of profeminism. *Social Alternatives, 12,* 32–36.

Fox, J. (2004). How men's movement participants view each other. *Journal of Men's Studies, 12,* 103–118.

Goodman, D. J. (2001). *Promoting diversity and social justice: Educating people from privileged groups.* Thousand Oaks, CA: Sage.

Hearn, J. (1993). The politics of essentialism and the analysis of the men's movement(s). *Feminism and Psychology, 3,* 405–409.

Youmans, S. (2004). *Always moving: Using memoir and theoretical constructions of masculinity to generate a unique perspective on mature male transformation.* Thesis, Goddard College.

Author Index

Subject Index